THE FIRST DOMINO

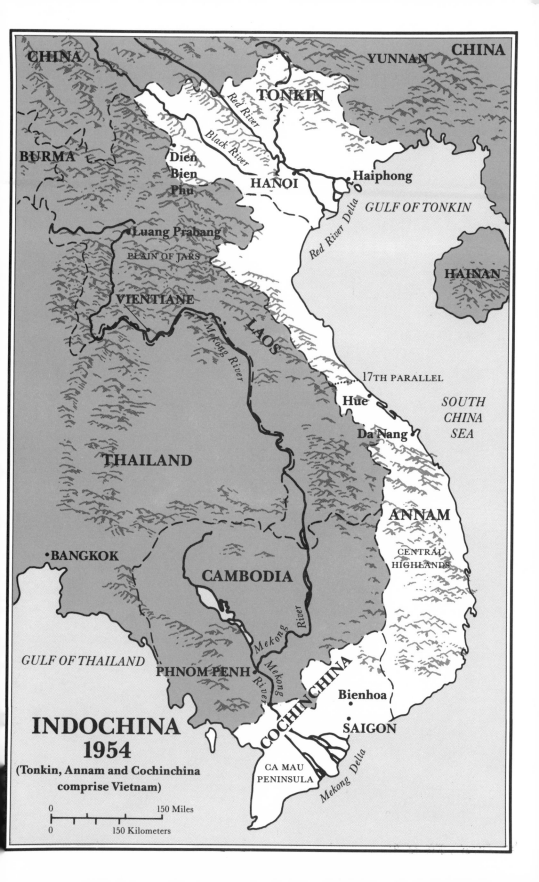

CHINA

CHINA

YUNNAN

TONKIN

Red River

Black River

BURMA

Dien Bien Phu

HANOI

Haiphong

GULF OF TONKIN

Red River Delta

Luang Prabang

PLAIN OF JARS

VIENTIANE

LAOS

HAINAN

17TH PARALLEL

Hue

SOUTH CHINA SEA

Da Nang

Mekong River

THAILAND

ANNAM

CENTRAL HIGHLANDS

BANGKOK

CAMBODIA

Mekong River

PHNOM PENH

COCHINCHINA

GULF OF THAILAND

Mekong River

Bienhoa

SAIGON

INDOCHINA
1954

(Tonkin, Annam and Cochinchina
comprise Vietnam)

CA MAU PENINSULA

Mekong Delta

0 —— 150 Miles
0 —— 150 Kilometers

THE FIRST DOMINO

Eisenhower, the Military, and
America's Intervention in Vietnam

James R. Arnold

WILLIAM MORROW AND COMPANY, INC.
New York

It is the policy of William Morrow and Company, Inc., and its imprints and affiliates, recognizing the importance of preserving what has been written, to print the books we publish on acid-free paper, and we exert our best efforts to that end.

Library of Congress Cataloging-in-Publication Data

Arnold, James R.
    The first domino : Eisenhower, the military, and America's intervention in Vietnam / James R. Arnold.
        p.   cm.
    Includes bibliographical references and index.
    ISBN 0-688-09640-9
    1. United States—Foreign relations—Vietnam. 2. Vietnam—Foreign relations—United States. 3. United States—Foreign relations—1945-1961. 4. Eisenhower, Dwight D. (Dwight David), 1890–1969. I. Title.
    E183.8.V5A93   1991
    327.730597—dc20   91-3398
                                                                              CIP

Printed in the United States of America

First Edition

1   2   3   4   5   6   7   8   9   10

BOOK DESIGN BY PAUL CHEVANNES
ENDPAPER MAP BY ARLENE SCHLEIFER GOLDBERG

To the archivists
of the National Archives
and Records Administration,
custodians of democracy's
greatest treasure, truth

ACKNOWLEDGMENTS

I am profoundly appreciative of the contributions made by friends, family, and associates. Thank you all:

Joyce B. Arnold for her archival research assistance at a moment of need; Dennis Bilger and the most cooperative staff of the Harry S. Truman Library, Independence, Missouri; my agent, Robert Gottlieb, whose curiosity stimulated this endeavor and whose business acumen saw it through; the people at William Morrow who had the confidence to support this project and, most important, Frank Mount, who provided skillful, meticulous editing, correcting flaws and reinforcing strengths, as well as an unflagging positive outlook for which I am particularly grateful; the staff of the National Archives; Herbert Pankratz and the staff of the Dwight D. Eisenhower Library, Abilene, Kansas, who patiently guided me through their archives.

I'm especially pleased to acknowledge my continuing relationship with the ever helpful reference librarians at the Handley Library, Winchester, Virginia.

At the National Archives, Dale Connelly efficiently helped locate photographs. Randy Hackenburg guided me to the Reeder, O'Daniel, and Williams photo collections at the U.S.

Army Military History Institute. Carl Teger reproduced the Institutes' photographs.

Finally, as has been the case now from Napoleon to Eisenhower, it was my life companion and wife, Roberta Wiener, whose support, interest in history and the craft of writing, and many talents proved indispensable to the writing of this book.

CONTENTS

Contents

THE FIRST DOMINO

CHAPTER I

DATELINE TO CONFLICT

There is, let me assure you, nothing in nature more egocentrical than the embattled democracy.
—GEORGE F. KENNAN

Part 1. ONCE AN ALLY

Whampoa, China, 1926

The founder of the Annamite, or Vietnamese, Communist party has been active in the anti-French struggle since the age of five. He is now thirty-six years old and has seen much of the world while working as a seaman and cook. Seven years ago, full of hope, he presented an appeal for Vietnamese independence at the Versailles Peace Conference, but the great powers ignored him, an experience that has helped him reach certain conclusions. Today, Nguyen Ai Quoc writes in his diary: "Only a Communist party can ensure the well-being of Annam."

For the next decade and a half he works to build the movement. In the aftermath of a failed insurrection in 1930, the French colonial rulers of Indochina sentence him to death but he evades capture. In the mid-1930s he attends a variety of leadership schools in Moscow, but does not entirely accept rigid Soviet ideas. By decade's end he submits a report to the Party that subordinates doctrine to pragmatic compromise. His goal is national independence, a goal that takes precedence over ideology.

He operates under a variety of aliases. The world will learn of him by the name Ho Chi Minh. The outbreak of World War II finds him in southern China working as a political commissar for a Chinese Communist guerrilla training mission.

Vichy, France, September 2, 1940

France has fallen to the Nazis and is now a mere rump state headquartered in Vichy but still controlling France's prewar colonial possessions. They include French Indochina, an area embracing Vietnam, Laos, and Cambodia. Vichy France has little military power to defend its colonies. The expanding Japanese military state enters into this power vacuum.

First Japan demands use of base facilities in Indochina. Alarmed, the American government urges Vichy to refuse. Absent armed United States assistance—assistance the Americans decline to offer—the Vichy head of state, the once great general of World War I, Marshal Petain, signs an order directing his colonial administrators in Indochina to negotiate terms permitting Japanese use of Indochinese military bases.

In Indochina, Vietnamese nationalists view this action as a further indication of the decay of French imperialism. Not only is France a harsh colonial power, it is a collaborationist state in league with Japan. A series of new insurrections against the French begins. The Indochinese Communist party is undecided whether these insurrections represent opportunity or are premature. While some Communists participate, many remain uninvolved. With Japanese aid, the French brutally crush the insurrections and by so doing eliminate all except the Communists as a viable national force.

South China, May 1941

At the Eighth Plenum of the Indochinese Communist party, a "United Front" is formed to work toward national liberation. Ho Chi Minh is placed at its head. The front is open to any group willing to struggle for Vietnamese independence: "Rich people, soldiers, workers, peasants, intellectuals, employees, traders, youth, and women who warmly love your country! At the present time national liberation is the most important problem. Let us unite together! As one in mind and strength we shall overthrow the Japanese and French."

While there are a variety of independence movements in Indochina, only the Vietnam Doc Lap Dong Minh—Vietnam Independence League, Viet Minh for short—will establish a nationwide reputation for military operations against the Japanese.

Washington, June 1941

American intelligence has cracked the Japanese diplomatic code. Intercepts reveal that Japan is pressing Vichy France for air and sea bases at Saigon and Cam Ranh Bay. American strategists and statesmen alike believe that while Vietnam is of little importance in and of itself, it is a stepping-stone that an enemy can use to gain more important objectives. This conclusion will endure and affect postwar decision making.

Tokyo, July 2, 1941

An Imperial Conference convenes and decides upon a policy of southward expansion "no matter what obstacles may be encountered." A joint protectorate will be established with the French in Indochina to provide the army with a base of attack northward against Nationalist China, west against Burma and Thailand, and south against British Malaya.

Vichy, July 19, 1941

Having gained base privileges, the Japanese make further demands tantamount to occupation of Indochina. At this point President Franklin D. Roosevelt tries to dissuade them by sternly lecturing the Japanese ambassador. He discounts all possible rationales for the Japanese action except one: "The occupation of Indochina was being undertaken by Japan for the purpose of further offense." When, with the aim of isolating China, Japan occupies southern Vietnam, the action precipitates the crisis leading to Pearl Harbor.

The Heavy Cruiser Augusta *off the Coast of Newfoundland,* August 12, 1941

After hazarding a voyage across U-boat–infested waters, Roosevelt and Prime Minister Winston Churchill meet for the first time. The two men reach an enduring understanding about international affairs. Among many topics discussed is the defense of the Pacific against Japanese aggression. Intelligence reports are alarming: The Japanese continue to mass their forces in Indochina. While the two leaders do not agree about everything—Roosevelt must attend to an American public rooted in isolationism, Churchill recognizes that Great Britain is fighting for her very existence. They agree on a philosophic statement of ideals, the Atlantic Charter, which says that the United States and the United Kingdom agree to certain "common principles . . . on which they base their hopes for a better future for the world." The policy states that the two great democracies "respect the right of all peoples to choose the form of government under which they will live; and they wish to see sovereign rights and self-government restored to those who have been forcibly deprived of them."

In northern Vietnam, Ho Chi Minh learns of the Atlantic Charter. To him, the charter is a ringing endorsement for Vietnamese self-rule. Perhaps America will favor Vietnamese independence.

Washington, July 26, 1941

Intelligence officers digest the news from Indochina. Yesterday, Japanese troops had marched across the Vietnamese border. Today the State Department announces a freeze of all Axis funds in the United States, and the Army recalls General

Douglas MacArthur to active duty to command American forces in the Far East. The recall indicates a major change in American strategy. The Philippines will be reinforced to form a strategic barrier blocking a Japanese drive on the oil-rich Dutch East Indies. This decision reverses a twenty-year-old strategic doctrine that kept America from making major military commitments west of Hawaii.

The State Department, August 2, 1941

Having failed to convince the French to undertake that which the United States felt unable to do, the Americans next try to shame Vichy into defending Indochina. Acting Secretary of State Sumner Welles criticizes Vichy acquiescence in a press release. Welles asks whether, given Japan's "expansionist aims," the French government "in fact proposes to maintain its declared policy to preserve for the French people the territories both at home and abroad which have long been under French sovereignty."

With this statement, a second enduring theme that will underlie American policy toward Indochina emerges. To protect a region seen as a strategic stepping-stone toward vital interests, America is willing to join ranks with the region's colonial power. For the remainder of World War II, whenever the United States negotiates for French assistance to fight the Axis powers, the French counter by asking about the nature of the postwar order. Prominent in the French view of this order is the rightful return of France as a great power, complete with the trappings of a great power, namely colonial possessions. Foremost in their thoughts is one of the colonial jewels, Vietnam.

In order to enlist French help, America pledges to support French claims to all of her overseas colonies. While this pledge makes many uncomfortable, not the least of whom is the anticolonialist American President, the hard need to mobilize all resources to resist the Axis powers supersedes the ideals espoused in the Atlantic Charter.

Washington, August 3, 1941

Kenneth Landon, a former missionary to Siam is asked by the head of the Office of Strategic Services (OSS), the government's main intelligence gathering and analysis entity, to report to Roosevelt on Japanese intentions in Indochina. To prepare himself he obtains access to government files and is taken to a set of file cabinets marked "Southeast Asia," which contain only one folder with four magazine articles. Landon is the author of all four. He asks the major in charge of the files what the government would do if it wanted to know something about Indochina. The major replies: "Oh, we'd ask our allies."

North Africa, November 1942

American soldiers are embarked at last to fight the Germans. It has taken great effort and an immense strategic debate to mount the attack. Operation Torch is intended as a first step toward the Allied return to German-occupied Europe. Allied weakness convinces strategists to begin by invading North Africa. The Vichy French government controls that territory. In hopes of avoiding French armed resistance, Allied statesmen meet with French officials. Citing their fears about the application of the Atlantic Charter to French colonial possessions, French officials inquire about Allied war aims. In response an American diplomat pledges that "the restoration of France to full independence, in all the greatness and vastness which it possessed before the war in Europe as well as overseas, is one of the war aims of the United Nations." He assures the French that "it is thoroughly understood that French sovereignty will be reestablished as soon as possible" everywhere, including in colonial territory. In the first year of the war, the United States reassures the French seven times on this subject.

Washington, March 1943

Anglo-American discussions concerning a new draft of the Atlantic Charter are becoming divisive. The Americans claim they wish to support national independence worldwide. The

British foreign minister, Anthony Eden, emphasizes the responsibility of the "parent" power toward native populations. He explains that the word "independence" troubles him and reminds the Americans that "the British Empire system . . . was built on the basis of Dominion and colonial status."

Given the more pressing need to cooperate to defeat the Axis powers, the two allies agree to disagree. Inability to work out a common policy precludes meaningful discussion on postwar colonialism.

The White House, January 24, 1944

President Roosevelt writes to Secretary of State Edward Stettinius regarding relations with France. For over a year the President has believed that Indochina should not be returned to French colonial rule, noting that: "France has had the country . . . for nearly one hundred years, and the people are worse off than they were at the beginning." It should be administered by an international trusteeship. Roosevelt notes that the British oppose trusteeship because of their own colonial goals. Nonetheless, Indochina should eventually become independent. Roosevelt concludes that "France has milked it for one hundred years. The people of Indo-China are entitled to something better than that."

The White House, March 17, 1944

Roosevelt meets with Stettinius to exchange views on an upcoming conference on postwar problems. The President urges him to raise the issue of an Indochina trusteeship under United Nations control. It is a plan designed to ensure peaceful order after the war. Roosevelt has been promoting trusteeship since the declaration announcing the Atlantic Charter, but it has not been well received even within the administration. The President maintains that "the white man's rule there is nothing to be proud of" and thus a trusteeship is the only reasonable solution. Roosevelt explains that he discussed this with the Chinese nationalist leader Chiang Kai-shek and the generalissimo agreed that trusteeship would be an ideal arrangement.

When Roosevelt tells Churchill that Chiang Kai-shek has no territorial ambitions in Indochina, the prime minister responds, "Nonsense." Roosevelt replies, "Winston, this is something which you are just not able to understand. You have 400 years of acquisitive instinct in your blood and you just don't understand how a country might not want to acquire land somewhere if they can get it. A new period has opened in the world's history, and you will have to adjust yourself to it."

Indochina, Early Summer 1944

The two-pronged American offensive drives through the Pacific toward Japan. From bases in southern China, bombers strike targets in Vietnam, but intelligence about Japanese movements is hard to obtain. Thus OSS agents consult with the Viet Minh because they are the only well-organized resistance group capable of providing reliable information and assisting in the rescuing of American airmen shot down over Indochina. While the OSS develops good relations with the Viet Minh, the British begin to stage their own commando operations in rivalry with the OSS.

Washington, July 6, 1944

Difficult, cantankerous General Charles de Gaulle arrives for an official three-day visit to see Roosevelt. Until the last day, meetings avoid controversy and concentrate on toasting traditional Franco-American friendship. Then de Gaulle's military aide corners Roosevelt's aide, Admiral William D. Leahy, and speaks of French intentions to recover Indochina from the Japanese. He asks for American help, but Leahy sidesteps the issue explaining that at this time Indochina cannot be "included within the sphere of interest of the American Chiefs of Staff."

Washington, October 10, 1944

American agents report that they are now certain that the British are secretly training and equipping French agents for clandestine missions into Indochina. Further investigation determines that British intelligence has received orders to have nothing to do with the Viet Minh or other nationalist groups, but to devote their support exclusively to the French. French agents will parachute into Vietnam to lay the groundwork for reestablishing French colonial rule. The State Department reports to Roosevelt that British and French strategy is to "win back and control Southeast Asia, making the fullest use possible of American resources, but foreclosing the Americans from any voice in policy matters."

Roosevelt responds to this news with a directive ordering the OSS to deny American support for such missions. However, he retreats from his previous strong statements regarding trusteeship. Instead, he wants the State Department to clearly inform the Allies that "we have made no final decisions on the future of Indo-China."

North Vietnam, Christmas Eve, 1944

Ho Chi Minh is certain America will defeat Japan. He also believes that the United States will support the Viet Minh since Roosevelt has sponsored the Atlantic Charter and denounced colonialism. OSS cooperation with his guerrillas provides further hope. Thinking that a show of strength will enhance his position, he orders his comrade, Vo Nguyen Giap, to form "armed propaganda teams" to attack isolated French outposts. Giap assembles a thirty-four-person team, including three women. Dressed as ordinary peasants, the team attacks two tiny French posts, kills the French officers, and captures many weapons. These skirmishes will be celebrated as the birth of the Vietnamese Army.

The Pentagon, January 1945

With the Axis powers reeling from Allied blows, the French are growing increasingly anxious about reestablishing their hold in Indochina. While the French administer the region's government and police and maintain small garrisons at various outposts, the Japanese retain overall authority. French military men tell the Americans that if the United States will transport two French divisions to Vietnam, they will be sufficient to overthrow this authority and to recapture Indochina. American strategists conclude that providing the resources to help the French will not promote the overall objective of defeating Japan. The United States refuses the French request for strategic transport.

Nonetheless, the President's resolve to impose a trusteeship over Indochina is weakening. On the first of the year he says: "I still do not want to get mixed up in any Indo-China decision. It is a matter for postwar."

American Embassy, Chungking, China, January 18, 1945

The embassy informs the military command that in a recent United States air raid over Saigon, nine airmen bailed out of their stricken aircraft. The Japanese have captured three. One is rescued by the Viet Minh and escorted to safety. The French have rescued the others, prompting a Japanese demand for their surrender. The French refuse.

This refusal annoys the Japanese. In addition, Japanese intelligence detects signs of French intent to stage an uprising. Given American opposition to their formal military return, the French are preparing an uprising as a means to lever themselves back into authority. Their plans are a poorly kept secret so the Japanese Army prepares a preemptive strike.

American Embassy, Chungking, China, February 1, 1945

French officers ask Major General Albert Wedemeyer, commander of United States forces in the China theater and chief of staff to Generalissimo Chiang Kai-shek, about possible American help should the Japanese strike. Wedemeyer greatly appreciates the fact that the French voluntarily furnish valuable assistance to the American 14th Air Force. However, "consonant with standing instructions from War and State Departments," Wedemeyer reports, he has "maintained non-committal policy vis-à-vis Indochina." Wedemeyer tells the French that policy is made in Washington and Paris, not Chungking. Two weeks later, the State Department cables Wedemeyer that his behavior "is good policy."

Yalta, February 8, 1945

Roosevelt has been urging Stalin to commit Russian resources to the fight against Japan. Today, Stalin presents his preconditions. One of them states that Indochina's fate will be left open to discussion. Roosevelt still wants a trusteeship as proposed in the United Nations draft charter. The next day when the President raises his cherished scheme, Churchill explodes and is on his feet immediately: "While there is life in my body no transfer of British sovereignty will be permitted."

With so many important issues to address, Roosevelt finds little opportunity to pursue trusteeship with his allies. The conference at Yalta has presented taxing challenges for all the world leaders. Weakened by disease, Roosevelt finds it difficult to attend to all details. Too many decisions to make, conflicting advice, physical infirmity, all conspire to defeat his trusteeship concept. The official American statement on the postwar trusteeship structure leaves the fate of all colonies in the hands of their prewar controlling powers.

Indochina, March 9, 1945

Two hours after issuing an ultimatum to turn over control of the colony and disarm the garrisons, Japanese forces attack French positions. Most defenders quickly surrender, but a few hard-core soldiers continue to fight. After overturning French rule in Indochina, the Japanese install a figurehead, the emperor of Annam, Bao Dai, as the head of a state independent of France.

This turn of events greatly helps the Viet Minh. The Japanese strike upsets nearly completed French plans to launch a decisive stroke against them. Furthermore, by attacking the

French the Japanese have created a great political opportunity for the Viet Minh. Quickly they establish a shadow government.

The White House, March 1945

General Wedemeyer arrives from China to discuss with Roosevelt the region's many problems. Roosevelt shows particular interest in Indochina and states that he is "doing everything possible to give the people in that area their independence." He explains his wish that America's allies abandon colonialism and admonishes Wedemeyer not to give the French any supplies.

The policy proves hard on American military men in the field. General Claire Chennault's airmen, the famous "Flying Tigers," are not interested in State Department policy concerning postwar French colonial rule. They are interested in killing Japanese and assisting anyone who shares this goal. Their airplanes bomb and strafe Japanese pursuit columns that are hounding the French from their positions in northern Vietnam. Eventually they receive permission to evacuate French women and children. Although they follow orders and do not provide supplies for the beleaguered French soldiers, they do not "relish the idea of leaving Frenchmen to be slaughtered in the jungle" while being "forced officially to ignore their plight."

The Pentagon, March 18, 1945

With increasing stridency, French representatives in Washington are requesting military support for French operations in Indochina against the Japanese. With the Pacific war all but won, American strategists see little military value flowing from French participation. Furthermore, they view French claims for "urgent" help as a transparent subterfuge for the real French purpose: reintroducing French troops into their Southeast Asian colonial possessions.

In Paris, de Gaulle increases the pressure by saying that if the French public learns that America resists restoring French rule in Indochina, there will be incalculable consequences including the possibility that France itself will fall into the Communist orbit. It is the first time a French official finds the key, American fear of communism, that will eventually unlock the floodgate restraining American aid. This time de Gaulle is premature and Roosevelt resists French appeals. Acting on his instinctive dislike for colonial powers, he maintains that a statement of support for the French position in Indochina is "inadvisable at the present time."

South China, Late March

The head of the OSS mission, Archimedes Patti, is invited to a rural teahouse where he might encounter the mysterious "Mr. Ho." As he arrives he sees a slender, short man approach, smile, extend his hand, and say, "Welcome, my good friend." Patti, like almost every American who encounters Ho Chi Minh during this period, is impressed with his "sincerity, pragmatism, and eloquence." Under orders to avoid politics, he still observes that Ho is not "a starry-eyed revolutionary or flaming radical, given to clichés, mouthing a party line.... This wisp of a man was intelligent, well-versed in the problems of his country, rational, and dedicated." Patti immediately sees that Ho seeks United States support for Vietnamese freedom from the French. This is beyond his authority to grant. However, "from a practical viewpoint, Ho and the Viet Minh appeared to be the answer to my immediate problem of establishing operations in Indochina."

France, March 20, 1945

While United States reports from China claim the French in Indochina are being systematically smashed and splintered—only a few garrisons continue to resist, including one in an obscure mountain valley named Dien Bien Phu—General Charles de Gaulle gives a more upbeat report: "I insist that there should be parachutages of [American] arms and munitions [in Indochina]. As long as we have arms and munitions, we shall hold. Aid us as much as possible. Morale is excellent. Vive la France."

Roosevelt's military advisers finally persuade him to permit the resupply of the French. In the coming weeks, Ho Chi Minh and his Viet Minh guerrillas observe from their jungle sanctuaries American planes parachuting supplies to French troops.

Paris, March 24, 1945

The recommendations of the special French colonial commission on Indochina are announced. It is an explicit statement of Indochina's future within the French Union. The existing artificial division of Indochina into five French-dominated "states" will continue, and the states will be governed by a mixed assembly comprising natives and Frenchmen who will report to a French governor general. In sum, the announcement gives the trappings of representative government while preserving colonial rule.

The result of Roosevelt's five years of concern over Indochina has been an incoherent policy that has angered allies and failed to assist colonial countries seeking independence. An OSS officer stationed in Vietnam will conclude: "In our neutral role we were thus a disappointment to both sides." The British remain deeply suspicious that America's continuing exploration of trusteeship threatens the very basis of their empire. The French worry that the United States intends to block their return to Indochina. Only Ho Chi Minh retains confidence in American policy, believing it will support his nationalist movement.

Part 2. THE NEW ENEMY

San Francisco, May 1945

One month into his presidency, Harry S. Truman first confronts the Indochina problem. At an organizational meeting concerning the establishment of the United Nations, the

French ask Secretary of State Stettinius about the restoration of French sovereignty within the French empire. The French reiterate their view that prior American statements imply that the United States understands such restoration to include Indochina. However, they ask if American press accounts reporting otherwise are accurate.

Stettinius is ill prepared for this question. Within the State Department the Asian specialists, who oppose French return to Indochina, have been feuding with the European specialists, who favor the French. They argue that now is the time to draw close to Great Britain and France as the strongest Western European powers and to remove sources of friction caused by French worries that the United States endorses eventual independence for French colonies. Subject to conflicting advice, Stettinius explains to the French ambassador that the record is clear of any American official statement that Indochina is different from any other French possession. Stettinius informs Truman that the French minister "seemed relieved and has no doubt cabled Paris that he received renewed assurances of our recognition of French sovereignty over that area."

Meanwhile, Archimedes Patti, the OSS officer running operations in Indochina, receives his first intelligence report from Ho Chi Minh. Included in the package are two political pamphlets Ho wants Patti to forward to the American delegation in San Francisco. Just as had been the case at Versailles in 1919, Ho's efforts to have the issue of Vietnamese independence placed on the great powers' agenda fail.

American Embassy, Chungking, China, May 21, 1945

Reassured by conversations in San Francisco, the French ambassador to China discusses Indochina with his American counterpart. Although French troops have suffered a punishing defeat at the hands of the Japanese, the ambassador speaks glowingly of Vietnamese cooperation with the French fighters: "The real trusteeship is in our hearts. It is a mutual confidence which exists between Indochinese and French."

Shortly thereafter, the State Department provides details

of the San Francisco Conference. The United States has
promoted "a progressive measure of self-government for
all dependent peoples looking toward their eventual independence." However, nothing is to take place without the concur-
rence of the parent power. Agreements reached in San
Francisco preclude the establishment of a trusteeship in Indochina unless the French promote such an arrangement, which
seems "unlikely." "Nevertheless," the President intends at
some convenient time to ask that the French begin the process
of establishing "civil liberties and increasing measures of self-
government in Indochina." This convenient time will never
come. Ho Chi Minh will cite the San Francisco Charter when
he appeals for American assistance against the French.

While Truman's Department of State awaits developments
before committing itself, an American diplomat in China informs the State Department that anti-French feeling in Vietnam is widespread and deep. Should the French try to crush
the nationalist movement, they will experience bloody failure.

Washington, June 23, 1945

A State Department study of Communist activities in Southeast Asia observes that Communists have effective control of
the nationalist-liberation movement in Indochina. It suggests
that "as long as the French seek to find a military solution, the
Communist and nationalist elements within the Viet Minh will
remain cohesive." Efforts by the French to provide a rallying
point for non-Communist elements in the Viet Minh have
failed. "It would seem that only outside intervention will prevent complete Communist victory."

Northern Vietnam, July 16, 1945

Six OSS agents, including three Americans and a Frenchman masquerading as an American, parachute into the remote mountains of northern Vietnam. Their mission is to
establish contact with a Vietnamese guerrilla group fighting
the Japanese. The ragtag guerrillas greet the Americans with

great enthusiasm. A bamboo arch leading to the guerrilla camp has a banner printed in English: WELCOME TO OUR AMER-ICAN FRIENDS. A frail black-haired man with piercing eyes introduces himself as C. M. Hoo, the group's leader. He immediately recognizes the French imposter and orders him escorted back to China.

The next day the leader speaks with the American officers in excellent English to explain his vision for Vietnam. While complaining about French tyranny, he says he wants to work with the French to gain their technical help. He foresees independence in five to ten years and cites John Foster Dulles's speech on self-determination at the UN conference in San Francisco: "Your statesmen make eloquent speeches about helping those with self-determination. We are self-determined. Why not help us?" He continues that for now he wants American assistance above all because his country is very poor.

The Americans listen, but they are not on a political mission. Their job is to assist the guerrillas in fighting the Japanese. Only later do they learn that the Vietnamese leader they met was indeed Ho Chi Minh.

State Department, July 14, 1945

Acting Secretary of State Joseph C. Grew asks the head of the OSS for information on events in Indochina, specifically the extent of anti-French sentiment and the possibility of effective armed opposition to French rule. One month later an OSS officer replies that anti-French feelings are shared by 100 percent of the population in many areas. Even Laos, a region that has seen few anticolonial actions, wants to be established as a free state under United States trusteeship.

Ho Chi Minh's Headquarters, Summer 1945

As time passes, Ho Chi Minh continues his talks with his new OSS friends about the fate of postwar Vietnam. He speaks of his admiration for the way America dealt with the Philippines: "You kicked the Spanish out and let the Filipinos develop their own country. You were not looking for real estate." He predicts the war will end soon and that the United States will emerge as the world's strongest nation. He compares himself with other nationalists: "Am I any different from Nehru, Quezon, even your George Washington? Was not Washington considered a revolutionary? I, too, want to set my people free." He asks the Americans to radio to Washington his plan, partially based on the U.S. Constitution, for a constitutional form of government for Vietnam featuring a gradual transition from French rule.

When these messages are sent, they receive either ambiguous replies or no answers at all. Thwarted, the seemingly gentle "Uncle Ho" briefly unmasks. With "his fierce eyes snapping" he says, "If you do not help us achieve our goal, I know a country that will be only too glad to come to our aid!"

Hanoi, Mid-August 1945

Upon learning of the collapse of Japanese power, the Indochinese Communist party meets. It decides to preempt Allied occupation of Vietnam by seizing as much power as possible as quickly as possible. Ho Chi Minh organizes a People's Congress comprising nationalists of varying political views. The congress creates the National Liberation Committee of Vietnam while the Viet Minh guerrillas become the Army of Liberation. These organizations are intended to form the nucleus of the new nation's government and army. On August 16 the first Viet Minh detachments enter Hanoi.

Their march route is lined with scorched villages. Viet Minh soldiers burn them to intimidate fence-sitting peasants into cooperation. Viet Minh leaflets and banners appear throughout the country, and mass demonstrations, dominated by Viet Minh speakers, celebrate liberation from the Japanese. Viet Minh political strategists promote the National Liberation Committee as a united front comprising all true patriots and claim it is the Vietnamese arm of the victorious Allied coalition.

Hanoi, August 18, 1945

Watching Viet Minh power expand, the soon to be deposed
Emperor Bao Dai writes to General Charles de Gaulle:

> Four years ago your country was invaded by foreigners.
> Therefore, you should understand that ... [we] will surely
> never accept any oppression or domination from any foreign
> nation. If you really see the actual situation of this country and
> the mighty strength of patriotism burning in every one of our
> people, you will understand better. Even if you should re-
> conquer the rule of this country, no one would obey you, every
> village will be a resisting force, each people will be your enemy,
> you will have to withdraw.

Like Ho Chi Minh's messages to Washington, Bao Dai's letter receives no reply.

Washington, Office of Strategic Services, August 22, 1945

The director of the OSS, William "Wild Bill" Donovan provides the secretary of state with his latest assessment of the
situation in Indochina. Based on agents' reports, he states that
the French have decided not to reoccupy Indochina because
they cannot do so in sufficient strength. Instead, they will
adopt a liberal policy and try to negotiate with the Indochinese Provisional Government. While explaining that the
Viet Minh are "100% Communist," he says that they have expressed a desire to have the status of an American protectorate and hope that the United States will keep the French from
reoccupying Indochina. They have publicly stated that they
will fight to prevent a return to French colonial rule. Donovan
ends his assessment by concluding that "the Indo-Chinese
would like to be placed on the same status as the Philippines."

Hanoi, August 26, 1945

Archimedes Patti arrives in Hanoi with a small Allied team
that includes a chief of French intelligence. The Viet Minh
propaganda apparatus is in full gear to impress the Ameri-

cans. The head of their reception committee, Vo Nguyen Giap, welcomes them to Vietnam. Giap and Patti converse and Giap asks why the French have accompanied the Americans. Patti tries to explain that although the United States does not intend to assist the French against the will of the Vietnamese people, the French as allies cannot be denied American friendship.

Giap is baffled by this answer. He asks why the Soviet Union is not represented. Patti explains that Stalin agreed at Potsdam not to be included in the Allied group who will accept the Japanese surrender. Giap seems surprised at Soviet disinterest in Vietnam.

He invites the Americans outside and points with pride to a Viet Minh honor guard. Waving in the breeze are all of the Allied flags, except the French, as well as one representing Vietnam. All except the Stars and Stripes are lowered and the Viet Minh band plays "The Star Spangled Banner" followed by the other countries' national anthems. Next, a long civilian procession including many children and students files past the reviewing stand and executes an "eyes right" while raising a clenched fist in the air. That night Viet Minh radio broadcasts speak of a free Vietnam and refer to Saigon as "the City of Ho Chi Minh." Thirty years in the future, although Ho will be dead, that is the name given to a newly conquered Saigon.

Hanoi, VJ Day, September 2, 1945

Ho proclaims the founding of the Democratic Republic of Vietnam (DRV). The Declaration of Independence is carefully modeled on that of the United States.

An OSS representative reports that he has spoken with the leaders of the DRV and is convinced that they are politically naive and being misled by Communist elements. He explains: "They seem to have no knowledge of the meaning of the terms they frequently use, such as nationalization, congressional assembly, liberalism, democracy."

Saigon, September 12, 1945

According to the terms of the Potsdam Conference, Chinese forces occupy northern Vietnam to accept the Japanese surrender. Upon reaching Hanoi they recognize the DRV as the local government. It is a very different situation when the British occupy Saigon; the local British commander is appalled at the collapse of public order. Various sects have stepped into the power vacuum caused by the successive collapses of French and Japanese power. French homes have been sacked and a priest murdered. With only a Gurkha battalion and a company of Free French at hand, the British commander—a traditional British colonial officer—tries to use the Japanese to help maintain order, which only increases tensions. Acting according to government orders, he steadfastly refuses to recognize the legitimacy of the DRV and defers to the French in handling colonial matters.

The existence of the DRV is an intolerable challenge to French aspirations to regain control of their colony. French officials claim they have little real fear that their efforts to reoccupy Vietnam will confront armed resistance. However, they wish to move fast before "fanatical nationalists" spread disorder. The only problem is how to get troops to Asia fast enough.

That same day the American ambassador cables the White House from China that "the fundamental issue in Asia today is between democracy and imperialism." He reports that Asian opinion is growing to believe that the United States supports European imperialism against native democratic movements. He reminds President Truman that this is contrary to Roosevelt's intentions.

Hanoi, September 16, 1945

The American OSS officer who first made contact with Ho when he parachuted into Ho's jungle base is invited to a good-bye dinner with Ho and Giap. The American has learned a great deal more about Ho Chi Minh since their first meeting. He asks him if he is a Communist, to which Ho replies, "Yes. But we can still be friends, can't we?"

Saigon, September 17, 1945

The DRV calls a protest strike. In the markets the Vietnamese refuse to sell to the French. The British commander's attitude hardens and he responds favorably when the French ask to be allowed to restore order. Martial law is declared, demonstrations outlawed, and Vietnamese are forbidden to carry weapons. When, a few days later, the British release and arm French prisoners of war formerly held by the Japanese, the liberated but poorly disciplined French run amok. They indiscriminately beat innocent Vietnamese and arrest Vietnamese politicians and public workers.

Saigon, September 23, 1945

With the connivance of the local British commander, French forces in Saigon completely overthrow the local DRV government. They declare French authority restored in the state of Cochinchina, which comprises most of southern Vietnam. Angered, the Viet Minh prepare a mass demonstration. An American OSS officer, Lieutenant Colonel Peter Dewey, warns the Viet Minh leader that it is sure to lead to violence. This leader replies that he intends to provoke French and British reprisals to focus world attention on the nationalist cause. Accordingly, two large, unarmed groups of Vietnamese march on Saigon. Former French prisoners of war repulse them with machine-gun fire. The next day the Viet Minh strike back, killing French and Eurasian men, women, and children. The British commander responds by ordering armed Vietnamese to be shot on sight.

Dewey protests French behavior and British collusion, but the cycle of terrorism and retribution has begun. The British commander declares Dewey persona non grata and orders him to leave. Meanwhile, fighting around Saigon among Viet Minh guerrillas, a gangster sect, and French forces escalates. In the ensuing violence, Dewey disappears three days later. His assailants are unknown and his body is never found.

Upon learning of his death, Ho cables President Truman a condolence: "We are touched by the death of any American resident in this country as much as by the death of our dearest relatives." He promises to spare no effort to find and punish the culprit.

The American Embassy, Moscow, September 26, 1945

From a great distance, diplomat George F. Kennan watches events in Indochina. He sees a link among the Vietnamese nationalist movement, French Communist party declarations calling for Indochinese independence, and Soviet expansion. He informs the secretary of state that the Soviet Union "now entertains a greater interest in Indochina" than it did during the war. Kennan warns ominously that the ideal situation from the Soviet standpoint would be complete Indochinese independence from Western influence "leaving native peoples completely open to communist penetration."

Hanoi, September 30, 1945

By Truman's order, the OSS is to be disbanded. He sees no place for an "American Gestapo." Archimedes Patti is thus recalled to the United States, but before he leaves, he and Ho Chi Minh have a farewell dinner. For the first time, Ho asks point-blank if America intends to permit the French to return to Indochina. Patti repeats that he and other Americans have orders to remain neutral.

Ho shakes his head, unable to reconcile United States statements, including the Atlantic Charter, with American inaction toward the events in Saigon. He predicts that French troops, armed and equipped by the Americans, will soon try to reconquer Indochina. He wishes instead that America would use its influence to restrain the French. He tells Patti that he places "more reliance on the United States to support Viet Nam's independence" than he places on the Soviet Union. He knows the United States considers him a "Moscow puppet" but claims he is not a Communist in the American sense. He considers himself a free agent who will take support from wherever it is offered.

Hanoi, October 4, 1945

An American official tours Hanoi. He finds Viet Minh political officers active throughout the city. They are "exceedingly anxious to cultivate American good will." For the Americans' benefit many of their colorful banners spanning the streets are in English. They announce INDEPENDENCE OR DEATH, DOWN WITH FRENCH IMPERIALISM, and INDOCHINA FOR THE VIETNAM-ESE. The official attitude toward Americans extends to the common people in the streets. In all contacts with Americans, the people of Hanoi "display a conscious effort to please and to be friendly."

London, October 9, 1945

Today the British formally recognize French civil administration in Indochina. They cede occupation rights to the French. In China, French diplomats reassure worried Americans that France intends to modify its rule for Indochina but that it would be an error to make changes until French authority is reinstated. The thirty-five thousand French military men already in Indochina are unable to restore order.

State Department, October 19, 1945

The State Department has just completed an analysis of Communist activity in the Far East. It concludes that throughout the region communism "may gain more adherents as the result of participation by Communists in nationalist independence movements" and revolts against European colonial control. In Vietnam, the Annamite Communist party dominates the newly proclaimed republic. Lurking in the background is the long hand of Russia: "The Soviet Union is in a position to encourage independence movements in colonial areas at very little cost to herself. This factor greatly heightens the significance of Communist movements, however small at present, in Southeast Asia." The department believes that potential Soviet involvement is of the utmost importance. The belief that even small nationalist movements can become Soviet pawns means that such movements will be viewed as dangerous.

Saigon, Late October 1945

As part of its policy of neutrality, the American government has refused to help French troops reach Indochina or to assist them once they arrive. The British step into the breach and provide the needed sea transport. The newly arrived French troops also lack ground transportation, so the British cede them some eight hundred American-built Lend-Lease vehicles. The American claim of neutrality is a fine distinction making little difference to the Vietnamese fighters opposing the French. They see an enemy armed and equipped by the United States.

The American consul in China reports to the secretary of state that the French can easily return to Indochina, "but it will be a mistake" unless they do so with overwhelming strength to crush Vietnamese resistance quickly. Absent overpowering forces and impressive air support, he predicts, "the struggle will be long and bloody."

The day after he sends this report, French armored columns sweep out from Saigon. Although they experience initial success, it soon becomes clear that French armor and airplanes cannot pacify the country. French troops control only the ground they stand on. The guerrillas control the rest.

Hanoi, November 1, 1945

Ho Chi Minh sends a message to the American secretary of state: "I beg to express the desire . . . to send to the United States of America a delegation of about fifty Vietnam youths with a view to establishing friendly cultural relations with the American youth. They have been . . . keenly interested in things American and earnestly desirous to get into touch with the American people whose fine stand for the noble ideals of international Justice and Humanity, and whose modern technical achievements have so strongly appealed to them."

Hanoi, November 3, 1945

Ho Chi Minh learns that the French are to represent Vietnamese interests on an important Advisory Commission established to plan for Asia's future. He telegrams Truman to protest the exclusion of his government from the commission. After two weeks, the State Department's Southeast Asian desk advises "that no action should be taken" to respond to Ho's appeal.

During the last three months of 1945, Ho sends numerous letters and telegrams to American ambassadors, generals, the chairman of the Senate Foreign Relations Committee, the secretary of state, and to the President himself. The French greatly fear these initiatives. Their worries are unnecessary; Ho never receives a reply from the American government.

Northern Vietnam, November 11, 1945

Following a three-day party conclave, the Indochinese Communist party announces a dramatic change: "In order to destroy all misunderstandings, domestic and foreign, which can hinder the liberation of our country, the Central Executive Committee of the Indochina Communist Party . . . has decided to voluntarily dissolve the Indochina Communist Party."

Ho Chi Minh is striving to broaden the Viet Minh popular base. He invites a prominent nationalist named Ngo Dinh Diem into his government. Diem, bitter toward the Viet Minh because they killed his brother and suspicious of the Communist domination of the Viet Minh, refuses.

The Yacht Williamsburg on the Potomac River, Year's End

Beset by the demands of an office unexpectedly thrust upon him, President Harry S. Truman doubts whether the Russians will ever deal in good faith, yet has no theory to explain Russian behavior. During most of the preceding year, he and his foreign policy advisers lurched from problem to problem, meeting each according to their abilities but totally lacking a cohesive strategy to further America's goals. Stalin's postwar actions are simply inexplicable to the amateur historian from Missouri. But their consequences are becoming clearer: an expanding zone of Russian hegemony. Dissatisfied with the most recent round of negotiation, Harry Truman has quite simply had enough. "I'm tired of babying the Russians," he exclaims to Secretary of State Stettinius.

Indochina, January–February 1946

Kenneth Landon, the former missionary who found the State Department's file bare of useful information about Vietnam in 1941, now is the assistant chief of the Department of State's Division of Southeast Asian Affairs. He receives the assignment to tour Southeast Asia to report on events there. Having drafted the American policy toward the region, he knows that the official American policy of neutrality is firm, but it is an open secret that the massive American aid intended for mainland France is being diverted to Vietnam.

In Saigon, Landon meets with the French high commissioner for Indochina, Admiral d'Argenlieu. The admiral says the world war is over and it is time to return to reality. America supports France, which necessarily means helping it worldwide. Why aren't the Americans consistent?

Continuing his fact-finding tour, Landon travels to Hanoi and meets with Ho Chi Minh. Ho is excited to meet, for the first time, a State Department officer. In the coming weeks they dine once or twice a day. Ho proves to be a smart and very well-read man. He talks of the French and American revolutions, democracy, and the U.S. Constitution. He claims he is not a Communist and that he has been unfairly branded one. He says his party uses Communist concepts merely to organize the people, but that the movement is nationalist. Landon just listens, later noting: "You don't tell a guy you think he's lying when you're trying to find out what he thinks. You let him think he's convinced you."

Ho explains that the French are willing to let the Viet Minh dominate the north if the French continue to dominate the south, Laos, Cambodia, as well as all Indochinese diplomatic and military affairs. This is unacceptable to Ho, who particularly wants the south with its rich agricultural resources and economic potential.

Before leaving, Ho hands Landon letters to President Truman and the secretary of state. The letters ask the President to support the idea of Vietnamese independence according to the Philippines example and warn that the French effort to reconquer Indochina threatens to bring on war. In Landon's view they are "the usual kind of guff that he handed to everybody. I brought them back and did what you'd expect me to do: I filed them away. Because our government was just not interested."

The American Embassy, Moscow, Washington's Birthday, 1946

Isolated from policy deliberations at home, George Kennan can no longer endure Washington's apathy toward the Soviet threat. He drafts a 5,540-word telegram analyzing Russian behavior and fires it off to his government. In it, he explains that communism is merely the most recent camouflage for the traditional Russian strategy: "to advance official limits of Soviet power." Russia views the United States as an implacable opponent of this strategy, Kennan warns. The question of the proper American response poses "the greatest task our diplomacy has ever faced." Kennan provides a simple strategy to thwart Soviet expansion. When confronted with force, the Russians will back down.

Kennan's analysis, celebrated as "the long telegram," establishes the intellectual basis of what will become known as the strategy of containment.

Vietnam, March 6, 1946

After intense negotiation, Ho Chi Minh and the French sign a treaty by which France recognizes Vietnam as a "free state with its own government, parliament, army, and finances," while the Vietnamese agree their country will form "part of the Indochinese Federation and the French Union." France promises a phased withdrawal of her troops so that by 1952 no French soldiers will be in Vietnam. Ho pledges that the Vietnamese will cease guerrilla warfare.

Ho's signature on the accord is a personal gamble. Many nationalists bitterly resent what they see as a sellout to the French and only with great difficulty does he manage to control the nationalist movement. He reassures his followers: "You know that I would rather die than sell our country."

French colonialists also resent the accord. Admiral d'Argenlieu, the French high commissioner, epitomizes their view, expressing his "amazement that France has such a fine expeditionary corps in Indochina and yet its leaders prefer to negotiate than to fight."

Exercising the accord's prerogatives, an advance guard of French soldiers occupies Hanoi twelve days later. The commanding French general meets with Ho and tells him that "there is no question of imposing ourselves by force on masses who desire evolution and innovation."

Saigon, March 12, 1946

A French official assures Saigon's colonial society that the recent agreement does not apply to the south. He calls it a "regional arrangement" applying only to the north and pledges that Cochinchina will remain a separate, French-dominated state within the French Union.

This statement marks the beginning of Admiral d'Argenlieu's campaign to thwart the March 6 agreement. When Viet Minh officials arrive to negotiate a cease-fire for the south, he orders them arrested and places a bounty on the heads of all Viet Minh leaders who do not surrender unconditionally by month's end.

Saigon, March 21, 1946

French officials have been reassuring the Americans that they plan on holding local elections to begin the process of Vietnamese self-rule. They claim a slight delay is necessary to restore order. Today d'Argenlieu issues a communiqué stating that "rebel activities have increased in the Bien Hoa area. . . . A French convoy has been attacked on the road between Bien Hoa and Tan Uyen. . . . A French detachment was ambushed at San Jay." Forced into a corner by d'Argenlieu's hard-line policy, the Viet Minh have struck back.

Despite such difficulties, the French prepare to return to northern Vietnam in strength. These arrangements mark the end of the period of Allied occupation of Indochina following

Japan's defeat. The postwar world in which the French are again the colonial power in Southeast Asia begins.

The United States, June 1946

In the beginning of the month, John Foster Dulles writes a two-part article for *Life* magazine warning about the spread of international communism. Politicians, Republican and Democratic alike, are quick to sense opportunity. Junior congressman Lyndon B. Johnson thunders: "We must have military strength to fulfill our moral obligations to the world." In Boston an earnest congressional candidate named John F. Kennedy finds he stirs audiences when he speaks of America's new destiny. In the Midwest a former military clerk, Joseph McCarthy, learns he too can arouse similar sentiments by describing communism's threat. In southern California, Richard M. Nixon begins to wear the mantle of anti-Communist crusader. These men share the belief that America should not withdraw into isolationism. They also see an issue that can propel them to power.

Fontainebleau, France, July 6, 1946

French and Viet Minh officials resume negotiations on the degree of independence France will accord Ho Chi Minh's Democratic Republic of Vietnam. Ho believes the French Union should merely recommend policies to its members, whereas the French construe federation to mean French control over diplomatic and military policy of each member state. The two views cannot be reconciled.

Worried about the outcome of the Fontainebleau conference, Admiral d'Argenlieu convenes a rival conference in Vietnam. He invites representatives from all over Indochina but excludes the Viet Minh. Accusing the admiral of undermining the proceedings concurrently taking place in France, the Viet Minh erect barricades to block French access to various key posts in Vietnam. The barricades become the scene of violent confrontations.

The White House, August 15, 1946

It might mean war with Russia. This is the message Assistant Secretary of State Dean Acheson conveys to the President as he explains the moves necessary to protect Turkey from Soviet aggression. United States global security requires taking a stand against Russia here and now. Acheson baldly states: "Turkey must be preserved if we do not wish to see other bulwarks in Western Europe and the Far East crumbling at a fast rate."

Truman listens and responds: "We might as well find out whether the Russians are bent on world conquest."

George Kennan's theory that the Russians will back down when facing strength is put to a test. Two weeks later Stalin backs down and containment passes its first test.

The White House, Fall 1946

Fed up with Russian behavior, Harry Truman requests one of his bright aides, Clark Clifford, to compile a report of international agreements the Russians have violated. Searching the State Department's archives, Clifford finds Kennan's "long telegram." Clifford and his assistant broaden their research mandate to examine the entire record of United States-Soviet relations. They present their key finding in one sentence: "The language of military power is the only language which disciples of power politics understand"; therefore the United States must be prepared "to wage atomic and biological warfare" as part of a global doctrine to "support and assist all democratic countries which are in any way menaced or endangered by the U.S.S.R." When Truman reads these words, he recognizes their incendiary nature and orders all copies of the report collected and locked up.

U.S. Army War College, Fall 1946

While politicians play with the words and images of Communist threat, one thinker tries to advance a concrete strategy to counter the threat. George Kennan, returned from his Moscow assignment, states: "There is no reason, in theory, why it should not be possible for us to contain the Russians indefinitely by confronting them firmly and politely with superior strength at every turn."

Haiphong, November 23, 1946

Two days ago, French bulldozers tried to knock down Viet Minh barricades. Fighting ensued and only with difficulty could French and Viet Minh officials agree to separate their troops to prevent further clashes. Admiral d'Argenlieu, in Paris at this time, recommends retaliation. The French premier agrees and authorizes the commander in Haiphong, General Jean E. Valluy, to "use all the means at your disposal" to become "complete master" of the city. When the Viet Minh fail to respond to an impossibly short two-hour ultimatum to evacuate key areas of Haiphong, a French naval sloop opens fire. After four days of heavy combat, French tanks and infantry, supported by air strikes and naval gunfire, drive the Viet Minh from the port city. An estimated five thousand Vietnamese civilians die.

Vietnam, Early December 1946

Abner Moffat, a Far East expert in the State Department, having left draft instructions in Washington governing his contact with Ho Chi Minh, arrives in Vietnam. If approved, the instructions will provide Moffat with an opportunity to establish meaningful, friendly relations with Ho.

Marking time, he talks with French officials and observes high-ranking Viet Minh officials. Conflict is imminent and he senses tragedy. In Hanoi, still without instructions, he meets with Ho. Absent guidelines, when Ho speaks of his hopes for a relationship with the United States, Moffat is forced to avoid serious discussion.

Upon returning to Saigon, he finds his instructions have finally arrived. They begin: "Assume you will see Ho in Hanoi. . . . Keep in mind Ho's clear record as agent [of] international communism." Written by Dean Acheson, the message summarizes American thinking about Ho Chi Minh and his movement. Recent violence causes "deep concern." America still sees the March 6 accord as the basis for resolving outstanding questions and wants everyone to avoid actions that might jeopardize it. Acheson advises that should Ho claim that French nonimplementation of the accord relieves him of compliance, the American response is that order must return before all else. Finally, Acheson says to tell Ho that "intransigence and violence" imperils American sympathy for Vietnamese freedom. Viewed plainly, Acheson is saying that America supports the French position. Acheson concludes with satisfaction that Franco-American policies "should obviate any danger that . . . Vietnamese might be turned irrevocably against West" and into the Communist camp.

Bitterly disappointed, feeling that American diplomacy, in its zeal to confront communism, has taken a step back to the wars of religion, Moffat goes out and gets drunk. He is the last official American governmental representative ever to see Ho Chi Minh.

Washington, December 17, 1946

Secretary of State James F. Byrnes sees the government of the Democratic Republic of Vietnam controlled by a small Communist group. This group represents the nationalist feeling of the Vietnamese, a sentiment running deep against the French and threatening to "turn against all whites." However, the French presence is important as both a counter to Soviet influence and to protect Southeast Asia from future Chinese imperialism.

Byrnes believes that the trouble in Haiphong in November might not have escalated had a different French commander been present. Although mutual distrust now rules the day, agreement cannot be reached by focusing on the past. Byrnes states that first and foremost, "basic Vietnam powers and relations with France" must be established. This requires new negotiators and probably neutral good offices or mediation.

The secretary's views are balanced and realistic and hint

that the United States has enough standing with both sides to mediate differences. But the State Department has arrived at this position too late. Events pass by Byrnes's good intentions.

Hanoi, December 19, 1946

Amid mounting tension, Viet Minh forces cut Hanoi's water and electricity and attack French posts. Two days later fighting spreads to the south. The issue of who is the aggressor is never resolved. It will take three months for the French to establish control in the northern urban centers. Meanwhile, the Viet Minh hold the countryside.

Western officials assessed the news from Vietnam and reacted according to their own agendas. The French premier addressed his nation about the outbreak of violence and, with predictable emphasis, said that order had to be established before all else. His successor sent a fact-finding mission to Vietnam. Its spokesman, archcolonialist Admiral d'Argenlieu, explained that "France does not intend in the present state of evolution of the Indochinese people to give them unconditional and total independence." However, another member of the commission, the dynamic, much decorated World War II veteran Jacques Leclerc, warned that by 1947 France would have insufficient troops to put down the revolt. He recommended negotiation leading to a political solution.

After listening to this contradictory advice, French leaders reached a decision on January 8, 1947. The overseas minister announced: "Before any negotiations, it is necessary to have a military decision." Led, ironically, by an all-socialist government, France decided to seek a military victory in Indochina.

In Washington, John Carter Vincent, director of the Office of Far Eastern Affairs, analyzed the situation and predicted the likely outcome. He told Dean Acheson, the man who would be Truman's principal foreign policy adviser, that to date the French had merely made "paper-concessions" toward Vietnamese autonomy. They had concentrated on undermining the powers of the nationalists. When the Vietnamese resisted, violence occurred. Vincent's French sources admitted that France lacked the military strength to recapture Indochina. Vincent concluded that given these facts, "guerrilla warfare may continue indefinitely."

From his remote sanctuary near the Chinese border, Ho Chi Minh reached the same conclusion. He issued an appeal to all Vietnamese:

> Those who have rifles will use their rifles; those who have swords will use their swords; those who have no swords will use spades, hoes, or sticks. Everyone must endeavor to oppose the colonialists and save his country.
>
> The hour for national salvation has struck! We must sacrifice even our last drop of blood to safeguard our country.

The war between the Vietnamese and the West, a twenty-nine-year contest for control of Vietnam, had begun.

CHAPTER II

A DIRTY WAR

*[Communism's power resides] in the infectious example of
a political movement successfully contemptuous and defiant
of old Europe; in the identification of the Marxist slogan
of imperialism with the national and racial resentments of
peoples emerging from colonialism.*

—GEORGE F. KENNAN

Part 1. A DOCTRINE TO SUPPORT FREE PEOPLES

President Harry S. Truman's train arrived at Washington's
Union Station following the 1946 midterm elections. Truman
had just seen his party drubbed at the polls and knew his fellow Democrats blamed his poor leadership for their fall. Although he did not know that members of his own Cabinet
plotted to circumvent his authority, he was acutely aware that
most Washington insiders held him in low regard. In FDR's
time it had been customary for the Cabinet to meet the presidential train when it returned following an election. The
proud Truman returned without that expectation, knowing
that in Washington, the most company of company towns, few
wished to be associated with him following the November debacle.

Yet on the platform stood a lone figure, formally dressed in
suit and hat, to greet him. Dean Acheson, an intellectual, a

most blue-blooded Washington insider, earned the Missouri dry goods salesman's undying loyalty for his gesture. He also earned the right to help draft Truman's most enduring foreign policy message the following February.

At the time Truman detrained to accept Acheson's greetings, he had been President for one and one-half years, but in many ways Roosevelt's ghost still haunted the White House and the nation. Truman had last seen Roosevelt at the end of March 1945, when the enormously popular leader left for a rest at Warm Springs. Thirteen days later Truman learned he was President. He had served as Vice President for three months. Although elected to Congress on a platform of unqualified support for FDR's policies, he had not been privy to many of Roosevelt's essential decisions. Roosevelt neither informed him about such major issues as the existence of the atomic bomb nor shared with him his future plans for such secondary considerations as Indochina. Not surprisingly, at his first Cabinet meeting the new President said that he intended to continue Roosevelt's foreign and domestic policies.

On his first evening as President he confronted, without realizing it, an issue having an important bearing on Indochina: the San Francisco Conference convened to establish the United Nations. Lacking knowledge of the details, Truman ordered State Department officials to proceed with the conference as planned. As it began, he labored hard to learn more about current diplomatic matters, asking Secretary of State Stettinius for a background report on the main foreign policy issues confronting the United States. The section of the report devoted to France began: "The best interests of the United States require that every effort be made by this Government to assist France, morally as well as physically, to regain her strength and her influence." The report explained that France was "unduly preoccupied . . . with questions of national prestige. . . . They have . . . in certain cases, notably in connection with Indochina, showed unreasonable suspicions of American aims and motives." It was probably the first time the new President read anything about the role of Indochina in American foreign policy.

On the sixth day of his presidency, Truman's Cabinet officers asked him to issue a directive to the American delegation in San Francisco on the subject of trusteeships for liberated territories. Truman welcomed this opportunity since he believed in the American ideal of fostering independence and self-determination. His instructions clearly stated that the conference should broadly delineate territories eligible for trusteeship and address the possible machinery for a system of trusteeships. French Indochina fell into the category of eligibility for trusteeship only if France voluntarily consented. Given Roosevelt's record, this position puzzled the French. As we have seen, French diplomats sought clarification of the American position and came away reassured that France essentially would have a free hand to regain her former colony.

As the weeks went by, Truman had an opportunity to reflect upon the fate of areas liberated from Axis domination. An amateur historian, he believed that when great powers fight, "pent-up fanatical nationalisms begin to stir everywhere." These nationalistic movements led to acts of belligerency and aggression fought under the justification of liberation. While the desire to gain freedom could not be suppressed, "unfortunately the wrong leaders too often undertake the role of liberators." Throughout the world there were thus many violent resistance movements against established colonial powers who happened to have been America's allies in the war. Truman concluded that American principle had to endorse the right of a people to determine their own political destiny. Having established this in his own mind, he quickly learned that the exercise of foreign policy was about much more than principle.

Within the State Department, experienced bureaucrats who should have assisted Truman's learning failed to do so. Instead, they engaged in a bitter battle to tilt United States policy toward France as the department divided into a pro-Asian versus pro-European camps. The latter camp, which consisted of men who had earned a professional reputation based upon their European understanding, men who retained profound respect for their European heritage, was dominant. America's capitalist tradition came from the still-venerated Old World. The value of tradition had just been demonstrated when America, allied with Great Britain and France, had vanquished world-threatening fascism. Moreover, under Stalin a new world threat was emerging. In the view of the European camp, it would have to be confronted by maintaining the successful alliance. Against all of this, the Asian specialists had little chance to promote the view that old-style European colonialism confronted an unwinnable task in Asia.

The chances of the pro-Asian camp diminished when their rivals executed a clever bureaucratic ploy. Recognizing that those who control the flow of information to a President can manipulate presidential decisions, after Roosevelt's death the Western Europe Office drew up a paper on Indochina policy that omitted discussion of Roosevelt's policy. Truman thus made decisions about the San Francisco Conference and American policy toward Indochina without benefit of knowing the entire record of United States thought and action concerning the region.

Undersecretary of State Joseph C. Grew and others urged Truman to do everything possible to improve relations with the French. In May 1945, to the immense satisfaction of Grew and the European specialists, Truman issued a ringing endorsement that said, in part, that France had emerged from catastrophe and "has demonstrated its determination and its ability to resume its rightful and eminent place among the nations which share the largest measure of responsibility in maintaining the future peace of Europe and the world."

During his first months as President, Truman had a very full plate. The San Francisco Conference, Germany's surrender, the Potsdam Conference, the birth of the atomic age, and Japan's surrender all occurred within a period of three months. It is little wonder that he could spare scant attention for an obscure region like Indochina.

♦ ♦ ♦

The year 1946 saw Soviet Russia replace the Axis powers as the major perceived threat to the United States. Many respected statesmen warned about the perils of isolationism at a time of Russian-dominated Communist expansion. One of those was the retired wartime ambassador to Russia, Averell Harriman. Harriman knew well that America was weary after its two efforts to save Europe. In Harriman's view, Americans wanted nothing more than to "settle all our difficulties with

Russia and then go to the movies and drink Coke," but he deeply doubted that now was the time for rest. He had tried, and in his own judgment failed, to find common ground for harmonious relations with Stalin. Unable to fathom the Soviet dictator's inner workings, Harriman returned home and told America that its work was not yet complete.

Having also reached this conclusion, in 1947 Truman took decisive action to thwart Russian expansion. He summoned congressional leaders to give their views on an important aid bill that would help Greece and Turkey resist communism. The meeting went poorly until Dean Acheson, now secretary of state, took command, telling the congressmen that a historical turning point was at hand. Not since the time of Athens and Sparta, of Rome and Carthage, had the world been divided into two such diametrically opposed camps. It was a mortal battle between the American democratic vision and Soviet dictatorship.

After a long pause, Senator Arthur Vandenberg of Michigan spoke: "Mr. President, the only way you are ever going to get this is to make a speech and scare the hell out of the country." The President agreed and told the State Department to draft the speech. The result was an uninspired report entitled "Public Information Program on United States Aid to Greece." But it contained at least one clear passage that concisely explained American strategic objectives, which Acheson lifted for presidential delivery: "It is the policy of the United States to give support to free peoples who are attempting to resist subjugation from armed minorities or from outside forces." Changing the wording only slightly—"I wanted no hedging in this speech," Truman recalled. "This was America's answer to the surge ... of Communist tyranny"—on March 12, 1947, the President delivered the speech, pronouncing what became known as the Truman Doctrine.

That spring congressional leaders debated the broad mandate presumed by the Truman Doctrine. During a congressional hearing, one congressman asked Acheson if it was "a first step in a consistent and complete American policy to stop the expansion of Communism," a question that Acheson evaded. Congressmen who considered Asia and China their special area of expertise logically inquired why the foreign policy goal of stopping the spread of communism was limited to Turkey and Greece to the exclusion of China; but Acheson could provide no convincing response. So it was that the United States embarked upon a worldwide campaign to resist communism.

Part 2. "IN GRAVE HAZARD"

Simultaneously, the teeth needed to enforce the Truman Doctrine decayed. The years immediately after World War II saw the rapid demobilization of the massive American military machine. The "boys" simply could not be returned home fast enough. Faced with unprecedented worldwide obligations at a time of substantial force reduction, military planners turned to nuclear weapons and strategic bombing as cheap alternatives to fighting costly ground wars against the Communist masses. In addition, policymakers sought allies to help stop the Communists. France figured to be an important partner in the anti-Communist coalition, which left the uncomfortable problem of how to deal with her desire to reimpose colonial rule in Indochina. Yet, with Germany occupied and Great Britain bled dry by the war, France stood as the only significant potential ally able to oppose Russia on the European mainland. The United States therefore had a tremendous interest in helping France recover her economic and military strength. Truman authorized Secretary of State Acheson to inform the French that America approved the sale of weapons and supplies to France "except in cases which appear to relate to Indochina." Soon thereafter, with an eye toward satisfying American interest in Indochinese self-rule, France decided to reinstate the Vietnamese emperor Bao Dai as a figurehead leader of Vietnam.

By the time the American President announced the Truman Doctrine, the nature of the awkward straddle that tried simultaneously to support French rebirth and the principle of anticolonialism, and address the concerns that Ho Chi Minh was a Communist had become apparent. The statement of the American ambassador to France reflected the uncertainty of the American position: "Frankly we have no solution of [the] problem to suggest." In mid-May 1947, the State Department instructed American embassies that given global strategic interrelationships, the United States would suffer from any French setback in Southeast Asia. The department summarized its policy with the observation that America was "essentially in [the] same boat as [the] French." While it was clear that this boat was a ship of war—fighting between the French and Ho Chi Minh's Viet Minh intensified with the passage of time—it was not at all clear who the enemy was or what was the conflict's likely outcome.

In the fall of 1948, the State Department's Office of Intelligence Research completed an examination of Communist influence in Southeast Asia. Finding evidence of Kremlin influence in all countries except Vietnam, it concluded: "If there is a Moscow-directed conspiracy in Southeast Asia, Indochina is an anomaly so far." The State Department remained eager for the French to align themselves with a Vietnamese nationalist. However, it worried that support of Bao Dai was inadvisable, as the United States had to avoid commitment to "a puppet government separated from the people and existing only by the presence of French military forces."

Such warnings could be overlooked given the specter of monolithic communism, a unified movement with grasping tentacles everywhere responding to one central Moscow brain. In January 1949, the Communists entered Peking. A year later, American intelligence reported that a Soviet think tank had examined opportunities in Southeast Asia and decided the time was ripe for accelerating Communist efforts there. Amid a growing sense of crisis, Truman's government began to reach a consensus regarding Ho Chi Minh and his movement. When the Soviet Union formally recognized Ho's government, Secretary of State Acheson announced: "The Soviet acknowledgment of this movement should remove any illusions as to the 'nationalist' nature of Ho Chi Minh's aims and reveals Ho in his true colors as the mortal enemy of native independence in Indochina."

Having branded Ho Chi Minh a participant in the Communist juggernaut caused the United States to view more favorably France's battle against the Viet Minh. The Truman administration had an unallocated sum of $75 million in military aid that the Senate had intended for use in the "general area of China." Anticipating that the funds would become available—indeed Congress eagerly authorized their use in January 1950—the Joint Chiefs of Staff (JCS) embarked upon a study of how best to spend the money in Southeast Asia. The study developed the intellectual basis for what would become known as the domino theory.

Heretofore, Southeast Asia had not figured prominently in American defense strategy. Concerned with a global war against Russia since 1946, military planners had chosen an island chain extending from Japan south to Okinawa, Taiwan, and the Philippines as a bastion from which to deliver air and sea attacks against the Soviet Union. Indochina had no role in this strategy. Now, faced with the loss of China to communism, an event nearly everyone believed a grievous defeat, the Joint Chiefs considered where the Communist flood would flow next. Southeast Asia was the obvious next place: "If Southeast Asia is also swept by Communism, we shall have suffered a rout the repercussions of which will be felt throughout the rest of the world."

More than ever, strategists saw the spread of communism in Asia as Soviet inspired. Therefore, they looked for a final position at which to draw the line against the Russians. The previously identified offshore island chain would have to serve as both an offensive platform and a last line of defense. Retaining it was vital to United States security. In turn, events in Southeast Asia took on new significance. Japanese airplanes based in Indochina had dominated the offshore waters during the beginning of World War II. Their sinking of two British battleships had marked the eclipse of the United Kingdom as a major Asian power. Now American military men—who, like their civilian leaders saw no distinction among Russian, Chinese, and Vietnamese communism—had to worry that Soviet planes could replicate the feats of Japanese aviators. Here was another reason to support the French, who were already manning the line in Indochina and fighting the Communists. So the JCS recommended military aid.

Army Chief of Staff J. Lawton Collins found the conclusion troubling. In World War II, Collins had won renown for his thrusting, aggressive leadership, but five years later, as he examined Far Eastern affairs, he uncharacteristically expressed caution. He doubted that Indochina was militarily as important to national security as the other Chiefs believed, declaring that the region's relevance "does not justify the seeking of a solution through a primarily military effort." Rather than an aid package restricted to military items, he preferred an integrated approach combining political, economic, and psychological programs. No one could question Collins's warrior credentials and when he emphasized nonmilitary means, the military took note.

His departure from Pentagon orthodoxy in late 1949 influenced the Joint Chiefs' next strategic assessment. Truman's secretary of defense wanted the JCS's opinion on how the United States could best prevent further Communist encroachment in Southeast Asia. They recommended the urgent dispatch of military aid, but, mindful of the unhappy experience of sending aid to China only to see it squandered, added important conditions. First and foremost, it should be carefully controlled and integrated with political and economic programs. American military officers should screen requests for equipment to ensure the coordination of aid with specific military operations. Moreover, the JCS wanted to understand and approve French operational plans before providing military aid. The Joint Chiefs appreciated that sending military aid to Indochina had political ramifications. They suggested that the United States insist upon Vietnamese independence following a phased French withdrawal, the same idea that Ho Chi Minh had promoted to American OSS men five years earlier. In sum, influenced by Collins's caution, the Joint Chiefs provided a carefully constrained program of military aid to the French. In the event, and much to the country's detriment, the program that evolved violated every proviso suggested by the Pentagon.

In part this occurred because the pace of events produced a crisis atmosphere. The decision to send aid had ascended to a new level of urgency after the Kremlin's recognition of Ho's government in early 1950. Obeying the imperative to counter all Soviet actions, it was clear that this dramatic Soviet action required a United States response. Truman's advisers recommended immediate help for the French because of the threat resulting from "an obviously Russian sponsored communist anti-government force under Ho Chi Minh." At the beginning of February 1950, Dean Acheson wrote a closely reasoned two-page memo for Truman on the subject of according formal recognition to the French-controlled governments in Vietnam, Laos, and Cambodia. Acheson explained that the French had undertaken legislative and political steps to transform their Indochinese colonies into states within the French Union. Few Americans had any understanding of such an esoteric subject as French colonial theory, and Truman was no exception. Acheson told the President that this French action was significant since it gave the Vietnamese considerably more freedom than they had previously enjoyed, words that largely reassured a man who considered himself a stout anticolonialist.

French Indochina comprised three Associated States. In French colonial theory a colony evolved from association within the French Union to becoming a part of Metropolitan France, whereas Associated States did not achieve independence. In Indochina one of the Associated States was Vietnam, which consisted of three regions: Annam, centered around Saigon, in the rich agricultural south where colonial life persisted the strongest; Cochinchina in the middle; and Tonkin, centered around Hanoi in the north. Of these, France most cherished Tonkin. Tonkin represented a century of costly effort to westernize Vietnam. Here stood the Bank of Indochina, guarding France's financial interests in Asia; and the University of Hanoi, imparting French culture and values through its French staff. In Tonkin, Catholicism flourished among the rural population. Although Cambodia and Laos also belonged to the Associated States, their only link to Vietnam was French rule. The Associated States were artificial divisions created for ease of French domination.

Acheson, overlooking the implications of continued colonial rule and dwelling instead on the Associated States' coming independence, also described for Truman strategic reasons for United States involvement in the region. Recognizing the Associated States as the legally constituted governments would serve as a role model for others in Southeast Asia, showing countries how nationalist aspirations could be channeled in a non-Communist path. In addition, the creation of stable non-Communist governments on China's borders would be a valuable asset. Finally, of course, it would help France, which was a signatory to the North Atlantic Treaty. All of this made a great deal of sense to Truman, and the day after reading Acheson's memo, he gave his approval to extending formal American recognition to Vietnam, Laos, and Cambodia. From this determination flowed the final decision to provide military aid to the French and French-controlled Indochinese forces.

Truman considered the advice of Acheson and others in a pressured environment, as the Central Intelligence Agency had told him the previous autumn that only about six months remained to rectify the situation before the French collapsed. Similarly, his State Department spoke of the decision as a matter of the greatest urgency. In mid-February 1950, the French formally requested immediate aid, and the President directed his secretary of state to ask if the aid could be coupled with steps granting greater independence to Vietnam. Although he concurred with the pro-French stance, Acheson worried that once the aid began, the United States would lose its leverage in promoting French reform. The French responded to Acheson with a private warning that absent American aid they would abandon Vietnam. Publicly, the French foreign minister derided American concerns, expressing amazement "that the United States insisted upon discussing future Vietnamese independence from France when Vietnamese independence from communism was at stake."

In Truman's administration, the president charged the National Security Council (NSC) with developing formal strategy statements. The NSC had originated in the fall of 1944 when Roosevelt requested General Donovan, the head of the OSS, to prepare a secret report on a postwar intelligence service. Donovan's plans fell afoul of a jealous J. Edgar Hoover, who leaked them to the press. The ensuing uproar forced Roosevelt to back off until April 1945 when he revived the plan. A week later he was dead and his successor was no friend of Donovan. Declaring that the United States could do without a peacetime "Gestapo," Truman disbanded the OSS.

The resultant fragmentation of intelligence gathering and analysis produced an unacceptable situation reminiscent of the divided authority that contributed to Pearl Harbor. In 1947 the National Security Act created a new defense organization. The Air Force became separate from the Army; the Joint Chiefs of Staff received a statutory basis. In hopes of coordinating all of the services, the act created a new Office of the Secretary of Defense. It also authorized a National Security Council to advise the President on high-level national security issues, and a new independent department, the Central Intelligence Agency, which reported to it. The NSC itself reported directly to the President. With this new organization, one of Truman's proudest achievements, the United States would fight the cold war.

The NSC would be the scene of many discussions in future years about American policy toward Vietnam since, for the first time, it gave the government a place where military and diplomatic problems could be studied and continually reassessed. The NSC comprised the President, Vice President, the secretaries of state, defense, army, navy, and air force, as well as the chairman of the National Security Resource Board. In sum, these positions encompassed many of the wisest, best-informed people the government could bring to bear on national security problems. However, the NSC operated in the same way as the Cabinet. It offered recommendations by making formal submissions to the President, but did not make policy. Only the President's signature on a National Security Council document made that document official policy. Since members of the NSC were one step removed from decision making, they could advance riskier suggestions than the man at the top. Nonetheless, the NSC frequently generated ideas that became the fundamental basis for presidential decision making.

National Security Council Document 64 was the first policy statement applicable to Indochina and it appeared nearly simultaneously with the French request for aid. It said that Communist aggression in Indochina was only one phase of a Communist plan to seize all of Southeast Asia. If Indochina fell, neighboring Thailand and Burma would go next. Worse, the "balance of Southeast Asia would then be in grave hazard."

World War II was the formative experience for the highest

echelon of American policymakers as they guided foreign policy into the 1950s. From their perspectives, the appeasement of the 1930s had led to war. In Europe they saw a straight chain of events from German reoccupation of the Rhineland, to the Austrian Anschluss to the dismemberment of Czechoslovakia at Munich, to general war in Europe. Almost everyone was less familiar with events in the Pacific, yet here too there had been a similar chain of events beginning with Japan's seizure of Manchuria, subsequent invasion of the rest of China, occupation of Indochina, and strike on Pearl Harbor. Viewed differently, after the toppling of the first domino, the remainder of the chain had inevitably collapsed leading to world war. Truman did not intend for this to happen again. He accepted NSC 64 and so committed his administration to a priority program to protect American security interests in Indochina, and then approved $15 million in military aid to support the French position there.

Acheson explained that underlying the aid program was the recognition that neither national independence nor democratic evolution could occur in an area dominated by Soviet imperialism. The program's goal therefore was to assist the French "in restoring stability" in order to permit Vietnam, Cambodia, and Laos the chance to "pursue their peaceful and democratic development."

♦ ♦ ♦

While the United States grappled with the mechanism for efficiently managing aid to Indochina, an event took place that seemed to illuminate the nature of the conflict in Asia with absolute clarity. At 4:00 A.M., Sunday, June 25, 1950, Russian-built tanks spearheaded a surprise North Korean invasion of South Korea. While two assault columns drove on Seoul, the United Nations Security Council met in emergency session and called for the North Koreans to withdraw. When the invaders pressed the attack, President Truman ordered General MacArthur to support the South Koreans with air and naval forces. At the same time, Truman announced, "I have similarly directed acceleration in the furnishing of military assistance to the forces of France and the Associated States in Indochina and the dispatch of a military mission to provide close working relations with those forces." He approved a JCS recommendation to increase military aid for Indochina to $31 million for the coming year. The Communist strike across the 38th Parallel had had immediate reverberations in Vietnam. Within two days the Americans more than doubled military aid to the French and decided to send a military mission to represent America on the ground. With this decision American soldiers returned to Vietnam to begin what would become a twenty-five-year effort.

In his memoirs Harry S. Truman expressed strong anti-colonial attitudes. Yet, as President, Russian expansion and the resultant cold war caused him to modify his views and begin to support France, a recognized colonial power. The Korean War confirmed his new attitude.

At the National War College, George Kennan reflected upon all of this and came to a very different conclusion. In August he wrote Acheson: "In Indo-China we are getting ourselves into the position of guaranteeing the French in an undertaking which neither they nor we, nor both of us together, can win." Unlike others who complained of the United States' Indochina policy, Kennan suggested concrete actions to change that policy. He recommended telling the French that after a closer view of the problem, the United States had concluded that the position was basically hopeless. The United States would stress that it had been and continued to be a French problem, but that we would do everything possible to avoid embarrassing the French while supporting any reasonable settlement of the conflict. He declared:

> We cannot honestly agree with them that there is any real hope of remaining successfully in Indo-China, and we feel that rather than have their weakness demonstrated by a continued costly and unsuccessful effort to assert their will by force of arms, it would be preferable to permit the turbulent political currents of that country to find their own level, unimpeded by foreign troops or pressures.

Kennan concluded that this path was preferable even at the probable cost of an eventual deal involving the Viet Minh and the resultant domination of the country by the Communists.

Part of the brilliance of Kennan's analysis lay in his recognition that a country lost more prestige by pursuing an unsuccessful policy than by ending that policy and accepting the consequences. But the more orthodox thinkers in the Truman administration could not accept Kennan's bold recommendations. Politically, doing so would have opened the administration to charges of abandoning an ally before America had even tried to help. Strategically, Kennan's advice went against the growing belief that Indochina was crucial to the United States.

Once the Truman administration accepted that events in Asia represented the next wave of Soviet expansion, it followed that Asian foreign policy could not be separated from that for Europe. The administration worried that a loss of territory in the Far East, especially if it seemed to result from an ally's failure of nerve, would adversely affect American public opinion. Americans would blame a country such as France, and then be unwilling to support her in Europe should the Soviets attack. While this worry perhaps underestimated public sophistication and resolve and overestimated the country's isolationist tendencies, it was a real concern for Acheson and Truman. They concluded that "in order to avoid this kind of reaction we must take a steadfast position in the Far East." A "steadfast" position required additional aid for the French.

The perils of this position could not be denied. Several senators, after completing a world tour at the beginning of 1951, warned Acheson that nationalism was sweeping through Southeast Asia. So strong was the drive to get rid of foreigners, native peoples preferred even bad rule by natives to better rule by foreigners. The senators warned that by helping "maintain a vestige of colonial rule," most Asians saw United States support for the French "as another instance of bolstering up the remnants of hated colonial regimes in this area." For reasons of grand strategy, Acheson and Truman decided to swim against the tide of nationalism.

The President explained his policy toward Korea and the Far East in a national radio address in the spring of 1951. He said: "The Communists in the Kremlin are engaged in a monstrous conspiracy to stamp out freedom all over the world. . . . If history has taught us anything, it is that aggression anywhere in the world is a threat to the peace everywhere." And so, for the remainder of Truman's presidency,

American policymakers saw events in Korea and Indochina as the intimately linked prongs of a Soviet-dominated effort to conquer Asia. Truman believed that the Soviets intended the Asian battles to prevent United States participation in NATO and the defense of Europe. The British would reinforce his opinion by claiming that Chinese intervention in Korea was a ruse to stop American aid in rebuilding Europe. Acheson concluded that the Soviets had embarked upon an all-out assault on the leadership of the United States. Its initial focus was to divide the country from its allies. Everyone expected Soviet pressure to intensify.

The fear of monolithic communism caused the administration to overlook opportunities for diplomatic subtlety. When British Prime Minister Clement Attlee suggested the time was ripe to try to drive a wedge between China and Russia, whom he suggested were natural rivals in the Far East, Truman refused to consider it. Stubborn and combative by nature, Harry S. Truman did not intend to let the Russians accomplish their grand designs while he was President. He preferred direct means, the essential component of which was military aid to foreign countries. He subsequently stated: "We could not deny military aid to a victim of Communist aggression in Asia unless we wanted other small nations to swing into the Soviet camp for fear of aggression which, alone, they could not resist."

To resist communism also required a united front. Accordingly, Truman's diplomats successfully promoted a basic tenet that none of the Western powers fighting the Communists would negotiate a separate cease-fire. The French respected this arrangement and broke off their continuing negotiations with the Viet Minh. The quid pro quo from the United States would be the assumption of much of the French financial burden for their war.

Part 3. UPPING THE ANTE

Saigon was the epitome of a torpid colonial city. White-suited French plantation barons, medal-bedecked French staff officers, and exotic Eurasian women mingled in bars and cafés. Untouched by war, usually unthreatened by Communist activity, it was a place where the white man sailed aloof on a sea of yellow. The United States established its embassy here instead of in Hanoi because Saigon was both the location of French military headquarters for all of Indochina and the seat of the Bao Dai government.

To preserve their rule, the French had already committed over 140,000 ground troops. Since the outbreak of fighting, they had suffered such heavy casualties that the French government concealed their extent from the French people. However, the French president wanted Truman to know and sent him a precisely tabulated accounting: 2,046 killed, including 70 officers and 281 noncommissioned officers in the first six months of 1950; 19,519 killed since 1945. In response to this grim news, Truman reiterated his determination "to bring this war to a victorious conclusion and to pacify the area." In addition he extended his condolences to the wives and families of the deceased servicemen.

How much had been gained by this sacrifice was very much open to question. When debating the merits of the aid package to the French, Acheson had told a senator that the situation compared most favorably to the previous year. He saw improvement in French morale, equipment, and overall efficiency. In the north, French troops manned a series of strongpoints along the Chinese border that interdicted the Communist supply line and, equally important in the American view, checked potential Chinese expansion southward. A considerable French force garrisoned the critical Red River Delta, northern Vietnam's rice bowl, which lay between Hanoi and Haiphong. Acheson believed French progress already included the pacification of the entire delta region and thought that American military assistance, comprehensive support short of actual fighting forces, would provide the last ingredient to a French mix that would win the war.

Politically, the United States supported the French-installed Bao Dai government. Bao Dai would drift in and out of the State Department's consciousness in the coming years as his perceived usefulness ebbed and flowed. Nominally emperor of Annam before World War II, he had been used, in turn, by the Japanese, the Viet Minh, and the French as a puppet ruler. Buffeted by forces stronger than himself, Bao Dai wavered between life as an international playboy and life as a contemplative, benign mandarin despot. After he returned to Indochina, the French had positioned him as figurehead leader of Vietnam. Lest he have any pretensions of exercising real authority, one of the first messages Bao Dai received from the French president tersely prescribed that "the annexation of Southern Viet Nam to the rest of the Empire shall be carried out in the following manner." As instructed, on March 8, 1949, Bao Dai signed a complicated series of articles forming the Associated State of Vietnam. Some of these articles granted elements of national sovereignty while others hinted at major future concessions. Neither did the French legislature ratify them nor did the government proceed with good faith negotiations regarding future sovereignty.

The foreign policy analysis branches of the American government assessed the significance of the March 8 agreement. The Central Intelligence Agency informed Truman and Acheson about perils it saw in an intelligence estimate submitted to the National Security Council that predicted continuing political instability as long as the French withheld full Vietnamese sovereignty. After months of further study, another CIA estimate flatly stated: "The Bao Dai regime cannot be relied on under any circumstances to gain true popular support." On a slightly different tack, the head of the State Department's Far East Division warned against the conventional analogy comparing the effort to resist Communist-dominated Asian nationalism to the recent conflict in Greece, where United States aid had been effective in repelling communism.

Asian leaders also warned American diplomats that French lip service to Vietnamese independence would not do. In the fall of 1949, Indian Prime Minister Jawaharlal Nehru told Acheson that "the Bao Dai experiment was hopeless and doomed to failure." The next year, when the United States formally recognized Bao Dai's government to counter Soviet recognition of the Viet Minh, the Philippine ambassador told Acheson that Asia now believed that America's zeal to fight communism caused it to espouse "the demonstrated inequity of colonial imperialism."

Sensitive to such criticisms, Acheson took every opportunity to press the French to ratify the March 8 agreement as an evolutionary step toward Vietnamese independence. At one meeting with the French ambassador, Acheson observed that the French had not even allowed Bao Dai to use Saigon's Imperial Palace. Instead, the palace housed the French high commissioner. The ambassador responded that it was difficult to ask Frenchmen to die in Indochina if they did not feel that they were dying for France or the French Union. This remark clearly expressed the heart of the matter.

American officials well knew there were additional French motives for withholding Vietnamese sovereignty. French prestige was at stake in Indochina. French leaders feared that any Indochinese concessions would cause unrest in her African colonies, most importantly Tunisia, Morocco, and Algeria where over one million Frenchmen lived. Local French interests in Vietnam also had to be protected. And finally, with true colonial superiority, the French believed that the Vietnamese were not yet ready for self-government.

Yet many influential men within the State Department managed to convince themselves that Bao Dai was a strong, anti-Communist nationalist leader to whom the French could make those concessions to Vietnamese independence necessary to subvert the Viet Minh. An American diplomat explained that "the United States is convinced that the Bao Dai government . . . reflects more accurately than rival claimants the nationalist aspirations of the people." Simultaneously, they recognized that more than in most wars, the fighting in Vietnam had a vital local political component. The free world could only win if it could convince Vietnamese peasants that they were "better off with Bao Dai than they are with Ho."

Other government officials doubted the wisdom of supporting Bao Dai but could see no alternative. The same CIA estimate that stated Bao Dai would never gain popular support rejected negotiations with Vietnamese Communists as too risky to be seriously considered. Nearly three years earlier, Secretary of State George Marshall had warned that supporting a Bao Dai government entailed great risk. Heedless, Dean Acheson and Harry Truman aligned the country with this playboy-philosopher-king who had virtually no popular support in Vietnam. So, the United States embarked upon a policy of urging the French to allow Bao Dai more freedom and authority while supplying their fighting forces with the tools for war. The French happily accepted the guns.

To do so they first had to deal with an American survey mission charged with determining the long-range goals of the aid program. Led by John F. Melby, a State Department official who had served with the American embassy in China from 1945 to 1949, the mission included a military section headed by Major General Graves B. Erskine. Erskine was a Marine Corps veteran of the Pacific campaigns who had commanded a Marine division on Iwo Jima. His job was to evaluate what equipment the French needed. He had little patience for anything French, pronouncing that they "haven't won a war since Napoleon so why listen to a bunch of second raters when they are losing this war." Erskine soon reached the sobering conclusion that the Viet Minh had pinned most French forces to widely dispersed defensive enclaves. Merely to travel by road from one post to another required an enormous escort. Such escorts tied down invaluable, scarce mobile units and prevented them from taking offensive action. Even in "pacified" areas, notably the region Acheson had highlighted some six months earlier as illustrative of pending French victory, Viet Minh dominance was apparent to Melby:

> It was a bit of a shock, therefore, to visit the Red River delta in July and see how the French interpret the word "pacification." . . . At 1,000-yard intervals along the road, they had built little beau geste towers, made of masonry, in which they had troops. As they swept the road, each tower, as cleared, would put up a white flag. When there were white flags as far down the road you could see, the convoys could pass that morning. It was impossible to get to the border posts except by air. Wherever we went . . . we were under armed guards—assassinations were a matter of daily occurrence.
>
> The French admit at night the Viet Minh control the countryside.

In addition to concluding that the French were losing, Melby, Erskine, and other members of the first American mission also determined that a military solution could not be decisive without concurrent political reform and economic aid.

With this assessment they echoed earlier sentiments doubting the popular appeal of Bao Dai. They went further and said that absent a political solution involving substantial French concessions, the French would be driven from Vietnam. Moreover, Melby privately informed Deputy Undersecretary of State Dean Rusk that high-ranking French generals in Vietnam said that France was incapable of granting the needed concessions.

Once again reports from the field flew in the face of determinations made in Washington. The State Department had to weigh the mission's pessimism against the mandate given by the National Security Council regarding the strategic importance of Indochina. Moreover, the Melby mission concurred with the NSC's strategic judgment in its final report that pronounced Indochina "the keystone in the arch of Southeast Asia without which, the balance of the area will likely fall." The State Department also had to take into account Truman's speech two days after North Korea's invasion of South Korea promising military assistance. Consequently, the department selectively accepted the Melby mission's conclusions and recommendations, largely ignoring the mission's political concerns while concentrating on the one concrete act possible in a difficult situation. The department arranged for military aid to be sent. In September 1950, the first members of a Military Assistance Advisory Group (MAAG) arrived in Saigon, and by the next month the MAAG began operation with some sixty-five American officers and enlisted men.

One serious consequence of the Military Assistance Advisory Group's small staff was that it had to rely upon French officials to handle most of the work. That was just fine with the French, who felt about the MAAG the same way that they had greeted the establishment of a full American embassy in Saigon. They welcomed all additional aid but worried about American information gathering and interference. In particular, they wished to limit American contact with the nascent Vietnamese military. Consequently, they forbade American officers from supervising the use of American equipment. When the Americans mentioned sending aid directly to the Vietnamese, the French said no. Threatening to resign, the French military commander in Indochina, General Marcel

Carpentier, stated: "I will never agree to equipment being given directly to the Vietnamese. . . . The Vietnamese have no generals, no colonels, no military organization that could effectively utilize the equipment." Carpentier did not explain that these Vietnamese military deficiencies resulted from deliberate French policy. The French wanted cannon fodder, not potential Vietnamese leaders, but the Americans missed this point. Carpentier also cited the unhappy American experience with Chiang Kai-shek as an example of sending aid to people unready to use it. Aware that American politicians were ever mindful of the Chinese debacle, the general knew that this reminder was certain to strike a responsive chord.

Accepting French constraints meant that most Americans were cut off from contact with Vietnamese soldiers, and especially the civilian population outside of Saigon. The Americans would be limited to selecting which French requests to meet and to verifying that supplies had been delivered. All military aid would be filtered through the French; only economic aid went directly to the Vietnamese. So, both the embassy and the MAAG had to rely upon the French for information and intelligence about the war's progress. This isolation effectively prevented their influencing policy. The inability to influence the policy of the recipients of American military aid would become a recurring theme of the American involvement in Vietnam.

Months earlier the Joint Chiefs had urged that military aid not be granted unconditionally, but that it be integrated with political and economic aid programs. Another condition the Chiefs recommended had been the close coordination between specific military aid and French military planning, which required the French to disclose their plans to American officers. Early on, however, the French had effectively refused. The JCS also had stressed the need for France to abandon her colonial policy. In the haste to halt the Communist tide, American military men overlooked their own wise words. By tolerating these oversights, they fell prey to a process that is the antithesis of long-range strategic planning. The great game of strategy, chess, requires foresight. Grand masters succeed because they look well into the future. Each move is linked by their strategy to an outcome that occurs many moves later. On the opposite end of the skill spectrum, the novice cannot foresee long-range consequences. He cannot link a series of moves to force a desired outcome. By concentrating entirely on the tactical merits of his next move, the novice plays what is called one-move chess. This is the game the Joint Chiefs allowed themselves to play when they made the first decisions to send military aid to the French in Vietnam.

♦ ♦ ♦

President Truman's famous meeting with General Douglas MacArthur on Wake Island in October 1950 gave a concerned mid-level State Department bureaucrat, Dean Rusk, an opportunity to probe the great general's mind about the situation in Vietnam. Rusk helped write official policy toward Indochina and on Wake Island he asked the general what he thought was the essential problem in Indochina. MacArthur replied, "They need to get an aggressive general." Rusk further queried about the impact of native popular support upon military operations. MacArthur answered, "Armed men passing through a village in Asia are treated with the highest respect." He explained that the "principal annoyance" that comes from a hostile population is in the "logistical support which it gives to the enemy," including the furnishing of food, water, the care of wounded, and, particularly, intelligence. The conversation made it clear to Rusk that MacArthur, one of the two or three most respected military men in the country, felt that with aggressive leadership the French could win.

The lack of aggressive French leadership became, however, an excuse to explain French setbacks. By late 1950 these setbacks occurred with alarming regularity in spite of the greatly increased deliveries of American arms and munitions. After a year of relentless training in the sanctuary provided by Red China, Vo Nguyen Giap committed his forces to the first direct showdown with the French. He chose as his target the French forts just over the Chinese border. Using entirely conventional tactics, backed by overwhelming firepower, the Viet Minh crushed the isolated forts one by one. When the campaign ended, the French had suffered their worst colonial defeat since Montcalm died defending Quebec in 1759.

The defeat caused the French defense minister to tell his

American counterparts that the current level of United States aid was inadequate. Truman agreed that the increased Communist threat required additional military aid and undertook the necessary measures. By the autumn of 1950, the size of the American military aid program grew until it was surpassed only by the support for the combat forces in Korea. While the arrival of massive American aid did not reverse the flow of French defeat, it did cause an all-important new factor to enter the equation: American prestige. State Department officials began warning that all of Southeast Asia was watching to see the outcome in Indochina. Over time, this warning expanded to the claim that the entire world looked to Vietnam to weigh the value of American aid and the strength of American resolve to fight communism. Prestige would rival security concerns as a reason for remaining in Vietnam.

Part 4. LA SALE GUERRE

The assembled diplomatic corps waited expectantly for the plane to arrive. The host of French and Vietnamese among them could not conceal their anxiety. The victorious Viet Minh campaign along the Chinese border had caused French morale to sag and apparently Giap was now massing his men for a drive on Hanoi. Communist leaflets posted the promise that Ho Chi Minh would be in Hanoi for Tet, the lunar new year coming in February 1951. The crowd was waiting for a possible savior. Marshal de Lattre de Tassigny, appointed to command French forces in the Indochina theater, was due to arrive this December day.

A large formation of immaculately dressed soldiers stiffened to attention. As the marshal's plane rolled to a stop, a nineteen-gun salute sounded. This was an American, not a French, tradition, but the marshal had grown fond of the ceremony. Attendants pulled the ramp to the door. The marshal walked onto the platform and stood motionless in his dress uniform. Slowly he put on his white gloves. The symbolism was unmistakable. The French called the fighting in Indochina la sale guerre, "the dirty war," and Marshal de Lattre had come to clean up the mess.

When the Viet Minh drive on Hanoi began, the marshal took personal command of the battle. His front-line leadership inspired the French Union forces to stand fast on hilltop positions as waves of Viet Minh infantry pressed the assault. The battle featured the first widespread use of American-supplied napalm, described by a Viet Minh officer whose unit was annihilated by it, as the fire that falls from the sky. Still, only by mobilizing every available airplane were the French able to resist the "human sea" attacks. When the battle ended, the Viet Minh had suffered a terrible defeat that clearly showed Giap had miscalculated. His forces were not ready for a general offensive to fight the French in the open.

Marshal de Lattre's victory restored the French position and greatly heartened most Americans concerned with affairs in Indochina. Here was vindication for the ever increasing amount of aid sent to the French, and here was a leader who proved MacArthur's claim about what an aggressive general could accomplish. Yet from a distance, at least one prominent general retained doubts.

General Dwight D. Eisenhower commanded Allied forces in Europe. His prime strategic task was to knit together a defensive alliance with enough manpower to hold Western Europe should the Russians attack. In March 1951 he met with de Lattre, who had returned to Europe to request French reinforcements for Indochina. That night Eisenhower entered his impressions of the meeting in his diary:

> The French have a knotty problem on that one—the campaign out there is a draining sore in their side. Yet if they quit and Indochina falls to Commies, it is easily possible that the entire Southeast Asia and Indonesia will go, soon to be followed by India. That prospect makes the whole problem one of interest to us all. I'd favor heavy reinforcement to get the thing over at once; but I'm convinced that no military victory is possible in that kind of theater.

In Indochina, the Military Assistance Advisory Group found de Lattre very difficult to work with. While lobbying for more aid, he frequently complained about American interference and claimed that there were entirely too many Americans in Vietnam. Lest there be any doubt about French primacy, when the U.S. Information Service—the propaganda

arm of the American government—tried to open a library, de
Lattre ordered it shut down. His high-handed action underscored a trend from the beginning of the Korean War. Until
then, America had preserved an independent policy toward
the French and, for a combination of idealistic and pragmatic
reasons, had pressured them for reform. Once the United
States decided that the French were doing the same thing in
Indochina that America was doing in Korea, the attitude
changed to one of more unqualified support. Marshal de Lattre shrewdly took advantage.

American officials in Saigon worried about de Lattre's failure to stimulate the same kind of response among his Vietnamese troops that he drew from his French soldiers. The
marshal had delivered "A Call to Vietnamese Youth." He said
that like it or not, the war in Vietnam was for Vietnam: "Certain people pretend that Vietnam cannot be independent because it is part of the French Union. Not true!" He contended
that in the modern world no nation could be absolutely independent; it was rather a world of "fruitful interdependencies."
He concluded by calling on the young men of Vietnam to defend their country. The American consul in Saigon reported
to the State Department that de Lattre's appeal elicited small
response. The choice of whether to fight on the side of Marshal de Lattre de Tassigny or of Ho Chi Minh did not prove
difficult for most Vietnamese youth.

So the *sale guerre* continued. The French fought it in their
own unique style in an effort to smooth its rough edges. An
American journalist accompanied de Lattre on a tour of
French outposts in the middle of a jungle. They arrived just
before lunch. After serving an aperitif, the head of the mess
escorted them to the table where name tags indicated everyone's assigned seat. The head of the mess announced the
meal. The journalist recalls: "The menu for August 14 at 1:00
P.M. Gentlemen . . . We will begin with soup. Then we will have
fish. Then we will have entrecote. Then we will have a salad.
Then we will have a tart. Then we will have coffee. . . . Meanwhile, on the perimeter the damn mortars are going off."

In September 1951, Marshal de Lattre arrived in New York
on a tour to request additional aid. He played the American
press brilliantly. After posing for pictures with Humphrey Bo-

gart and Lauren Bacall before the Statue of Liberty, he told reporters that the French war was not to support colonialism but rather, as in Korea, to fight against communism for liberty and peace. *Time* magazine, in a cover story on de Lattre, agreed. De Lattre continued his campaign to teach Americans to equate Korea with Vietnam during visits to West Point and Annapolis, the Tomb of the Unknown Soldier, and on television's *Meet the Press.* He pledged that with American support the war would be won in at most two years.

His whirlwind tour coincided with deep public frustration over both the Korean War and American foreign policy. Only a year earlier, when Chinese armies routed American forces along the Yalu River in Korea and the Viet Minh drove on Hanoi, a poll revealed that fully half of all Americans believed World War III was imminent. Little had occurred since that time to allay public fears. This made the country all the more susceptible to forceful, positive views expressed by generals like de Lattre and Douglas MacArthur.

Following his recall as commander in Korea, MacArthur had spent part of the summer telling the Senate that Asia, not Western Europe, was the decisive area in the fight against communism. Republican politicians picked up on this theme and used American setbacks in Asia to bludgeon Truman and the Democrats. It was thus a receptive White House audience who met with de Lattre to discuss Indochina. The marshal told them that the previous season's victory outside Hanoi "marked the turning of the tide." He described his plans to increase the size of the Vietnamese Army, knowing that it was a cherished goal of the American mission in Saigon. He would utilize the youth of Vietnam, whom he called "as numerous as the rice shoots, as ready for plucking and as useful." He spoke with great enthusiasm about Bao Dai's enhanced authority, referring to him as the "ablest statesman in Vietnam." Finally he reiterated that victory would come in one to two years.

It was a bravura performance that succeeded in earning an increase in the volume and speed of American support and a statement from Truman that the United States "would not let Indochina fall into enemy hands." Congressman John F. Kennedy from Massachusetts did not fall sway to de Lattre's aura. He saw things differently, saying: "In Indochina we have allied ourselves to the desperate effort of the French regime to hang on to the remnants of an empire."

De Lattre's visit to America had little effect upon the role of the Military Assistance Advisory Group in Saigon. Frustratingly, it continued to be a mere supply clearinghouse. Officers spoke disdainfully about French waste and inefficiency. One incident among many occurred when an American officer stumbled upon a vast stockpile of United States-supplied rifles. The French had told the MAAG that new French Union battalions were either underequipped or poorly equipped. The MAAG then informed Washington that it was "somewhat surprised to learn upon the arrival of the rifles that they might be kept indefinitely in storage." Americans in Vietnam also complained about tactics that condemned enormous numbers of soldiers to defending strongpoints and garrisoning forts. They argued, with good evidence and despite de Lattre's claims, that the French were not effectively utilizing Vietnamese manpower. So grew the attitude that the American military could do better.

The year 1952 began on a somber note with the death of Marshal de Lattre from cancer. A second blow came when the Viet Minh staged a very sophisticated offensive featuring field and antiaircraft artillery partially directed by Chinese advisers. To buttress flagging morale, the French staged an exhibition of captured Viet Minh equipment, but an American diplomat in attendance reported that it failed "as a propaganda project." Instead of increasing confidence in the French Union forces that captured the weapons, the display heightened Vietnamese discouragement and fatalism because the spectators had not realized how well armed the Viet Minh were.

Everywhere the French mood worsened and talk began about stalemate and even defeat. The State Department concluded that de Lattre's promised war-winning offensive had died stillborn. The CIA predicted that the strain of France's dual commitments to Europe and to Indochina would cause her to withdraw from Vietnam. The French minister for relations with the Associated States said that France had no hope of winning. If Indochina was really the "keystone" in the arch of Southeast Asia—and this was the view expressed by National Security Council strategy documents—then something had to be done. As before, when confronted with ambiguous choices, American planners seized upon something concrete that they could understand and accomplish. This time top American military leaders recommended that the United States undertake to train indigenous forces in Vietnam. Initially, Washington officials rejected this suggestion, but the germ of an idea had been planted.

At this time Admiral Arthur Radford, the United States commander in chief in the Pacific, turned his considerable energies to the conflict in Vietnam. He proposed that Great Britain, France, Australia, and New Zealand meet with the United States to study the military problems posed by the Chinese threat to Southeast Asia. The first of the so-called Five Power Meetings, held in January 1952, quickly exposed the self-interested positions of the two most important of America's partners. France wanted all the help and commitments it could get on Indochina. Britain was primarily interested in avoiding any actions that might arouse Communist China and prompt her to attack Hong Kong. New Zealand and Australia indicated greater willingness to take military action to resist communism, but felt overshadowed by Britain.

An eager interventionist, Radford prepared a military advisory committee in association with Australia and New Zealand. The Joint Chiefs of Staff feared that Radford was overstepping and might commit the country to military actions it wanted to avoid. Radford's view was that "the JCS did not fully face up to the importance of the Far East as a whole and Southeast Asia in particular," focusing instead on Europe and NATO.

Nonetheless, the JCS directed Radford to prepare defensive plans for Southeast Asia based upon the Five Power Meetings. Since the powers were unable to agree even upon terms of reference, and the only forces the United States could commit to the plan were already engaged in Korea, planning faltered. The only thing the powers could agree on was that Indochina was a most likely target for further Chinese aggression.

Lack of French and British cooperation angered most American military men, who felt that they did not appreciate what America had done for them in World War II. To Radford and the JCS, they seemed reluctant to spend their own money and grasping toward American aid. With hindsight, Radford realized that two additional factors heavily influenced French and British attitudes. They looked to Korea, where almost half of the entire United States military lay bogged down in a stalemate. In the European view, this made America a less useful military ally. More important, both countries were war-weary and demands for military resources were extremely unpopular.

Radford and his fellow officers' incomprehension about the French military effort increased during the admiral's visit to Hanoi. He saw a French armored column begin an offensive designed to destroy an important Viet Minh base area. French generals briefed him about the operation and predicted great results. When the operation failed dismally, Radford could not learn why. Neither his intelligence officers nor the voluminous letters of explanation from the French could explain the defeat. Radford concluded that the French had probably lost their nerve. In fact, the political pressure on the French generals to limit manpower losses had caused them to be overly cautious. But, in the American view, the important lesson from the operation was that the French lacked guts. Just as had occurred to the officers serving with the MAAG in Saigon, in the top military echelons the attitude grew that the United States could do the job better.

At the beginning of summer 1952, the French prime minister and his principal advisers met with Secretary of State Acheson and British Foreign Minister Anthony Eden. The aggressive French negotiating position surprised Eden. The French complained about the paucity of American support, even though Acheson reminded them that already the United States underwrote one third of the war's cost. The French argued for more aid. They stated that its absence would prejudice ratification of the European Defense Community, a linchpin in American strategy to resist Russian expansion, as well as continued French effort in Indochina.

Eden spoke privately with French officials, observing that such pressure tactics were unnecessary and could only frustrate the United States. He was wrong. To his amazement, later in the summer Acheson told him that the United States had agreed to a 40 percent increase in aid. Eden "had been wrong in doubting the French method." Clearly the Americans remained an easy touch, and the French understood how to deal with them. When offering another $150 million in aid, Acheson also offered United States assistance in training native forces. Always skittish about potential American interference, the French rejected this idea. American assistance did not seem to make any difference as the remainder of the year saw further deterioration in their situation.

Meanwhile, in Washington Dean Acheson reflected on what was going wrong. He complained about the lack of French aggressiveness while pursuing military operations. He worried about growing French public opinion that saw the war as a lost cause and a draining sore that undermined the possibility of Franco-German equality in European defense. He concluded: "The central problem in Indochina was the fence-sitting by the Population. They would never come down on one side or another until they had a reasonable assurance of who would be the victor and that their interests would be served by the victor."

The secretary of state was in error about this. Most Vietnamese had already decided that their interests lay with the Viet Minh. Those who sat on the fence did so to protect themselves from French reprisal.

At about the same time, President Truman signed his last National Security Council document articulating American strategy toward Southeast Asia. He believed that the country had been well served by the earlier NSC policy as described by NSC 64. A progress report on NSC 64 concluded that United States military aid had been crucial to France's ability to maintain her position and that further improvement depended upon continuing American material and financial aid. Communist China's entrance into the Korean War required an update of formal NSC policy. The Chinese intervention had lent support to American policymakers, military and civilian alike, who viewed Communist operations in Korea and Indochina as a coordinated assault on Asia as part of a Moscow-inspired scheme for world Communist domination. By the summer of 1952 this view evolved into NSC 124/2.

NSC 124/2 provided a strong statement of why the region

was important: "Communist domination, by whatever means, of all Southeast Asia would seriously endanger in the short term, and critically endanger in the longer term, United States security interests." It focused on the Chinese as the root of the problem, declaring that the loss of any countries owing to covert or overt Chinese aggression would lead to the

> swift submission to or an alignment with communism by the remaining countries of this group. Furthermore, an alignment with communism of the rest of Southeast Asia and India, and in the longer term, of the Middle East . . . would in all probability progressively follow. Such widespread alignment would endanger the stability and security of Europe.

The toppling dominos, although they were not yet called this, would cast a wide circle of destruction.

It was thus imperative to prepare for a Chinese attack. While the risk of an overt military attack against Southeast Asia was inherent in the existence of a hostile, aggressive Communist China, "domination through subversion" was the greater risk. This risk came from "the inability of the governments of France and the Associated States to continue to oppose the Viet Minh rebellion." The NSC proposed to strengthen propaganda and cultural activities, continue economic and technical assistance, encourage expanded commercial trade, enhance covert operations, promote a coordinated defense, and make clear to the American people the importance of Southeast Asia to national security. The council also devoted much thought to how best to confront direct Chinese intervention even though it believed this to be an unlikely contingency. The focus on China derived, of course, from the exceedingly unpleasant surprise of Chinese intervention in Korea. The NSC laid out a clear policy stating that the United States would become directly involved in Vietnam only to counter direct Chinese intervention. In passing, the council addressed the ticklish political situation in Vietnam. It wanted to continue to pursue constructive measures that would eventually allow France to reduce her colonial presence, but this was more a vague hope than a concrete plan.

In the final analysis, the National Security Council merely

endorsed the aid programs already in place. The heart of the American effort remained increased aid to develop the Vietnamese armed forces so they could maintain internal security without foreign assistance. This policy, and its variants, would remain the United States' strategy for the next twenty years, evolving into the "Vietnamization" program implemented by President Richard Nixon in 1969.

While the Truman administration had often emphasized the importance of political reform, by the end of its second term many had grown discouraged. The New Zealand ambassador visited Acheson to voice his worries. He pointed out the difficulties inherent in supporting France given the strength of Asian anticolonial feeling. Acheson responded that "France had done all that it could be expected to do in transferring responsibility for government to the Associated States." Regrettably, native Indochinese leaders had proven "inefficient and unwilling to assume the responsibilities of government." In fact, Bao Dai had given up hope that the French ever intended to cede real authority to the Vietnamese. In despair, he had returned to the life-style of an indolent international playboy.

The assistant director for mutual security, Theodore Tannenwald, Jr., made the last inspection tour of Vietnam during the Truman presidency. He spent a mere three days in Saigon in the late fall of 1952, but came away with strong impressions. An economic specialist, he found the behavior of local French businessmen particularly annoying. They received 95 percent of the business generated by United States aid. Many imported the aid at the official exchange rate and resold material at the black market rate thus garnering a neat 250 percent profit. This was symptomatic of the overall situation. In spite of American economic aid, the Vietnamese economy remained poorly developed and unstable with the French still controlling banking, currency, and transportation. A local Indochinese owner of an airline—precisely one of the entrepreneurs United States aid strove to help—complained that he could not get permission to fly passengers from Saigon to Hanoi because it would compete with a rival French-owned airline.

The most important conclusion Tannenwald reached regarded the political situation. He observed that the French showed little real intention of granting the Vietnamese sovereignty while doing everything possible to perpetuate colonial control. Simultaneously, they took steps to create a facade of reform to satisfy the United States. Tannenwald reported that he departed disillusioned, with "the feeling we have been kidding ourselves" about French intentions to cede colonial control. He recommended that American policy either adjust to the reality of French control or force the French to undertake immediate major reforms.

In 1950, from outside the government, John Foster Dulles had pondered this same problem. He focused on what the United States could do to remedy the conditions that allowed communism to flourish. Responding to a letter critical of American policy, he described Indochina as one of the "most difficult of all" international situations. While not condoning French colonialism, he wrote: "It seems that, as is often the case, it is necessary as a practical matter to choose the lesser of two evils because the theoretically ideal solution is not possible for many reasons." Two years before becoming the most influential Cabinet officer in the Eisenhower administration, Dulles had decided that support for the French was the only realistic policy.

Also in 1950, the Joint Chiefs of Staff had reported to the secretary of defense about the future in Indochina. The Joint Chiefs had clearly stated: "The fundamental causes of the deterioration in the Indochinese security situation lie in the lack of will and determination on the part of the indigenous people of Indochina to join whole heartedly with the French in resisting communism." Without popular support, the Joint Chiefs predicted that the French would fail.

That same year, John Melby, the head of the American team that laid the groundwork for the military mission in Vietnam, had returned home and given a speech about the situation in Indochina as he saw it. Melby described aid programs in Vietnam as disjointed, uncoordinated, and wasteful. He predicted a great debacle unless two fundamental questions were answered: "What is it worth and what are we prepared to pay for it?"

Much of what would become known as the "domino theory"

was in place when the Truman administration left office. By the time Eisenhower became President, America was already entangled in a military alliance in Asia. It would be up to him to answer what Vietnam was worth and what the nation would pay for it.

CHAPTER III

PRESIDENT EISENHOWER

*[Our faith] confers a common dignity upon the French sol-
dier who dies in Indochina, the British soldier killed in Malaya, the American life given in Korea.*
                              —INAUGURAL SPEECH, 1953

Part 1. FROM BATTLEFIELD
TO WHITE HOUSE

Lame-duck President Truman invited President-elect Eisenhower once more for a visit and a briefing. It was an encounter neither man relished. More than three years earlier,
Eisenhower had severed his ties to the Truman administration
because of disagreement over the defense budget. Truman
wanted to cut it; Eisenhower vehemently disagreed. It was the
beginning of a deterioration in their relationship. Although
both grew up in small midwestern communities much alike,
and Eisenhower the general loyally served Truman the President, the mechanism for handing over control of the government now caused great strain. Back in August, during the
heat of the campaign, Truman had invited candidate Eisenhower to a Cabinet luncheon for a briefing on the current
international situation. Regarding it as poor politics, Eisenhower declined, and this slap in the face infuriated Truman.

The man from Missouri immediately wrote a personal "Dear Ike" note in which he said that for reasons of partisan politics Eisenhower had allowed his advisers, "a bunch of screwballs," to lead him into "a bad mistake." This exchange made their encounter following Eisenhower's electoral triumph difficult.

Accompanied by John Foster Dulles, his designated secretary of state, Eisenhower came to the White House in response to Truman's second invitation. After unsuccessfully trying to set a reluctant, unsmiling Eisenhower at ease, Truman began the formal meeting. He invited the President-elect to discuss his foreign policy, but Eisenhower declined, at which point Truman requested his own secretary of state, Dean Acheson, to talk about current world problems. Acheson spoke about Korea, the United Nations, trouble in Iran, and the difficulty in getting France to accept the European Defense Community treaty, and then turned to Indochina. He described the Truman administration's long involvement, observing that the French seemed to have recently lost their will to fight. The people of Indochina, in turn, waited, unwilling to commit themselves until they could see a clear victor. Acheson concluded that although the United States had steadily increased its support for the French, the new administration had to prepare itself for a French attempt to seek a war-ending political solution.

As the meeting ended, Truman worried about Eisenhower's "frozen grimness." He did not understand it and concluded that the President-elect was "awestruck" by a new awareness of the many problems confronting him. Eisenhower recorded his reactions differently, later writing that the meeting "added little to my knowledge, nor did it affect my planning." From others such an assertion might be construed as arrogance; spoken by Eisenhower it showed confidence that he was ready to tackle the job. Few men in American history embarked upon the presidency with more practical experience at the highest echelon of leadership.

On June 6, 1944, he commanded the most complex endeavor in world history, the invasion of Normandy. It had been as much a political as a military task. Differing Anglo-American objectives needed reconciliation and prickly French pride assuaging. It demanded the ability to forge and manage a close-knit international command team, which, in turn, required measured doses of criticism, encouragement, and tact. When the moment of decision came, the responsibility had been his alone. In a word, the success of D Day required leadership.

Many of the people with whom he worked during the war held high office in their governments in 1953. Familiarity, particularly with the country's key European allies, Great Britain and France, imparted great advantages to the new President. He believed he also well understood, from experience, the mind of the country's greatest enemy. At the time he commanded the Allied occupation force in postwar Germany, Eisenhower had tried to cooperate with the Russians, but his efforts failed. Confrontations with Soviet imperialism dashed his hopes that the end of World War II would bring a better world. By the autumn of 1947 he concluded that Russia was bent on world conquest. When he entered the 1952 presidential campaign, he was every inch a cold warrior. Yet, compared with his party's conservative branch and its foreign policy, he was almost a liberal.

The Republican party's platform for the 1952 campaign was an extreme right-wing document. It charged that the Democratic party had "shielded traitors to the Nation in high places," and proclaimed that "there are no Communists in the Republican Party." The foreign policy planks, written by John Foster Dulles, lambasted the passivity of Truman's containment policy since it abandoned "countless human beings to a despotism and godless terrorism." It pledged that there would be no yielding to communism in the Far East. In the interest of party unity Eisenhower accepted this platform. Although his failure to mention foreign policy during his acceptance speech underscores his disapproval of such a messianic anti-Communist viewpoint, Republican conservatism nonetheless constrained his own foreign policy.

This became very apparent during the subsequent campaign. Having spent the last twenty years out of power, the Republican party entered the 1952 election full of frustration and anger and its leaders gave voice to these emotions in a most negative way. Mere criticism was the least of their rhetorical excesses. Many Republicans charged the Democrats with "twenty years of treason," as witnessed by those great "infamies," Yalta and the loss of China. Because of his leadership roles—FDR's commander in Europe when the Soviets absorbed Eastern Europe into their empire, Truman's Chairman of the Joint Chiefs of Staff when Peking fell to the Communists—Eisenhower stood vulnerable. So, sometimes against his better judgment, he joined the Republican chorus of criticism. He denounced Yalta, blamed the Democrats for the loss of China, and charged that Truman was too soft on communism both at home and abroad. When Senator Joseph McCarthy began a relentless assault upon George C. Marshall's reputation, claiming that the great soldier-statesman had knowingly tolerated Communists in the government and worse, Eisenhower failed to repudiate him. Such an astonishing failure of character—Marshall had been his foremost benefactor, guiding him from the rank of lowly colonel at the beginning of the war to five-star general—reveals how severely the Republican right wing intimidated him.

During the presidential campaign, Eisenhower's advisers found that their man did not have to explain his foreign policy in any detail. They anticipated that "with his great grin and good-natured professions of pious intention, his prudent equivocation about McCarthyism, and his invulnerable status as a national hero," he could defeat a divided Democratic party. Their confidence proved well founded: After five successive Democratic victories beginning in 1932, Eisenhower easily won the 1952 election, receiving 442 electoral votes to Stevenson's 89.

In spite of his need to accommodate conservative Republicans and their isolationist tendencies, Eisenhower retained a strong belief that America had an obligation as a leading participant in world affairs. Central to his foreign policy as he entered office were the two beliefs that the country had a historic mission to provide international leadership and that it should act in close cooperation with its allies. America could not afford to act alone; rather it needed friends and allies united in recognition of common interests.

Eisenhower knew that the Soviet Union presented the greatest threat to the United States. Only it had the capacity to launch atomic war upon the country, so all foreign policy decisions had to take this threat into account. The American counter was nuclear deterrence. At the time Eisenhower took office, only airplanes carried atomic weapons; nuclear-tipped missiles had yet to be developed. Bases ringing the Soviet Union provided the launch points for these aircraft, requiring vast sums to be spent for both military assistance and economic development to maintain their security. Thus, for reasons of nuclear strategy, foreign aid played a large role in Eisenhower's international policy.

His second major foreign policy concern was the defense of Western Europe. After strategic deterrence, its security overshadowed all other considerations. To oppose the Russians, in 1949 the United States had created the North Atlantic Treaty Organization (NATO) with Eisenhower as its first commander. NATO marked the beginning of European rearmament. So strongly did Eisenhower feel about it that he told a friend, "I rather look upon this effort as about the last remaining chance for the survival of Western civilization."

During his tenure as NATO commander, Eisenhower had confronted what most Americans perceived was French obstructionism. Committed to an expanding effort in Indochina, France worried she lacked the resources to offset simultaneously Germany's rearmament. The United States, on the other hand, worried about the extent of the French commitment to fight communism. America pressed France both to increase her NATO contingent and to reinforce her effort in Vietnam. To complete the circle, the French understood American concerns and played them off brilliantly. With each decision about European or Southeast Asian defense, France extracted concessions from the United States. She successfully demanded either increased aid or reduced pressure for political reform in Asia, or both.

Now came an American President who believed that although European defense required colossal expenditures, the alternative was far worse. Loss of Western Europe to the Russians would require total war mobilization at infinitely greater cost than the price of foreign aid. He believed the cost of foreign alliances actually made economic as well as strategic sense.

The Far East came a decided third in Eisenhower's priorit-

ies. If there was an area in which he lacked knowledge, it was
Asia. Not since Pearl Harbor had Eisenhower directly dealt
with Asian affairs. However, in the prewar years he had the
formative experience of service in the Philippines. He sailed
for Manila in late 1936 to join General Douglas MacArthur's
staff. For three years he labored to build a Filipino army to
defend the island nation against the growing might of Japan.
During his work he acquired knowledge and attitudes directly
relevant to the Indochinese situation of the 1950s, encountering at first hand colonialism and nationalist urges for self-
government. He studied the relationship between defense
against aggression and sovereign rule. Describing his mission
to the Philippines in his diary, Eisenhower observed that European nations viewed their overseas possessions as "opportunity for their own economic betterment." This contrasted with
the American concept of "government only by the consent of
the governed." He was proud of America's helping to lead the
Filipinos toward self-government. However, he found them
completely unprepared for immediate independence, since
they could not meet the fundamental obligation of sovereign
government, defense. He wrote in his diary: "We have learned
to expect from the Filipinos . . . a minimum of performance
from a maximum of promise." While not lacking intelligence,
"they are unaccustomed to the requirements of administrative
and executive procedure." In meetings they seemed to grasp
detail and agree to whatever decision was reached, but then
they did nothing. "Moreover, it often develops that the decision itself has not really been accepted by them, even though
at the time they appeared to be in full agreement. . . . These
peculiar traits we are learning to take into account, but obviously, they impede progress." Eisenhower's early Army experience in the Philippines molded his attitude toward Asia. Like
many Americans he believed in the stereotype of the inscruta-
ble Oriental: "There's one thing I learned in the five years I
served the Army out there—we can never figure out the workings of the Oriental mind. You just can't tell how they will
react."

More important, he reached conclusions regarding the significance of Western influence upon a developing nation. First
and foremost, the United States could give military instruction

to enable a native government to meet its "fundamental obligation" of national security. Independence should follow once a nation possessed this ability. This would turn out to be precisely the French view toward Vietnam.

Eisenhower had first seriously analyzed the fighting in Indochina while serving as military commander of NATO in 1951, when the shortage of manpower in Indochina forced the French to deplete their NATO contingent. At that time, he strongly urged the French to state publicly that the war was a contest between freedom and communism. He knew that this could only be done if the French assured the Vietnamese that ultimately they would gain political self-determination. As we have seen, the French could not oblige Eisenhower because French leaders believed that doing so would remove the rationale for their nation's sacrifice.

Many responsible French leaders had told Eisenhower that they completely agreed with him. Their comments, and the carefully constructed "concessions" that the French granted, went a long way toward convincing Eisenhower that a fundamental change in French policy was not needed. Rather, he thought French policy merely required clarification because "the matter was still subject to misinterpretation." On the other hand, the issue of communism required no such clarification. Communist goals were clear.

When he became President, Eisenhower confronted a war in Vietnam growing in size and importance. He viewed the fighting in Indochina in simple terms as a conflict between the "lawfully constituted" government and the Communists. He thought of Asia in us-or-them terms. Asia's natural resources, its rubber and tin, were available either to the West or to the Communists. Asian peoples either supported the West or were potential recruits to march under the Communist banner. More important was Eisenhower's sense of Vietnam's strategic location. He believed Communist expansion ultimately threatened Japan, a view that grew in importance as he became more familiar with the region.

Eisenhower had no respect for the opinion that the Viet Minh might be nationalists, describing them as "so-called patriots." When the Chinese began providing substantial support to the Viet Minh after 1949, the war began "to assume its true complexion of a struggle between Communism and non-Communist forces." Accordingly, immediately after his inauguration Eisenhower directed his administration to devise plans for strengthening the French in Indochina.

Part 2. THE NEW ADMINISTRATION

In his first State of the Union Message, Eisenhower cited four principles he planned to use as beacons to guide his administration. He told the nation that he wanted to apply "America's influence in world affairs with such fortitude and such foresight that it will deter aggression." The aggression he wished to deter was monolithic communism. He declared that world communism was engaged in a global offensive, and that therefore the free world needed a united, global defense. This strategic assessment colored all subsequent decisions regarding Vietnam.

The high cost of global deterrence was readily apparent and clashed with the Republican campaign vow of fiscal responsibility. Eisenhower's defense plans, with their associated high cost, upset the party's conservative wing, most notably Ohio's Senator Robert A. Taft. The twin pillars underlying Taft's philosophy were opposition both to a President's right in peacetime to deploy military force and to deficit spending. Right from the beginning, Eisenhower's foreign policy violated Taft's deeply held views. Not a shy man, the senator argued to Eisenhower's face with great heat that the President proposed to spend almost as much as Truman had spent, and demanded a complete reassessment of the military budget. In response, after aides had intervened to give their leader a cooling-off period—he was quite capable of "blowing his fuse" when angered—the President explained his reasoning by reviewing the world situation. Quite simply, there were too many dangers to justify Taft's approach. The President ticked them off. Among the first threats he described was that in Indochina where the Viet Minh had invaded Laos as the war in Vietnam continued. Against this background, he told Taft that "regardless of consequences, the nation's military security will take first priority in my calculations."

In spite of these words, Eisenhower saw a clear connection between the nation's economic and military strength. He wanted the best defense for the money and this meant a greater reliance on atomic weapons delivered by the Strategic Air Command and the emerging technology of long-range ballistic missiles. It also meant continued use of Military Assistance Advisory Groups, which, although costly, were substantially cheaper than direct American intervention as in Korea. Taft, and fellow isolationists in Congress, grumbled about all of this, but for the moment no one had the stature to challenge a popular President and war hero over matters of national security.

♦ ♦ ♦

Eisenhower's secretary of state, sixty-two-year-old John Foster Dulles, shared Eisenhower's belief that America had a decisive role to play in international affairs. Dulles had spent much of his adult life trying to inform his countrymen that global developments affected fundamental American interests. Having calculated the chances of the rival Republicans and cast his lot with Eisenhower, Dulles now had the opportunity to practice what he preached. Eisenhower delegated to him "the responsibility of developing the specific policy, including the decision where the administration would stand and what course of action would be followed in each international crisis." Eisenhower believed that Dulles possessed more experience and knowledge in the diplomatic field than any other living American. The President often said, "Foster has been in training for this job all his life." Indeed, it was only the truth.

At the age of nineteen, Dulles served as a secretary at the Second Hague Peace Conference of 1907. He worked as a counsel for the United States at Versailles following World War I, where he closely observed President Woodrow Wilson's failure to establish a lasting peace. It was a formative experience that prejudiced his view toward disarmament talks specifically and compromise discussions with militarist states in general. During the 1930s he provided brilliant analysis of the economic roots of conflict. Unlike more pedestrian thinkers, he looked beyond immediate events to conceptualize and articulate underlying global trends. In 1942, referring to the havoc caused by the Great Depression, world war in Europe and the Pacific, and unrest in colonial areas, he concluded that "the old politico-economic order has failed."

By 1946 he had arrived at an understanding of Soviet foreign policy, which he saw as designed to promote international revolution as a means to achieve national expansion. Dulles's participation in negotiation with the Soviet Union taught him that the Soviets negotiated aggressively to try to divide the Western allies and to maneuver the United States into sacrificing weaker allies. To cooperate with the Russians under such circumstances was to continue World War II "war appeasement" with "peace appeasement."

The proper response to the Russians was deterrence. The free world needed "to develop the will and organize the means to retaliate instantly against open aggression by Red Armies, so that, if it occurred anywhere, we could and would strike back where it hurts, by means of our choosing." Dulles contended that American foreign policy under Truman had been reactive, featuring a series of rear-guard actions against Soviet initiatives. He wanted a more positive approach, and Eisenhower agreed.

Dulles was not as concerned about Europe as were his predecessors. He felt that the combination of the Marshall Plan and NATO had convinced the Soviets to look outside of Europe to achieve their expansionist goals. Asia was the next crucial contest and Dulles very much shared the conventional wisdom that Moscow directed Mao Tse-tung's Chinese forces. Like Ho Chi Minh's Viet Minh, they were pawns in the Russian global game. In Dulles's view, Russia utilized indirect aggression—class war, civil war, guerrilla war—to advance her aims. The war in Indochina was an example of the latter.

In 1952, before Eisenhower's election, Dulles presented his answer to Soviet indirect aggression, calling it "peace through deterrence." He explained it to an attentive French audience in Paris, using French involvement in Indochina as an example. He described how the threat of air and naval bombardment of the Chinese mainland would deter direct Chinese intervention in Vietnam. What his grand strategy overlooked was that the Viet Minh did not require Chinese intervention to win.

While Eisenhower possessed a trusted subordinate in John Foster Dulles, he had a less easy relationship with the leaders of the American military. Few things annoyed him as much as criticism from military men, in part because of the habit of command. Most often critics had been junior officers who, during the war, had obeyed his orders. Another factor was his political insecurity. In the new arena of politics, he had to listen to civilians, whether he respected them or not. He was intolerant of an additional burden imposed by ex-subordinates, not wishing to be ambushed from the flank of those who should, in his mind, be most loyal. Accordingly, he made a significant change in the way the Joint Chiefs of Staff performed their duties.

Eisenhower regarded the Chiefs as members of his administration's team. He wanted the JCS to consider the views of their civilian superiors, and preferred that they avoid debate in front of Congress and the public while refraining from making recommendations contrary to his own policy. In a word, he did not want them to embarrass him. By appointing his Joint Chiefs of Staff for no specified term, he implicitly held over them the threat of dismissal. This went a long way toward ensuring loyalty and conformity. However, it risked isolating him from the candidly expressed opinions of other military men. Paradoxically, the general as President relied more upon civilian advice than had his civilian predecessors.

For most of his administration, the man upon whom he would rely to hold together a supportive consensus within the JCS was Admiral Arthur Radford, whom Eisenhower first encountered while sailing home from Korea in late 1952. Radford's reputation preceded him; during World War II the admiral had commanded in the Pacific the aircraft carrier *Enterprise,* arguably the most successful combat vessel of the war. He had displayed aggressive, innovative leadership and had risen in rank accordingly. Since 1949, he had been the Commander in Chief, Pacific. He was an officer who firmly believed that events in Indochina had a great bearing upon American security. While other military men had been engrossed with the war in Korea, Radford had twice taken time to tour Vietnam. His attention to a region others overlooked was characteristic of the man. Fellow military officers regarded him as a farsighted thinker.

Radford impressed Eisenhower most favorably since he seemed to possess a rare character combining strongly held convictions with a willingness to change when presented with new information. Eisenhower came away from his first encounter convinced that Radford could be most useful in Washington. While serving as a general, the President had acquired tremendous knowledge about European affairs. Radford, on the other hand, had served in the Pacific and was considered an Asian expert. Eisenhower thus welcomed Radford onto his team, believing that together they possessed global expertise. The admiral became Chairman of the Joint Chiefs of Staff in the summer of 1953.

He took up this post at a time when American military men continued to ponder the capabilities, limitations, and political implications of atomic weapons. It had been a process going on since Hiroshima. Atomic weapons' appeal was their combination of tremendous destructiveness at a cheap price. Reliance upon strategic bombers delivering nuclear weapons for defense offered an alternative to fighting costly ground wars against the Communist masses. In the Eisenhower administration this strategy evolved into the New Look.

The New Look was Eisenhower's promised alternative to Truman's military policies. It relied upon massive nuclear retaliation and proposed to show clearly to any potential aggressor that he could not count on superior conventional military power to overwhelm an American ally without considering the possibility of receiving a nuclear attack. Its partisans argued that never again would American forces become locked into a bloody conventional war.

Eisenhower's determination to create a leaner, more efficient military machine required military leaders to absorb new economies. When Radford became Chairman of the JCS, he found his fellow chiefs embroiled in a strategic debate over how to economize. Eisenhower had specifically requested each branch of the military to take a fresh look at national defense, but instead, the service chiefs—the heads of the Army, Navy,

Marines, and Air Force, engaged in a parochial defense of their turfs.

To force a consensus, Radford took the other chiefs on an open-ended Potomac River cruise. He believed that the cruise would permit frank, man-to-man discussion and would prevent interference from their swollen staffs. Consensus came after two solid days of debate and analysis. The Army representative, General Matthew B. Ridgway, proved the most intransigent. He based his opposition upon the fact that the New Look kept the Army's mission intact while cutting its manpower by 20 percent. Nonetheless, by the end of the second day Ridgway accepted the joint policy.

Radford had led the Joint Chiefs in exactly the manner Eisenhower intended, managing an enormously divisive issue to a seemingly happy consensus. The resulting policy, the New Look, was "a reassessment of [U.S.] strategic and logistic capabilities in the light of foreseeable developments, certain technological advances, the world situation today, [and with] considerable estimating of future trends and developments." By trying to take a longer view of the country's military needs, the New Look sought to rationalize military expenditures with likely threats given finite economic resources. By the end of 1955, the New Look was America's strategic doctrine, and continued as such through 1972.

Even as it was being developed, formidable and articulate dissenters emerged. Foremost among them was General Maxwell Taylor, who, citing recent history, feared that massive retaliation was inappropriate for all circumstances. Taylor argued that despite possessing overwhelming air and naval superiority and nuclear weapons, it had been American infantry deployed along Korea's rugged hilltops who had determined the issue of victory or defeat. Shortly after the Korean armistice he wrote his World War II comrade Matt Ridgway:

An outstanding impression from the operations in Korea has been the ineffectiveness or inapplicability of many of our modern weapons to the requirements of the Korean type of limited war. . . . The enemy, terrain, and weather combined to nullify in a large measure much of the costly equipment assembled during and after World War II in preparation for a possible World War III, to be fought principally in Western Europe.

Taylor contended that unwillingness to use nuclear weapons in Korea indicated that future wars would still rely on conventional means. Taylor's letter to Ridgway marks the beginning of his departure from Pentagon orthodoxy regarding limited wars. His thinking would prove particularly important when he served as the most influential military adviser to Presidents Kennedy and Johnson as well as ambassador to South Vietnam during the crucial period when American ground forces entered the war.

◆ ◆ ◆

During his service as Commander in Chief of the Pacific, Radford had received many orders from the Joint Chiefs pertaining to Southeast Asia. He understood the history and evolution of the Joint Chiefs' strategy. Beginning in 1950, the JCS had recommended military aid to the French in Indochina. When first considering Chinese military aid to the Viet Minh and, later, direct Chinese military intervention, the Joint Chiefs' recommendation had consistently been for more military aid. They had also recognized that that alone was not enough, having stressed early and often the paramount need for French political reform. In addition, being prudent men, they prepared contingency plans. As early as 1950 the JCS had charged Radford with preparing for the possible intervention of American planes and ships in Vietnam. At all costs they wanted to avoid a ground commitment, an aversion reinforced by the Korean War's demand upon scarce American manpower.

In the fall of 1950, the war in Korea seemed about to be won, making available substantial American forces. While some high-ranking officers advocated that the United States should, under certain circumstances, be prepared to enter the Indochinese war with its own forces, the JCS pushed for a clear statement of American policy toward Indochina. Then the Chinese surprise counteroffensive struck in Korea forcing their attention elsewhere and prompting them to oppose committing forces to Indochina for the foreseeable future.

For the remainder of the Korean War, American military analysts debated whether the Chinese would or would not intervene in Vietnam. There was general agreement that even a small Chinese force, together with the Viet Minh, could drive the French out of Indochina. Accordingly, the Joint Chiefs ordered Radford and his staff to prepare for two contingencies: air and naval assistance to cover a French evacuation; and air and naval intervention to prevent a French defeat. Everyone hoped any intervention would be in association with the British and in cooperation with the French. However, because of French and British waffling over how to confront China, the JCS had also required planning for unilateral United States action to save Indochina. Consequently, Radford had overseen contingency plans for covering the French evacuation of the Tonkin Delta, a naval blockade of Communist China, and for military action against selected targets in mainland China.

At least one veteran warrior, General of the Army Omar N. Bradley, doubted that air and naval attacks alone could accomplish U.S. objectives in Indochina. As the outgoing Chairman of the Joint Chiefs of Staff he accepted plans calling for limiting intervention to air and naval forces not because he thought this approach would work, but rather because it was vastly preferable to American involvement in another Asian ground war.

Part 3. KOREAN ARMISTICE

Although the last significant territorial obstacle to peace had been overcome by negotiation in early 1952, bloody, indecisive fighting continued in Korea as Eisenhower took office. The sole remaining negotiable issue separating the adversaries was the postarmistice exchange of prisoners. Yet because resolution of this issue would determine who gained a moral victory—both sides had long ago abandoned serious hope for a military victory—negotiation was bitterly contentious and seemingly without end.

Late in the presidential campaign, when Democratic candidate Adlai Stevenson showed small gains in the polls, Eisenhower's advisers coined a clever phrase that passed into the textbooks of American politics. When their man said that after his election "I shall go to Korea," it implied that by undertak-

ing a personal mission he could find an honorable way to conclude the war. In fact, he had no clear idea how to end the
war. It did not matter. His electrifying pledge sealed victory.
Following the election, he did go to Korea—during the return
voyage he met Admiral Radford—but it was upon entering
office that he had to make good his promise.

Toward this end he undertook measures to put Communist
China on notice that unending stalemate was unacceptable to
the United States. In essence, his message was that either the
Chinese would negotiate in earnest or risk having the war extend beyond the borders of Korea. His threat was in keeping
with his belief that the Chinese Communists, like all Communists, respected only force. It also fit Dulles's celebrated threat
to "strike where it hurts by means of our choosing." A concurrent technological development reinforced the threat when
American scientists detonated the world's first nuclear weapon
small enough to be fired by artillery. The era of tactical atomic
weaponry was born. If employed, tactical atomic weapons
could decisively break the Korean stalemate.

While discussing the topic of a possible Korean armistice, an
adviser informed the President that Secretary of State Dulles
opposed an armistice, reporting that Dulles had said, "I don't
think we can get much out of a Korean settlement until we
have shown—before all Asia—our clear superiority by giving
the Chinese one hell of a licking." Such a licking could only
be administered with atomic weapons. Eisenhower's head
snapped angrily around and he glared at his adviser:

> All right then. If Mr. Dulles and all his sophisticated advisers
> really mean that they can not talk peace seriously, then I am
> in the wrong pew. For if it's war we should be talking about, I
> know the people to give me advice on that—and they're not in
> the State Department. Now either we cut out all this fooling
> around and make a serious bid for peace—or we forget the
> whole thing.

It is arguable whether or not Eisenhower would have authorized the use of atomic weapons in Korea, but he was certainly willing to threaten their use in a high-stakes game of
bluff. When his first threats seemed to have no impact, a frustrated Eisenhower authorized Dulles to send a warning to the
Chinese that absent satisfactory progress, the United States

might employ its atomic arsenal and would no longer be responsible for limiting hostilities to Korea.

This time the threat of massive retaliation worked. After two years of negotiation, during which United States forces suffered nearly half their total number of Korean casualties, serious discussion resumed. On July 27, 1953, peace came to Korea.

In accepting the armistice, the United States broke faith with France. Years before, the Truman administration had insisted that no Western power fighting the Communists negotiate a separate cease-fire. The rationale was that such an arrangement would increase the burden upon those countries still fighting. Peace in Malaya would make worse the situation in Indochina; peace in Indochina would increase the difficulties in Korea. Accordingly, the United States had convinced France to break off talks with the Viet Minh. With the Korean armistice, the United States violated its own position.

The Korean armistice had quick, drastic repercussions in Vietnam. Just as the war's outbreak in 1950 had triggered an immediate doubling of American assistance for the French, so its end led to a massive increase in Chinese support for the Viet Minh. The transfer of logistical support from Korea to Vietnam did not surprise the American government. Back in 1952, Winston Churchill had warned Truman that an armistice agreement in Korea would intensify the Indochinese problem. Months before the armistice, Eisenhower delivered his first State of the Union speech, which included a statement recognizing that resolution of the Korean War would inevitably affect Indochina. In an address in the spring of 1953 he said: "Any armistice in Korea that merely released aggressive armies to attack elsewhere would be a fraud." The principal American negotiator in Korea acknowledged "that it was known in advance that a Korean truce would release Chinese troops to attack French Indochina." For the Eisenhower administration the armistice was a calculated risk.

Later, Eisenhower described the impact of the Korean peace: "The Chinese Communists now were able to spare greatly increased quantities of material in the form of guns and ammunition . . . for use on the Indochinese battle front. More advisors were being sent in and the Chinese were making available to the Viet-Minh logistical experience they had gained in the Korean War."

The flow of support from Korea to Vietnam was not entirely one-sided, however; a battalion of stalwart regulars, France's contribution to the United Nations effort in Korea, transferred to Vietnam. They would be annihilated in a spectacular ambush a little more than one year hence.

♦ ♦ ♦

Just as had been the case in Truman's government, the National Security Council served Eisenhower by crafting formal strategy statements on national security. Upon entering office, Eisenhower found American policy toward Indochina still governed by an NSC document, NSC 124/2, signed by Truman the previous year. Its main objective was to prevent Southeast Asia from passing into the Communist orbit. Eisenhower had found much fault with Truman's handling of foreign affairs, but found nothing to quibble with in this NSC document bearing Truman's signature. It remained in effect through the first months of his administration. Only the pace of events caused his National Security Council to modify Truman's prescription.

While the American President began his administration by embracing Truman's policy toward Vietnam, in Europe his two most important allies were arriving at very different conclusions regarding Indochina. In the autumn of 1951 a man who would have tremendous influence on American policy, Anthony Eden, returned to the Foreign Office to serve as the United Kingdom's foreign minister. It was the view of the British Foreign Office that in 1950 the French position had taken a dramatic turn for the worse. Eden argued that France's chances for winning the war were slender. He received reports from the British ambassador to Paris describing a pessimistic French mood. Senior officers of the French general staff admitted that evacuation was inevitable, but felt that the military situation had to improve before terms for evacuation could be negotiated. They also complained that both Great Britain and the United States should give more help since France could not be expected to single-handedly defend the interests of the free world in Indochina and also contrib-

ute to the defense of Europe. Eden correctly sensed that underlying this French argument was the fear that her
commitment in Indochina would make her militarily inferior
to a rearmed Germany if the proposed European army came
into being.

Eden understood all of this and came to a conclusion substantially different from that held by Eisenhower and Dulles;
stating that "the best hope for France was a general settlement
in South-East Asia which would include a cease-fire." To accomplish this Eden decided that negotiations on Indochina
should follow a Korean armistice and skillfully set about conducting British foreign policy toward this end. Eden's "best
hope" was an outcome that Dulles would strain every nerve to
oppose.

In France, an increasing number of politicians called for
negotiations with the Viet Minh to end the war. French papers
reported that some high-ranking generals, including men who
had served under Eisenhower and whom he considered
friends, now believed the price to retain Indochina too high
to bear. The newly elected premier, René Mayer, the latest
leader of France's revolving-door government, disagreed. He
planned to visit Washington to request more aid.

In Vietnam, the French looked back at 1952 and concluded
that at best they had achieved a stalemate. The commander
in Tonkin, General François de Linares, described the war's
frustration: "This is not like the warfare we know. We are accustomed to success if we have superior firepower." De Linares elaborated that in past wars the French established a
front, massed men and material, and if they advanced ten or
twenty miles knew they had achieved something. "But that's
not the way it is here. We establish our front. We push ahead
as we had hoped . . . but no use! There is no enemy ahead
of us. By this time he is behind us, breaking up our lines of
communication. When we turn back on him, he disappears.
We can't find him."

For the future they could only hope for one massive, set-
piece battle where firepower, mobility, and air power could be
brought to bear.

Vo Nguyen Giap looked at the past year rather differently.
He had learned his lesson against Marshal de Lattre during

the fight for Hanoi in 1951. He did not intend to repeat his mistake of challenging the French to an open fight on their terms. Henceforth his men would fully utilize their rapid cross-country ability to concentrate from dispersed bases, strike from ambush an enemy unfamiliar with jungle fighting, and retire before the inevitable counterattack. In this manner Giap intended to stretch French defenses. Eventually, when the time was ripe, he would strike across the inland hill country, far from French bases where enemy air power could not be decisive. By the fall of 1952, about the time Americans went to the polls to elect Dwight D. Eisenhower, Giap and his fellow commanders "decided upon a military strategy from which no French initiative and no amount of American military aid were going to cause it to deviate."

The year preceding Eisenhower's election saw four important trends emerge. The threat of Chinese intervention in Vietnam began to dominate other concerns over Indochina. The United States began to consider unilateral action, even while striving mightily to cooperate with the British and the French to defend Southeast Asia. Washington, not Paris, became the decision-making capital for Indochinese strategic planning. It was Washington that hosted meetings to plan the expanding military aid program and where numerous tripartite and bilateral conferences devoted to Indochina convened. Lastly, France was beginning to crack under the triple strain of war in Indochina, European rearmament, and governmental instability.

During Eisenhower's first year in office a fifth trend emerged. Eisenhower's public support for the French war effort and his statements linking the outcome in Vietnam with American national interest put American prestige on the line.

CHAPTER IV

STEADY AT THE HELM

We are supporting a government here which does not represent the majority of the people. It is difficult to be on a losing team, and know it.
—HERMAN HOLIDAY (MUTUAL SECURITY ADMINISTRATION OFFICIAL STATIONED IN SAIGON),
1953

Part 1. A "WORKABLE" PLAN

By 1952 the mounting casualty list brought home to the French people the severity of the fighting in Indochina. Although the fact that many of the losses were among her colonial troops made the burden somewhat more bearable—few in France wept when a unit comprising *"les noires"* suffered heavily; the Foreign Legion was paid to die—the losses of officers and noncommissioned officers were hard to ignore. France had already paid a staggering cost to defend Indochina. Native Frenchmen killed included 3 generals, 8 colonels, 18 lieutenant colonels, 69 majors, 314 captains, 1,140 lieutenants, 3,683 NCOs, and 6,008 enlisted men. This attrition meant that every three years the equivalent of an entire class from Saint-Cyr, France's West Point, died. Only the professional army incurred the cost. French politicians refused to force draftees to serve in Indochina.

105

Accordingly, France turned to three other traditional sources to fulfill her manpower needs: Foreign Legion mercenaries; soldiers recruited from French colonies; and native Asian troops. The French Union Army in Indochina comprised a minority of European-born Frenchmen; the fight to retain the jewel of France's colonial empire was waged by forces including North Africans from Morocco and Algeria, Africans from places like Senegal, and 20,000 Foreign Legionnaires. They bore the brunt of the war. Some 12,000 Legionnaires and Africans and 14,000 native soldiers had died to maintain French rule. Over 20,000 soldiers were missing—many of them Indochinese who deserted at first opportunity—and more than 100,000 soldiers of all nationalities had been wounded or had contracted tropical diseases requiring discharge from military service. While France relied upon mercenaries to restore her colonial estates, in a broader sense the entire French Expeditionary Corps was a mercenary army, for America paid the bill for nearly all of them. Yet a vexing manpower shortage continued to impede the French war effort. To the Americans in Vietnam the obvious solution was to increase the Indochinese contingent.

French leaders always resisted any perceived erosion of their authority to the Americans. They worked hard to limit the Americans in Vietnam to bookkeeping duties. They claimed that creating a Vietnamese Army was an internal matter between France and the Bao Dai government, which limited Americans serving with the Military Assistance Advisory Group (MAAG) to such ineffective measures as distributing a propaganda booklet entitled "Phu Joins the Army." Intended to stimulate volunteers, the booklet posed a laughably unrealistic scenario in which the hero learns of the establishment of the state of Vietnam under Bao Dai, joins his fellow villagers in a spontaneous oath of support to the army and Bao Dai, awakens following a severe wound suffered in battle against the Viet Minh to see Bao Dai's picture over his hospital bed, and is deeply moved to prayer for Bao Dai's health. Few Vietnamese youths rushed to join the army after reading "Phu Joins the Army."

By the middle of 1952 highly placed French officials began to change their minds and envisage a stronger American role in raising a Vietnamese Army. They certainly wanted the Americans to equip any newly raised troops. Reluctantly they considered allowing the Americans to train them as well. As one Frenchman observed: "The rapid creation of the [native] army would not itself solve the problem, but it would open the way to its solution." The equipping and training of native forces appealed to many American statesmen and military men alike. Truman's State Department believed that a strong Vietnamese Army would enhance Bao Dai's authority. Later, John Foster Dulles also promoted this idea.

But the American general who commanded the MAAG in Saigon disagreed that Americans should actually undertake a training role. He cited the language barrier and observed that the training mission would require more than four thousand American officers and men. Official Washington discounted his reservations. Raising and training a Vietnamese Army was something concrete that could be done to protect what was by now widely perceived to be a region crucial to United States security. The arrival of Brigadier General Thomas J. H. Trapnell as the new commander of the MAAG in the summer of 1952 brought to the scene an officer more than willing to expand the American role.

There was one enormous hurdle to overcome—it was one that the Melby mission to Vietnam had identified and reported on in 1950. At that time, General Erskine had suggested to the French commander in Vietnam, General Carpentier, that he increase his number of armed Vietnamese. Carpentier retorted that they were unreliable, untrustworthy, and would never make good soldiers. Erskine replied: "Who in hell are you fighting but Vietnamese!" Found out, the French general had shifted his ground and observed that if more Vietnamese soldiers were used, "greater concessions to Vietnam would also be required." French unwillingness to accept the consequences of creating a Vietnamese military persisted into the Eisenhower administration.

At the beginning of Eisenhower's term, an official with the Mutual Security Administration completed a three-month assignment in Hanoi. He reported that the French felt pessimistic about their chances for military success because of their shortage of manpower, but that "French-Viet combination cannot succeed because Viets under French command will never have [the] will to fight their Viet Minh brothers." To raise an effective native army required steps counter to the very reason the French fought the war. Vietnamese would fight for independence but would not fight to maintain French rule.

French setbacks in the fall of 1952 prompted General Trapnell to overlook the daunting obstacles. To increase the strength of the French Union forces, Trapnell suggested raising forty to fifty so-called light battalions. They would be lightly armed to enable them to find and fight the Viet Minh in areas otherwise inaccessible to most French forces. The French commander liked the idea but pointed out that the financial cost was too high for his nation to bear. This meant that the United States would have to increase its aid. The Army Chief of Staff, J. Lawton Collins—"Lightning Joe" of World War II fame—was enthusiastic. He thought it an excellent mechanism for the French to grant added responsibility to the native governments. The United States had developed a very successful training program for South Koreans. Ignoring the very different nature of the two wars, Collins suggested that the French utilize proven American training methods. Less than a decade later, a different Vietnamese Army would collapse against the Viet Cong assault and critics would complain that the United States had inappropriately trained the South Vietnamese using irrelevant Korean War methods.

American planners pressed for the light battalion proposal in hopes that the additional units would be ready for the fall 1953 campaign. Events would show that even when large numbers of Vietnamese were conscripted, their lack of officers prevented them from becoming an effective military force. The educated Vietnamese middle class—the class that provides most armies' officers—had no desire to fight for the French against Vietnamese who, even if Communist-dominated, still represented nationalism. Absent motivation and leadership, the great majority of Vietnamese Army units were poor; except when stiffened by French officers, they could not oppose their countrymen. The Americans in the Military Assistance Advisory Group in Saigon failed to comprehend the roots of this deficiency. By the end of the French war, the Vietnamese contingent reached the impressive number of some three hundred thousand men, yet it conquered very little territory from the Viet Minh and freed few French Union soldiers for mobile operations.

♦ ♦ ♦

The French Air Force in Vietnam never fielded more than about 275 planes, a small number by later American standards. Yet even this number exceeded the capacity of French ground crews. At the end of 1952 the French government formally requested Americans to help service and maintain the planes. In Saigon, General Trapnell and other American military men had pointed out to the French the substantial aircraft maintenance problems that existed including a faulty supply system, poor location of facilities, lack of preventive maintenance, and absence of inventory control. The French responded by noting that the real supply bottleneck, the Korean War, had been removed. They therefore requested massive logistical support so that their own inefficiency would not be noticed.

With this argument, once again the French finessed American criticism and turned it to their advantage. General Trapnell strongly endorsed the request for maintenance help. Technically, the American airmen were intended as a loan for one month only. In the first month of 1953, twenty-eight Americans arrived in Vietnam. In July, fifty-five more would be sent for a six-month tour of duty. Although it represented a change in the way the United States chose to participate in the fighting in Vietnam, at the time the arrival of a handful of American airmen in Vietnam hardly seemed significant. From any viewpoint they could scarcely make the difference in the war's outcome, so Eisenhower and his administration focused on longer-term measures. Deputy Secretary of Defense William C. Foster believed that the French effort in Indochina promised at best continued stalemate and asked the Joint Chiefs to reevaluate the American role. The JCS recommended against active United States combat participation because American forces were already stretched too thin. They believed that to take the offensive, the French needed more men and that those men could only be raised from native troops. Furthermore, they recommended that the United States pay the cost to raise those troops.

American and French military thinking thus converged. It boiled down to a matter of money. The French commander in Vietnam estimated that he would need $1.5 billion for each of the next two years, a colossal request surpassing all previous appeals for aid. Heretofore, aid had been provided on a largely ad hoc basis. Although Americans had urged the French to develop a long-term strategy to assist the United States in planning its aid package—indeed the Joint Chiefs had stated this as a precondition for aid back in 1950—the French had characteristically resisted. This time the United States insisted that further aid be contingent upon full knowledge of French political and military plans.

In part this condition stemmed from Eisenhower's insistence on a new national frugality. The country could not be expected to absorb comprehensive trimming of the military budget while remaining unquestioning and openhanded toward the French. Consequently, Secretary of State Dulles laid down new conditions. He told the French that Congress would grant more money only if it were convinced that the French possessed a sound strategy promising the elimination of most Viet Minh forces within two years. In times past when the French asked for more help, the Americans had sometimes grumbled about political reform or the need for aggressive leadership but in the end had always anted up. Dulles seemed to have raised the level of American expectation. The French wondered whether this too was a bluff they could call.

The death of Joseph Stalin in March 1953 brought a wave of diplomatic visitors to Washington to discuss the new world scene. Among them were Premier René Mayer; his foreign minister, Georges Bidault; and his minister for Indochina, Jean Letourneau. Eisenhower and Dulles entertained their French visitors aboard the presidential yacht. The American President had high hopes for this cruise. He wanted cooperation over the European Defense Community treaty (signed by France but not yet ratified by the French parliament), a pledge regarding political reform in Indochina, and a strategic plan that would at least give hope of ultimate victory. Because of his strong feeling of comradeship with Bidault, a courageous resistance fighter during World War II, Eisenhower believed he would hear frank and flexible French responses.

Instead, Bidault disappointed Eisenhower. On the European issues, Bidault spoke on "both sides of the question." On Indochina, "he evaded, refusing to commit himself to an out-and-out renunciation of any French colonial purpose." Only on the question of strategic planning did the French oblige Eisenhower. The minister for Indochina knit together an improvised scheme that prominently employed newly raised, American-financed light battalions. It called for an offensive spreading from south to north with the light battalions occupying pacified territory, permitting the mobile troops to continue into Viet Minh territory to secure additional ground. Ultimately all of this would lead to a decisive battle against the Viet Minh regulars in the north. Designed to bring victory in 1955, the plan depended upon an effective Vietnamese Army.

Letourneau's plan was not entirely satisfactory to the Americans. Although the State Department accepted its political implications, or lack thereof, it wanted the Department of Defense to determine if it was acceptable from a military viewpoint. Captain Arleigh A. Burke, head of the Navy's Strategic Plans Division, believed it was not. It was too costly and of doubtful efficacy. He compared the French effort to the American Indian Wars. Like the Indians, the Viet Minh flowed around static garrisons to strike vulnerable targets in the rear, avoiding stand-up combat. Burke wrote to the Chief of Naval Operations: "When the French win a battle, it doesn't stay won. The enemy disperses and builds up for another attack."

In private meetings the Joint Chiefs also found much fault. Representing the Army, General Collins criticized French failure to use American training methods proven successful in Korea. The Air Force Chief described the need for "a 100 degree change in French political and military affairs in Indochina." However, in their public recommendation the Joint Chiefs said the plan was "workable." Similarly, the head of the Military Assistance Advisory Group in Saigon expressed criticism but accepted Letourneau's strategy as preferable to stalemate and inaction.

Ultimately, only the opinion of the man at the top mattered. Eisenhower viewed the global picture and inevitably looked at Europe first. The unification of the free states of Western Europe in a scheme like the European Defense Community had long been one of Eisenhower's cherished dreams. He considered his 1951 speech to the English Speaking Union on that topic as the best he ever wrote and delivered. In 1953, his concern over French participation in European defense still superseded all else. This was not to say that the President lacked concern over Indochina. Eisenhower again declared that unless the Communists were "checked decisively and promptly," disaster would ensue and that the United States "could not stand aloof—unless we were ready to allow free nations to crumble, one by one, under Communist pressure." Eisenhower concluded that whatever the flaws in the French position, aid could not be delayed.

On May 5, 1953, the President sent a special message to Congress on the Mutual Security Program explaining that the program's basic purpose was "the long-term security of the United States living in the shadow of the Soviet threat." It asked for $5.25 billion for military weapons and support for America's allies. Eisenhower assured Congress that he had carefully scrutinized all elements of the program, which had led to certain fundamental determinations including the need for a greater United States effort in the Far East. He proposed "substantial additional resources . . . to assist the French and the Associated States in their military efforts to defeat the Communist Viet Minh aggression." He warned that failure to adopt his program could disunite the free world "at a moment of great peril when peace and war hang precariously in balance."

In addition to bringing a host of foreign visitors to Washington, Stalin's death stimulated American foreign policy experts to reassess their conception of communism. The government's various intelligence branches submitted their thinking to the National Security Council in April. The central security problem in the Far East continued to be an aggressive Chinese Communist regime closely aligned with the Soviet Union. However, Marshal Tito of Yugoslavia had, since 1948, demonstrated something heretofore unsuspected: the possibil-

ity of non-Russian Communist leaders defecting from the
Kremlin's control. The analysts observed that Mao resembled
Tito in many ways. It was thus possible that Mao retained the
capability of independent action and that China might too
split from the Soviet camp. The State Department believed,
however, that unless the Soviets displayed a high-handed attitude toward the Chinese or a prolonged leadership battle developed in Moscow, Mao would continue his allegiance to the
Soviet Union. Only in the long term might ideologic and nationalistic forces reave the Sino-Soviet entente.

So the United States government determined that Stalin's
death did not fundamentally alter the current strategic situation, but while reaching this conclusion analysts had entertained for the first time the possibility that communism was
not monolithic. Further reflection along these lines might have
suggested that what was true for Tito and Mao was equally
true for Ho Chi Minh, but that did not occur. Instead, with
regard to Vietnam, the analysts repeated the empty recommendation that the French undertake political and other measures to increase the effectiveness of the Vietnamese armed
forces and improve the people's morale.

Part 2. A DETERIORATING SITUATION

In the early spring of 1953, Admiral Arthur Radford, at
the time still Commander in Chief, Pacific, made another visit
to Hanoi "to find out why our best efforts to aid the French
had resulted in so little military success." He found a remarkable and shocking deterioration in the French position. He
thought somebody must be at fault, but found it difficult to
ascribe responsibility. The admiral's quandary stemmed from
his preconceptions; he recognized poor French leadership and
searched for specific culprits. His focus on leadership ob-
scured the underlying problem of Vietnamese nationalism.

In mid-April the President delivered his famous "Chance
for Peace" address. Responding to Soviet peace propaganda,
Eisenhower tried to avoid denunciations and instead offer
something positive. He challenged Russia to prove its peaceful
intent by agreeing to such measures as a free, united Ger-

many. He described the terrible dangers associated with a continuing arms race and spoke about a better way for the world to live. He cited clear principles that guided United States conduct in world affairs, one of which was the right of any nation to choose its own government and economic system.

At about the same time, the French government repeated a previously successful tactic to preempt criticism from the new American administration regarding colonialism in Indochina. Amid great fanfare, French officials claimed they had practically granted independence to the Associated States. The falseness of this position showed itself within a month of Eisenhower's "Chance for Peace" speech. May saw a devaluation of the local currency arising from a decision made in Paris without consultation with native leaders. The devaluation caused heavy financial losses in all three Associated States and proved continued French economic domination.

Like Roosevelt and Truman before him, Eisenhower chose to overlook the inconsistency between his statement of principles and his policy toward the French. A new Viet Minh offensive with three divisions against Laos again reinforced his opinion that larger issues were at stake than mere adherence to ideals.

When the President examined a map of Southeast Asia, the strategic position occupied by Laos loomed large. Its loss had all the same negative consequences as the loss of Vietnam plus a set of additional ones. Communist control of Laos would permit a hostile drive west as well as south. He told his National Security Council that "if Laos were lost we were likely to lose the rest of Southeast Asia and Indonesia. The gateway to India, Burma and Thailand would be open." About eight years hence, as a new war expanded into Laos, he was to tell President-elect Kennedy very much the same thing.

In fact, the 1953 Viet Minh invasion of Laos had limited objectives. In keeping with his long-term strategy, Giap intended the invasion to force the French to spread their forces even thinner by drawing them into the hinterland where they could be fought on more even terms. He withdrew his soldiers in early May once these objectives had been accomplished. The Viet Minh lacked the logistical capacity to entertain the larger purposes that Eisenhower feared. Nonetheless, the invasion greatly disappointed Eisenhower. Before it occurred, he had thought that in due course, however slowly, the French would win. The Laos invasion shattered his confidence.

Radford reacted differently. Looking at the map, and thinking in conventional terms, he believed that with more troops and, most importantly, aggressive leadership, the French could attack the long and presumably vulnerable Communist line of communications. Meanwhile, to help the French defend Laos, he responded in a typical American way by recommending a technological solution. He recommended sending the French six C-119 "Flying Boxcar" transports immediately. This newest type of military cargo plane could carry tanks to the isolated Laotian outposts. The tanks could provide a tactical trump card to which the Viet Minh had no answer. When making this recommendation, Radford reported to his superiors that the United States must send additional help quickly if it was to recoup any part of its large military and economic investment. He also concluded that "if we had to supply most of the help . . . we had a right to be in on the planning."

The President authorized an emergency loan of the Flying Boxcars. However, he turned down the French prime minister's request for United States military personnel to fly the planes, recognizing that approval would put Americans in combat positions. Instead, he authorized Dulles to pursue the option of having former American military men fly the planes. He knew that the aircraft loan could only be a stopgap measure. Something more substantial had to be done.

Nine days later, at a meeting with the National Security Council, Eisenhower decided to demand two major changes: a new, dynamic French general; and a French guarantee of independence for the Associated States once the fighting ended. On the subject of political reform, the secretary of the treasury added that French Foreign Minister Bidault had apparently reversed his earlier equivocal attitude and was now asserting that France intended to free ultimately the Associated States. However, lower-echelon French officials seemed to want to perpetuate colonialism. Eisenhower responded that unless this attitude changed, nothing could save Indochina and "continued United States assistance would amount to

pouring our money down a rathole." Vice President Richard
M. Nixon added that the dilemma in Indochina seemed "to
boil down to the fact that the native peoples were unwilling to
fight Communism in order to perpetuate French colonialism."

Regarding the leadership question, Eisenhower believed
that most of the French generals sent to Indochina had been
poor. What they needed was an aggressive, inspirational
leader. The President had several officers in mind including
General Jean E. Valluy, the officer who had issued an unreasonable ultimatum and then ordered the bloody bombardment of Haiphong in 1946. Before Eisenhower's recommendations reached Paris, the French government announced
its candidate for command in Vietnam, Lieutenant General
Henri Navarre.

Fifty-four years old when summoned to lead the French Expeditionary Corps in Indochina, Navarre came from the cav-
alry branch, the traditional elite of the twentieth-century
French military. His first combat experience came in a guerrilla war against Moroccan tribes in the 1920s, an experience
taken into account when choosing him. He had served in staff
and intelligence positions before World War II, and in 1945
had led a spearheading French armored unit into Germany.
After the war he honed his administrative talents while serving in Algeria. He held a staff position in NATO when he
learned of his appointment. Navarre protested that he was totally unqualified for the assignment because he had never
served in Indochina. Prime Minister René Mayer, who had
already searched far down the army list to find an acceptable
general, was in no mood to listen to a refusal. He wanted Navarre to go to Indochina and find an honorable way out of
the war. Furthermore, Navarre would have to make do with
the resources at hand because reinforcements from France
were a political impossibility.

Navarre returned to his post in Germany to plead with his
superior officer that he be allowed to stay in Europe. His superior replied, "It is your duty to accept, somebody must take
on the job." He was little known to most Americans, yet his
strategy would bring the United States to the brink of war the
next year.

During the Franco-American talks in March, Premier Mayer had invited the Americans to dispatch a military mission to Indochina to assess French requirements for extra aid. The Joint Chiefs selected Lieutenant General John W. "Iron Mike" O'Daniel, a World War II and Korean War veteran who derived his nickname from his proven combat toughness. A man of action, he was somewhat impetuous and not known for being a good listener, particularly if he had a different idea in mind. This was an unfortunate characteristic because his mission's centerpiece was discussion with General Navarre.

O'Daniel was to talk with Navarre about French requirements for and utilization of American military aid, French strategic plans, and in particular progress in strengthening native forces. He was to influence the French to be more aggressive on the battlefield while simultaneously expanding their training efforts to develop "loyal, aggressive, and capable indigenous forces." Finally, O'Daniel was supposed to devise ways to promote American influence on French operations without impinging on French responsibilities, an instruction that spoke to the old aid-without-influence problem. Everyone from the secretary of state on down had tried and failed to solve it. Perhaps O'Daniel could do better.

O'Daniel arrived in Saigon one month after Navarre had assumed command. Although possessing very different temperaments, essentially the difference between a combat officer and a staff officer, the two got along exceedingly well from the start. A French Army magazine published in Indochina described the man with whom O'Daniel had to cooperate: Navarre "advanced toward the small group of officers standing at attention who had come to greet him and coldly shook the hands of two or three of them. . . . General Navarre is the happy owner of a Persian cat . . . and hides from no one the fact that he adores cats because they prefer to be alone and because they have an independent way of thinking."

The magazine portrayed his character as shy sensitivity combined with iron nerves. It reported he was a man who would not tolerate sloppiness and would admit to no extenuating circumstances. One critical French reporter saw him a little differently: "He was physically and morally a feline . . .

simultaneously cordial and distant, debonair and icy."

A capable, if cold and uninspiring leader, Navarre found his command demoralized with the bulk of its resources tied to static defensive positions. While the French Union forces, with their superior firepower, could dominate any stand-up fight, such battles proved maddeningly infrequent. Fighting remained at the level of *la sale guerre,* "the dirty war." The Viet Minh held the initiative.

Navarre brought a fresh perspective to the French war effort. After soliciting recommendations from his more experienced subordinates, and with frequent prodding from O'Daniel, he devised a plausible strategy to arrest the deteriorating situation. He told his subordinates: "My principal aim is to break the force of habit. The Expeditionary Corps lacks aggressiveness and mobility. I am going to do my best to give it back these qualities." To regain the initiative, he planned to gather a general reserve, which would come both from troops currently scattered in small garrisons and, in spite of his prime minister's previous refusals, reinforcements from France. Navarre planned to implement another conventional step as well. Instead of continuing to operate in 2,000- to 3,000-man mobile groups, he wanted to organize his striking forces into division-size units, which would be better able to compete with Giap's 10,000-man infantry divisions. His emphasis upon recognized military principles—mass, initiative, offense—was certain to earn the praise of military men.

Once he had completed the reorganization and expansion of his forces during the 1954–55 campaign season, Navarre intended to launch a full-blown offensive in the summer of 1955. While limited offensives and spoiling attacks were permissible before that time, a major battle was to be avoided until all was ready. Three years after the Joint Chiefs of Staff had recommended requiring, as a precondition to providing aid, that the French prepare and share their military plans with American officers, the French obliged.

O'Daniel reported through Radford to the Joint Chiefs his extremely positive impressions of Navarre's strategy. He told the JCS that Navarre and his subordinates had instilled a new aggressive spirit and were determined "to see this war through to success at an early date." O'Daniel predicted decisive defeat of the Viet Minh by 1955. Other American military officers applauded Navarre's organizational steps, having long urged the formation of division-size units and better utilization of native troops. As to Navarre's intentions for his forces, the idea of regaining the initiative greatly appealed to the offensively oriented American officer corps.

Radford, in one of his last decisions before becoming Chairman of the Joint Chiefs of Staff, cautioned that proof of the pudding would be in the tasting, but nonetheless recommended full American support for the Navarre Plan. The outgoing Chairman of the JCS, General Omar Bradley, had reservations based on past French performance. However, he judged it to be a marked improvement over previous French plans and sufficiently promising to warrant additional United States aid.

The arrival of yet another new French government caused American optimism to soar even further. In June 1953, Premier Joseph Laniel entered office. He pledged to push the war to an early, victorious conclusion and recalled Navarre for consultation. The general offered three alternatives: holding the Associated States within the French Union; internationalization of the war to involve America, Great Britain, and additional minor allies; or withdrawal. Navarre well knew that his government would choose the first. He advised his government that the preservation of the French Union required military success sufficient to create a favorable negotiating position. Laniel accepted Navarre's strategic vision as his government's blueprint for victory. At Navarre's private farewell dinner before he returned to Vietnam, the general pledged, "I shall not make the same mistakes as my predecessors."

At the end of July, Premier Laniel put a price tag on the Navarre Plan. He told the United States that France required an additional $400 million to finance the war effort for the coming year. It amounted to a doubling of the previous aid package, yet the State Department quickly recommended approval. The department was again greatly influenced by the hope that more aid would help win French ratification of the European Defense Community treaty, underscoring the link between American global strategy and events in Indochina. The Eisenhower administration calculated that the money saved by a military merger of the European countries in the EDC would repay the investment in Indochina many times over. It was in keeping with the administration's search for military economy. Virtually any aid program was cheaper than an alternative requiring the presence of United States forces.

When the National Security Council deliberated over the latest French request, it recognized a difference from past requests: "The situation in Indochina has reached the crossroads. For the first time, the French program offers a real hope of solving this problem which is also at the core of the French weakness and hesitation in Europe." Unlike previous requests, this one had benefited from O'Daniel's coaching and included the type of information that made American policymakers most comfortable. It had detailed estimates for force buildup and described tactical and strategic objectives to buttress the request. The council decided that despite risks and uncertainties, it was in the nation's own security interests to furnish the additional aid.

The NSC based this conclusion on the belief that "the Laniel government is almost certainly the *last* French government which would undertake to continue the war in Indo-China." Eisenhower wanted to seize the opportunity provided by the Laniel government, for if it failed the next government would seek a negotiated settlement inevitably leading to an undesirable outcome. The previous spring he had placed political and military conditions upon the aid, which the French now accepted. Bowing to American pressure, Laniel had promised the Associated States a chance "to perfect their independence" within the French Union through the exercise of selected trappings of self-rule. Militarily, Navarre had presented the United States with a detailed victory plan.

Having found leverage to move the French once, Eisenhower now decided to increase the pressure. This time further assistance would be conditional upon a public French commitment to gain the support of the native peoples, a French invitation for close American military advice, and a renewed promise to ratify the European Defense Community. The National Security Council added one more condition, endorsing increased aid provided the Department of State and the Joint

Chiefs of Staff certified that the Navarre Plan held a promise of success.

The State Department had already passed the onus for such certification into the hands of the Joint Chiefs. Initially the JCS recommended giving the aid, but shortly thereafter backed away from an unqualified endorsement of the Navarre Plan. It wanted to amend an assessment that had said the plan held "a promise of success" because it now viewed this statement as overly optimistic. During the days intervening between the endorsement and the hedge, General Trapnell—the commander of the Military Assistance Advisory Group in Vietnam—had reported that the French were not taking any of the steps they had discussed with O'Daniel. Trapnell told the Joint Chiefs that the French had no plans for a large fall offensive, had not reorganized as promised, had sent reinforcements amounting to a few battalions instead of the promised two divisions, and had generated no sense of urgency in the training of Vietnamese officers. Apparently O'Daniel, in his enthusiasm for his new assignment, had fallen for French blandishments, a mistake made by many other American diplomats and military men.

Trapnell's cautionary judgment also coincided with a change in the membership of the JCS. Now at its head was Admiral Arthur Radford, while the new representative of the Air Force was General Nathan Twining, a firm proponent of strategic air power and thus a partisan of the New Look. A perhaps apocryphal story popular in Air Force circles explained Twining's views. Responding to an Army critic who denigrated Air Force claims about strategic bombing, Twining asked how many men the Army had lost during the invasion of Japan. Twining believed air power had brought Japan to her knees and that it could achieve almost any military objective. Radford and Twining dominated strategic debate and, along with the new Navy appointee—Admiral Robert B. Carney—gave the President three reliable boosters inside the Joint Chiefs of Staff. Completing the new membership was the Army's General Matthew B. Ridgway, who would prove to be a dissenter from the uniform party line Eisenhower wanted from his Joint Chiefs.

So the new Joint Chiefs assessed the Navarre Plan. Only

weeks earlier, before his appointment to the JCS, Radford had backed without qualification aid to support the Navarre Plan. A judgment he felt comfortable with when serving at a lower level now seemed a little different with the admiral potentially accountable. Consequently, under his guidance the JCS substantially altered its stance, declaring that a basic requirement for success was the creation of "a political climate . . . which will provide the incentive for natives to wholeheartedly support the French." The Joint Chiefs had been emphasizing the political side of the equation since 1950 and Radford insisted that they go on record once more with this proviso. Furthermore, they recommended that additional aid be contingent upon actual French performance and French willingness to act upon United States military advice.

Radford's qualified support served two purposes. It represented the Joint Chiefs' candid thinking and it covered the Chiefs' flanks. They knew that such protection was as relevant to the political infighting in Washington as to conflict on the battlefield. However, disentangled from all else, the bottom line was clear. The Eisenhower administration endorsed the Navarre Plan and the Joint Chiefs of Staff concurred.

Part 3. LIGHT AT THE END OF A TUNNEL

The Governors' Conference in Seattle in early August 1953 provided Eisenhower with the opportunity for relaxed reflection upon a variety of national concerns. Eisenhower saw an informed citizenry as crucial to the American way of government. State governors had the important task of explaining programs and policies to the citizens. All chief executives, presidents and governors alike, had access to information unavailable to the public. It was the chief executive's duty to digest this information and inform the public about the major problems of the time so that citizens would support reasonable programs. This belief brought Eisenhower to Seattle, where he intended to inform the governors about pressing problems. He wanted them, in turn, to take his views to their people. A particular topic the President wished to speak about was Indochina, because his audience did not "know, really, why we are so concerned with the far-off southeast corner of Asia."

When Eisenhower explained American policy, he spoke at a time of relative calm in foreign affairs. His explanation was not the result of crisis thinking but rather the product of steady reflection. He was not making a partisan appeal, so his words were largely untainted by political overtones. Nor was he speaking over the head of his audience, directing his words for a foreign government. These factors made his speech notable, a simple, clear statement of his beliefs at the time.

He began by noting that the war in Indochina was variously described as "an outgrowth of French colonialism" and a contest "between the communists and the other elements in southeast Asia." He passed quickly on to the strategic importance of the area and in so doing did not say which view he held, thus implying that the war's origins no longer mattered. He told the governors the situation was fraught with peril for the United States: "If Indochina goes, several things happen right away." The Malay Peninsula, with its valuable tin and tungsten, would become indefensible. India, Asia's last great remaining population undominated by the Kremlin, would be "outflanked," and the free world could not "hold the rich empire of Indonesia."

Eisenhower concluded that "somewhere along the line, this must be blocked. It must be blocked now. This is what the French are doing." The money the United States gave to the French to pursue the war represented "the cheapest way . . . to prevent the occurrence of something that would be of the most terrible significance for the United States of America—our security, our power and ability to get certain things we need from the riches of the Indonesian territory, and from southeast Asia."

The President had articulated his rationale for American involvement in Vietnam and given a preview of the "domino theory." That same month the American people received an alternative viewpoint. *Life* magazine featured a cover article entitled "Indochina, All But Lost." Famed photographer David Douglas Duncan had spent eight weeks in Indochina to research the article. Then, the magazine's dominant force, renowned conservative Henry Luce, had tried to squash the resultant article because it was so critical of the American effort.

Only Duncan's willingness to stand up to the magazine mogul in a face-to-face encounter had allowed the article to be published. It provided some rare firsthand accounts of the situation from Americans living in Indochina.

An American agricultural expert in charge of administering aid spoke of his shame and embarrassment because the aid did not reach the people for whom it was intended. He blamed corrupt Indochinese officials appointed by the French because of their political affiliations rather than their competence. Another American economic specialist told how millions and millions of aid dollars were being given away without any American gain in friendship, respect, or trust. Douglas toured Saigon and reported something that the strategic thinkers on the National Security Council and at the State Department overlooked, writing: "In the background of this war is a society that has become corrupt."

Turning to the military situation, Duncan wrote about the French plan to turn over an increasing share of the war to the Vietnamese themselves; "Other nations will be asked to help support the new Vietnamese battalions. To me, and many people in Indochina, 'other nations' means the U.S." Duncan warned that Indochina seemed all but lost.

Duncan could not know it, but earlier in the summer the Central Intelligence Agency had reached a similar conclusion. The Agency submitted its estimate of probable developments in Indochina through the middle of 1954. It stated quite bluntly that the French position was likely to deteriorate and that after mid-1954 "the political and military position could go very rapidly."

Eisenhower and his government understood the risks, but like the Truman administration, could conceive of no acceptable alternative to supporting the French. By the fall of 1953, this meant bankrolling the Navarre Plan. In early September the French asked for $385 million. The National Security Council endorsed the request, provided that the French aggressively carried out the Navarre Plan and granted true sovereignty to the Associated States.

By mid-month, Secretary of State Dulles spoke before the United Nations. He told its General Assembly that a midsummer French declaration showed that the French planned to

grant independence to the Associated States and concluded
that this pledge undercut Communist claims of being the true
champions of independence. Reassured if not confident about
French intentions toward political reform, at month's end Eisenhower authorized the aid expenditure. Since Congress was
not in session, and since his advisers told him that asking Congress for a supplemental authorization—the normal method
for handling such large requests—was politically unwise, Eisenhower approved a scheme whereby funds earmarked for
other foreign assistance went to Indochina instead.

This less than candid approach aroused concern among
some congressional leaders. Massachusetts Congressman John
W. McCormack, already an influential Democratic leader in
the House, wrote to the appropriate official in the federal government to say that he worried that if the Navarre Plan failed,
the United States might feel obliged to send its own troops to
Indochina. He saw support for the Navarre Plan as a calculated risk and hoped the administration recognized it as such.
No politician could challenge a national military hero, particularly one who had recently won overwhelming election, on a
judgment of military risk, so McCormack, after expressing his
concern, deferred to Eisenhower's desire. However, the way
the Eisenhower administration handled the aid request
marked a change. Rather than risk political damage, the President found it easier to pursue his policy in Southeast Asia
through less public, bureaucratic maneuvers.

A warning about the nature of calculated risk appeared
shortly thereafter when the Vietnamese National Congress
seized upon the French government's own words and decided
that they knew best how to "perfect their independence."
Their chosen method was refusal to cooperate with the
French under the existing political system and a demand for
withdrawal from the French Union. This action undercut both
Dulles's claim to the United Nations and one of the major
American requirements—support from the native peoples—for backing the Navarre Plan. A defeat on the battlefield
soon undermined a second precondition.

Reliance upon native levies, particularly the much heralded
Vietnamese light battalions, was an important component of
the Navarre Plan. A small campaign tested the light battalions

in the forge of combat and found them wanting. In a show-case operation, regular French Union forces cleared a province in Tonkin. As called for by the Navarre Plan, they turned over responsibility of this "pacified" province to the light battalions. The Viet Minh responded in a manner that would recur with regularity when the U.S. Army employed a similar approach in the next decade. Their leaders thoroughly understood the threat posed by successful pacification efforts, particularly ones employing native troops. The Viet Minh and the Americans agreed on this: The support of the Vietnamese people would tilt the balance of victory. Accordingly, the Viet Minh massed regular forces and local guerrillas to squash the province's native garrison regardless of cost.

In the event, the cost proved small. Lacking the fighting abilities of regular French Union forces, the light battalions put up a poor fight. The resulting mauling might have signaled to American observers that the Navarre Plan rested on a very unsure base, but did not because of a new, dramatic distraction. As the Americans had urged them so often to do, the French undertook a new autumn offensive.

♦ ♦ ♦

Back in the summer, Senator John F. Kennedy had spoken before the Senate. His speech marked a return to a subject he had addressed two years earlier: French failure to grant Vietnam meaningful political freedom. He observed that regardless of American efforts, the war would not be won until the Vietnamese people supported it. Victory would only come after the French made the "concessions necessary to make the native army a reliable and crusading force." The senator also caustically noted how the French manipulated the United States. Each year they gave the Americans three assurances: independence of the Associated States is now complete; independence will be accomplished under steps "now" being undertaken; and military victory is just around the corner. The way in which French leaders negotiated for American assistance for the Navarre Plan supported the senator's opinion.

A contrasting viewpoint appeared that fall in one of the country's most influential magazines when *Time* magazine featured a cover story on General Navarre. It was full of the trademark quotations the magazine employed when building support for a favored "good guy." The article concluded with a quote from an anonymous United States official: "A year ago none of us could see victory. . . . Now we can see it clearly—like light at the end of a tunnel."

Toward the end of 1953 a flurry of Americans traveled to the Far East to assess progress in what was now, with the termination of the fighting in Korea, the major military hot spot in the world. The first of them, Iron Mike O'Daniel, responded to the invitation of General Navarre to assess progress since his first visit back in the summer. What he found concurred with *Time*'s upbeat appraisal. Navarre staged an impressive display of bustling activity that solidified O'Daniel's faith in French leadership. He reported to Washington: "We should fully support General Navarre, in whose success we have such a large stake."

When Pentagon planners received O'Daniel's report, with its claim that the French had "wrested the initiative from the enemy," they concluded that based on "real military progress . . . prospects for victory are increasingly encouraging." The Army's representative on the Joint Chiefs of Staff, General Ridgway, now demonstrated his independence by objecting to this "overly optimistic" conclusion. He managed to have the Joint Chiefs tone down their endorsement of O'Daniel's report. However, it remained an endorsement nonetheless.

Vice President Richard Nixon spent six days visiting the Associated States as part of an extensive Asian tour. He received the standard French treatment replete with champagne toasts, sumptuous dinners, inspections of spit-and-polish drill units, and the mandatory visit to "the front." Unlike many, he was not completely taken in. A French officer introduced Nixon to a Vietnamese unit and Nixon later recalled: "I saw immediately a basic problem of the war. The French did nothing to hide the disdain they felt toward the Vietnamese." He toured a refugee camp at Sontay—a place that seventeen years later would house American prisoners of war—where the peoples' stoicism and determination to survive greatly moved him.

He concluded that French failure was due to their inability to inspire the Indochinese to defend themselves against communism. But this very weakness made it all the more important to support the French, for should they withdraw, "Vietnam—and possibly Laos and Cambodia as well—would fall like husks before the fury of the communist hurricane."

In December the JCS Chairman, Admiral Radford, traveled to the Philippines where he met with General Trapnell, chief of the Military Assistance Advisory Group in Vietnam. He found, as before, that the tremendous United States aid effort "seemed to have little or no effect." Trapnell reported that when Americans promoted the expansion of the MAAG to include training Vietnamese in order to ensure that American equipment was properly used, the French consistently rebuffed them.

By the end of 1953, Eisenhower had a variety of different military analyses of the situation in Vietnam. O'Daniel was optimistic. He reported that the French held the initiative and that the Navarre Plan would bring victory. Except for Ridgway, the Joint Chiefs largely agreed. The Commander in Chief, Pacific, Admiral Felix Stump, considered O'Daniel too optimistic and felt that his report did not give enough attention to political and psychological factors. Stump reiterated that the Vietnamese people had to support anticommunism before the French could win. The U.S. Army attaché in Saigon presented a bleaker picture. He said the French were on the defensive, there were no signs this would change, and he doubted they could win in the foreseeable future.

While sorting out which of the views to believe, the President could look for little help from his government's intelligence community. Such was its sorry state resulting from dependence upon French sources, that at an early December briefing for the National Security Council, the head of the CIA reported that "no Westerner really knows whether or not Ho Chi Minh is actually alive."

During his first year in office, President Eisenhower formally spoke in public about Indochina some ten times. His last statement came on the twelfth anniversary of Pearl Harbor: "We salute the valiant forces of France and of the three Associated States of Indo-China fighting within the French Union to protect the independence of Cambodia, Laos, and Viet Nam. We recognise the vital importance of their contribution to the defense of the free world." Many times in the past year he had thought about Vietnam. Rhetorical flourishes aside, these words well reflected his conclusions.

Seventeen days earlier, three thousand French Union paratroopers had tumbled from their American-built transport planes on a remote river valley near the Laotian frontier. The drop centered on a small village whose name meant "Seat of the Border County Prefecture." In Vietnamese, the village's name was Dien Bien Phu.

CHAPTER V

∧∧∧∧∧∧∧∧∧

CRISIS AT DIEN BIEN PHU

Strike to win, strike only when success is certain.
—Vo Nguyen Giap

Part 1. A DARKENED ROOM

The conference in Berlin, on January 25, 1954, was the first meeting in five years between the "Big Four" World War II allies: France, Great Britain, the Soviet Union, and the United States. The conference's lack of an agenda worried the American representative, Secretary of State Dulles. He anticipated that the Soviets would try to use Indochina to drive a wedge between the United States and France in order to disrupt Allied unity, prevent French ratification of the European Defense Community (EDC) treaty, and derail Franco-German reconciliation.

Events at the conference confirmed Dulles's fears. Soviet Foreign Minister V. M. Molotov—a wizened, veteran diplomat who had somehow managed to emerge on top during Moscow power struggles—he would serve Khrushchev with the same dedication he gave Stalin—hinted to the French that peace in

130

Indochina might be obtainable if the French rejected EDC and German reconciliation. Although French Foreign Minister Bidault initially refused, by week's end he had begun to weaken. Over Dulles's opposition, he accepted a Soviet proposal that the Korean Political Conference, planned for the coming April in Geneva, include consideration of Indochina.

In Berlin, Dulles again grappled with the problem of how best to influence but not alienate France. For months he had bluntly warned the French that ratification of the EDC was crucial to further United States support for her position in Indochina. At the meeting of the Big Four, he also tried to keep the French from talking peace because he feared such conversations would lead to a compromise with the Communists. Yet when push came to shove, Dulles relented and accepted that Indochina would be discussed at the forthcoming conference at Geneva. He did so because of his anxieties that too much pressure against peace discussions would create a moral obligation for the United States to sustain the French military effort on an even grander scale. He doubted that Congress would approve more aid without conditions unacceptable to the French. The French, in turn, would be angered, and a wave of anti-Americanism might well sweep France.

Therefore, Dulles did not push the French to the limit and accepted a Geneva conference devoted to the entire Far East. It proved a fateful decision. There was now a finite amount of time during which the French and Viet Minh could be expected to try to improve their negotiating positions by striving for success on the battlefield. It would be an unequal contest as the French had already committed most of their reserves while the Viet Minh had not. Amid divided counsel at the highest levels of the French government, General Navarre had received the impression that the loss of the Laotian capital would shock French public opinion and perhaps terminate public support, such as it was, for the war. Moreover, it would certainly topple Laniel's fragile government. So Navarre launched Operation Castor, the code name for the drop on Dien Bien Phu, in the belief that the occupation of the strategic valley was the best way to defend Laos.

Originally, he intended to establish a base in the valley to serve as a mooring point for wide-ranging raids against the Viet Minh's lines of communication leading to Laos. This was exactly the type of aggressive maneuvering that many American officers, up to and including members of the Joint Chiefs, had recommended over the years. Neither they nor Navarre, however, had accounted for the terrible terrain in Vietnam. Trackless jungles, mountains, and streams prevented movement by Western-style forces who depended on heavy weapons and vehicles. The French Union forces at Dien Bien Phu soon found themselves limited to movement within range of their artillery emplacements. Instead of maneuvering, they dug bunkers and fortified, beginning a transition from raider base, to entrenched camp, to fortress.

On December 3, 1953, Navarre gave orders to hold the entrenched camp at all costs. In so doing he completely reversed his earlier scheme, as described in the Navarre Plan, to avoid battle while building up a strategic reserve. Now he planned to accept battle in remote northwest Vietnam. He might have ordered an evacuation, as Operation Castor had patently failed in its stated purpose to serve as a "mooring point" for strikes against the Communist supply line to Laos. Had he done so, he would have sacrificed scarce material and tarnished his prestige, but would have undone the Viet Minh's even more tremendous effort to concentrate resources at Dien Bien Phu. Then he could have called the operation a successful spoiling attack, one that thwarted Giap's plans while allowing his own forces to continue to build along the original lines of the Navarre Plan. Instead, he chose to stay.

Clouding his judgment were the opinions of his critics, particularly his chief subordinate, Brigadier General René Cogny. If he withdrew, Cogny and others would say that they had told him that the operation was flawed from the beginning. Only by remaining could Navarre put to the test his strategic judgment. Holding steadfast to his plan, ignoring his own niggling doubts and the minority view of dissenters, Navarre—the detached, calculating "feline"—demonstrated that military men are not machines implementing their government's decision, but rather men subject to the range of human emotions. While he clung to his decision for a variety of reasons, one transcended all others: He thought he could win.

He believed that the open valley floor and the rolling slopes descending toward the valley provided an ideal place for the French to utilize their superior firepower. If Giap attacked, his men would be consumed by French cannons.

Three days after Navarre made his decision to hold Dien Bien Phu, Giap issued a mobilization order to concentrate Viet Minh forces around the valley. Like the French generals, he recognized that logistics were the key to the battle's outcome. Unlike the French, he believed his men could surmount the terrible physical impediments: "You must repair the roads, overcome all obstacles, surmount all difficulties, fight unflinchingly, defeat cold and hunger, carry heavy loads across mountains and valleys, and strike right into the enemy's camp to destroy him and free our fellow countrymen."

◆ ◆ ◆

When Eisenhower wrote about his first year in office in his memoirs, he observed that "the passing of 1953 did not eliminate our troubles in Vietnam; far more serious ones were still to come." At the time he was more sanguine. On January 7, 1954, the date of his second State of the Union Message, he felt encouraged about the world situation in general and optimistic about Vietnam in particular. He told Congress and the nation that in the past year there had been "a great strategic change in the world." Dulles had frequently denounced Truman's containment policy as passive and reactive to Communist initiatives; Eisenhower now told the country that America held the initiative. He pointed to Indochina, where American assistance permitted "the vigorous resistance of France and the Associated States" to Communist aggression. He intended to continue material assistance to hasten final victory. In passing, he noted that American aid would bring closer the day when the Associated States gained the "independence already assured by France."

The President's confidence that the French could hold stemmed largely from the misleadingly optimistic reports he received from two of the three most important Americans in Vietnam, General O'Daniel and the American ambassador, Donald R. Heath. Ambassador Heath had been hearing nothing but expressions of confidence from French circles in Sai-

gon. He informed Washington that the French command
hoped that the Viet Minh would attack Dien Bien Phu. Although the next several months would be an "anxious period,"
Navarre had not in any way modified his opinion that within
twelve to fifteen months his forces would "inflict decisive military defeat on Viet Minh." Thereafter, all that would remain
would be "a police clean-up operation."

Also buttressing Eisenhower's confidence were the attitudes
of many of his top advisers in Washington. The day after his
State of the Union address, Eisenhower's CIA director, Allen
Dulles, briefed the National Security Council on the situation
at Dien Bien Phu. He pointed out that three enemy divisions
surrounded the entrenched camp but that it was not yet clear
whether they would launch an assault. Admiral Radford commented that Navarre had told him that the Viet Minh could
take the camp if they committed three full divisions and were
willing to take heavy losses. The admiral doubted the Viet
Minh were willing to pay this price.

Allen Dulles responded: "The only purpose to be served by
a Vietminh attack on this fortress would be the psychological
damage which they could do to the French will to continue
the war in Indochina. This political and psychological advantage might seem to the Vietminh to be worth the military loss
that they would suffer."

Everyone present might well have recalled the words of another French general, Napoleon Bonaparte, who said that
"the morale is to the physical as three is to one." Viewed this
way, the psychological effect on France of losing her elite
troops could be predicted to be fatal. Instead, Eisenhower and
his advisers counted the garrison's soldiers—it represented
some 5 percent of total French Union forces—and decided
their loss would not be too grave, particularly if the Viet Minh
suffered heavily in the process of killing them.

Besides, there appeared to be no valid military reason that
Dien Bien Phu should succumb. Although isolated, it was
linked to the balance of French forces by the unbreakable umbilical cord provided by air power. Admittedly, at the beginning of the year General Trapnell had reported that for the
first time Viet Minh antiaircraft gunners were shooting down
French fighter-bombers on a regular basis. This led Admiral

Radford to speculate that American pilots, with their ability to suppress antiaircraft fire, could reclaim aerial dominance in a mere afternoon. His was an amazing suggestion considering that the administration had been so careful to avoid direct intervention. Now, the head of the Joint Chiefs of Staff proposed to risk all merely to knock out some antiaircraft guns.

The National Security Council ignored Radford's bold musings, but also sidestepped the issue of what would be done if the French capitulated. The next week CIA director Allen Dulles told the NSC that although the garrison was down to six days' supplies, unless the Viet Minh could stop the airlift, neither he nor the French generals anticipated any difficulties. The Viet Minh had never displayed the capacity to prevent a French airlift.

An updated formal policy statement adopted by the National Security Council reflected American confidence in the French position. Approved on January 16, it said in part: "With continued U.S. economic and material assistance, the Franco-Vietnamese forces are not in danger of being militarily defeated by the Viet Minh unless there is large-scale Chinese Communist intervention."

However, as was often the case, by the time a formal strategy statement had been approved, events overtook it. Such was the case when, two weeks after his State of the Union address, the President again talked about Southeast Asia with his National Security Council. The situation, as candidly discussed among his close advisers, was not quite as rosy as the picture he had presented during his address. Nagging doubts had emerged. According to the meeting's agenda, the head of the Joint Chiefs of Staff was supposed to describe possible further measures to support the Navarre Plan. Before doing this, Admiral Radford spoke about contingency planning to cover the withdrawal of French forces from Tonkin. He mentioned that three years earlier, when confronting the possibility of a Korean-style Chinese intervention in Vietnam, Marshal de Lattre had told him that before the French could ever get out, they would be massacred. Radford said that this was still a sound conclusion. He saw no point in talking about a French abandonment of Indochina; it was too grim a possibility to entertain. The admiral also wanted to delay presenting the Joint

Chiefs' latest assessment of the Navarre Plan, claiming that it had been written hurriedly and needed refinement. Furthermore, General O'Daniel would soon be reporting from Indochina and his input would improve the assessment. Clearly, Admiral Radford sensed trouble and, concerned with Pentagon prestige, was beginning to distance the Joint Chiefs from overly enthusiastic claims about French success.

Eisenhower was not taken in by Radford's prevarication and wanted the Joint Chiefs to finish their report as soon as possible. He insisted that Indochina not be lost through American inaction if it was within the United States' means to support the Navarre Plan. More bombers and more American technicians to service them could be sent. Regarding the situation at Dien Bien Phu, Eisenhower criticized French strategy that tied down so much strength in the Tonkin Delta while the Viet Minh massed around the entrenched camp.

With anxiety rising, Eisenhower and the NSC waited for the Joint Chiefs' report. This "hurriedly written" document had been completed the day before Eisenhower's State of the Union speech. An analysis of American objectives and possible courses of action in Southeast Asia, it stated the policy choice in the bluntest terms. Given that the region was a critical area, a conclusion reached by the Truman administration and endorsed by Eisenhower, the JCS report considered what military actions the United States would undertake in the case of overt Chinese aggression or internal subversion in Indochina asking: "Will the U.S. employ . . . military force sufficient to destroy Communism" in the region?

In that the country had only just disengaged from Korea, posing this question was brave yet logical. Answering it proved beyond the first efforts of the CIA-JCS team assigned to the problem, who gave responses ranging from, Why consider such a hypothetical situation since France would never permit herself to be defeated? to sending seven American divisions to replace the French. There was agreement that the United States had to do everything possible to support the Navarre Plan and to discourage any negotiated settlement. The analysts doubted that sending American ground forces to fight a "limited war" in Indochina was "to the net security advantage of the U.S." They asked if the region was of such critical importance that it should override the certain costs and possible risks and generally believed that the United States should not become involved in ground combat. If, however, American forces did engage, enough troops should be sent to ensure victory. Furthermore, the JCS stated, "the military judgment is that only the commitment of *large* U.S. forces will ensure victory."

American military intervention in Indochina had first been debated in 1950 by the Truman administration. Less than two months after the outbreak of the Korean War, the French ambassador asked Secretary of State Acheson if the United States would provide tactical air support in the event that China intervened in Indochina. Acheson replied that American intelligence discounted the likelihood of such a Chinese action but would study the situation. After the Chinese entered the Korean War, most discussion centered around a similar Chinese move into Vietnam. The first American contingency plans called for supporting the French with air and naval units. But, as early as November 1950, Pentagon planners feared the potential consequences of even a limited intervention: "While minor commitments of United States military forces might be sufficient to defeat the Viet Minh in Indochina it is more probable that such commitments would lead to a major involvement of the United States in that area similar to that in Korea or even to global war."

In spite of Pentagon fears, formal United States strategy called for limited intervention if the Chinese provided overt support to the Viet Minh. This strategy remained in effect through 1952. By that time Secretary of State Acheson had concluded the country could not afford to use ground forces in Indochina, but should counter Chinese intervention with air and naval units.

When American officials discussed these ideas with their British and French counterparts, they found them distinctly unwilling to commit to specific plans. Thus the Joint Chiefs had directed Admiral Radford, as Commander in Chief, Pacific, to prepare plans for both cooperative Allied action and unilateral American intervention. Radford's strategy had called for a naval blockade of China, naval support of a French evacuation from the Tonkin Delta, and air strikes against selected targets in mainland China. In early 1954, Radford and his staff dusted these plans off to take another look.

It was this reexamination that delayed the JCS report to the National Security Council. The CIA and military experts could not agree what should be done if sending more aid to the French failed to stop the Viet Minh or if the French decided to pull out of Indochina. Some argued that it was necessary to make a decision whether or not to intervene immediately, which seemed to accord with the Eisenhower-Dulles foreign policy approach that stressed initiative and action rather than Truman-style reaction. However, Eisenhower and his advisers balked at plans to send Americans to war. Attacking Democratic failure and flaying the passivity of containment made good politics. Contingency plans, particularly those involving bold actions, were well and good in the abstract, but in the breach, the key leaders in the Eisenhower administration preferred to defer decision making until learning more about the actual situation. Much now depended upon what O'Daniel found in Vietnam.

♦ ♦ ♦

Since Giap had made the decision to accept battle at Dien Bien Phu, his forces had made a prodigious effort to bring men and supplies to the hills overlooking the entrenched camp. French radio-intercept teams detected the Viet Minh's buildup. To stop it, French air power attacked the trails leading to Dien Bien Phu. During two consecutive days at the end of December, twenty-three fighter-bombers dropped twenty-three tons of bombs on a strategic chokepoint. Photo reconnaissance determined that on the following day, road traffic had been restored. The photos did not reveal how it was taking place.

Along numerous primitive paths, stern Viet Minh commanders grouped the local inhabitants into road maintenance crews. Once the bombers passed, out came every able-bodied person to repair the damage. If the French had dropped small delayed-action bombs, the villagers first drove a herd of water buffalo across the ground to explode them. The local commissar called for volunteers to undertake the risky process of attaching a grapple to the larger bombs so that they could be hauled away. Then the villagers repaired the damage with shovels and pickaxes. They brought tons of earth and rock in baskets on their backs to fill bomb craters. In this fashion, employing very little mechanical power, even the worst bomb damage could be fixed in less than two days and the flow of truck-borne supplies resumed. Although the French did not yet realize it, if the Viet Minh were to be halted it would not happen until they reached the base's perimeter.

There the garrison's next line of defense would be its artillery. A high-ranking French technical expert, who had seen how the Americans used massed artillery in Korea, visited Dien Bien Phu and inquired whether the camp had sufficient artillery. The commander of the artillery, Colonel Charles Piroth, responded with surprise, "Look at my plan of fire, M. Minister. I've got more guns than I need."

French confidence was apparent again when O'Daniel flew into Dien Bien Phu in early February. Whereas his last tour had been at Navarre's invitation, this time General O'Daniel went in spite of Navarre's opposition. Navarre need not have worried. By and large, French defensive arrangements impressed O'Daniel. He could not help but feel attracted to the garrison's top officers. Many were brother warriors—kindred spirits who, like O'Daniel himself, had seen war up close. The artillerist Piroth, for example, had fought the Germans in Italy during World War II, just as had O'Daniel, and had lost an arm during that campaign.

In a report to the Joint Chiefs, much cited in subsequent histories, he wrote that the position "can withstand any kind of an attack that the Viet Minh are capable of launching." O'Daniel had seen the obvious advantages of the surrounding high ground and asked the garrison's commander, Colonel Christian de Castries, why he had not included this dominating terrain in his defensive scheme. The colonel replied that the artillery fields of fire were better in the valley than on the heights. Encouraged by the garrison's high morale, O'Daniel reported that it could repulse any attack.

Following the Dien Bien Phu disaster, French military men and historians would claim that American officers had approved of their position. Overlooked is a crucial caveat

O'Daniel included in his report to the JCS. After stating that
the post could withstand attack, he added: "However, a force
with two or three battalions of medium artillery with air observation could make the area untenable. The enemy does not
seem to have this capability at present." O'Daniel's confidence
about the garrison's ability to hold rested on knowledge of
Viet Minh capability. However, for this intelligence, Americans in Vietnam were entirely dependent upon French
sources. The French had worked hard to keep Americans
from developing their own sources of intelligence and now
their labors came to fruition.

The day after O'Daniel's visit to Dien Bien Phu, President
Eisenhower held a news conference in Washington. Reporters
had learned that American Air Force mechanics were being
sent to Vietnam. It was a sensitive political issue. Senate leaders had warned that opposition was so great that it threatened
aid appropriations for all of Southeast Asia. The administration crafted a compromise that promised a departure date by
mid-June. Unaware of this, a reporter asked Eisenhower if the
American airmen were servicing planes in Vietnam. Although
a first group had been sent for exactly that purpose one year
ago and a new group had the same mission, the President
claimed ignorance about their mission. Asked whether the situation was critical, he replied that it had been critical for a
long time, but that ultimately success hinged on Vietnamese
desire to be free. He concluded with a deliberate understatement: "We have had some evidence that there is a lack of enthusiasm" on the part of the Vietnamese to fight the
Communists. In fact, at the National Security Council meeting
that same day, CIA director Allen Dulles had told the President "that the majority of the people in Vietnam supported
the Vietminh." Eisenhower mentioned that he too had gained
that impression a few days earlier when receiving the Vietnamese ambassador. Upon being asked how many Vietnamese
believed French promises of genuine independence, the ambassador replied "perhaps two or three percent."

Shortly thereafter, two very different field assessments arrived in Washington. O'Daniel's optimistic report predicted
sure victory. In sharp contrast was an evaluation submitted by
the Military Assistance Advisory Group's Army attaché. The

head of the MAAG found the situation at Dien Bien Phu very troubling. The previous month he had informed his superiors that the French had only an even chance of holding the position. Reading O'Daniel's report, he thought that once again Iron Mike was overconfident. So he sent his Army attaché to Dien Bien Phu for a second opinion and that officer gave a very pessimistic appraisal.

The two reports created quite a stir in Washington, very much the same as occurred in the next administration when two officers toured Vietnam and provided President Kennedy with completely different assessments. Kennedy greeted them by asking if they were sure they had visited the same country. In 1954 the secretary of state similarly demanded clarification and invited MAAG commander General Trapnell to provide his views.

Trapnell welcomed the opportunity, having experienced enormous frustration at the way O'Daniel seemed to have access to policymakers while Washington ignored his own opinions. Seizing his chance, he told the Joint Chiefs and Dulles that "despite the confidence reposed in Navarre and the French forces by visiting U.S. political notables and military missions . . . the current campaign season has been dominated by the Viet Minh." Staff planners in the Department of the Army concurred. They argued that even if the French won out at Dien Bien Phu, the United States would still not attain its objectives in Southeast Asia. Additional military aid would not solve the underlying, persistent lack of Vietnamese fighting spirit owing to the population's doubts about true political reform.

O'Daniel, on the other hand, had reported favorably on the continued development of Vietnamese forces, contending that because of their contribution the military situation was well in hand and would improve rapidly. Trapnell knew that this was very misleading. Since the announcement of the Geneva Conference, the Vietnamese Army had begun to collapse. For example, in spite of the threat of court-martial, only 5,400 of 94,000 Vietnamese men summoned obeyed mobilization orders. In April 1954 alone, there would be nearly 4,000 documented cases of desertion from the Vietnamese Army. Six months after the formation of the light battalions, in which everyone up to and including Eisenhower held such stock, a quarter of their strength was gone although they had barely been in combat.

Trapnell understood how newly appointed Vietnamese officers preferred the supply and administrative services where they could line their pockets with American goods. Fifty thousand piasters bought a man an exemption, so only the poorest, least capable joined the fighting troops. What possible motivation could they have? Neither the figurehead imperial ruler Bao Dai, nor Nguyen Van Tam, the nominal head of the government, nor Tam's son, the army's chief of staff, commanded respect. The people of Saigon saw their military leaders bedecked in medals, driving American cars to their lavish cocktail parties. In the bitter words of a French journalist who observed them: "Their hatred for Communism was governed by the advantages which capitalism offered them: medals, women, money."

Trapnell only partially appreciated the enormity of the problem, but, unlike those in Washington and those who came on inspection tours, he based his knowledge on longer field observation. He described what he saw, but his observations were not what some of the hawks in the Pentagon and in the Eisenhower administration wanted to hear. Admiral Radford discounted the negative assessments from the field by saying that members of the MAAG took an overly parochial view and "tend to become frustrated as a result of continuously being on the scene." Along with Undersecretary of State Walter Bedell Smith, he assured Congress that there was no basis for the "alarmist interpretations of recent military operations" in Vietnam. Eisenhower clearly believed O'Daniel over Trapnell. He cabled Dulles, who was in Berlin completing arrangements for the Geneva Conference, that "O'Daniel's most recent report is more encouraging than given to you through French sources." Recognizing the way the wind was blowing, the United States ambassador in Saigon requested that the Army attaché stop sending pessimistic reports. That officer courageously declined.

While no one within the executive branch felt deeply alarmed at the situation, outside, Mississippi Senator John Stennis spoke up. When the Pentagon had formally announced the dispatch of two hundred Air Force mechanics to Vietnam, Stennis identified grave consequences: "First we send them planes, then we send them men. . . . We are going to war, inch by inch." Republican leaders met privately with Eisenhower and expressed similar concerns, to which the President reacted sharply: "But we can't get anywhere in Asia by just sitting here in Washington and doing nothing—My God, we must not lose Asia—we've got to look the thing right in the face."

At his weekly news conference on February 10, reporters asked if the Air Force mechanics could be considered combatants. Eisenhower responded that there was no chance that they would be touched by battle. Citing Stennis's speech, a reporter persisted. The President answered, "No one could be more bitterly opposed to ever getting the United States involved in a hot war in that region than I am; consequently, every move that I authorize is calculated, so far as humans can do it, to make certain that that does not happen."

Daniel Schorr, of CBS Radio, asked if the President's remarks meant that he was determined not to become more deeply involved in Indochina regardless of how the war was going. Eisenhower replied that although he could not predict the drift of events, he could not "conceive of a greater tragedy for America than to get heavily involved now in an all-out war in any of those regions, particularly with large units."

Finally, a reporter noted that Stennis had complained that the Senate Armed Services Committee had no advance knowledge about the dispatch of additional Air Force technicians to Vietnam. The President assured the reporter that "there is no attempt here to carry on the affairs of America in a darkened room."

Part 2. SIEGE

February 1954 brought little change in the military situation in Indochina, a lull that reinforced those in Washington who believed the Navarre Plan was progressing satisfactorily. In fact, February, like January, was a time of immense toil for the Viet Minh. Since the dawn of warfare, sieges had been a matter of supplies and of artillery. The attacker maneuvered to isolate the garrison while preserving his own supply line. The defender husbanded his resources and attacked the besieger's supply line, hoping that friendly forces outside the fortress could bring relief. The attacker entrenched his artillery—mechanically powered catapults in ancient times, gunpowder-propelled shells in the modern era—so as to protect it while it battered down the defenses. The defender employed his artillery to try to destroy the hostile guns before they created a fatal breach. More than any other style of warfare, a siege was subject to near mathematical precision. In January and February, Giap and his staff performed the calculus of combat better than their French adversaries.

The French high command based its confidence for the defense of Dien Bien Phu on what it presumed was sound military analysis of three conventional factors: logistics, weaponry, and terrain.

The Viet Minh's logistical lifeline stretched to the Chinese border some one hundred miles distant. Supplies had to travel across nearly trackless mountains, jungles, and rivers. Everything had to be carried by coolies. French intelligence officers knew an Asian's carrying capacity and knew the weight of munitions required for a major offensive. Simple algebra proved that the Viet Minh would need tens of thousands of porters, a mass of men that surely could not escape aerial bombardment. The French Air Force alone would prevent a major Viet Minh effort.

Furthermore, the Viet Minh lacked the heavy weapons needed to support a major attack against an entrenched camp. Heretofore, enemy artillery had been used only rarely. Comprising nothing larger than 75-millimeter Japanese and Chinese guns, Viet Minh artillery had only been used along the Chinese frontier and in the Red River Delta. Such small-caliber guns could not compete with the garrison's heavier artillery commanded by Colonel Piroth.

Finally, local terrain conditions around the valley dictated that any Viet Minh artillery had to be set up on the forward slopes facing the French position. They could not fire from the safer reverse slopes because the increased range and angle of trajectory would prevent shells from hitting the base. The

French artillery fire plan, relying upon its heavier weight of metal, would dominate these forward slopes.

Simply put, the Viet Minh could not bring sufficient munitions to the nearly inaccessible valley, they had never possessed a formidable artillery, and the French artillery dominated the surrounding hills. Within the French military, this assessment went virtually unchallenged. After all, Navarre had been an intelligence officer, and his subordinates had trained at France's finest military schools. How could Giap, a former history teacher, know better?

The problem was that each assumption was wrong. Regarding logistics, the Viet Minh relied upon thousands of bicycles to multiply the carrying capacity of each man. Modified with reinforcing wooden struts to strengthen the frame and front fork and bamboo poles to extend the handlebar, each bicycle carried 400 to 500 pounds. For three years the Viet Minh had utilized bicycle transport. French military intelligence calculated that each bicycle could carry about two times the weight of the man pushing it, underestimating their ability with the modified bicycle by a factor of two or three. The real carrying capacity of a small team of porters was a matter of tons, not pounds, as the French figured. Furthermore, against all odds the Viet Minh managed to build roads to carry Russian-supplied trucks.

Similarly, although the French had indications that the Viet Minh possessed formidable artillery, they did not make use of the information. On January 19, French radio-intercept teams learned that the Viet Minh high command had ordered absolute priority to the transport of 81-millimeter mortar shells and, much more ominously, 105-millimeter shells. Such shells were only useful if the Viet Minh had the guns to shoot them, a notion too incredible to take seriously. Nonetheless, by January 27, although the French did not know it, the Viet Minh had already emplaced most of their twenty-four 105-millimeter cannon in firing positions overlooking the French defenses. That task had required an amazing labor even more difficult than the hauling of supplies. Escaping aerial detection through impeccable camouflage discipline, trucks brought the cannon as close as possible to the firing positions. Then, teams of soldiers manhandled them up steep slopes. They averaged a yard a minute on the steepest slopes, and had to put huge wooden wedges behind the wheels every step of the way to prevent them from backsliding. Political officers inspired the men with the story of one soldier who, when all the drag ropes had broken, wedged his body behind the wheels to prevent it from rolling downslope. So they toiled and sang a soon to be famous song:

> The ravines are deep,
> But none of them deeper than our hatred.
> Let us pull the guns behind us
> And the battlefield will become the graveyard of our
>   enemies.

They dragged the cannon from one concealed position to another until they finally came to firing positions tunneled into the forward slope overlooking the French camp. Covered with vines, protected overhead by yards of earth and rock, the cannon awaited the signal to open the battle. Weapons the Viet Minh were not supposed to have went into positions the French could not see while twenty thousand peasants, some volunteers, some conscripted at gunpoint, maintained the roads that slowly brought the shells forward to accumulate for the decisive moment.

◆ ◆ ◆

In the valley below, the garrison waited, ignorant of the coming storm. The American Army attaché reported to Washington that the French had ceased patrolling. To American "alarmists" this was a sure sign of overconfidence. In mid-February a French war correspondent visited. The Viet Minh opened fire with a brief barrage from their light artillery—as yet they had not revealed the positions of their heavier 105-millimeter cannon—and caused extensive damage. The correspondent expressed concern to the post's commander, Colonel de Castries, who replied, "What of it? I wear my red forage cap so that they can see me better."

On February 19, Minister of Defense René Pleven toured the camp. Noting the fragile combat shelters—all construction material had to be airlifted to the valley causing most dugouts to be poorly constructed—and recalling reports that the Communists had artillery, he asked a battalion officer if the situation was dangerous. The officer replied, "We shall fight as at Verdun." To the surprise of everyone, a mere lieutenant added, "M. Minister. It would be a catastrophe if we didn't fight. We've got a unique opportunity to crush the Viets."

During the remainder of Pleven's inspection, the glow of confidence affected everyone. Rather, it affected everyone except General Fay, the chief of air staff, whose silence contrasted with the others. Fay was renowned for his quiet, calm judgment. Pleven inquired, "And what about you, General?"

Fay replied, "Minister, I am afraid I cannot join in today's concert. What I have seen has only confirmed me in an opinion which I shall express, bluntly, in full awareness of my responsibilities. This is it: I shall advise General Navarre to take advantage of the respite . . . to evacuate all the men he can, for he is done for. That is all."

Fay proved true to his word. He told Navarre his view upon his return to Saigon. Navarre maintained his position declaring, "Dien Bien Phu was chosen deliberately, and it is there that we shall win the battle." Rebuffed publicly, Fay met Navarre that evening in private and expressed a willingness to assume personal direction of the evacuation and defend Navarre from all critics of the retreat. Navarre declined. It was the last chance for the garrison of Dien Bien Phu and with it began a series of catastrophic Western defeats at Giap's hands that would not end until the unseemly American helicopter evacuation from the United States embassy roof in Saigon twenty-one years hence.

While most were taken in by the French high command's confidence, several French journalists retained grave doubts. On February 24, Navarre held a press conference and assured journalists that the Viet Minh offensive had peaked and "exceeded its logistic possibilities." One doubter, a special correspondent for *Le Monde,* had recently completed a rail journey through the hinterland. He told his colleagues: "The Commander in Chief has just explained everything to us dogmatically, and I, a humble journalist, would stake my life on it that he is either making a terrible mistake or lying to us. I would be ready to swear that the situation he has described has noth-

ing in common with reality." In the 1960s, there would be
military briefers addressing a different set of journalists, but
the effect would be very similar. The American press would
call the briefings the Five O'clock Follies, and they too would
be convinced that the military was either lying to the reporters
or so sadly out of touch that they were lying to themselves.

♦ ♦ ♦

At the end of February, the major foreign policy focus for
the Eisenhower administration was the upcoming Geneva
Conference. It was to comprise two distinct sections: one devoted to final resolution of the Korean War; the other devoted
to Indochina. First, Secretary of State Dulles had to go to Capitol Hill to report to the Senate Foreign Relations Committee
on the Berlin Conference. He could expect sharp questioning.
Although they could not know it, the personal destinies of several of the interrogators, Senators William Fulbright and Hubert H. Humphrey, were to become forever linked with
Vietnam.

Republican Senator William Knowland believed he understood the Korean portion of the Geneva Conference but regarding the Indochinese negotiations he had many questions.
He quizzed Dulles on decision making and the secretary gave
a candid answer: "I suppose that in the last analysis these
things come down to the question of who has the power to
make a settlement." Dulles accepted that the United States had
that power and sought to maneuver to permit its most effective use. Senator Hubert H. Humphrey asked if a negotiated
settlement would prove favorable to the West. He acknowledged that Dulles had faced a difficult situation in Berlin, but
argued that the odds of anything constructive coming out of
the Geneva Conference were poor because the West was negotiating from a position of weakness. When pressed by the debate with Dulles, the senator from Minnesota went one step
further, asserting that it was "patently obvious that we just do
not have any plan" in the event of a military disaster in Indochina. This lack was wrong because the President and Dulles
had repeatedly said that Indochina was of critical importance
to national security.

Other senators picked up on this theme. Dulles had told

them that Indochina was more important than Korea. They argued that if the nation had gone to war for the less critical Korea, it was inconsistent to avoid war for Indochina. The senators were skillfully turning the administration's own rhetoric against it, and while so doing several were beginning to have grave doubts about the course of American policy in Vietnam. Dulles tried to reassure them that the Navarre Plan, and the strong American support for this plan, would successfully achieve American goals but Senator Fulbright sharply questioned his assumptions. Senator Humphrey pointed out that some administration officials, including Admiral Radford and Bedell Smith, had claimed that the military situation was fine, whereas Dulles was now saying that all along the situation had been uncertain. This charge of inconsistency, and possible duplicity, caused something that seldom happened at such meetings; John Foster Dulles lost his temper. He recovered fairly quickly with a graceful apology. Senator Mike Mansfield, the future Senate majority leader in the Johnson administration, smoothed things over saying, "It is good to see you with your Scotch-Irish up once in a while; it relieves the tension."

Knowland provided calming perspective. Referring to Humphrey's criticism that the administration lacked a plan, he said, "The big job we have got is to keep out of war if we can . . . but we are in a changing world, and Indochina is just one point on the perimeter. It is pretty difficult."

Dulles agreed. At the next National Security Council meeting he told the council to expect a difficult, frustrating negotiation at Geneva, much like the lengthy talks leading to the Korean armistice. However, he now felt confident that the conference presented opportunities for the United States to improve its global position. As he reported to Vice President Nixon, the present position "offers the fair probability of salvaging both French membership in EDC and the continuation of the struggle in Indochina."

Since the beginning of the year, official United States policy had aimed at preventing the French from negotiating with the Communists unless there was a marked improvement in the military situation. Dulles feared that negotiations would lead to neutrality, which "would eventually turn the country over to Ho Chi Minh with no opportunity for the replacement of the French by the United States." The secretary of state, by late winter 1954, believed that matters were progressing satisfactorily. He did not anticipate a French push for a negotiated settlement, "provided there was no real military disaster in Indochina prior to and during the conference." Neither he nor anyone else attending a National Security Council meeting that addressed the situation in Vietnam anticipated any significant military reverse. They believed that lavish American aid was about to pay off.

Among the many groups studying Vietnam was the President's Special Committee on Indochina. Chaired by Undersecretary of State Walter Bedell Smith, the President's close and trusted wartime chief of staff fondly called "Beetle," the committee submitted its findings on March 2. The Special Committee's mandate was to suggest a program whereby the Viet Minh could be defeated without resort to overt combat operations by United States forces. Its starting point was the assertion that "Indo-China is considered the keystone of the arch of Southeast Asia." This phrase had originated in the Truman administration and had seldom been challenged since. It invariably preceded a second premise that Indochina must not be permitted to fall to the Communists, and such was the case when the Special Committee addressed the problem.

The Special Committee recognized that its suggestions would not affect tactical operations around Dien Bien Phu and, instead, focused on longer-term problems. Foremost remained the inability of the French to develop effective native forces. As had been stated so many times, this was the key to success. The United States had either sent or was preparing to send sufficient equipment and supplies to win the war. There was also an ample untapped reservoir of manpower in the Associated States. Therefore, the Special Committee concluded, the continued failure had to be due to French bungling. They presented detailed suggestions to reverse the present trend and concluded that without armed Chinese intervention, those suggestions "give promise of leading to an ultimate victory in Indo-China without overt use of U.S. military forces." However, the committee hastened to add that since the recommended actions could not take effect immediately, a drastic reverse in the near future could derail the program. In that event, the country would have to consider direct military action in Southeast Asia. To cover such a misfortune, its last recommendation was for the Department of Defense to develop contingency plans for the use of American armed forces in Indochina.

On March 11, 1954, Allen Dulles told the National Security Council that the most serious developments in Indochina were the Viet Minh raids against airfields in the Tonkin Delta. He explained that the raids were obvious Viet Minh attempts to create incidents that would involve U.S. Air Force mechanics stationed at airfields within the delta.

In fact, they were part of a series of long-planned raids Giap hoped would disrupt the French aerial supply line to Dien Bien Phu. The first such raid struck an airfield near Hanoi in the predawn hours. Just as they were to do a decade later against American airfields, Viet Minh commandos penetrated the base without incident. They attached explosives to twelve planes and escaped, losing one man. American airmen sat in shelters during the raid.

Four days later another predawn raid hit an airfield where forty-four American airmen worked servicing the big Flying Boxcar transport planes. A spectacular firefight ensued. The Viet Minh destroyed four bombers, but the Americans escaped unharmed. Such incidents were exactly what Congressmen and reporters had in mind when they had queried the President if the dispatch of mechanics to Vietnam would place them in the line of fire. Rapidly unfolding and dramatic events prevented anyone from following up on this presidential inconsistency.

The day of the second raid, Giap wrote a proclamation to inspire his men on battle's eve. It explained what was at stake: "Winning the battle of Dien Bien Phu means exterminating the major part of the best enemy forces . . . smashing the Navarre Plan, and dealing a terrible blow to the schemes of the Franco-American capitalists who are financing the war. The victory of Dien Bien Phu will have immense consequences both at home and abroad." Communist rhetoric aside, in the spring of 1954 the United States government indeed had a large investment of money and prestige riding on the battle's outcome.

Part 3. ASSAULT

On the afternoon of March 13, the long-expected Viet Minh assault on Dien Bien Phu began. To the garrison's vast surprise, a tremendous artillery bombardment began the action. A French Foreign Legion sergeant described the scene: "We are all surprised and ask ourselves how the Viets have been able to find so many guns capable of producing an artillery fire of such power. Shells rained down on us without stopping like a hailstorm on a fall evening. Bunker after bunker, trench after trench, collapsed, burying under them men and weapons."

Colonel Piroth's French and African gun crews manned their cannon to return the fire. Although bravely served, their guns failed to silence the Viet Minh artillery. When the bombardment shifted to the all-important airstrip—the garrison's lifeline to the outside world—French aircraft scrambled to take off and evade the shells. Heretofore well-camouflaged Communist antiaircraft batteries opened fire from hilltop sites just off the runway's end. Their accurate fire dominated the air over the fortress.

At dusk, the assault cries of *"Tiên-Lên!"* or "Forward!" carried to the defenders of a critical French strongpoint named Beatrice that guarded the airstrip. The attackers crumpled under intense machine-gun fire until squad leader Phan Dinh Giot threw his body against a bunker's firing slit to shield his comrades and permit them to advance. He posthumously became the first hero of the Viet Minh siege force. An hour later the last radio message from Beatrice announced its loss to the enemy.

The next day the battle resumed. Heavy Viet Minh artillery fire soon rendered the airstrip unusable. That night Viet Minh infantry attacked another key French strongpoint named Gabrielle. The Algerian defenders resisted odds of eight to one and beat back attack after attack. Their success depended upon heavy supporting fire from Colonel Piroth's artillery, but Piroth no longer commanded the guns.

That evening the once confident commander of the garrison artillery was a shattered man. Tears streaming down his face he told a fellow officer, "We're done for. . . . We're heading for a massacre, and it's my fault." This brave but misguided officer who had always maintained that his artillery could destroy that of the enemy, who had declined reinforcements, and constantly doubted the ingenuity of the enemy, retired to his dugout. Taking a grenade with his one arm—the other he had lost in combat during World War II—he pulled the pin with his teeth and held the grenade against his heart.

Worried about the effect of Piroth's suicide on the garrison, Dien Bien Phu's commander concealed it. His dispatch to Hanoi simply stated: "Colonel Piroth died on the field of honor." Hours later the Viet Minh resumed their assaults and overran strongpoint Gabrielle.

In the opening round of combat, both sides fought with enormous gallantry and both suffered heavy losses. A lull ensued as they recovered from the shock and prepared for the trials of strength at other key strongpoints. After these first days the battle's pattern was clear. As in any siege, stout defenders could extract heavy casualties from the attacker's ranks, but in the end superior numbers and superior artillery would tell.

Dien Bien Phu's extreme peril was not immediately apparent in Washington. In the past, the Viet Minh had surrounded other French garrisons and been unable to capture them, and it was difficult to imagine that this should be any different. That attitude changed when, one week after the first Viet Minh assaults, the head of the French armed forces staff, General Paul Ely, arrived in Washington for extensive consultation with his American counterparts. Ely had toured Vietnam and Dien Bien Phu before the assaults began. Upon returning to Paris he and the French chiefs of staff concluded that the Navarre Plan could not lead to victory and that the best the French Union forces could accomplish was the creation of a favorable bargaining position for the upcoming Geneva Conference. Even to gain this modest objective, he planned to request substantial additional American aid. To plead for more help Ely went to Washington.

His presentation surprised and dismayed the Eisenhower administration. The massive American support for the Navarre Plan had been predicated upon its achieving its stated goal: military victory in Indochina. With battle joined at Dien

Bien Phu, the President and his staff focused on winning that battle. The day Ely arrived in the United States, Eisenhower met with Dulles, Radford, and Secretary of Defense Charles E. Wilson for one and a half hours. After the meeting, a close aide noted in his diary: "Indo-China problem getting graver." However grave, no one anticipated Ely's bombshell.

On Ely's first night in Washington, Vice President Nixon, General Ridgway, Allen Dulles, and Radford held a working dinner with the French general. Radford expressed an opinion held by most of the American military. He told Ely that he saw no theoretical reason why the French should not be able to crush the Viet Minh, provided they had the will and the material assistance to do so. Victory still hinged on sound, aggressive planning and well-trained native troops. The admiral vigorously promoted these ideas at the dinner. In particular, he strongly pushed the idea that the United States assist in training native soldiers. Ely doused much of this optimistic talk. In ensuing meetings he told his hosts that Dien Bien Phu had a fifty-fifty chance of holding and took advantage of the Americans' consternation to press for more aid. He rejected American appeals to become more involved in training the Vietnamese Army on the grounds that it would adversely affect French prestige and the political scene in France at a delicate time.

In addition to asking for more aid, Ely made one other enormous request. He formally asked Secretary of State Dulles whether the United States would intervene with aircraft should the Chinese Communists send jet fighters over Vietnam. Dulles responded that he could not make such a decision as the American constitutional process had to be followed. However, he told Ely:

> If the United States sent its flag and its own military establishment—land, sea or air—into the Indochina war, then the prestige of the United States would be engaged to a point where we would want to have a success. We could not afford thus to engage the prestige of the United States and suffer a defeat which would have worldwide repercussions.

He added that if the French wanted American military participation, the United States ought to have a greater say in granting independence to the Associated States and in training indigenous forces.

Admiral Radford sensed that the United States was on the cusp of a critical decision. He urged Ely to extend his stay in Washington for a few more days to examine the situation at Dien Bien Phu in more detail and told Ely that the United States was considering intervention with air and naval power. They discussed the mechanics and details of air intervention: "Next General Ely asked what America would do if the French needed help to avert a disaster at Dien Bien Phu. I said . . . if the French government requested such aid and our government granted it, as many as 350 aircraft, operating from carriers, could be brought into action within two days."

Before Ely left Washington, he and Radford agreed to push their planning as far as possible to reduce to a minimum the time lapse between a decision to intervene and the actual strike. Ostensibly, this was in case Red Chinese jet aircraft intervened over Dien Bien Phu.

Informally, they recognized that such contingency planning would also apply to intervention to save Dien Bien Phu.

While Radford told the President's Special Committee on Indochina that the United States must intervene to save the garrison in any event, Ely departed with the belief he had the admiral's pledge to save the fortress. His was not an unreasonable assumption; the Americans had never turned down any French request of substance, particularly an emergency request.

On March 19, 1954, the day before Ely's arrival in the United States, an American carrier task force received orders to maintain a twelve-hour alert in preparation for steaming to the waters off Vietnam, the Gulf of Tonkin. The Chief of Naval Operations, Admiral Robert B. Carney, informed the task force commander that although no approved plan for intervention had been reached, the task force should be ready just in case. The next day Radford briefed the President about the carriers' capabilities. Then, Eisenhower issued orders for the fleet to put to sea. Ostensibly, it was to conduct routine training operations. In fact, the carriers sailed toward a position within striking range of Dien Bien Phu.

CHAPTER VI

THE FALLING-DOMINO PRINCIPLE

Of course, we were brought to the verge of war. The ability to get to the verge without getting into the war is the necessary art.

—JOHN FOSTER DULLES

Part 1. TIME FOR DECISION

Throughout its history, the United States Army abstained from creating elite units. Unlike most of the world's armies, which had traditional, designated elite-status units, such as Great Britain's Coldstream Guards, the more egalitarian U.S. Army forbade the practice. The paratroops came as close to being an elite force as regulations permitted. Their origins dated from the years before the country entered World War II. At that time, select officers had been charged with creating units capable of performing like no others in American military history. Its soldiers would fly over conventional battle lines and descend to the ground using parachutes. Once they landed, they would have to be ready to confront an enemy in all directions without benefit of a safe rear area or line of supply. The newfangled paratroop units attracted some of the most imaginative combat leaders the country had to offer.

156

During the war, the Supreme Allied Commander learned to trust, and the nation learned to celebrate the exploits of units led by Generals Matthew B. Ridgway, Maxwell Taylor, and James Gavin. By definition, paratroop leaders had to think in unconventional terms. In 1954, all three turned their thoughts to the conflict in Southeast Asia. As a group, their influence on American policy toward Vietnam would persist through the middle of the next decade.

Maxwell Taylor was perhaps the most intellectual of the three. At the beginning of the year, with Dien Bien Phu already under siege, he hosted one of his famous biweekly debates after the evening meal. The exercise was intended to keep his staff alert and the topic he chose was "Resolved: That the United States Should Intervene Militarily in Indochina." The debate was so ably conducted that when the issue was put to a vote, the result was a tie. Taylor himself only voted to break ties, and, accordingly, all eyes turned toward the head of the table. After thinking for a moment, Taylor voted with the negative. His vote had no bearing on national policy; Ridgway, his former comrade-in-arms on the Joint Chiefs of Staff, would have much more influence on the conduct of national affairs. What Taylor could not know was that he had begun an association with a far-off land that would lead him to the pinnacle of influence within the administrations of two Presidents who committed the nation to war. His prominence would cause him to become a chief target for those who opposed American involvement in Vietnam.

While Taylor and his staff debated intervention as an intellectual issue, the National Security Council prepared for a meeting where formal policy regarding intervention would be determined. In anticipation, Admiral Radford and Secretary Dulles readied their cases. Characteristically, Radford seized the initiative the day before the council met.

To Radford the need for American military intervention was obvious, but he could not carry his fellow Joint Chiefs with him. The lessons of Korea loomed large in their thinking. With overwhelming air and naval superiority and the commitment of ground forces, the United States had been unable to win. The Chiefs could not see how air and naval forces alone would do any better in Vietnam. In particular, they doubted the effectiveness of air strikes against targets concealed in the jungle. Admiral Carney felt air strikes would provide modest tactical benefits to the garrison of Dien Bien Phu but not prove decisive. The Chiefs worried about what would happen next if the air strikes were indeed indecisive. Intervention had to be balanced against the military and political consequences of United States combat involvement in the war.

Undaunted, Radford summarized for the President his own view of the Ely talks:

> The measures taken by the French will prove to be inadequate and initiated too late to prevent a progressive deterioration of the situation. The consequences can well lead to the loss of all Southeast Asia. . . . I consider that the United States must be prepared to act promptly and in force, possibly to a frantic and belated request by the French for U.S. intervention.

The next day, March 25, the National Security Council met. CIA director Allen Dulles told the President and the council that little had changed at Dien Bien Phu. Eisenhower asked why the French had been unable to prevent the Viet Minh buildup around the beleaguered fortress. General Ridgway explained that, according to Navarre, Viet Minh guerrilla resistance kept the French Union forces from operating in the hinterland. The President observed that if the French could only move by air, "it seemed sufficient indication that the population of Vietnam did not wish to be free of Communist domination." His sobering words were not lost on the council's hawks.

Plunging ahead, John Foster Dulles read from a Joint Chiefs of Staff memo regarding the extent to which America should commit its resources to Indochina. He recommended that the Planning Board, the group charged with drafting strategy statements for the NSC, prepare a contingency plan. The Planning Board was one of Eisenhower's administrative innovations. Its role was to coordinate the NSC's actions in an effort to make the council function more like the British War Cabinet. Specifically, Eisenhower had wanted the Planning Board to have on hand appropriate contingency plans for all likely world events. A trusted personal assistant, General Robert Cutler, headed the board. Cutler now spoke.

He asked if Dulles's request envisaged a contingency plan for American intervention with military force. He reminded the council that such a plan had already been developed and that the council had so disliked it that it had been withdrawn and all copies destroyed. Cutler's intercession might have derailed planning for intervention except that Eisenhower himself now made it clear that he wanted to know whether the United States should pursue a policy that might lead to the employment of ground forces in Vietnam.

The NSC turned to the question what to do if the Communist Chinese sent MiG jet aircraft over Vietnam. Cutler pointed out that official NSC policy stated that United States jets would intercept them. Dulles interjected that the President would still have to secure congressional approval before intervening. He reminded the council that the attorney general was preparing an opinion "with respect to the prerogatives of the President and of Congress in the matter of using U.S. military forces to counter aggression."

Eisenhower observed that it was time to start sounding out the likely congressional reaction to American intervention. Dulles disagreed, thinking it premature until the NSC had decided for itself. As Dulles saw the situation, because of the seasonal monsoon the fighting season would end before a clear military decision had been reached. The Chinese were unlikely to send their MiGs in advance of the Geneva Conference. Therefore, the decision the United States had to focus on was a political one: Who would fill the void left by the global collapse of France as a great power? "Would it be the Communists, or must it be the U.S.?" He believed that the French had already made the decision to abandon Indochina. The United States thus might have to force the French into line, but this would risk ratification of the European Defense Community.

Secretary of Defense Wilson tried to cut the Gordian knot. In his previous job as head of the General Motors Corporation, he had said that what was good for General Motors was good for the country. Regarding Vietnam, he had similar confidence that he knew what was best: He suggested that the United States forget about Indochina and concentrate on preparing the remaining free countries of Southeast Asia to resist communism. Eisenhower firmly rejected Wilson's idea. He explained that "the collapse of Indochina would produce a chain reaction which would result in the fall of all of Southeast Asia to the Communists."

This remarkable meeting adjourned with the decision to direct the Planning Board to prepare contingency plans for American military intervention in Vietnam. During the discussion, the participants addressed almost every major issue that was to characterize all subsequent debate over Vietnam. How could victory be attained when the civilian population seemed to support the Communists? Should the country pursue its objectives in Southeast Asia at risk of committing ground forces? What were the limitations on presidential war powers? Could enough Allied support be mobilized to make the defense of Indochina a united effort? Could the war be won without involving China? Given the enormously complex issues, was Vietnam worth defending?

The administration had to grapple with all of this amid a growing crisis as the Viet Minh embrace of Dien Bien Phu squeezed tighter with each day and while the Geneva Conference drew inexorably closer.

◆ ◆ ◆

Responding to the increasing urgency, the Eisenhower administration acted on both the military and diplomatic fronts. From the flight decks of American carriers operating in the Gulf of Tonkin, U.S. Navy planes took off to reconnoiter Chinese airfields along the North Vietnamese border as well as potential targets along the Viet Minh line of communications leading to Dien Bien Phu. In Washington, Air Force Chief of Staff Twining briefed the President about the capabilities of the B-29 bomber. This was the plane that had dropped the atomic bombs on Japan. Although aged, it remained in 1954 the Air Force's strategic long-range bomber. If the Air Force was to intervene in the skies over Vietnam, its pilots would fly the venerable B-29.

Meanwhile, Secretary of State Dulles delivered a speech designed to prepare the American public for a new war and to pursue Eisenhower's desire for united action to save Indochina. Dulles had won renown among professional diplomats for his forceful speeches and this one was no different. He had prepared during an entire career for moments like this.

The threat of massive nuclear retaliation had worked once before when Eisenhower authorized Dulles to use it to unstick faltering negotiations over Korea. In the previous autumn, Dulles had given it another try. At that time, speaking to the Council on Foreign Relations, Dulles outlined the administration's foreign policy and national security plans. He explained that the aggressor in Korea had begun serious negotiation only when faced with the American atomic threat. He warned that any new aggression by the Communist Chinese in Indochina would similarly produce grave consequences that might extend beyond the borders of Vietnam. The press had focused on Dulles's phrase "massive retaliatory power ... by means and places of our choosing." They understood the strategy to be the President's "New Look," but were not sure what it really meant in practice. Although they bombarded Eisenhower with questions for clarification in subsequent news conferences, the President responded with deliberate vagueness.

Now, on March 29, Dulles gave a similar speech to New York's Overseas Press Club. He detailed Soviet and Chinese support for the Viet Minh. He described the consequences of the loss of Southeast Asia and how it endangered the Philippines, Australia, and the entire western Pacific. He then reminded his audience about his earlier speeches regarding retaliation in places and by means chosen by the free world. He said that if the political system of Communist Russia and Red China were imposed on Southeast Asia, it "would be a grave threat to the whole free community. The United States feels that the possibility should not be passively accepted, but should be met by united action. This might have serious risks, but these risks are far less than would face us a few years from now if we dare not be resolute today."

Dulles's speech dramatically signaled a new American policy. No longer was the possibility of military intervention limited to responding to an overt Chinese invasion of Vietnam. De facto Communist hegemony over any substantial part of Vietnam might trigger a massive United States nuclear strike against China. Yet balanced against this hawkish warning was the call for "united action." This was an apparent effort to reassure American allies and Congress that the United States would not act without their foreknowledge.

No one quite knew what to make of Dulles's speech. Speaking for many foreign observers, *The Times* of London commented that it was always difficult to permit Dulles's words to speak for themselves because he operated in a manner so unlike that of other foreign ministers. Most used public statements to hint at policy. Dulles seemed to reverse this pattern and to make statements stronger than the policy itself. One thing at least was clear: The United States was willing to take unprecedented steps to save the French position in Indochina.

The same day that Dulles spoke in New York, Paul Ely briefed the French Committee of War on his conversations in Washington. The French had assigned a code name to American intervention, Operation Vautour, or Vulture. Ely told the committee that Vulture was available for the asking, an assessment that received support when the committee learned of Dulles's speech. At first they greeted Dulles's words with elation; however, further reflection convinced them that the decision to ask for Vulture was not so simple. They considered the consequences if single or multiple United States raids failed to alter the situation. In either event, would Vulture trigger Korean-style Chinese intervention? Finally, how would Vulture affect hopes for a peaceful settlement at Geneva, scheduled to start in less than a month? After pondering these questions, the committee decided to send a staff officer to Vietnam to describe to Navarre what they believed was a concrete American offer to intervene. The committee would defer to his judgment whether Dien Bien Phu's situation was desperate enough to warrant the risks of Operation Vulture.

Part 2. TO FORGE UNITED ACTION

No major presidential decision is without political ramifications and President Eisenhower had to attend to the political side of the decision to intervene. He knew he retained the strong backing of the American people. He also knew they were not eager to embark upon another Asian war. According to an opinion poll taken in November 1953, just over half of the public supported the idea of employing the Air Force to prevent the Communists from taking Indochina. Only a third supported ground intervention.

The nation's most prominent newspapers and magazines also demonstrated a mixed attitude toward intervention. Since the time the press became aware of Indochina, influential newspapers including *The New York Times* and *The Washington Post* had endorsed the belief that the region was a critical, strategic location. As far back as 1950, *The New York Times* had concurred with the view that its loss would trigger a collapse to communism of all neighboring countries. On March 12, 1954, *The Washington Post* complained in an editorial that Eisenhower was being overly cautious in believing he had to secure congressional approval before entering the war in Indochina. In April, *Newsweek* would write that Indochina's raw materials were "essential to Western industrial civilization."

In contrast, the conservative *Chicago Tribune* had viewed American involvement with deep suspicion. It attacked the administration in an editorial in 1953 charging that it was duping the American people by claiming that "in opposing the native rebellion, it is fighting Communism." Overall, while there was disagreement in the press about American policy, the establishment media was prepared to buy into the official policy as long as it received due consideration from the federal bureaucracy and from Congress. Given Eisenhower's popularity, the media did not present a significant constraint on the administration's freedom of action.

Congress was another matter. Some of Eisenhower's sharpest critics spoke from the ranks of his own party. Senate Majority Leader William Knowland worried that support for the French would lead to involvement as in Korea. In April 1954, when Democratic Senator John F. Kennedy would make a comprehensive denunciation of American policy, Knowland and his oratorical helpmate, Senator Everett Dirksen, spoke up to agree with Kennedy. Another Democrat, Senator Hubert Humphrey, complained that in the present critical situation the executive branch was failing to keep Congress informed.

Eisenhower understood that Congress would probably resist unilateral American military intervention. But united action, authorized by the country's most trusted military leader and President, was another matter. No congressman would risk the charge of losing another country to communism.

On April 1, Eisenhower and his National Security Council met again. For the first time, no one doubted that the French faced defeat at Dien Bien Phu. Viet Minh artillery interdicted the airstrip. Surprisingly accurate antiaircraft fire, some of it radar-directed and employing Chinese technicians, made aerial resupply and reinforcement increasingly hazardous. Radford acknowledged that absent American intervention, the garrison was doomed. The President understood that of the five Joint Chiefs, only Radford and perhaps Twining supported American air strikes to save the garrison. Nonetheless, he wanted formal study of intervention to continue.

So delicate was the decision to intervene that Eisenhower did not explore everything he had in mind during the NSC session. Instead, with a small group that remained after the meeting and at lunch with two friends he mused about alternatives. He speculated that surreptitiously the "U.S. might have to make decision to send in squadrons from two aircraft carriers off coast to bomb [the] Reds at Dien Bien Phu." The President added that if he undertook such a course, "we'd have to deny it forever."

In the chambers of the Joint Chiefs of Staff, Admiral Radford argued for direct American intervention. His aggressive position worried Matt Ridgway, who believed that Radford was overstepping the Joint Chiefs' mandated authority by volunteering recommendations to the President and the Cabinet. The Joint Chiefs were supposed to offer advice only if formally asked by the President or secretary of defense. To do otherwise, to advocate a certain foreign policy, was inevitably to involve the Chiefs in politics. Ridgway cautioned Radford to play by the rules and to observe the proper chain of authority. The other Chiefs joined him in his rebuke of Radford's freewheeling style.

Dissatisfied, Radford formally convened the JCS, asking them to consider, if proper authority asked, what their recommended response to a French request for intervention would be. Ridgway correctly saw this as a hypothetical question, another Radford effort to outflank the formal constraints imposed upon the JCS. Quite simply, Ridgway wanted to keep the nation out of a war and he played the game strictly by the rules to prevent a hasty, and in his mind dreadful, decision. Accordingly, he insisted that the Joint Chiefs not respond. The next day the admiral returned with the proper written request from the secretary of defense requesting the Chiefs' recommendations.

When put to a vote, Ridgway and Carney were against intervention. Marine Corps Commandant General Lemuel C. Shepherd, Jr., joined them and said the United States "could expect no significant military results from an improvised air offensive against guerrilla forces." He predicted that the inevitable consequence of aerial intervention was either failure or further intervention. Only the Air Force's General Twining gave qualified assent. As he later explained: "You could take all day to drop a bomb, make sure you put it in the right place . . . and clean those Commies out of there and the band could play the Marseillaise and the French could come marching out . . . in great shape." So in spite of all Radford's efforts he had persuaded only one other member to support what he and Dulles believed was so necessary.

The place of decision now shifted to Capitol Hill. Responding to growing congressional criticism that Congress was not being kept informed, Eisenhower decided to send his two most aggressive hawks, John Foster Dulles and Admiral Arthur C. Radford, to Capitol Hill to persuade congressional leaders. Dulles hoped the meeting would lead to a joint congressional resolution authorizing the President to employ naval and air units to assist the French. He showed a suitable draft statement to Eisenhower. Had Congress approved, it would have restricted presidential freedom much more than did the Gulf of Tonkin Resolution, which ten years later granted President Lyndon B. Johnson authority to employ "all necessary measures to repel any armed attack." In the event, Eisenhower believed that it was politically wiser to sound out Congress before showing them Dulles's draft resolution.

Dulles assented. He also observed that he wanted the resolution in hand so that he and the President would have another card to play in the high-stakes game of bluff designed to deter the Communists. He told Eisenhower that Admiral Radford, on the other hand, seemed to want the resolution so as to be able to send in air strikes to save Dien Bien Phu. Dulles harmonized his and Radford's views and headed to a secret meeting with congressional leaders. For seventeen years an informal coalition of conservative Republicans and southern Democrats had dominated the Senate. The meeting included the leaders of that coalition: Majority Leader William F. Knowland and two other Republicans; and five Democrats. Chief spokesmen for the latter group were the minority leader, Texas Senator Lyndon B. Johnson; and his mentor, the extraordinarily powerful Senator Richard B. Russell of Georgia.

Russell disliked the administration's foreign policy, believing it too risky. He explained, "I am weary of seeing American soldiers being sent as gladiators, to be thrown into every arena around the world." Russell was consistent. He had objected when Truman first sent aid to the French in Vietnam. At that time, he believed the policy ineffective because the Vietnamese lacked the will to fight on their own behalf. Nothing had transpired in the succeeding four years to alter his views. However, when Dulles and Radford arrived for the meeting, it was Russell's protégé who spoke on his behalf.

As soon as he had been elected to the Senate, Johnson had cultivated Russell, the undisputed leader of the Senate's inner club. By dint of his considerable talents and tireless pandering, Johnson joined the important Armed Services Committee and ascended to Senate minority leader in 1952. He took his marching orders from Russell, but increasingly was becoming a powerful man in his own right. He firmly believed in a bipartisan foreign policy, declaring: "If you're in an airplane, and you're flying somewhere, you don't run up to the cockpit and attack the pilot. Mr. Eisenhower is the only President we've got." He also recognized the political reality of the President's enormous popularity. To attack Eisenhower would be "like telling children that their father was a bad man." Given these attitudes, Dulles and Radford had reasonable grounds for optimism as they entered the secret congressional meeting.

Radford and his aides outlined the military aspects of possible intervention. They explained how air strikes from the two carriers operating in the Gulf of Tonkin could buttress the French ground forces at Dien Bien Phu. In addition, their fighters would escort B-29s flying from the Philippines to deliver saturation bombing on the Viet Minh positions. Led by Johnson, the members of Congress had many questions, very similar to those the French War Committee had raised, regarding possible Chinese reactions and the ultimate commitment of United States ground forces. The congressmen's persistent questioning uncovered one pertinent fact. Undoubtedly forewarned by a leak from Radford's opponents on the Joint Chiefs, a congressman asked the admiral if the JCS unanimously agreed about intervention. He had to acknowledge that they did not. With Russell's consent, Johnson forged the congressional attitude of "no more Koreas with the United States furnishing 90% of the manpower." The congressmen then articulated the conditions under which they would support intervention.

Dulles returned from the meeting to inform Eisenhower that Congress would endorse intervention under three conditions: united action with Allies to include the United Kingdom; an unequivocal French declaration of intent to grant the Associated States independence; and a promise that the French would stay the course.

Partisan memoir writers and sympathetic biographers would later claim that Eisenhower never intended to commit American forces to combat in Vietnam. Instead, they maintain, he went through the exercise of consulting Congress and requesting Allied support in full knowledge that both would reject bold action. He did this, they reason, to protect his political flank from the inevitable fallout stemming from French defeat. Those who had cried, "Who lost China?" would predictably turn their thundering rhetoric to "Who lost Indochina?" The President's actions the day after Radford and Dulles returned from Capitol Hill make this case untenable.

However much Eisenhower wanted authorization to intervene, he—unlike Dulles and Radford—was acutely aware of certain political facts bearing on the situation. As his close aide Sherman Adams later explained: "The President knew that the American people had no appetite for another prolonged

war in Southeast Asia. He was determined not to become involved without the approval of Congress and without the participation of the British." Accordingly, he set about trying to
meet congressionally imposed conditions for intervention.

♦ ♦ ♦

Dien Bien Phu's stalwart defense had stirred France like no
incident since World War II. Consequently, the French government began to operate at a speed surpassing previous experience. In Washington, the French ambassador quizzed
Dulles about his congressional meeting. He understood the
American decision-making process well enough to appreciate
the critical congressional role in war making. Twice he asked
Dulles whether the Eisenhower administration and Congress
would be prepared to go it alone if the British declined to join
in united action? The secretary of state gave an oblique answer to the effect that lack of British participation would
greatly increase the difficulties of American intervention but
not render it impossible.

Meanwhile, General Paul Ely's aide arrived in Vietnam to
brief Navarre about Operation Vulture. At first Navarre rejected Vulture because he feared the Chinese reaction. But
over the next two days tremendous Viet Minh assaults stag-
gered Dien Bien Phu's garrison and seized several more
strongpoints. Only by the narrowest did the French Union
forces hold. On April 4, Navarre radioed Paris his approval
of Vulture.

That Sunday night, two secret meetings convened to determine Dien Bien Phu's fate. In Washington, President Eisenhower held an off-the-record meeting on Indochina. Five of
his most trusted subordinates met to discuss strategy. The
group included three people—Dulles, Radford, and Beetle
Smith—who held very firm, aggressive views on what needed
to be done. Together they agreed on a plan to send American
forces to Vietnam subject to certain conditions that the President insisted upon. First, action had to be joint or "united"
with the British, and to include Australian and New Zealand
troops. If possible, Asian forces from the Philippines and
Thailand would also be involved to avoid the taint of an exclusively "white" intervention. Second, the French would have to

see the fight through to the end. Third, to avoid the criticism
that the intervention was intended to prop up French colonial
rule, the French would have to guarantee the future independence of the Associated States. In essence, these were the conditions Congress had insisted upon the previous day.

State Department Counselor Douglas MacArthur II departed the meeting and checked his mail for any late messages. At 10:15 P.M. he read a top-secret telegram from the
American ambassador to France, Douglas C. Dillon, which reported startling news. The ambassador had received an urgent summons to attend a French cabinet meeting. He arrived
at eleven to be told that while fully cognizant of the gravity
of its decision, the Laniel government had decided to request
formally that the United States launch Operation Vulture. As
Foreign Minister Bidault concluded, "for good or evil the fate
of Southeast Asia now rested on Dien Bien Phu." The French
now believed that the conference at Geneva would be won or
lost depending on the battle's outcome.

Eisenhower's secret meeting had broken up by the time
MacArthur read this message, but he hastened to inform the
participants. When Admiral Radford learned of the French
request, he must have recalled with grim satisfaction his prediction that any French request for intervention would be
"frantic and belated."

In the President's mind, the best way to meet the French
request was to forge united action as quickly as possible.
Therefore, he and Dulles worked until midnight on a letter
to Prime Minister Winston Churchill that amounted to a request for war. Eisenhower was not usually given to oratorical
flourish, but in this letter he invested his considerable personal
prestige in an emotional appeal to his old wartime colleague
and friend. He knew his man and believed he knew how to
move him. The letter began by noting Dien Bien Phu's "gallant fight" and saying its plight was not "hopeless." He re-
counted the domino-like consequences of losing Indochina to
the Communists. This "has led us to the hard conclusion that
the situation in Southeast Asia requires us urgently to take
serious and far-reaching decisions." He argued that somehow
the United States and the United Kingdom must contrive to
force a Communist retreat from the region. He quoted his

secretary of state's recent speech on the need for action and then he proposed the formation of an international coalition that "must be willing to join the fight if necessary." He specified that he did not envision the employment of significant American or British ground troops for this fight.

He wrote that the situation was analogous to that which Churchill described in his military history *Their Finest Hour,* a book recalling the near fatal consequences of early Allied failure to oppose Hitler. Lest the point be lost on his audience, Eisenhower concluded with a passage he felt sure would stir the old warrior in Churchill: "We failed to halt Hirohito, Mussolini, and Hitler by not acting in unity and in time. This marked the beginning of many years of stark tragedy and desperate peril. May it not be that our nations have learned something from that lesson?"

The next morning the top officials in the administration grappled with what to say to the French regarding their request for intervention. The President reiterated to Dulles, who passed the message on to Radford, that intervention without congressional support would be "unconstitutional and indefensible." As Eisenhower, Dulles, and Ambassador Dillon reconstructed the events leading to the French request, Eisenhower realized that Admiral Radford's personal assurances had greatly influenced the French decision. The President said that Radford had made a mistake, but Dulles defended the admiral. Dulles claimed that during the Ely talks he and Radford had clearly explained the American position, yet his defensive reaction to the President's implied criticism coupled with the tone of the message he now sent to the French show that he recognized the blunder.

He replied to the French: "As I personally explained to Ely in presence of Radford," the United States could not commit belligerent acts without first securing certain preconditions. The administration was doing everything possible "to prepare public, Congressional and Constitutional basis for united action in Indochina." In spite of Dulles's protestations, he himself had contributed to the French misconception regarding how far and fast the United States was prepared to go. In his last official contact with the French ambassador before the request, Dulles had said that unilateral intervention was not "impossible." French leaders knew that heretofore the Americans had never turned them down. Radford had led Ely to believe that once the French requested it, American bombers would appear over Dien Bien Phu in short order.

Now French leaders learned that much more was involved and that a significant time lag would ensue. After learning of the American rejection, Foreign Minister Bidault told Dillon to tell Dulles that the time for formulating coalitions had passed and Dien Bien Phu's fate would be decided in the next ten days. Ely told one of his military aides that he feared Operation Vulture would come too late.

♦ ♦ ♦

For many in the Eisenhower administration the month of April proved very hard. The siege at Dien Bien Phu created a month-long crisis atmosphere. Weekly, tension mounted. It reached recurring peaks with each meeting of the National Security Council since everyone knew that during one of those meetings an irrevocable decision to go to war or to refrain from intervention would be made. Probably not since the critical days of early June 1944, when Eisenhower met with his staff at Southwick House near Portsmouth, England, to ponder gloomy weather forecasts for the all-important Normandy coast—a time when he alone had to decide whether to cancel or continue the pending D-Day invasion—had the President faced such strain. Referring to "the tremendous tensions" of the moment, the President remarked to a close aide that if the French managed to endure he would forgive them for the worries they had imposed upon him over the last four years.

Events were moving so fast that the NSC had to revise a two-day-old report in order to examine in detail the consequences of possible American military intervention in Southeast Asia. This examination considered specific alternative means of intervention and their likely consequences. Worried that things were spinning out of control, Ridgway produced an "Army position" on intervention. It began: "There are important military disadvantages to intervention in Indochina under the assumptions set forth" by the NSC. It continued by stating that neither could intervention with air and naval units alone ensure victory nor would the use of atomic weapons reduce the number of ground forces required. It estimated that seven American divisions would be needed, provided the Chinese did not intervene. By predicting such high manpower requirements, the Army position guaranteed that planners would take notice. Everyone agreed that once the United States committed its prestige by intervention of any sort, victory had to result. The Army position clearly told planners that such victory would involve a major war.

The next day the NSC met for an unscheduled emergency session. The entire Joint Chiefs of Staff was requested to attend. CIA director Allen Dulles set the meeting's tone. He said that everyone on the special Indochina intelligence committee recognized that if the United States intervened in sufficient force to defeat the Viet Minh, there would be great danger of overt Chinese Communist intervention. He then proceeded to describe the situation at Dien Bien Phu, where the garrison was short of food and ammunition, wounded could not be evacuated, and the air dropping of supplies was very difficult.

Seeking to preempt the anticipated hawkish, pro-intervention statements of Dulles and Radford, Robert Cutler—the head of the NSC's Planning Board—observed that the board saw no evidence that the French had decided to accept a negotiated settlement, something the United States continued to oppose, or that a military decision in Indochina was imminent regardless of what befell Dien Bien Phu. With this statement Cutler was implying that there remained time to make a carefully considered decision. He was trying to prevent the possibility of a hasty plunge to war.

Vehement disagreement greeted his claim. The secretaries of defense and state, CIA director, and JCS Chairman all felt Cutler was being overly optimistic. But Cutler had not spoken for their benefit. His words were meant for Eisenhower, who now spoke. The President said that even the loss of Dien Bien Phu could not be described as a military defeat because the French would have inflicted enormous losses on the Viet Minh. Then, with great emphasis, he said there would be no unilateral American intervention. With this statement, Eisenhower showed that he "had backed down considerably from the strong position he had taken on Indochina the latter part of the previous week."

No one challenged the President's decision, but neither could they agree what therefore should be done. A wild and lengthy argument ensued with the hot-tempered participants, a category that included the President, barely able to contain themselves. At one moment Eisenhower said that the loss of Indochina did not necessarily mean the balance of Southeast Asia would fall. Later, he took the opposite view saying "Indochina was the first in a row of dominoes. If it fell its neighbors would shortly thereafter fall with it." With great warmth he asked where did the process end.

Vice President Nixon seemed to have acquired confidence in his expertise and standing within the administration following his Asian trip. He participated in the debate to a much greater extent than had been his norm. The situation he saw was much like the situation he would confront as President fourteen years in the future. The NSC's talk had focused on the desirability of forging a defensive organization to resist overt Communist aggression. Nixon interjected that at some point the United States "must decide whether it is prepared to take action which will be effective in saving free governments from internal Communist subversion."

Secretary of State Dulles agreed with the Vice President that the danger lay in subversion rather than Korean-style naked invasion. The secretary of defense made the unpopular but accurate observation that Dulles and others well described the danger but had not said what the country could do to thwart Communist aggression.

For the first time at this high level, someone outlined an alternative that would become the new policy. Eisenhower had selected Harold Stassen, the former governor of Minnesota, to serve as his mutual security director, the man in charge of the country's foreign aid program. Stassen proposed that in between the extremes of intervention and loss of Indochina lay a third possibility: to try to hold the southern part of Indochina and establish a new line of defense there.

The secretary of defense and Admiral Radford argued that such a stance was to accept the loss of North Vietnam, the most valuable portion of the country. Radford called it "a very temporary solution at best," which left the NSC back at square one. Some feared that conceding Dien Bien Phu meant con-

ceding all of Southeast Asia. Their opponents argued that the
United States could not defend all countries worldwide from
both external and internal aggression, that it would amount
to "a policy of policing all the governments of the world." At
one point in the long debate, all participants were frustrated
into silence.

At last the National Security Council and the President decided to defer a decision and to accept congressionally imposed constraints. The President authorized an effort to
satisfy congressional conditions so that intervention could be
launched if necessary. Secretary of State Dulles noted that the
position of the United Kingdom was key. If the British would
join in united action, other countries would follow and Congress would be placated. Dulles expected the British to be
most difficult.

While the National Security Council argued policy, an
equally lively debate ignited in the Senate. Senator John F.
Kennedy provided the tinder. He said he was reluctant to
undercut either the French defenders of Dien Bien Phu or
Secretary Dulles, who was about to embark on the delicate deliberations at Geneva. "But," Kennedy continued,

> the speeches of President Eisenhower, Secretary Dulles, and
> others have left too much unsaid. . . . For if the American peo-
> ple are, for the fourth time in this century, to travel the long
> and tortuous road of war—particularly a war which we now
> realize would threaten the survival of civilization—then I be-
> lieve we have a right . . . to inquire in detail into the nature of
> the struggle in which we may become engaged, and the alterna-
> tive to such struggle.

It was time for the American public "to be told the blunt
truth about Indochina." Kennedy proceeded to recite the misleading claims that both the Truman and Eisenhower administrations had issued to Congress regarding the war in
Indochina. It was a litany beginning in 1951 when the head
of the Military Assistance Advisory Group in Indochina told
Congress that events had taken a favorable turn and victory
seemed possible in less than two years, and continuing
through recent months with descriptions of the Navarre Plan's
war-winning strategy. Given this record, and in view of administration statements about the need for united action, the sena-

tor concluded that "to pour money, material, and men into the jungles of Indochina without at least a remote prospect of victory would be dangerously futile and self-destructive."

Kennedy had no illusions about Indochina's fate if there was a negotiated peace leading to partition or a coalition rule with Ho Chi Minh. He concluded, as had the Central Intelligence Agency and the National Security Council, that either situation would result in eventual Communist domination. But, "no amount of American military assistance in Indochina can conquer an enemy which is everywhere and at the same time nowhere, an 'enemy of the people,' which has the sympathy and covert support of the people." Kennedy saw hope only if the French granted true sovereignty to the Associated States so that the native peoples rallied to the cause of resisting communism.

Kennedy's words received much support from his senatorial audience. Significantly, the first to join the chorus was the Republican majority leader, William Knowland. The Senate debate sent a clear message to the White House: Democrats and Republicans alike were suspicious of administration claims regarding the war. While they supported the general concept of united action, they were dubious about the merits of its exercise in Southeast Asia.

The combination of an NSC meeting held two days earlier than normal and Senate opposition to intervention in Indochina attracted press attention. The following day a reporter asked the President to explain what Indochina meant to the free world. In his response, Eisenhower for the first time publicly articulated what became celebrated as the "domino theory." After mentioning several secondary considerations—the region's economic importance, the plight of human beings passing under Communist dictatorship—he said: "Finally, you have broader considerations that might follow what you would call the 'falling domino' principle. You have a row of dominoes set up, you knock over the first one, and what will happen to the last one is the certainty that it will go over very quickly." He then listed the dominos in order: Indochina, Burma, Thailand, Malaysia, Indonesia. One after another, the shock wave of their fall would extend all the way to Japan, Formosa, the Philippines, Australia, and New Zealand. He concluded: "The possible consequences of the loss are just incalculable."

A follow-up question asked if the President agreed with Kennedy's statement saying that the Indochinese people must be guaranteed independence before any American intervention. Eisenhower replied that no outside country could be helpful unless the local people wanted what the foreigner had to offer. In a moment of surprising candor, he stated he did not know what the Indochinese wanted, but that their aspirations had to be met if there was ever to be a final solution.

Meanwhile, Army Chief of Staff General Ridgway continued his campaign to dampen war fever. He wrote to the other Joint Chiefs to express his strategic notions regarding Indochina. Like other strategic thinkers, he followed the accepted logic that sought to keep Southeast Asia from falling to the Communists. The problem was how to obtain that end. It was the Joint Chiefs' duty to describe the military measures necessary to obtain a national objective. Ridgway said that such military measures should be on a broad multinational basis. Only under the most extreme circumstances, if at all, should the United States intervene alone. Here was a clear distillation of his previous statements. His thinking had, however, progressed one important step further. He concluded that just because the objective was to defend Indochina from the Communists, it did "not follow that the military measures required to attain that objective would find any decisive objectives in Indo-China itself." If the United States went to war and wanted to win, it would have to attack the source of Viet Minh military power, Communist China. Anything short of that would be a diversion of limited American military resources to a nondecisive theater for the attainment of nondecisive local objectives.

The point of Ridgway's letter was to alert the country's top strategic thinkers that they could not achieve national objectives by employing naval and air units in some kind of surgical strike designed to influence the outcome at Dien Bien Phu. Such an intervention would have nearly the same risks as a much more massive intervention without compensating results. The country would then face the decision of the next step. When Ridgway studied the map of Indochina, he saw no worthwhile or "decisive" objectives to attack. So it came down to a decision to attack China or accept defeat. Ridgway was careful not to pass judgment on the consequences of an attack on China except to say that if China failed to heed a warning to desist supplying the Viet Minh, the United States would have to mobilize for general war. The general wanted everyone to realize the enormous consequences of intervention in Vietnam. He knew he was in a high-stakes competition with Radford to gain the President's ear. He played his hand in the style reminiscent of his leadership during World War II paratroop operations: careful preparation followed by a bold move.

When Ridgway undertook the necessary measures to assure that his advice reached up the chain of command, Dulles's prediction to the NSC on April 6, regarding the British position on united action, proved accurate. Churchill replied three days after receiving Eisenhower's impassioned plea recalling . the great days when the enemy was fascism. The delay itself spoke volumes, and indeed his message expressed a distinct lack of enthusiasm for Eisenhower's clarion call for war. However, out of respect for the President, he said that his government would discuss the entire matter with Dulles on April 12 in London.

The diary of Eisenhower's press secretary, James C. Hagerty, provides a fair barometer of the White House mood during the crisis. For April 7 he wrote: "Indo China really getting rough." On that day, the administration pressed forward on all fronts to secure the necessary conditions for intervention.

No one exerted himself more than Admiral Radford, who continued to maneuver outside authorized JCS channels. He sent his special assistant to the State Department on a "most delicate matter." The assistant wanted to convey to Dulles on a strictly confidential basis the secret conclusions of a Pentagon study group. That group had determined that three tactical atomic bombs could smash the Viet Minh at Dien Bien Phu. Radford wanted Dulles to know that the employment of atomic weapons was a viable means of intervention. Although he had briefly discussed this with Secretary of Defense Wilson, Radford now presented this information to Dulles in a manner clearly indicating he did not want anyone else to know his views, most importantly Ridgway. The admiral was playing a deep game indeed.

That same day he accompanied several White House aides on a return visit to Capitol Hill. This too was a secret, closed-door meeting. Since they had last been there, Senator Lyndon Johnson—acting on behalf of his mentor Senator Richard Russell—had sounded out some fellow Democrats on the subject of intervention. During a discussion, one senator said the country would lose face if it did not act with force. An Oklahoma senator ended the discussion by pounding on the table and saying he "was more concerned with losing another part of his anatomy if we did go in." Given these attitudes, Radford's aides reported back to the President that Congress was lukewarm at best toward intervention.

On one other front, perhaps the most significant one of all, the United States stepped back from war. Now that the President had decided against unilateral intervention, Admiral Carney informed the Pacific Command that there would be no combat operations from the flight decks of the two carriers poised for action in the Gulf of Tonkin. On April 7 they reversed course and by the next week had returned to the Philippines. The country had come close to direct military conflict in Vietnam. If it had dodged one bullet, there were to be several more in the coming weeks. Dulles and Radford, two very skilled partisans of intervention, had not given up hope.

Toward this end the secretary of state departed for London and Paris. He had a difficult task ahead. In spite of Eisenhower's personal rapport with Churchill, the British seemed unwilling to take decisive action, preferring to see what the conference at Geneva would bring. Dulles had to persuade them otherwise. In Paris, General Ely was disappointed and embarrassed by the American refusal to intervene alone. It was clear that the French still wanted fast United States military action to save Dien Bien Phu. If it did not occur and the fortress fell, there was a good likelihood that the French and possibly those Vietnamese who supported them would exclude the United States from any further role in Indochina. To satisfy Congress, Dulles had to persuade the French to continue the fight regardless of the fortress's fate while simultaneously granting the Associated States true sovereignty. The challenge tapped his many talents and vast experience.

Part 3. SHUTTLE DIPLOMACY

The United Kingdom's foreign minister, Anthony Eden, prepared for Dulles's arrival with great trepidation. Increasingly, the burden of leadership was falling on his shoulders. At eighty years of age, Prime Minister Winston Churchill was fast losing his legendary physical and mental energy and had come to rely upon Eden to fill the void. Eden had long operated in the great leader's shadow and welcomed the increased responsibility. However, he did not look forward to negotiating with Dulles.

Anthony Eden had experienced a warm relationship with many American diplomats including previous secretaries of state. He did not get along nearly so well with Dulles. Eden possessed, as did so many British diplomats, a conceit that only the British and selected other Europeans had the experience to understand and conduct intricate diplomacy. He believed that the Americans tended toward impatience and naivete, which often led to misguided bluster. Dulles's anti-Communist zealotry compounded this American tendency and blinded him to realistic appraisal of the world stage.

The astute foreign minister did not know that American diplomats, on the other hand, believed that the British filtered all Asian strategy through a colonial perspective. Dulles thought that his British counterpart focused on how events in Southeast Asia influenced the imperial position in Hong Kong and Malaya. Sensitivity toward Hong Kong made them unwilling to risk confronting the Chinese. Concern for Malaya made them willing to draw an anti-Communist barrier well south of a line preferred by the United States. Both countries more or less accurately recognized the other's biases without appreciating their own. It made for a difficult relationship.

By February 1954, Eden decided that the French needed to hold their ground to assist their bargaining position at Geneva but that they should not escalate the fighting. At the same time, the Eisenhower administration was straining every nerve to ensure that the Navarre Plan led to outright French victory. Eden knew that the American and British positions were different and believed the American strategy unworkable. Finally, he did not share the American sense of urgency regarding French actions in Indochina. He declared that the "French cannot lose the war between now and the coming of the rainy season however badly they may conduct it."

Therefore, Eden focused on the upcoming Geneva Conference. It was clear to him that any negotiated settlement would either produce a Communist share in the government of most of Indochina or complete Communist control of some part of Indochina. He thought the second alternative preferable. Although he sympathized with American reluctance to accept either of these outcomes, he simply thought it unrealistic to expect that a victor's terms could be imposed upon an undefeated enemy.

Dulles's speech on March 29 in which he stated that the imposition of a Communist system in Indochina "should not be passively accepted but should be met by united action" troubled the British diplomat. American officials had already told the British that the United States would not intervene unilaterally with ground forces. British military experts doubted that any lesser means could be effective. Eden fretted that Dulles's strong words might falsely encourage the French. On April 1, he instructed the British ambassador in Washington to inform Dulles that "after earnest study of military and political factors, we feel it would be unrealistic not to face the possibility that the conditions for a favourable solution in Indo-China may no longer exist." Therefore, Eden recommended that planning should begin so as to be ready for a compromise at Geneva. In other words it was high time to prepare for the "least damaging solution," and this was a partition of Vietnam.

Dulles responded to Eden the same way Radford had responded to Stassen during the National Security Council meeting. He told the British ambassador to relay to the British foreign minister that the United States had examined the partition solution but rejected it since it would ultimately lead to Communist domination. The best hope, Dulles said, was to compel China by threat of military action to stop aiding the

Viet Minh. That had been the point of his March 29 speech. It was better to take risks now in order to avoid even larger risks of world war in the future. Furthermore, he explained, the atomic balance of power vis-à-vis Russia was most favorable—the world was just learning of America's successful hydrogen-bomb detonations on Bikini Island—and this situation would not last. Dulles clearly showed he was ready to put to the test the deterrent effect of massive retaliation.

Before Dulles arrived, Eden prepared his country's position. He reckoned that there was a fundamental difference between threatening retaliation for some future Chinese action—the proper use of deterrence in his opinion—and threatening retaliation for something the Chinese were already doing, namely supporting the Viet Minh. The latter policy would force China to swallow a humiliating rebuff, something no nation was likely to do. Then the threat would have to either be withdrawn—a diplomatic defeat that the British did not wish to share in—or implemented. If implemented, the Chinese might invoke the Sino-Soviet Treaty, possibly resulting in world war. That disaster had to be avoided. In conclusion, Eden judged Dulles's plan wrong and very risky. He recommended, and Churchill's cabinet concurred, that the United Kingdom not sign on for ill-considered "united action."

Thus, there was good reason for Eden's anxiety as Dulles's plane landed outside London on April 11. In the first meetings, when confronted by British opposition, Dulles withdrew his plan calling for a warning to China. Dulles explained, however, that the United States had concluded that the French could no longer deal with the situation on their own. Consequently, he proposed an ad-hoc coalition that might lead to an organization to defend Southeast Asia. He maintained that this in itself should deter the Chinese and strengthen the Western position before Geneva.

Eden replied that he agreed in principle with the idea of collective security but that it required careful preparation and should not be rushed. In any event, such an organization could have little influence on the immediate fate of Dien Bien Phu. Eden advised that any solution to the immediate problems would have to come at Geneva.

Over the next days Dulles argued that the situation in Indo-china was analogous to the Japanese invasion of Manchuria in 1931 or Hitler's occupation of the Rhineland. Such aggression had to be met with firmness and a willingness to employ force. If the conflict could be put on an international basis, by which he meant British participation, intervention had a chance of success. Dulles said that with the British on board he was confident Congress would authorize Eisenhower to use American air and naval forces and possibly even ground forces. Eden reiterated that his country was opposed to becoming involved before Geneva.

They compromised and issued a joint announcement, which stated that the United States and Great Britain were ready to examine the possibility of collective defense in Indo-china. The British would yield nothing more to Dulles's passionate plea for united action. Having extracted the most he could, Dulles journeyed to Paris on April 14.

He found French leaders confused, despondent, and in near panic over the fate of Dien Bien Phu. The day Dulles had arrived in London, General Navarre had suggested that rather than delay Operation Vulture, the Americans conduct bombing sorties by unmarked aircraft, an idea that Admiral Radford turned down. Next a French official asked for a loan of American B-29 bombers. When the Americans examined this idea, they found that the French had no qualified pilots to fly the big bombers. Desperate, Navarre asked for American nocturnal raids against the Viet Minh supply line, but this too the United States rejected.

Against this background Dulles arrived in Paris. French Foreign Minister Bidault showed the secretary of state a personal letter from General Navarre. It described the desperate condition of the garrison, but putting forward the view that the fortress's fall should not be considered a defeat but rather the end of an operation that had achieved much by extracting a terrible toll from the Viet Minh. Navarre did acknowledge that the pro-French Vietnamese showed signs of defeatism. Dulles reacted to Navarre's letter by returning to the familiar ground of urging the French to grant the Associated States sovereignty as a goad to encourage their fighting spirit. Yet even now, with the empire in collapse, Bidault responded as the French had responded all along: The French public and parliament would never support continuing a war that was not intended to keep Indochina French.

Bidault asked Dulles point-blank if the United States would reconsider unilateral intervention to save Dien Bien Phu, contending that only American intervention could save the garrison. Dulles answered by describing the need for collective security and united action. Bidault responded that these would be too late to save Dien Bien Phu.

At this point Dulles allegedly asked, "And what if we gave you two atomic bombs to save Dien Bien Phu?" Dulles had studied French at the Sorbonne during his youth. Bidault, prior to entering politics, had taught English. They could not have misunderstood one another over something so serious. Bidault apparently replied that atomic weapons could not help the garrison since it would destroy it as well as the Viet Minh. Nonetheless, he passed on this offer to Premier Laniel. Later that afternoon, following a formal meeting with Laniel, Bidault said that it was important for Dulles and the French premier to meet alone. Everyone left the room except one of Dulles's aides, who observed the two statesmen speaking briefly to one another. No one knows what they said, but there is little doubt that the subject was Dulles's offer of atomic weapons.

It seemed likely to be a moot question as another tremendous Viet Minh assault stood poised to overrun the French Union forces. On April 18 the American chargé in Saigon cabled Washington to say the situation had worsened. Viet Minh trenches extended across the end of the airstrip, the area held by the garrison was not extensive enough to permit parachute resupply, and most of the parachutes drifted tantalizingly just out of reach of the garrison to fall into Viet Minh hands. In an effort to raise the garrison's morale, its commander, de Castries, received a promotion to general. When Major General Cogny sent his own general's stars along with a bottle of champagne to be parachute-delivered to de Castries, they too fell outside the weakening grasp of the garrison.

Against all odds, the garrison held through Easter weekend and beat back wave after assault wave during the following week. Their last tanks led elite paratroopers into the counterattack, supported by the remaining artillery firing off its nearly depleted stock of ammunition. When the smoke cleared, a month-long struggle for three tiny strongpoints ended in mutual exhaustion. The Viet Minh had suffered thousands of casualties to capture "three laughable squares of rice field" and some eight hundred yards of vacant airstrip. The defenders had lost ground, but their resistance forced Giap to order a pause while he collected reinforcements and gathered new supplies from China. There could be no doubt, however, that this was merely a breathing spell between attacks.

On Easter Sunday, April 18, a paratroop leader visited his chaplain for confession. When asked about the tactical situation, he told the chaplain, "We are headed for disaster."

◆ ◆ ◆

Curiously, while battle raged at Dien Bien Phu, and Dulles conducted his shuttle diplomacy, in Washington the Eisenhower administration relaxed. While the attacks that everyone expected would capture the fortress were taking place, President Eisenhower departed the capital for a golf trip to his cherished Augusta, Georgia, vacation haunt. On the day it took two French battalions ten hours to fight through to an isolated strongpoint in order to deliver water and a handful of ammunition, presidential aides released to the press a message he had sent to the president of France and to the chief of state of Vietnam, Bao Dai. It was a heartfelt salute to Dien Bien Phu's gallantry and stamina. In part, the message said that the garrison was "defending the cause of human freedom and are demonstrating in the truest fashion qualities on which the survival of the free world depends."

That same day, Good Friday, April 16, the Vice President substituted for the President at the American Society of Newspaper Editors' luncheon. Speaking for over an hour, he declared that the Vietnamese lacked the ability to either govern themselves or to fight the war. A French withdrawal would mean Communist domination inside of a month. Responding to a question on whether he thought the United States should send troops to Indochina if the French withdrew, he replied, yes, America should "take the risk now by putting our boys in." The next day his words were headlines throughout the nation.

Widely interpreted at the time as an administration-sanctioned trial balloon, Nixon's statement certainly represented his own viewpoint and that of many others, including Dulles and Radford. Upon his return from Paris, Dulles joked that he saw the Vice President got his name in the paper. When Nixon hastened to say he had not meant to interfere with Dulles's negotiations, Dulles reassured him that his statement might prove to be beneficial and had made a favorable impact in Paris. Although apparently unauthorized, the Vice President's words also seemed to reflect Eisenhower's judgment. Dulles told Nixon that the President was not disturbed by his statement and, indeed, shortly thereafter Eisenhower told his aides to fix any political damage but not to undercut the Vice President. Furthermore, when the President was back in Washington the next week, he defended Nixon to Republican critics. So Nixon's intemperate words had no long-lasting effect, except perhaps to open a window into the inner thoughts of the administration at a moment of crisis. Had any critic known what was taking place in the skies over Dien Bien Phu, the uproar would have lasted more than a mere day's headlines. American Air Force officers were flying reconnaissance missions in preparation for launching Operation Vulture.

♦ ♦ ♦

At the beginning of April, Lieutenant General Earle E. Partridge, commander of the U.S. Far Eastern Air Force, landed at Saigon's Tan Son Nhut airport to discuss Vulture with his French counterpart. Accompanying him was Brigadier General Joseph D. Caldara, the officer who would personally command any mission. The French lack of preparation to support Vulture appalled them. Nowhere in Indochina did the French possess the type of navigational radar necessary to direct precision bombing by heavy bombers. Given that the Viet Minh trenches closely hugged the French Union positions, this was a crippling deficiency. Vulture called for raids by sixty to ninety-eight B-29s. A small navigation error that altered their release point could mean that hundreds of tons of high-explosive bombs would rain down on the French instead of the Communists.

There were other risks as well. For example, mission planning called for any disabled bomber to do its utmost to reach the open ocean before ditching in order to prevent Communist discovery of a wrecked American plane or, worse, Communist capture of American flyers. To test the mission's feasibility, General Caldara flew three nocturnal recon missions over Dien Bien Phu. During one subsequent planning meeting, Franco-American bickering reached such a tense level that an American diplomat tried to lighten the atmosphere with a joke. His effort offended Caldara, who turned to him and said, "If that mission takes place, I'm going to be riding the lead B-29 into the goddam flak, and you're welcome to the right seat."

The head of the MAAG found his encounters with the French officer corps in Vietnam very frustrating as well. General O'Daniel had replaced Trapnell as commander of the American advisory effort at the end of March. Thereafter, he met periodically with Navarre and managed to extract one important concession. Arguing that the French still failed to utilize native manpower, O'Daniel finally heard the words he had long wanted to hear when Navarre said that twenty-five to fifty or even more American officers could begin instructing soldiers in the Vietnamese Army. O'Daniel began immediately to plan how to train the Vietnamese to an effective fighting pitch. He drew up plans for a large Vietnamese force that, commanded by American officers, would engage in a sweeping nationwide offensive. Within half a year, he believed, it could replace the French. Unaware of O'Daniel's grand plans—knowledge that would have confirmed his worst fears regarding loss of control to the Americans—Navarre conceded this much because he believed it necessary to get the Americans to launch Vulture. So the battle at Dien Bien Phu also had the effect of creating a breach in French resistance to the United States effort to take over training responsibilities.

The strain of combat told heavily on Navarre. By April 21 he was convinced that nothing could save Dien Bien Phu. O'Daniel reported that the French commander failed to appreciate the importance of the Vietnamese Army, did not grasp significant tactical matters, and in sum was unable "to wage war here on a scale that is necessary to win." Nearly all

American military men in Vietnam shared O'Daniel's frustration with the French. They knew a decisive battle was taking place in the faraway north and were certain the French were mishandling it. General Partridge told the American ambassador in Saigon that, without speculating on policy implications, it would be possible to build modern airstrips in Vietnam inside of six months. Then American jet aircraft could make the Viet Minh "feel what real air power is."

In Saigon, bickering between French and American officials and military men intensified, fed by a French suspicion that the Americans were stalling. They were right. Operation Vulture hung fire while Dulles completed his shuttle diplomacy and returned to Washington. Although his meetings had proven as difficult as expected, the secretary felt encouraged. He thought the British had agreed to a coalition to defend Southeast Asia and that the French, however reluctantly, would permit an internationalization of the war. Consequently, as soon as he arrived home, he proposed an international meeting for April 20 with concerned American allies to examine the possibility of a collective defense for Southeast Asia and the western Pacific.

The British were unprepared for the speed with which Dulles acted. They had not had time to consult with members of their commonwealth. Dulles's precipitous action angered Eden, who informed the British ambassador in Washington that the "Americans may think the time past when they need consider the feelings or difficulties of their allies." In what was probably a deliberate attempt to embarrass Dulles, and to slow down what the British considered his erratic diplomacy, the British ambassador waited until after the United States had announced the meeting to inform the State Department that he had instructions not to attend. The British boycott fatally compromised the establishment of any meaningful ad-hoc group for the collective security of Southeast Asia before the Geneva Conference. Eden, with Churchill's compliance—the next week the prime minister would say he had suffered many defeats in World War II, and now the French would endure their own defeat—believed an international meeting, indeed any commitment to action, premature. Their delaying tactics had won out, and thus the American plan for united action collapsed. Remarkably, it did not yet bring about the demise of Operation Vulture.

While Dulles flew back to Europe to attend a NATO meeting and then the Geneva Conference, the French government cast around desperately to try to promote Vulture. Hoping to force the American hand, they insisted that they would accept whatever compromise arose from the Geneva Conference even if it meant a partition of Vietnam. While Eisenhower still refused to sanction intervention, he did react to the French threat by authorizing ever closer cooperation between the two governments. Instead of merely providing the supplies and contributing aircraft, American Air Force "technicians" busily fixed the planes and packed the parachutes for the Dien Bien Phu aerial supply efforts. In an unprecedented move, United States Air Force planes began to ferry French reinforcements to Indochina. The secretary of defense assured Congress that the planes would land outside of combat zones and depart as soon as they unloaded. Yet, the increased American effort was not enough.

On April 22, Dulles met with the French foreign minister to discuss the still unratified European Defense Community as well as Indochina. Bidault told him that the situation was virtually hopeless without massive United States aerial intervention and he would now drop his opposition to internationalizing the war effort if such a step could save the garrison. His concession encouraged Dulles to try one last time for immediate united action.

A message arrived for the secretary from Eisenhower in which the President expressed a clear understanding of the situation's irony. The French had finally agreed to ask for internationalization of the war only after the situation was almost irretrievably lost. Moreover, British failure to comprehend the danger now blocked united action. The President mentioned that Churchill had invited him to a meeting in May, but pronounced "I am bound to say that I see no profit in it unless they are ready to look facts in the face and take and support obviously necessary decisions." The President concluded his message to Dulles with an expression of thanks "on behalf of America, that we have in you such a skilled and devoted representative to support our interests in these fateful days."

Even at this last moment, Eisenhower was willing to go to war to save Dien Bien Phu. Press secretary Hagerty's diary entry for this day reveals the tension level pervading the White House:

> Staff on an hour's call to return to Washington because of Indochina. Situation getting very grave, and it may be necessary to support French troops at Dien Bien Phu. . . . French would like us to send in these planes for a quick strike. Of course, if we do use them, we probably will never admit it, but decision to assist the French by use of American planes will be a very calculated risk and could lead to war.

Buoyed by his leader's ringing endorsement, Dulles met the next day with Bidault and Eden. Bidault told Dulles that Navarre described the situation at Dien Bien Phu as desperate. Navarre saw hope in only two alternatives: a massive American bombing mission in the next seventy-two hours or a ceasefire. Dulles, in turn, told Eden about Navarre's assessment. To John Foster Dulles, everything he had worked so hard to accomplish came down to the British reaction.

According to Eden, although Dulles appeared to share his doubts about intervention, the secretary of state said he was prepared, with Eden's backing, to recommend that the President ask Congress to authorize intervention. Eden demurred. He told Dulles that United States intervention would certainly compromise the Geneva Conference and might trigger a third world war. Eden later wrote about his emotions: "I am fairly hardened to crises, but I went to bed that night a troubled man."

The crisis atmosphere was taking a toll on others as well. The strain of knowing that what they decided would determine the fate of the garrison brought Bidault close to the breaking point. While Eden slept fitfully, Laniel discussed with Dulles the consequences of losing Dien Bien Phu. He predicted his government's fall and asked again for direct American intervention. Dulles replied that intervention required congressional approval, which he would request if the British joined forces.

The next day, Eden met with Dulles and Radford, who had

just arrived. Before leaving Washington, Radford—with presidential approval—had ordered the American aircraft carriers, which by now had docked in the Philippines, to return to the Gulf of Tonkin. After Dulles repeated that Eisenhower was ready to ask Congress for intervention provided the British joined in, Eden asked what specific actions the United States required of the United Kingdom. Radford said that there had to be some military effort to assist the French immediately and explained what the Royal Air Force could do. Eden asked if the Americans really believed aerial intervention could save the garrison. At this time American, French, and British experts all believed the fortress would fall in a matter of days. Radford acknowledged that there could be no guarantee. However, he explained that above and beyond Dien Bien Phu, American intervention would have a very beneficial psychological impact on the Vietnamese. It would prevent them from collapsing and turning on the French.

Eden inquired how China would respond to united action in Vietnam. Radford replied that he doubted the Chinese would intervene but that if they attempted aerial intervention, American naval airplanes could bomb Chinese airfields and easily eliminate this threat. The British foreign minister observed that there was a Sino-Soviet alliance. Radford said he did not think the Russians wanted a world war at this time. Eden, realizing the futility of arguing grand strategy with Radford, concluded that the United States was forcing Britain into a very difficult corner and that he had to return to London to consult with his colleagues.

Before doing so, he wanted to clear up several important discrepancies between the American description of French policy and what the French told the British. Accordingly, Dulles and Radford met Eden, Bidault, and Laniel. Dulles opened the meeting by asking the French position if Dien Bien Phu fell. Bidault equivocated, making it evident that the French had been telling the American secretary of state something substantially different from what they told the British. Eden had shrewdly seen how they manipulated the Americans in order to obtain immediate intervention. Nonetheless, Dulles showed Eden a draft letter stating the United States was ready to intervene under certain conditions, most importantly if

Great Britain was alongside. Eden emphasized that the United Kingdom was not committed to intervention in the Indochina war. Believing that this required a "decision of first-class importance," Eden hastened back to London to discuss it with the British cabinet.

While Eden returned home for consultation, in Washington the President too had reached certain conclusions. Returning from his golf vacation to address the American Newspaper Publishers Association in New York, he found that the publishers had convinced Hagerty that the American people did not understand the significance of what was taking place in Southeast Asia. At dinner they told the President, "You have to educate the people more on Indochina . . . the average citizen does not know where Indochina is, does not realize why we will have to move in eventually." Accordingly, Hagerty persuaded the President to address these issues the next day during a political visit to Kentucky.

In his folksy manner Eisenhower said, "The words 'Dien Bien Phu' are no longer just a funny sounding name, to be dismissed from the breakfast conversation because we don't know where it is, or what it means." It is "a testing ground between dictatorship and freedom" where one side is trying to give the people the right to live as they choose and the other side is trying to "make them mere additional pawns in the machinations of a power-hungry group in the Kremlin and in China." In his speech the President returned to the image of an expansionist Russia and the rhetoric of the cold war, symbols and language he believed the public well understood, to describe how he viewed the situation in Vietnam.

Indeed, although his administration had focused on the Chinese role as major supplier for the Viet Minh, Russia always lurked in the background. The United States ambassador in Moscow had reported that *Pravda* had printed the Soviet response to Dulles's March 29 speech. *Pravda* claimed that Dulles was infuriated at his inability to provoke Chinese intervention in Vietnam because he badly wanted a pretext to commit American forces. There was enough truth in this assertion to make for very good propaganda. The ambassador analyzed the *Pravda* article and concluded that Dulles's firm stance had produced characteristic Soviet uncertainty when confronted with strength. However, he doubted that the Soviets could wield much influence over Chinese policy toward Vietnam.

Even as the United States pursued a foreign policy based upon opposition to monolithic communism, that monolith was splintering. Yet Eisenhower did not yet appreciate this. Relating events to an aide he said, "The French have asked us to send planes to Dien Bien Phu, but we are not going to be involved alone in a power move against the Russians." In a similar vein he told Republican congressmen that it was important not to show any weakness to the Russians during this crisis lest they try to employ the Viet Minh's subversive tactics in other parts of the world. Although his misperception had implications for long-term global strategy, his soldier's eye remained clear. On April 24 he requested an aide to draft a suitable statement for him to deliver after the fall of Dien Bien Phu.

◆ ◆ ◆

After Eden left for London, the American ambassador to France, Douglas Dillon, tried to sort out what had transpired amid the emotional, complex discussions. He sent his conclusion to the State Department: "In short we must in making our decision realize that military intervention by US Forces in next few days prior to fall of Dien Bien Phu appears to be the only way to keep the French Union Forces fighting in Indochina and so to save Indochina from Communist control." Then he, like Dulles and Eisenhower, awaited the British decision.

In London, Eden explained the American position. In his view, Dulles and Radford recognized that intervention could not save Dien Bien Phu, but now favored action to rally French and Vietnamese morale and to avoid a general disintegration. He later wrote: "The Americans had therefore proposed that the United States and the United Kingdom Governments should give the French a joint assurance that they would join in the defense of Indo-China, and that, as an earnest of this, they should be given immediate military assistance, including token British participation." Eden found Churchill and his military advisers in substantial agreement

with his own view that air intervention alone would be ineffective. Churchill also agreed that once aerial intervention had
been tried, it was likely to lead to a ground commitment. The
British military chiefs did not subscribe to the total collapse
predicted by the domino theory. They believed Malaya could
be held regardless of what happened in Indochina, and
Churchill considered this to be a sufficient contribution to
stopping the spread of communism in Southeast Asia.

The prime minister understood that defeat in Vietnam
might have far-reaching effects. However, as he would explain
to Admiral Radford at a dinner the next evening, the Indochina situation had to be viewed in context. Seven years earlier
the United Kingdom had relinquished its 250-year control of
India. Since that time its once vast empire had withered further. To ask his country to squander its limited resources to
bail out the French in Indochina, a region in which it had no
historic connection, was impossible. As Eden wrote: "Sir Winston summed up the position by saying that what we were being asked to do was to assist in misleading Congress into
approving a military operation, which would in itself be ineffective, and might well bring the world to the verge of a major
war."

The next night, April 25, Eden met Dulles in Geneva. He
reported that the British Chiefs of Staff opposed intervention
on the grounds it would prove ineffective. Therefore,
Churchill and his cabinet had rejected intervention. So the
United States stood alone. If it intervened and Dien Bien Phu
fell anyway, as seemed probable, the French government
might topple. The new government would likely either repudiate American participation in the war or withdraw leaving
the United States to continue alone. Dulles accepted defeat.
From Geneva on the evening of April 25, he telegrammed
Washington that he recommended against intervention.

On April 26, Eisenhower told congressional leaders that
Franco-British failure to agree to a unified policy meant that
Dien Bien Phu would fall. He frankly admitted he did not
know what would happen next but that it might well mean
the French would abandon Indochina. While some American
forces might get involved—referring to air cover against Chi-

nese jets—he was not going to "carry the rest of the world on our back" by sending ground forces.

The same day, Eisenhower told Republican legislative leaders that the country must keep pressing for collective security and display the free world's determination "to oppose [the] chipping away of any part of the free world. Where in the hell can you let the Communists chip away any more? We just can't stand it."

It wasn't easy for the former general to watch brave French soldiers slowly lose at Dien Bien Phu. It became harder to stand by when Dulles reported a "tragic" situation, with France "visibly collapsing" while America looked on. Perhaps hardest of all was the need to resist the plaintive appeals for intervention from his old wartime colleagues in the French resistance. He expressed his frustration to General Alfred Gruenther: "As you know, you and I started more than three years ago trying to convince the French they could not win the Indochina war and particularly could not get real American support in that region unless they would unequivocally pledge independence to the Associated States upon the achievement of military victory." He continued by saying that no Western power could act in Asia except in concert with other nations, including, most importantly, local Asians. Otherwise, the Western nation would be vulnerable to charges of imperialism, colonialism, or paternalism.

In a letter the next day to a boyhood friend from Abilene, Eisenhower reiterated this theme: "For more than three years I have been urging upon successive French governments the advisability of finding some way of 'internationalizing' the war; such action would be proof to all the world and particularly to the Vietnamese that France's purpose is not colonial in character but to defeat communism in the region and to give the natives their freedom." He complained about the French use of "weasel words" when they promised independence, and concluded that this made them unreliable partners for united action. The British, on the other hand, could not be counted on because they feared angering the Chinese and then losing Hong Kong.

On April 27, the JCS presented its formal position regarding the latest French request for intervention. It declared:

"The question resolves itself really to whether or not we are, under the guise of a last minute effort to relieve Dien Bien Phu, to commence active participation by U.S. forces in the Indochina war." The JCS answered no.

By the summer of 1954 the United States had provided aid to Indochina at an original cost of $2.6 billion, a staggering sum for the time. Military shipments had included 1,800 combat vehicles, 30,887 motor vehicles, 361,522 small arms and machine guns, 438 naval craft, 2 World War II-era aircraft carriers, and some 500 aircraft. This colossal armament had been in vain. Now the United States had to seek at the conference table in Geneva what had been lost on the battlefields in Vietnam.

The Allies went to the Geneva Conference confused and divided. As the President later observed: "The Geneva Conference could not have begun or been conducted under worse conditions."

CHAPTER VII

❮❮❮❮❮❮❮❮

CONFERENCE IN GENEVA

I should like to express our admiration for the gallant men
who so heroically defended Dien Bien Phu against insuper-
able odds. . . . Those brave men made their sacrifice in or-
der that individual freedom and national independence for
the people of Viet-Nam should not be lost to Communist
enslavement. We of the Free World are determined to re-
main faithful to the causes for which they have so nobly
fought.

—Dwight D. Eisenhower, May 7, 1954

Part 1. DEATH OF A FORTRESS

John Foster Dulles arrived in Geneva on a cloudy, gray day that matched his mood. He had toiled long and hard to avoid having Indochina's fate decided at an international conference. When the war-weary French insisted, he labored to ensure they had the strongest negotiating position possible. Now that the conference had come, he found the Western alliance confused and in disarray. Worse, as French Foreign Minister Bidault told Western diplomats, the French negotiating hand had hardly a card to play, "perhaps just a two of clubs and a three of diamonds." Dulles embarked upon a round of meetings and sent his first findings back to Washington.

Armed with Dulles's intelligence, Secretary Bedell Smith accurately described the situation at Geneva during a National Security Council briefing. He observed that the United States entered the conference with a lesser degree of common un-

196

derstanding with its allies than it had had approaching any
previous international meeting. However, several things were
clear. The French intended to negotiate a settlement to retain
enclaves in northern Vietnam and all of the south. The British
would support any settlement satisfactory to the French as
long as it also protected Her Majesty's possessions in Hong
Kong and Malaya. However, the fear of a world war influenced all British calculations, and those fears were not base-
less. Following a meeting with Molotov, the leader of the
Soviet delegation, Dulles reported that open American intervention in Indochina would be met by open Chinese intervention and general war.

After Smith's presentation, Radford described the military
situation in Vietnam. The area held by the French at Dien
Bien Phu had shrunk to about fifteen hundred yards in diam-
eter. Their situation was desperate. Harold Stassen told the
council that it was time to decide once and for all whether to
intervene. Even if the French folded, and the British refused
to participate in united action, he recommended that the
United States go into southern Vietnam alone to save the situation. That should be done, he concluded, to exhibit strength
and determination and save the rest of Southeast Asia from
Communist domination.

The President shredded Stassen's logic, pointing out that
his assumptions "leaped over situations of the gravest difficulty." Central to the President's argument was his belief that
the United States assumption of the French role would, in the
eyes of many Asiatic peoples, merely replace French colonialism with American colonialism. Stassen countered that the Associated States wanted American intervention. If the French
withdrew from Indochina in phased steps, it would permit the
orderly insertion of substitute American forces.

Eisenhower recognized merit in this idea and said what he
most feared at Geneva was a hasty French withdrawal that occurred in "such a way so as to prevent the United States from
taking over the French responsibilities." But the President
would not accept Stassen's arguments for unilateral American
intervention. There was too much risk of a general war with
China and the Soviet Union. He might rail against British
shortsightedness and hear Dulles complain about Churchill's

fear of atomic incineration, but when confronted with military realities, Eisenhower reached the same conclusion as the British. Furthermore, he argued, unilateral intervention would also fail as a demonstration of leadership, for "without allies and associates the leader is just an adventurer like Genghis Khan."

In the final analysis, the President believed that "there are plenty of people in Asia, and we can train them to fight well. I don't see any reason for American ground troops to be committed." So the meeting concluded with the council agreeing that while the United States could not afford to send ground forces into Vietnam, there was an ample potential fighting force already present. What was needed was for the United States to undertake the training of the indigenous peoples to forge an effective army to resist communism.

Meanwhile, from Paris on April 28, General Paul Ely sent a top-secret message to Navarre informing him that there was no chance of an American air strike to save Dien Bien Phu. The much weakened garrison was not told this. They subsisted on hope of intervention supplemented by a meager diet permitted by the few parachutes that fell safely within their perimeter. While thousands of disheartened soldiers abandoned the fight to seek shelter in deep underground bunkers, a hard knot of elite paratroops and Foreign Legionnaires continued the fight. Nightly they received a handful of reinforcements—there was no lack of volunteers including many who had never jumped before—who parachuted into the fortress to join in the hopeless struggle.

Transport planes, flown by American pilots belonging to the Civil Air Transport group, delivered them to their fate. These pilots, nominally civilians, most of them retired military men, flew twenty-four of the twenty-nine Flying Boxcars that dropped supplies and reinforcements to the garrison. They were noncombatant mercenaries attracted to the CIA-sponsored Civil Air Transport by a mixture of money, adventure, and idealism. In times past, mechanical problems and poor weather had been the main danger. At Dien Bien Phu it was different. The risks of maintaining the tenuous aerial lifeline increased daily as the Viet Minh emplaced more antiaircraft weapons and their gunners improved with practice. The

American pilots complained that they flew at lower altitudes to ensure accurate parachute delivery than did the French Air Force pilots who were supposed to suppress the antiaircraft fire. Yet still they flew.

Pilot James B. McGovern joked with a fellow American aviator about who was the more powerful magnet attracting fire. McGovern was a living legend, a nearly three-hundred-pound daredevil known as Earthquake McGoon, a character in the popular *Li'l Abner* comic strip whom he resembled. He had flown with the Flying Tigers in China and then signed on with the Taiwan-based Civil Air Transport. His jokes had a hard edge after his plane lost its elevator controls following a hit in early May, but he kept flying until his forty-fifth flight to Dien Bien Phu when his plane received fatal damage. With the leading edge of one wing in tatters, an engine shut down, and oil leaking everywhere, he radioed for a compass bearing over low country toward Haiphong. He did not make it. The crash killed both him and his copilot: the first Americans killed in combat in Vietnam since an OSS officer had died in an ambush outside of Saigon in 1945.

At last Giap ordered the final assault. Following a punishing artillery bombardment, on the night of May 1 the Viet Minh's famous "Iron Division" spearheaded the attack. It proved to be the first in a relentless series of powerful blows. During the day, monsoon rains filled the trenches and collapsed the remaining bunkers; at night came the attacks. One nocturnal Viet Minh assault featured seven battalions with over three thousand soldiers against a French strongpoint defended by eighty-nine Legionnaires and Moroccans. Heedless, Navarre sent his last parachute reserves to reinforce the garrison in a desperate gamble that it could be held until diplomats negotiated a cease-fire at Geneva. His gamble, like almost every other command decision he made in Indochina, failed. On May 7, 1954—one day short of the ninth anniversary of VE Day—Dien Bien Phu surrendered.

In Nice, on the French Riviera, the chief of state of the non-Communist Vietnamese regime, Bao Dai, took time from his pursuit of the gaming tables to thank France for her sacrifice.

In Saigon, many young Vietnamese had anticipated the debacle. During the spring draft, only 2,000 able-bodied draftees responded to the 120,000-man call-up. Older, and presumably wiser, people had awaited certain news about Dien Bien Phu before reaching a decision. Then there was a fevered exodus from Vietnamese and French banks to safer vaults in Hong Kong.

In Hanoi, Navarre issued a statement blaming the loss on Chinese aid, which "suddenly allowed the enemy to inaugurate a type of modern warfare that was entirely new to the Indochinese theater." He said that the garrison's gallantry contributed "one of the most glorious pages" to the French armed forces, and concluded that "the struggle of the free peoples against slavery does not end today. The fight continues."

Ho Chi Minh waited more than a week before issuing a victory proclamation. It was a typical mixture of modesty and determination:

> Let me first of all express to you my affectionate solicitude to the wounded and to all of you . . .
> We have the intention of distributing to each of you the insignia of "Combatant of Dien Bien Phu." Do you agree with this? . . .
> Do not underestimate the enemy and remain ready to accomplish everything the Party and the Government might ask of you.
> I embrace you affectionately. Your uncle, Ho Chi Minh.

Giap's proclamation was also true to his proud personality and doctrinaire views:

> The Dien Bien Phu victory is the most prestigious which our Army has ever achieved. . . .
> We have brought failure to the Navarre Plan and struck a rude blow against the intrigues of the French colonialist warmongers and the American interventionists who wanted to expand the Indochina War.

Giap also made an important decision regarding what to do with the close to ten thousand French prisoners captured at Dien Bien Phu. He interspersed them with his own infantry and artillery columns as they marched rapidly toward the next battlefield, the Red River Delta. That left the French with the choice of bombing the massed, vulnerable columns and killing their own men, or letting them pass. The French chose the latter, thus negating Dien Bien Phu's last reason for existence, tying down and punishing Viet Minh forces for as long as possible.

While the French Air Force did not kill the prisoners, the march itself did. The prisoners shared the experience that befell Americans captured by the Japanese in the Philippines and by United Nations soldiers captured by the North Koreans and Chinese. They underwent a terrible death march to distant prisoner of war camps where the vast majority died in the three months before repatriation began as a result of the Geneva Accords.

In the United States, Senator Joseph McCarthy's ongoing investigation of alleged Communist infiltration of the Army received front-page headlines. Editors pushed news of the fall of Dien Bien Phu to the back of their newspapers. Vietnam became, and continued to be for the remainder of the decade, a subject that received little attention from the media. But first, Eisenhower had to endure one withering rhetorical barrage from Senator Lyndon Johnson. Speaking on May 6 at an annual Democratic political dinner, Johnson asked: "What is American policy in Indochina? . . . All of us have listened to the dismal series of reversals and confusions and alarms and excursions which have emerged from Washington over the past weeks. . . . It is apparent only that American foreign policy has never in all its history suffered such a stunning reversal." Referring to the abortive efforts at intervention, the senator continued: "We have been caught bluffing by our enemies, our friends and Allies are frightened and wondering, as we do, where we are headed." Fourteen years in the future, during a trying battle around an American Marine base at Khe Sanh, Johnson would demand of his generals, "No Dien Bien Phus." In 1954, his harsh criticism of Eisenhower's policy toward Southeast Asia was one of many influences prodding the President to undertake a new burden in Vietnam.

The defeat at Dien Bien Phu stemmed from many French blunders. French intelligence had failed to foresee that the Viet Minh could bring superior artillery to the hills that dominated the airstrip in the valley below. French artillerists had failed to foresee that these guns would be so superbly concealed that they could not be eliminated. French airmen failed to foresee that morning fogs, afternoon rains, and a powerful antiaircraft force would greatly limit air power over the valley. Finally, no one predicted that thousands of Vietnamese porters could carry enough munitions over extremely rugged terrain to provide the ammunition necessary to win a conventional siege.

In contrast, the Viet Minh high command had foreseen everything of consequence and prepared accordingly. Military historians debate what is and what is not a decisive battle. If a decisive battle is one in which a world power is overthrown and replaced as a result of martial combat, then there were two in Vietnam in a twenty-one-year span beginning in 1954. Vo Nguyen Giap and the Vietnamese Communists won them both.

Part 2. NEGOTIATION AND INTRIGUE

On May 7, 1954, Eisenhower carefully edited his secretary of state's draft speech, intended for delivery on nationwide television, concerning the fall of Dien Bien Phu. He believed that Dulles needed a little restraint just now. A few days ago, in his first NSC meeting following his return from Geneva, Dulles had urged that a decision be made whether the United States was willing to commit forces to prevent the loss or partition of Vietnam. Referring to atomic weapons, he said, "We have the military means to redeem the situation." Eisenhower made his attitude crystal clear when he added an insert reading: "The United States will never start a war." The subject of intervention might have thus been closed, except for two things.

The first had to do with the peculiar workings of any large bureaucracy. Just as in war the men at the front are often the last to learn of command decisions, within the Eisenhower administration important units forged ahead heedless, and so threatening to bring on war. Although Eisenhower had turned away from intervention, the policy had acquired a momentum of its own.

At various times, the President and his National Security

Council had asked for studies and contingency plans for military intervention. One such study in May, following the fall of Dien Bien Phu, comprehensively examined the economic, legal, military, and budgetary consequences of intervention. By the time appropriate groups finished their studies, the options had acquired partisans. This process was in the nature of contingency planning; someone asked to draw up a plausible scheme might well have to defend his product to critics. A defense of a plan easily became a defense of its creator's judgment, influencing the architect's future within the organization. Thus someone who begins as a detached student can end up an advocate. This is even more likely when someone knows his superiors hold certain ideas and promote certain actions. In the case of military intervention in Vietnam, hawkish planners received support from important hawks at the top: Radford in the Pentagon and Dulles at the Department of State.

Requests for planning guidelines and contingency studies, made in late winter, appeared before the NSC in May. One detailed plan called for sending six American infantry and one parachute division to Vietnam. When summed with air and naval units, it amounted to a 322,000-man expeditionary force. There were others as well. On May 19, Admiral Radford submitted his conclusions in a paper entitled "U.S. Military Participation in Indochina." It maintained that air and naval units could act alone and would be particularly effective if targeted against China, "the principal sources of Viet Minh military supply." In essence Radford and many others believed that Indochina presented an opportunity to test the New Look.

Promoters of intervention offered another reason for action now as opposed to later. In the near future, increased Soviet nuclear capacity would inhibit American action. Therefore, a general told Secretary of Defense Wilson that "the U.S. Government must decide whether to take the steps necessary to contain Communism in Asia within Red China by intervention in Indo-China or accept the probable loss of Asia to Communism."

Such thinking greatly alarmed the secretary of the army, Robert T. Stevens. He reacted by writing a letter of his own to Wilson, stating: "I am becoming increasingly concerned over the frequency of statements by individuals of influence within and without the government that United States air and sea forces alone could solve our problem in Indochina." Armed with information provided by Ridgway, Stevens noted that from a logistical standpoint alone, dispatching American forces to Vietnam would be very difficult. Furthermore, in a prescient warning that anticipated how much manpower United States forces would actually employ during the 1960s in a static-base defense role, he added: "If United States land-based forces are projected any appreciable distance inland, as would be essential, they would require constant local security at their every location." Stevens concluded that consideration of logistics alone "explodes the myth that air and sea forces could solve the Indo-China problems."

Of all the concerned institutions in Washington, it was the U.S. Army who worked hardest to avoid combat intervention in Vietnam. While the Army secretary submitted his objections, from the Joint Chiefs General Matthew Ridgway continued to argue that air and naval intervention would inevitably lead to a ground commitment. Like the Army secretary, he thought that none of the people advocating intervention had any realistic idea what it would cost in blood and money. While he acknowledged that America could defeat the Viet Minh, he believed the price would be tremendous. Ridgway concluded that it was essential that those involved in such a grave decision should understand the problem.

He sent a technical team to Vietnam to obtain the answers "to a thousand questions that those who had so blithely recommended that we go to war there had never taken the trouble to ask." It was led by a career engineer officer who had supervised logistics for the immense Leyte invasion in World War II. This officer took note of such facts as the depth of the water over the sand bar at Saigon, storage facilities to house the thousands of tons of supplies an American fighting force would need, the available road net to move inland, and the tropical diseases that would attack combat soldiers in a Vietnamese jungle. The survey team reported that the infrastructure to support modern war was almost nonexistent. The team confirmed the requirement for a tremendous engineering and logistical effort just to introduce American soldiers into Vietnam, let alone support the fight once they arrived.

This report received an important endorsement from the third in the trio of former paratroop generals who had served under Eisenhower in Europe. Lieutenant General James Gavin was well regarded by Eisenhower and was known as an innovative, thinking general. Like Ridgway, Gavin strongly opposed any interventionist policy in Indochina. His views placed him in a very difficult position. Gavin knew that to emphasize the difficulties associated with sending the Army to Vietnam played right into the hands of the partisans of the New Look who foresaw little need for an army. If the Army balked over obstacles to fighting in Vietnam, this would give the New Look's advocates more ammunition. They could point to Indochina as evidence of the Army's uselessness. Thus, opposition to intervention risked further emasculation of the Army's budget. Furthermore, at this time Washington was full of malicious gossip about the Army's combat readiness. Given this climate, Gavin recalled, "it was not an easy position for the Army to take . . . but it seemed to be a commonsense one, so Ridgway and I stuck to our guns."

Before Ridgway's survey team completed their study, alarming intelligence from the French reached Washington. In May, following the loss of Dien Bien Phu, French intelligence warned that Chinese jet fighters, to which the French had no counter since their Indochinese air force was exclusively propeller-driven, were massing on airfields along the border. It was thought that those planes would undertake the short flight to Hanoi to support the Viet Minh in their final offensive. Consequently, French leaders requested American guarantees that when the jets appeared, the United States military would immediately oppose them.

Back in January, the National Security Council had considered the possibility of Chinese MiGs intervening in Vietnam. It approved a policy specifying that the United States would counter the move by providing air and naval support to the French. If these measures failed, the United States—hopefully in conjunction with the United Kingdom and France, but alone if necessary—would strike targets inside China. Now that the feared intervention appeared more likely, Eisenhower's foreign policy specialists again united in recommending that the military prepare to defend the French.

Radford's interventionist attitude was predictable. Later he described the situation: "We were well prepared militarily for intervention. The JCS had drawn up and were putting the finishing touches on plans to cover every contingency. They had the strategy worked out, the command structure, the force contributions, plans for training native troops. They awaited only the political agreement at the top."

Dulles, too, said that a Chinese sortie into Vietnam "would be like a declaration of war against the United States." More surprising was the view of Robert Cutler, the man in charge of NSC planning. He said that the NSC staff had concluded that should China intervene, there would be little point in discussing the collective defense of Southeast Asia, since the United States would be forced to bomb China with atomic weapons. Here was a most serious war scare; the Chairman of the Joint Chiefs, State Department, and NSC were ready to respond with unprecedented force.

The President greeted this bold advice with an even bolder proposal. He would, of course, not act without congressional authority. However, if he requested that war be declared, he "would not ask any half-way measures." In addition to attacking China, he warned, there should be a strike against the enemy head as well. That head was Russia. He wanted to make sure that everyone understood the enormity of what they recommended. Therefore, he summoned the Joint Chiefs and told them that in view of the Sino-Soviet treaty, an atomic attack on China would inevitably mean war with Russia. Suppose, he postulated, that given our country's nuclear superiority, a preemptive attack succeeded. He fixed Radford with a stare and said, "I want you to carry this question home with you: Gain such a victory, and what do you do with it? Here would be a great area from the Elbe to Vladivostok . . . torn up and destroyed, without government, without its communications, just an area of starvation and disaster. I ask you what would the civilized world do about it?"

While Radford pondered, his fellow naval officer on the Joint Chiefs, Admiral Robert Carney, made a warlike foreign policy speech. Carney said that the United States was "approaching a fork in the road. . . . Do we want to turn into the smooth dead-end or take the rougher road that offers us a good destination if we have got the guts and strength to manage it."

Seemingly unfazed by Eisenhower's question about the consequences of an atomic attack on Russia, Radford informed the secretary of defense that the Joint Chiefs believed there were two ways to defend Indochina. One would be a static, reactive defense, which they believed unsound because it repeated the unhappy strategy used in Korea. The favored alternative benefited from the lessons of Korea: an offensive against the source of Communist military power in Southeast Asia, China. In support of this strategy, Radford submitted a JCS analysis that ended with the statement that "Indochina is devoid of decisive military objectives." In other words, there was no worthwhile target for American bombers inside of Vietnam, implying that the only military scheme that made sense was to strike China.

If Admiral Radford had not blinked at the prospect of nuclear war, the President's thinking had clarified with the passage of time. On June 3 he told the National Security Council that any thought of attacking China alone was contrary to all basic United States objectives. He said he "did not wish the United States to stand alone before the world as an arbitrary power supporting colonialism in Asia." Nonetheless, Eisenhower signed an NSC action that formally committed the President to ask Congress for military intervention against China should Chinese jets appear over Southeast Asia.

At least one of the President's principal deputies continued to believe that intervention remained a live possibility. Until the middle of June, Secretary of State Dulles told the American delegation in Geneva that the French "want, and in effect have, an option on our intervention but they do not want to exercise it and the date of expiry of our option is fast running out."

During the entire time the debate over intervention occurred, the President received reports on current popular opinion bearing on the administration's Indochina policy. They were based on regular surveys and showed the American public to be consistently divided into three groups. One quarter, the "activists," felt the United States was not doing enough to stop the spread of communism. They supported any proposal involving American military action. Balancing this segment of the population were the "isolationists," who just as consistently believed that it was more important to stay out of war than to stop Communist aggression. The majority of the public supported some proposals and opposed others; this was the group that a politician had to enlist. In the summer of 1954, they were willing to have the United States join the fight if the Communists were likely to conquer all of Indochina, provided there were significant allies ready to join in. They preferred, however, to have a truce signed, and favored an agreement for the collective security of Southeast Asia. In essence, the moderate middle segment of the American population supported the President's moderate instincts.

Eisenhower knew he could count on the public should he have to commit the nation to war, but it was a step he did not have to take. In the following weeks Chinese jets failed to appear in the skies over Vietnam. Chinese forbearance resulted from a combination of fear of United States retaliation and the fact that the Viet Minh were doing very well without them. Then Ridgway received his survey team's report and hastened to present it to the President. The report, which declared there could be no military solution short of an all-out effort including national mobilization, proved the last link in the President's decision making. It was the decisive evidence that put an end to further talk and planning for American intervention in Vietnam during the 1950s. Whatever was going to happen would take place without American combat participation. Whatever was going to happen would be decided at the conference tables in Geneva.

♦ ♦ ♦

Since the time of Julius Caesar, the city of Geneva had managed to avoid the ravages of war. Somehow, centuries of European conflict swirled around its walls and left it untouched. In the twentieth century it became a center of peace, a place where statesmen of the world gathered to conduct negotiations ostensibly aimed at creating a better world. Here, on the shores of tranquil Lac Leman, stood the Palais des Nations, the former headquarters of the ill-fated League of Nations.

It stood as a reminder that the base instincts of international aggression often triumphed, even over good-faith peaceful resolves. Few statesmen who gathered in Geneva on April 26, 1954, believed that their foreign counterparts intended to negotiate in good faith.

Bitter division reaved the Western allies. The United States and France blamed the British for the failure of united action. France felt betrayed by an American offer for intervention, withdrawn just when it was most needed. The United States reciprocated with the sense that the French were abandoning the greater good, the imperative to defend Vietnam, the first domino, and were instead compromising with communism. Senate Majority Leader Knowland labeled the conference a potential "Far Eastern Munich."

While mutual recrimination characterized the Western camp, confronting them across the table appeared to be a united front comprising the Soviet Union, China, and the Viet Minh. In fact, although few realized it, further cracks in world communism had occurred. In Moscow the post-Stalin power struggle continued. Nikita Khrushchev was on the ascent, rallying the party around his insistence that the Soviet Union had to develop military superiority over the United States before undertaking aggressive moves. Chinese leaders also perceived they had to proceed cautiously. They had recorded Dulles's threats, observed American naval maneuvers in the Gulf of Tonkin, and judged that the United States just might be looking for a pretext to attack. Because the Soviets and the Chinese considered themselves weaker than America, they might not back to the hilt the demands of their junior partner, the Viet Minh. But as the conference convened, it was an open question whether the disunited Western allies possessed the wit to uncover Communist weaknesses.

The opening phase at Geneva addressed a political settlement for Korea. This provided an opportunity for the real action to take place outside the conference room. Private meetings among diplomats in Geneva, Paris, and Washington produced a bewildering intrigue. Even Dulles, as experienced and sophisticated a statesman as the United States could hope to bring to bear on the problem, was nearly overwhelmed. He reported: "Developments have been so rapid and almost every hour so filled with high-level talks that evaluation has been difficult."

The secretary of state's anger at the British impaired his judgment and made an already tense relationship exceptionally difficult. Further hampering American diplomacy was the fact that the United States did not recognize the People's Republic of China as a legitimate nation. This led to the ludicrous spectacle of Dulles refusing to even look at the Chinese diplomats during formal sessions, let alone discuss matters in private. Given these conditions, a reporter asked Eisenhower at a news conference in Washington what outcome he would accept from Geneva. The President declined to answer in specifics, but made it clear that given Communist progress on the battlefield, something less than what he had hoped would have to be accepted.

While it appeared that Eisenhower was giving a cagey answer in order to retain negotiating flexibility, in fact he and his administration did not yet have a position. The State Department was so busy with intervention and regional coalitions that it had not prepared for the negotiations at hand. A Pentagon officer connected with the forthcoming conference wrote to the State Department: "This department is becoming increasingly concerned regarding the lack of a U.S. position in preparation for the Indochinese phase of the conference." So indecisive was the Eisenhower administration that the American delegation did not receive instructions on how to conduct negotiations until May 10. In the meantime the delegation lost its leader when John Foster Dulles decided that his presence in Geneva served no good purpose and went home.

This came about largely because of British behavior. On May 1, Eden met with Bedell Smith and Dulles. The arrival of Bedell Smith in Geneva significantly improved the negotiating atmosphere among the three Western allies. It helped a great deal that Smith and Eden, unlike Dulles and Eden, had a warm relationship based upon mutual respect. Smith was one of the few Americans whom Eden considered capable and level-headed amid the crisis atmosphere.

Smith had experienced military crisis many times while serving as Eisenhower's chief of staff. Unlike Dulles, he did not become caught up in the emotionally charged atmosphere caused by Dien Bien Phu's pending fall. He demonstrated his analytical abilities during the first evening's discussion when he commented that he felt the British Chiefs of Staff took an unduly pessimistic view of the situation while the American Chiefs were overly optimistic. While he and Eden calmly discussed the consequences of intervention versus loss of Vietnam, Smith's American colleagues spoke with the kind of fiery passion that Eden so scorned.

Walter Robertson, the assistant secretary of state for Far Eastern affairs, kept returning to the "fact" that Dien Bien Phu was a symbol and what was really in the balance were the three hundred thousand armed Indochinese anxious to carry on against the Viet Minh. To this Eden caustically inquired why, if they were so eager to fight, did they not do so.

It was a question of proper training, the Americans answered. In this the French had failed dismally, so the United States would have to undertake the burden. It might take two years for training to have a beneficial effect. A British diplomat asked what would happen during those two years. Did it not mean that "things would remain on the boil?" Dulles replied yes, and that this outcome "would be a very good thing."

Recognizing that the Americans, except for Smith, felt deep anger at the British refusal to join in united action, Eden reported to London that the United States had no plans of its own, but was searching for some expedient that would serve to stabilize the situation. However fair this characterization, it overlooked Eden's role. One of Eden's advisers observed that Dulles had grounds for his anger, noting that "we are getting very near having cheated the Americans on this question of starting talks on SE Asian security."

British diplomacy had foiled Dulles's efforts to forge united action. Then, he had suffered the humiliation of listening to Communist invective at the conference table while the British sat silent. It was too much and, on May 3, he turned the delegation over to Smith and departed Geneva never to return. As negotiations unfolded, the United States worked behind the scenes to develop a regional coalition to defend Southeast Asia, giving its Geneva delegation little influence on the agreements worked out in Geneva.

Negotiation and intrigue would continue for more than another two and one-half months. It would not be a contest for intangibles such as prestige or vaguely defined influence. Rather, it was about very real matters: where national borders would be drawn and who would rule within those borders. Anthony Eden, not John Foster Dulles, would represent Western interests. Eden, not Dulles, would chart the future of a region that the United States, but not the United Kingdom, considered vital to Western security. Strangely, the man Eden found easiest to work with was Soviet Foreign Minister Molotov.

During a dinner on May 5, Eden found that he and Molotov shared a problem. They agreed that they "both had allies whose views on the situation in Indo-China might be more extreme than our own," so they set about arranging proceedings to outflank their meddlesome allies. Toward this end Molotov and Eden became joint chairmen of the conference. The day after Dien Bien Phu fell, the first session on Indochina convened.

Two days later the American delegation finally received formal instructions approved by the President. They forbade United States negotiators to talk with the Communist Chinese or Viet Minh and directed that the United States participate in the Indochina phase as "an interested nation . . . neither a belligerent nor a principal in the negotiation." Eisenhower intended the limited American participation to give maximum freedom of action in order to promote "territorial integrity and political independence under stable and free governments" of the Associated States. In essence, Eisenhower's instructions recited aims without suggesting means. They were a formula of intent without substance because the President himself still groped for a way to achieve his strategic goals in Southeast Asia.

Under Eden and Molotov's patient leadership, negotiations proceeded slowly. Some progress had been made when, on May 15, Swiss papers reported on Franco-American discussions of military intervention. Fear of American intervention and world war blocked further progress. Eden reported the conference nearer to breakdown than ever before. The Americans were impatient. The head of the delegation, Bedell Smith, reported to Washington that the Communists had "not budged an inch" on any substantive issue and furthermore doubted they would make meaningful concessions because "they have a big fish on the hook and intend to play it out." Eisenhower too feared a repeat of Communist Korean-style delaying tactics. He believed such tactics aimed at paralyzing the West by creating policy divisions among the nominal allies. Therefore, he urged Smith to bring the conference to an end as rapidly as possible since "the Communists were only spinning things out to suit their own military purposes."

Having invested his own prestige in the conference, Eden redoubled his efforts to find compromise. The puzzling Chinese attitude posed the largest obstacle. Even to as experienced a diplomat as Eden, the Chinese delegation's leader, Chou En-lai, took positions that were difficult to fathom. Eden worked hard to establish some personal rapport with Chou En-lai, but it proved tough sledding. It was even more difficult for the United States delegation to appreciate the Chinese position for the simple reason that they had orders forbidding recognition of the Chinese. A junior American diplomat recalls inadvertently finding himself in the same elevator with a young Chinese diplomat. They had attended college together and now the Chinese delegate served as an "American expert" for his foreign ministry. Neither spoke, but looking at one another they first began to smile and then laugh at the absurdity. Convulsed with laughter, they arrived at the conference floor where they "hastily recovered our composures and studiously avoided looking at each other from that moment on."

On June 8, Secretary of State Dulles declared categorically that the President did not intend to ask Congress to authorize American intervention. Although it was a less than candid statement—even at this time, if the French agreed to American conditions, intervention remained, in Dulles's words, "an option"—fear of war receded among the delegates in Geneva.

Still, it took a dramatic event in France to break the logjam at Geneva. On June 12 the continuing disaster in Indochina—casualties had been considered unacceptably high in 1953, and during the first months of 1954 they ran six times higher—caused the fall of the Laniel government. Radical Socialist Pierre Mendès-France formed a new government based on the pledge that he would negotiate a settlement at Geneva within thirty days or resign.

Even while negotiations accelerated, so did the pace of the fighting in Vietnam. Once again displaying unsuspected mobility, Giap hurried his battered veterans of Dien Bien Phu east to the crucial Red River Delta. His rapid concentration gave him a two-to-one manpower advantage and forced the French to evacuate the southern half of the delta. It was another electrifying gain for the Viet Minh. In the Central Highlands of southern Vietnam—around Kontum, an area that would feature much combat for American troops in the 1960s and would be the location of Giap's war-winning final offensive in 1975—a series of well-executed ambushes destroyed France's elite Groupe Mobile 100 and the Korea battalion.

Americans, too, experienced the consequences of the heightened Communist effort. When five American servicemen assigned to maintain French aircraft left their base at Da Nang to go for a swim, local Viet Minh guerrillas captured them. The incident had no particular importance except to the Americans involved—they would not be returned until after the Geneva agreement—and perhaps as a refutation of the President's claim that American servicemen could be sent to Vietnam, assist the French, yet stay out of harm's way. Regardless, the wave of Viet Minh military successes did not translate into clear-cut advantages at Geneva. Pressured by their Chinese allies, the Vietnamese Communists accepted a key compromise: partition.

Part 3. A NATION DIVIDED

In the spring of 1954 the United States had been absolutely opposed to partition and the resultant loss of any part of Indochina. The domino theory held that should a section of Vietnam fall to the Communists, the balance of Southeast Asia would follow. Thus, the Special Committee on Southeast Asia had recommended that United States policy accept nothing short of military victory and oppose any negotiated settlement. Dulles had pursued these recommendations as far as humanly possible. When, in late May, American delegates in Geneva informed Washington that partition appeared inevitable, he pragmatically shifted the American position. During his speech on June 8, in which he announced the United States' intent to avoid intervention, he also said that Southeast Asia could still be held even with the loss of the northern portion of Vietnam.

In contrast to his American allies, partition was an outcome Anthony Eden had long anticipated. Even though it was acceptable to the British, Eden still tried to obtain the best deal possible for all Western interests. Although they disagreed about Vietnam, the Anglo-American position toward Laos and Cambodia was in harmony. It asserted that the civil war in Vietnam was very different from the Viet Minh's direct invasion of Laos and Cambodia and that therefore each country had to be considered separately rather than covered by one blanket agreement. In spite of Chinese and Russian opposition, Eden held firm on this and managed to win an important Communist concession. The senior Communist delegates accepted Eden's argument for separate settlements and pressured the Viet Minh delegation to concur. When the Viet Minh bowed to that pressure, they abandoned their Laotian allies, many of whom had fought long and hard, some of whom had manned the siege lines around Dien Bien Phu. The Viet Minh agreed to three separate treaties, one for each of the now defunct Associated States.

The French and Viet Minh concluded agreements on the cessation of hostilities in Indochina on July 21, 1954, conveniently backdating their signatures to accommodate Mendès-France's pledge to have a treaty within thirty days or resign. In Vietnam, the cease-fire agreement called for the rivals to regroup on opposite sides of a provisional demarcation line along the 17th Parallel. The regrouping would be completed within three hundred days. During that time, any civilians residing in one zone could migrate to the other zone. The agreement also prohibited the introduction into Vietnam of all types of war material, the establishment of new military bases, and any commitment of additional military personnel. An International Control Commission (ICC), neatly balanced between a Western, a Communist, and neutral member (Canada, Poland, and India, respectively) would supervise the cease-fire. A second part of the agreement tried to specify how and when Vietnam's partition would end. This "Final Declaration" called for elections in July 1956 to furnish "democratic institutions" in Vietnam.

At the conclusion of the conference, Undersecretary of State Smith stated the United States position toward the agreement. Neither he nor Dulles had wanted to be there to witness defeat and humiliation. Dulles objected to having the United States once again enter into the "Yalta business of guaranteeing Soviet conquests," but domestic political considerations came into play. On a late afternoon in July, after Eisenhower had finished hitting some golf balls on the White House lawn, the President spoke with his press secretary James Hagerty, about Geneva. Hagerty mentioned that if the United States failed to send Dulles or Smith back to the conference, "America would look like a little boy sulking in his tent." He advocated using the forum at Geneva to express the country's objections to the settlement. Eisenhower saw merit in the suggestion, but observed that since the settlement was not going to be one the United States should support, the choice was to become a party to the agreement or to express disapproval by not returning top diplomats to Geneva. He worried that if he accepted Hagerty's suggestion and sent a representative to "sound off against the settlement, as we should," the United States would divide the free world by publicly splitting with its allies.

Often Eisenhower seemed to let Dulles dominate him, but when deciding what to do about the Geneva settlement he was his own man. The day after talking with Hagerty he ordered Smith back to Geneva. Overnight, a deciding factor had entered his calculations, politics. He told his Cabinet that if the United States did not go on the record as opponents of the settlement, the Democrats would claim in the coming congressional elections that "we sat idly by and let Indochina be sold down the river."

Accordingly, Smith was present at the end of the conference where he announced that the United States did not concur with the Final Declaration. Selecting appropriate words from the United Nations Charter, he said that his country would refrain "from the threat or use of force" to interfere with the agreements and "would view any renewal of the aggression in violation of the aforesaid agreements with grave concern." These words would be cited by President Kennedy to justify expanded American intervention in Vietnam. Smith also restated the American policy toward nations divided against their will when he said the United States would support United Nations-supervised fair elections as a means to achieve unity. He reiterated the traditional American policy of support for all peoples to determine their own future and pledged that the United States would not hinder such efforts.

The newly created South Vietnam also did not sign the Final Declaration. Its own armistice proposal, advanced as an alternative, had been rejected without international consideration. South Vietnam meekly protested the fact that the French had set the date for future elections without conferring with South Vietnamese leaders. Indeed, the French commander in chief signed the cease-fire agreements with the Viet Minh on behalf of Vietnam and Laos, thus giving final testimony to the hollowness of French claims that they had granted the Associated States substantial self-rule. Even at the end, the French remained high-handed in their dealings with their erstwhile Indochinese allies.

While American statesmen would have objected strenuously to the comparison, in reality the United States behaved in a similar fashion. The United States and France together made plans and signed agreements that would determine the fate of the people of Indochina. Occasionally in public the French would talk as if the Vietnamese were independent, but in private talks and through their actions it was clear they considered them colonial subjects. In contrast, in both public utterances and private discussion American leaders spoke about true independence for the Indochinese. However, the President himself held a paternal attitude toward the Vietnamese. When asked at a Cabinet meeting if the successful policy employed in Greece might not work in Vietnam, he replied that the situation was different. The Greeks "were a sturdy people with a will to win," while the Vietnamese were "a backward people."

The American chargé in Saigon shared the President's paternalism. He referred to the Vietnamese as clients, saying:

"If they were to be made independent they should be made to act like independent people" by severing "the umbilical cord . . . to make the baby grow up." Along these lines, days before the completion of the Geneva Accords, Dulles flew to Paris to coordinate the Western position with French leaders. He found time for lengthy meetings with Mendès-France but could only manage a brief discussion with the foreign minister of Vietnam. No influential American asked the Indochinese what they wanted. Like the French, the United States imposed its will upon Vietnam.

While the delegates from the Associated States were treated like figureheads, the Viet Minh delegates also departed Geneva full of frustration. So rapid and complete were their battlefield successes that they believed they deserved much more than they got. They had attempted to secure an autonomous zone in northern Laos for their Pathet Lao allies. They had pressed for partition well south of the 17th Parallel in fullest expectation that at least the ancient capital city of Hue would fall within their lines. They had tried for early elections confident they would win. Instead, bullied by their larger Communist partners, they gained none of these.

Eisenhower too was not happy with the final outcome, but, having resisted intervention, he had no choice except to accept partition. As he candidly told reporters, the agreement had features unsatisfactory to the United States, but he was hard-pressed to suggest an alternative solution given the circumstances. He stated therefore that he would refrain from criticizing what the French had signed. His acceptance acknowledged a setback to nearly ten years of American Far Eastern policy. There was no disguising the fact that another country had fallen to the Communists. The calculated risk taken to support the French had failed.

Worse, one of the main reasons for taking that risk proved unjustified within a month of the Geneva Accords. Both Eisenhower and his predecessor tolerated much from the French because they believed France a crucial partner in the Atlantic alliance against Russia. Both Presidents moderated their demands for French political reform toward the Associated States because of the higher need for French participation in NATO and ratification of the European Defense

Community. At the end of August, the French National Assembly rejected the European Defense Community. It was a bitter blow to Dulles and Eisenhower.

Before this occurred, the President instructed Dulles to throw himself into negotiations to create an alliance to defend the non-Communist remainder of Southeast Asia. This led to the South East Asia Treaty Organization (SEATO). Eisenhower intended to make as firm a national commitment to SEATO as the United States had made to the NATO countries. It was quite a departure from his campaign criticism of Truman's policy of containment. At one time he and Dulles had argued that containment was reactive and passive. They had promoted a more dynamic approach to foreign policy featuring united action. United action failed to save the northern portion of Vietnam. In the coming months, the President and his secretary of state would exert themselves to see if collective defense could save the south.

The crisis at Dien Bien Phu and subsequent negotiations at Geneva tested everyone in the Eisenhower administration. There had been a wide divergence of opinion within the administration. Reviewing events, Admiral Radford provided a fair summary:

> President Eisenhower, in my opinion, thoroughly agreed with the position taken by congressional leaders. In the Defense Department, I feel that a majority of senior officers familiar with the details of the Vietnam problem also agreed that it was preferable to have additional allies if we were to intervene militarily. On the other hand there were some, including myself, who thought we should intervene by ourselves if we could not get additional help.

The first half of 1954 had been a profound test of Dulles's skills. For the first time since joining the administration, he received much press criticism for the way he handled negotiations. His boss went out of his way to refute this criticism, saying, "Foster Dulles . . . is the greatest Secretary of State in my memory." Considering Eisenhower's enormous respect for George C. Marshall, who had once served Truman as secretary of state, that was high praise indeed.

At the beginning of 1955, Dulles reviewed the lessons of the previous year. He told an interviewer that "the ability to get to the verge without getting into the war is the necessary art. If you cannot master it, you inevitably get into war . . . if you are scared to go to the brink, you are lost." His critics coined the term "brinksmanship" to characterize this approach to foreign affairs.

Preceding the Geneva Conference, Dulles had tried and failed to paper over differences among the Allies in order to achieve united action. Before leaving Geneva, he tried to hide these differences from the Communists during negotiations, but Molotov's keen powers of observation penetrated to the underlying Allied dispute. Comprehending their disunity, Molotov exploited it. Furthermore, throughout the crisis Dulles failed to appreciate and resolve fundamental contradictions: how to obtain indigenous support for a French fight to preserve colonial rule, particularly against an opponent widely viewed as a nationalist force fighting for self-rule; how to press reform upon the French—which had to mean granting independence—while keeping them in the fight; and how to convince influential neutrals and dubious allies of the United States' peaceful intentions while threatening massive retaliation. American negotiators at Geneva, acting under Dulles's authority, blundered by sending confusing signals to the French. As Secretary Smith complained: "We make strong statements, then qualify them." At a minimum this could lead to misunderstanding; more likely it could lead to mistrust.

Just as he failed with France, so he did not succeed in enlisting the British for united action to save Dien Bien Phu. At a meeting with the French and British in 1953, Winston Churchill compared France's attitude toward Indochina with the British position toward India. It should have been apparent thereafter that if the United Kingdom was willing to relinquish her greatest colonial treasure, India, without a fight, she would not fight to help the French hold Vietnam. In his zeal to halt the Communists, Dulles overlooked this and by so doing ignored the factors molding what should have been an entirely predictable British refusal to enter into united action.

At a May Cabinet meeting, Dulles responded to a question comparing Communist expansion with the Axis expansion before World War II. He said; "The nibbling has already reached the point where we can't see much more territory go to the Communists without real danger to ourselves. The problem, of course, is where to draw the line," and Dulles proceeded to explain the special difficulty of "drawing a line" in Asia. Employing subversive tactics, the Communists could "burrow under it," causing it to appear to be a civil war, and thus making it difficult to marshal international support for resisting the subversion. Whatever his failings during the difficult late spring days of 1954, with these words Dulles displayed great prescience.

After Dulles, within the Eisenhower administration Admiral Radford had been most prominent in decision making during the Dien Bien Phu crisis. While he advocated policies Eisenhower did not undertake, like Dulles he emerged with the President's confidence in him intact. Such was not the case with General Ridgway. However highly the President regarded his combat leadership, in Eisenhower's opinion Ridgway had displayed troublesome signs that he would not be a team player.

In the summer of 1954, Ridgway, supported by Gavin, used his authority to present the Army's opposition to armed intervention in Indochina. For the rest of his life Matt Ridgway believed that his actions had kept the country out of a war. Twelve years later Gavin's beliefs would gain prominence again. He would participate in the debate over American strategy in Vietnam and would announce his opposition to that strategy. His former commander, Ridgway, would concur, putting them at bitter odds with Maxwell Taylor, once a fellow paratroop comrade and in 1966 one of Lyndon Johnson's most hawkish military advisers.

♦ ♦ ♦

On June 3, 1954, French officials signed a treaty with Bao Dai giving Vietnam full independence and sovereignty. This act, taken eight years earlier, might have provided an effective rallying point for nationalist forces and a counterpoise to Ho Chi Minh's communism. In 1954 it seemed more like a cruel joke. Having stirred up tremendous armed opposition over an eight-year fight, the French seemed willing to hand the mess over to the small group of French-loyal Vietnamese, as if to say, "You wanted independence, here it is." Two weeks later

Bao Dai offered leadership of the new nation to a man who had left Vietnam rather than serve as part of the puppet state he considered Bao Dai's government to represent. His name was Ngo Dinh Diem.

There was no doubt that Bao Dai's choice was Vietnam's most prominent non-Communist nationalist. As far back as 1947, American diplomats who took the time to meet provincial Vietnamese learned that many who wanted an independent country also did not want a Communist Vietnam. When queried about who they preferred, most replied Diem.

Born the son of a mandarin on January 3, 1901, Diem entered into a family that belonged to the Vietnamese elite. His family was strongly Catholic; his own spiritual side so powerful that he took a vow of chastity and never married. He attended the same school as Ho Chi Minh, ten years after Ho left, and qualified to enter the civil service. Disillusioned with French unwillingness to reform, he quit the government and schemed with non-Communist nationalists to achieve independence. Both Ho Chi Minh and Bao Dai offered him important roles in their governments. He declined Ho's offer because of his suspicions concerning the Communist domination of the Viet Minh. In 1946, Ho Chi Minh had Diem's fate within his hands. At that time Ho controlled Hanoi and was using his superb intelligence service to locate and eliminate many opposition leaders. Diem went into hiding in a monastery, but Ho undoubtedly knew Diem was there. His presence was such a poorly kept secret that a junior American diplomat attended mass with him. But Ho chose to leave him alone.

Diem survived but declined his next offer to join Bao Dai's government, believing the French would use Bao Dai as a puppet. In 1950, unable to support either the French or the Viet Minh, he left Vietnam. His departing statement said that Vietnamese national aspirations would be satisfied only when Vietnam obtained true sovereignty. He recommended that posts in the future government of a new Vietnam should be reserved "for those who have deserved best of the country; I speak of those who resist." So, just as Ho had spared him, he expressed a willingness to have the Viet Minh participate in the future leadership of Vietnam.

He came to the United States and met a small group of

influential Americans who were concerned with Vietnam. He greatly impressed New York's Cardinal Spellman, who began to dream of a Vietnamese government led by the devout Catholic, Diem. For two years Diem lived in two East Coast Maryknoll seminaries, while he lectured at prominent universities and visited Washington, D.C. There he encountered sympathetic listeners and won the support of some important administration officials and politicians, particularly Senators Hubert Humphrey, Mike Mansfield, and John Kennedy.

In May 1954, while the battle of Dien Bien Phu determined Vietnam's fate, Diem met with Bao Dai once more. Bao Dai offered leadership of Vietnam's new government to Diem. At this time Diem had no serious rival. He accepted the offer but only after persuading Bao Dai to grant him full civilian and military powers. On June 26, 1954, Diem returned to Vietnam. Greeting his plane in Saigon were some five hundred well-wishers, mostly government officials, Catholic dignitaries, and aged mandarins. His arrival generated little popular enthusiasm.

Apparently, Diem's new nation was to be a battlefield between the Viet Minh and the Americans. One day after the Geneva Conference concluded, Ho Chi Minh announced: "The struggle will be long and difficult; all the peoples and soldiers of the north and south must unite to conquer victory." The next day Dulles gave his view, declaring: "The important thing for now is not to mourn the past but to seize the future opportunity to prevent the loss in northern Viet-nam from leading to the extension of Communism throughout Southeast Asia."

With conflict looming, Diem possessed few resources. He found himself a ruler in name only. His control extended to a few blocks of central Saigon. Battered by war, the country's transportation and communications systems—its roads, rail lines, canals, telephone and telegraph services—were in disrepair. Much of the arable land lay fallow, its peasants having fled to the cities where they found themselves unemployed with little in the way of social services. The bankrupt government, administered by a corrupt or incompetent civil service, provided for neither the peasants nor the stream of refugees from the north. The few sound businesses had grown rich based on their relationships with the French, and the new regime threatened that relationship. Many of the army leaders opposed Diem. A hostile sect, the Binh Xuyen, controlled the Saigon police, making their opposition apparent when they ruthlessly dispersed a pro-Diem rally organized by his Catholic supporters. The Viet Minh had impressed the entire nation with their victory over the French and they, too, opposed Diem. Diem's prospects were stunningly bleak.

A year earlier Vice President Nixon had met with Bao Dai in Vietnam. Bao Dai had said that negotiations with the Communists were pointless, pronouncing that "at the least we would end up with a conference which would divide my country between us and them. And if Vietnam is divided, we will eventually lose it all."

The Geneva Accords had proven Bao Dai half right. The accuracy of the rest of his prophecy depended upon the skill of Ngo Dinh Diem.

In 1946 Ho Chi Minh travels to Paris to negotiate Vietnam's future. The activities of French colonial leaders undermined the talks. By year's end the First Indochinese War began.

ABOVE: During a 1948 campaign stop in Omaha, President Truman impulsively joins the veterans of his World War I unit as they parade.

LEFT: One of the principal architects of U.S. Cold War strategy, Dean Acheson is sworn in as Secretary of State for Truman's second term in 1949.

Weakly fortified blockhouses and towers provided a defensive barrier in northern Vietnam along the Chinese border. In 1950, when the Viet Minh employed artillery for the first time in the war, the position crumpled, producing the greatest French colonial disaster since Montcalm's defeat outside of Quebec.   U.S. ARMY MILITARY HISTORY INSTITUTE

Chronically short of manpower, French strategists exacerbated the problem by tying down large numbers of men in static garrisons to preserve lines of communication. Artillerists aboard an armored train fire at concealed guerrillas during an ambush in central Vietnam.   U.S. ARMY MILITARY HISTORY INSTITUTE

ABOVE: The MAAG and Pentagon officers put great stock in the light battalion concept. A French officer urges members of a Vietnamese light battalion forward to assault a village in the Red River Delta in 1953. NATIONAL ARCHIVES

BELOW, LEFT: In a false display of unity, a French officer (*middle*) introduces an American MAAG officer to a Cambodian officer in 1952. In fact, the French worked hard and successfully to prevent Americans from getting to know native Indochinese officers.
RIGHT: American strategists considered the fighting in Indochina and Korea to be two prongs of a unified Communist assault upon Asia. It was a view the French strongly encouraged, so detachments of French infantry joined the U.N. effort in Korea. BELOW, RIGHT: General Matthew Ridgway presents a medal to the commander of the French battalion in Korea in 1951. When transferred to Vietnam, this unit would be annihilated in a spectacular Viet Minh ambush. NATIONAL ARCHIVES/NATIONAL ARCHIVES

ABOVE: Poorly motivated and poorly equipped, Vietnamese light battalions provided small support for the French war effort. The MAAG response was to lavish additional equipment upon them and to question French training methods.

LEFT: During a speech in March 1954, Ho Chi Minh accused the United States of taking "another step toward direct intervention" in the Indochinese War. That same month the Eisenhower administration debated Operation Vulture, an American aerial bombardment of Viet Minh positions around Dien Bien Phu.

BELOW: The Emperor Bao Dai meets with the French General Juin in 1953. Bao Dai's adaptation to Western styles distanced him from the people he nominally ruled, yet many American diplomats put great stock in the "Bao Dai" solution.

RIGHT: Truman doubted Eisenhower really understood the complexity of the task he was about to undertake. In spite of their deteriorating relationship, Truman greets the new President at the White House on inaugural day, 1953. NATIONAL ARCHIVES

BELOW: French Union paratroopers descend into the valley at Dien Bien Phu during the opening assault, November 1953. Failure to secure the heights overlooking the drop zone and airfield ultimately proved fatal.

BOTTOM: Using Dien Bien Phu as a "mooring point" for wide-ranging mobile operations, the garrison sortied into the hinterland. The difficult terrain defeated them, yet across these same mountains the Viet Minh performed logistical miracles. A French Union patrol buries its dead before moving on.

U.S. ARMY MILITARY HISTORY INSTITUTE

U.S. ARMY MILITARY HISTORY INSTITUTE

Defeated in its attempts at mobile operations, French Union soldiers convert the valley floor to an entrenched camp. Already Viet Minh mortars from the nearby hills (*background*) have accurately registered on the artillery emplacements, airstrip, command posts, and ammunition dumps.

Before the bombardment begins, the airstrip at Dien Bien Phu services American-supplied Bearcat fighter bombers and the all-important Dakota transports landing at left.

The "paratroop mafia." Major Marcel Bigeard (*second from right*) and his fellow airborne officers conducted the tactical defense of Dien Bien Phu from this bunker headquarters. Their professional skill and their men's tough fighting qualities extracted a terrible toll from the attackers.

ABOVE: The Viet Minh bombardment begins. Casualties are rushed to a helicopter while a flag of truce is vainly displayed. Soon the airstrip will be completely interdicted by Viet Minh artillery.

RIGHT: French Union soldiers counterattack to seal off the first Viet Minh penetrations.

ABOVE: Viet Minh prisoners captured during a counterattack.

Free to move only between bombardments, soldiers repair their flimsy fortifications. The basket in the foreground holds dirt and rocks for emergency repair. The plane in the upper left is a transport knocked out by accurate artillery fire. The airfield is now closed.

U.S.-provided "Flying Boxcars" (shown here over Laos in perfect flying weather without antiaircraft fire), often flown by mercenary American pilots, parachuted supplies to the garrison. It proved a tenuous link that could not adequately support the defenders.

As the Eisenhower administration debated intervention, Admiral Arthur Radford promoted a variety of bold schemes, including Operation Vulture.

Meetings of the Joint Chiefs of Staff proved critical during the debate over intervention. Radford (*seated left, back to camera*) failed to persuade his fellow Joint Chiefs (*clockwise*) Ridgway, General Lemuel Shepherd, USMC, and Admiral Robert Carney. Only the Air Force's General Nathan Twining (*to Radford's right*) endorsed intervention.

BELOW LEFT: John Foster Dulles (*left*) poses with Soviet Foreign Minister Molotov in 1955. A year earlier, during the conference at Geneva, Dulles proved disinclined to involve himself in failure and left the U.S. mission in Walter Smith's hands. Molotov played an important role and correctly assessed Western rifts but proved surprisingly indifferent to Viet Minh aspirations.

RIGHT: Contemptuous of American anti-Communist ideologues, Anthony Eden (*left*) distrusted Dulles (*middle*) and foiled Eisenhower's quest for united action to intervene in Indochina.

RIGHT: Abandoned by the French, hundreds of thousands of Vietnamese fled the north. The U.S. Navy transported many during Operation "Passage to Freedom." Sailors toss candy to Vietnamese children during a voyage south.

BELOW LEFT: Immediately upon taking office in the summer of 1954, Ngo Dinh Diem confronted stiff challenges from Army Chief of Staff Hinh, here awarding a medal to a South Vietnamese soldier, and from the sects.

BELOW RIGHT: Ably stage-managed by Edward Lansdale, Diem (*in suit, waving to crowd*) embarked upon a Western-style campaign during South Vietnam's first presidential election. General O'Daniel (*to Diem's left in civilian clothes and hat*) was taken in by the apparent depth of Diem's support.

ABOVE: Rewarded for his work in Vietnam, Colonel Lansdale (*second from left*) receives the Distinguished Service Medal in 1957 from Air Force Chief of Staff Twining (*far right*), while CIA Director Allen Dulles (*to Lansdale's right*) and Deputy Director General Charles Cabell (*to Lansdale's left*) attend.

General J. Lawton Collins went to Vietnam in 1955 as Eisenhower's special ambassador. Lansdale foiled his efforts to distance the United States from Diem.

RIGHT: Lansdale helped Diem splinter the United Sect Front. These Cao Dai soldiers rallied to Diem in March 1956.

BELOW: In open depots, millions of dollars of equipment and munitions deteriorated in the heat and monsoon rains. The need to recover U.S. equipment that the French had abandoned provided a useful subterfuge for introducing more U.S. advisers into Vietnam.

BOTTOM: Although the French had always asked for more aid, their poor inventory control and maintenance procedures meant that a tremendous volume of the aid went unused, as these abandoned engines, transmissions, and axles testify.

By the time of Eisenhower's reelection, South Vietnam seemed secure from communism. The President with his grandchildren and Vice-President Nixon with his children enjoy their victory during the 1957 inaugural parade.

The high-water mark of the Diem regime came during his triumphal visit to the United States in 1957. Dulles (*right*) and Eisenhower believed that they had backed a winner.

The head of the MAAG since the autumn of 1955, General Samuel Williams (*left*) stressed training the South Vietnamese to defend against a conventional invasion from the north. He failed to appreciate the real threat from the guerrillas in the south.

Nearly every American military officer believed that the South Vietnamese Army was ready to fight. Displays of conventional military prowess, such as this engineer demonstration in the summer of 1957, helped persuade traveling military and political VIPs (*seated on raft at left*) that the MAAG training program was working.

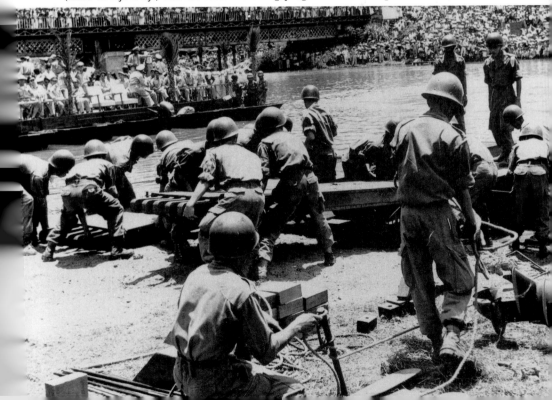

By the late 1950s, the South Vietnamese had skillfully learned how to manipulate the flow of U.S. aid. A confident banner greets touring American VIPs at the entrance to a newly built agroville.

When Eisenhower briefed the new President, John F. Kennedy, he warned about Communist advances in Laos but said nothing about Vietnam.

CHAPTER VIII

~~~~~~~~~~

PASSING THE BATON

*No nation can be saved to the free world unless it itself
wants to be saved.*
—DWIGHT D. EISENHOWER, 1954

Part 1. "THE GREAT EQUATION"

The President called it "the great equation." Back in 1952,
while crossing the Pacific on his return from Korea, he and
his advisers grappled with the calculus. Truman's budget for
fiscal 1954 admitted a $10 billion shortfall in revenues, an
anathema to the Republican party. The President-elect reckoned the budget could be balanced only by cutting the biggest
spender, the Department of Defense. But given his party's
commitment to meeting the Communist threat worldwide,
cutting proved difficult. By recognizing a monolithic Communist movement eager to strike at any weakness, containment
understood a world filled with virtually unlimited threats.
Limitless threats versus limited resources was the President's
"great equation." With containment threatening to eat end-
lessly into national resources, Eisenhower demanded that a
way be found to defend the country's strategic interests at a

lower cost. In this belief was the origin of the New Look.

Dulles too contributed to the strategy. He argued that since the country could not afford to position military forces around the globe, it would have to deter attack by relying on nuclear bombs. Bombs required a means of delivery, so strategic bombers had to be built. Bombers cost money, requiring conventional forces to be pared considerably. Eisenhower's budget message of January 21, 1954, clearly stated defense priorities: further development of atomic weapons; expansion of continental defense against worst threat, air-delivered nuclear bombs; assistance to allies for developing military strength in friendly nations; and preparation for rapid mobilization in event of an emergency. Within this scheme, expenditures for the Air Force were the highest since World War II, while monies for the other services declined. Since conventional forces were relegated to a secondary role, the use of surrogates, such as the French, took on added importance.

The Geneva Accords meant many things, among them an apparent refutation of the New Look. The threat of massive retaliation failed to defend the French position. Ridgway's study of the mechanism of ground intervention proved that a substantial ground force could not be sent to foreign shores without a general mobilization. If atomic war and ground intervention were undesirable or unfeasible, limited intervention with air and naval units remained. In the event, this too had been deemed impossible. As the Pentagon adviser at Geneva commented, "The U.S. should not be self-duped into believing the possibility of partial involvement—such as 'Naval and Air units only.' One cannot go over Niagara Falls in a barrel only slightly."

Although Ridgway and most Army officers had concluded that the loss of North Vietnam further discredited the New Look, other members of the Joint Chiefs disagreed. In May 1954, Admiral Radford defended the New Look before the Naval War College. He asked rhetorically what it meant and then answered, "It means that atomic forces are now our primary forces. It means that actions by other forces, on land, sea or air are relegated to a secondary role." His endorsement of the New Look before an important, potentially hostile audience cemented his easy relationship with the President. If Eisenhower had any ill feeling because of Radford's personal, out-of-bounds diplomacy with the French, the admiral's endorsement of the New Look overcame it.

Indeed, Eisenhower never said anything negative about Radford's performance during the crisis. He considered him the only JCS member capable of laying aside parochial service interests in order to further the national good. Accordingly, the admiral continued to be a trusted confidant until the end of his term in 1957. His replacement would be the officer who emerged during the crisis at Dien Bien Phu as the second most hawkish member of the JCS, the Air Force's General Twining. Under Twining's leadership, the country would greatly expand the Strategic Air Command. In October 1960, Army General Lyman Lemnitzer became Chairman. That gave the Army, which had been outvoted during the Radford-Twining reign, a tying vote in JCS decisions. The Air Force/Navy-versus-Army rivalry, which found much ammunition in the debate over the New Look, and the fact that New Look partisans held sway in the Joint Chiefs until 1960, influenced how the United States became involved in Vietnam.

With monies spent elsewhere, the Army cast about for a role in Eisenhower's "New Look." It hit upon the idea of counterinsurgency, but there were insufficient funds to pay fully for the development of an American antiguerrilla fighting force. Then, in 1960, having achieved parity in the Joint Chiefs, important Army officers promoted the new, untried doctrine. A new President would eagerly employ an untempered weapon in Vietnam. These decisions lay in the future, but they stemmed from strategies and attitudes born in 1954.

♦ ♦ ♦

Eisenhower's concept for the Joint Chiefs brooked little dissent from his policies. When Eisenhower outlined his views in the beginning of 1955, he asked for a manpower reduction in the armed forces for the coming year. The New Look and the 1954 budget had been blows against the Army. When new budgets further degraded the Army, Ridgway took his objections to Congress, where he testified that such reductions would jeopardize national security. This angered the President and began a public debate over strategy.

Eisenhower defended his position by talking about the likely course of a new major war. He said that a World War II-type response to hostilities abroad, whereby convoys carried soldiers from the United States to Europe and Japan, would be totally unrealistic. Enemy submarines would prey on the convoys while the massed troops would be sitting ducks for atomic weapons at the embarkation and debarkation ports. Nuclear weaponry required new thinking. Eisenhower responded to Ridgway's claims by saying that Ridgway was doing his job in looking out for Army interests, but that the President, as Commander in Chief, had to look at the broader strategic picture. "The only thing we fear is an atomic attack. . . . Suppose that attack were to occur tomorrow on fifteen of our cities. Goddamn it, [it] would be perfect rot to talk about shipping troops abroad when fifteen of our cities were in ruins." During the first days of an atomic war, Eisenhower went on, the troops would be needed to restore order at home. The idea of shipping troops overseas during the opening stages of an atomic war was nonsense. "That's the trouble with Ridgway. He's talking theory—I'm trying to talk sound sense."

Ridgway argued that spending so much for nuclear forces was preparing for the least likely eventuality. Russia, he predicted, would avoid pushing things to a point where the United States would launch a nuclear war. Instead, it would fund wars on the periphery where the United States would have great difficulty deploying force. Such profound disagreements could not persist and Ridgway resigned. He charged in his memoirs, published in 1956, that Eisenhower's policy was based on economic considerations rather than national defense. Although the President's State of the Union speech declared that the Joint Chiefs unanimously consented to the administration's defense program, Ridgway claimed it was "a directed verdict."

Ridgway discussed how Eisenhower's strategy required the military to be capable of putting "out big fires or little ones wherever the Communists might set them," a task that eventually required foot soldiers. Ever the infantryman, he wrote: "Despite all the new and terrible techniques of killing that our generation has devised, the foot soldier is still the ultimate weapon. Wars are still fought for little bits of bloody earth, and they are only ended when the enemy's will to resist is broken, and armed men stand victorious on his home soil."

Because of Ridgway's efforts, and because of Eisenhower's ultimate prudence, Americans had not contested the bloody earth of Vietnam in 1954. With the conclusion of the Geneva Accords, the armed men standing victorious were Viet Minh soldiers. They had conquered half of Vietnam; the fate of the remaining half hung in the balance. The Geneva settlement had suspended the fighting but failed to eliminate the sources of conflict. It gave the Vietnamese people neither unity nor freedom. In the north, the struggle for economic survival furnished the Communist party with an excuse to continue the harsh dictatorial policies it had adopted during the war's final years. In the south, incipient civil war provided an excuse to impose authoritarian rule.

Part 2. WATERSHED DECISION

A soldier examining the chessboard of Southeast Asia in the summer of 1954 saw a unified, victorious Viet Minh force opposed by fragmented, demoralized anti-Communist units. Victory had attracted thousands of new recruits to the Viet Minh ranks, while newly conquered territory provided expanded opportunity to conscript by force the less eager. The Viet Minh Army was swollen to about 230,000 mostly veteran soldiers backed by at least 100,000 local guerrillas. By the conditions established at Geneva, those forces had free rein over Vietnam north of the 17th Parallel, the area that was to become North Vietnam. They were a formidable threat to the south. When the French evacuated Hanoi that autumn, disturbed American observers saw the Viet Minh's "grim efficiency" on parade. They witnessed a notable contrast "between the silent march of the victorious Viet Minh troops in their tennis shoes and the clanking armor of the well-equipped French whose western tactics and equipment had failed."

The French had failed to stop the Communist juggernaut; now it might well be the turn of the National Army of Vietnam, a force that had nearly collapsed since the cease-fire.

With a nominal establishment of 150,000 men, it was in fact much weakened by desertions and defections to the Viet Minh. In the short run the French would defend the south, but long-term security depended upon the National Army. For many years Americans had recognized that this would be so. Military officers and statesmen alike had said that stopping the Communists depended upon native troops. The majority of the funds allocated to support the Navarre Plan had been intended to build up indigenous forces. It appeared to many that it would be a race to create a solid National Army before the French withdrew completely from Vietnam and the Viet Minh attacked again. The large unexpended balance originally earmarked for the Navarre Plan could be redirected to the Vietnamese National Army and thus perhaps influence the race's outcome. Many Americans believed that the money could be spent most effectively if the United States undertook to train the South Vietnamese military.

The decision to do so was the end result of a logical progression beginning with the early American presence in Vietnam. In 1950, the first American military mission to Vietnam had focused on the role of national armies in defending Southeast Asia. The Melby mission had predicted that a properly trained and equipped force would establish internal security and deter external aggression provided there was "a practical solution to the political problems." In spite of crippling manpower shortages, during the ensuing years the French failed to find such a solution and so did not create effective national forces.

In 1952 the three service secretaries representing the Army, Navy, and Air Force suggested to the State Department that the Military Assistance Advisory Group (MAAG) in Vietnam undertake the direct training of the Vietnamese Army. The State Department liked the idea, but the head of the MAAG and most of his Army officers serving in Vietnam at that time did not. They argued that it should remain a French responsibility because Americans lacked the language and cultural skills to communicate with Vietnamese—there were probably only three or four Americans in the world who were fully literate in Vietnamese. As happened so often, Washington officials discounted the views of the men in the field.

However, regardless of what any American wanted, it was the French who decided what they could and could not do. As late as the end of March 1954, when Dien Bien Phu's defenders still clung to their precious bit of "bloody earth," Admiral Radford had told General Paul Ely that the MAAG in Vietnam, now led by a different officer, wanted to assist the French in training the Vietnamese both to improve the quality of the training and to release French officers for combat duty. Radford reported: "General Ely was most unsympathetic to any encroachment on French responsibilities or significant expansion of the MAAG."

When the hard-charging General O'Daniel became head of the MAAG in April 1954, he quickly came to certain conclusions. As the Geneva Conference began, he urged Washington to act soon before any agreement constrained American options. Furthermore, O'Daniel retained faith that the war could be won and submitted that nine Vietnamese and three Cambodian divisions might be created by October. He and his staff conceived a general offensive against the Viet Minh, Operation Redland, using these troops. A State Department official in Saigon warned: "I have the greatest admiration for General O'Daniel's faith, tenacity and bulldog courage. I fear, however, he may be oversanguine as to possibilities of making an effective Vietnamese fighting force in six months' time." He cited pervasive Vietnamese apathy, internecine rivalries, and lack of leadership from Bao Dai and his ministers. He concluded: "I do not say the job cannot be done but that we should take a close look at its dimensions before we come in."

While the negotiations at Geneva continued, the French agreed to have the United States train Vietnamese units. Now the U.S. balked because nearly everyone who had dealt with the French had become wary. Dulles suspected that sudden French acquiescence might be a ploy to draw the U.S. into the conflict without having to accept previous American conditions. Rather than stumble piecemeal into an enlarged role, Dulles wanted a comprehensive agreement on all the American preconditions before the U.S. began to train the Vietnamese. At the same time Ridgway—always vigilant about a drift toward a ground commitment in Asia—gave O'Daniel explicit orders forbidding him from making any training promises.

As was now typical of the Franco-American relationship, the French could not understand why the United States did not begin to do that which they had wanted to do for so long. O'Daniel, deeply frustrated, could not understand it either. He thought he had accomplished his mission splendidly by setting up training plans and getting the French to agree to them. He appealed directly to the Joint Chiefs of Staff for permission to begin training. Reluctantly, Radford had to tell him that the request had been passed on to the "highest authority," Eisenhower, and there it stood.

Following the conclusion of the Geneva Conference, Ridgway prepared a set of conditions regarding training that became official JCS policy. First and foremost, there would have to be "a reasonably strong, stable, civil government in control." Otherwise, "it is hopeless to expect a U.S. military training mission to achieve success." In the summer of 1954 few expected that a strong, stable, civil government would emerge.

While the debate over training continued, the United States government maintained an equivocal attitude toward the current leader of the government of Free Vietnam. The secretary of state described the American position: "We do not wish to make it appear that Ngo Dinh Diem is in our pocket or that we are irrevocably committed to him. On the other hand, we do believe the kind of thing he stands for is a necessary ingredient of success."

◆ ◆ ◆

When Ngo Dinh Diem assumed office, his real military control extended to only a few blocks of Saigon. He was cut off from his natural source of strongest support, the large Catholic population living in North Vietnam. The French did not support Diem since he espoused Vietnamese nationalism. Worse, they still controlled the South Vietnamese Armed Forces and had installed General Nguyen Van Hinh, a French citizen, as its chief of staff. Hinh became Diem's hated rival. Outside the city, warlords acted in feudal style to profit from the chaos of a crumbling state. They preferred to deal with one another and had no desire for a competent central government.

Three religious/ethnic sects controlled much of the countryside. Perhaps the least bizarre were the Buddhist Hoa Haos who, operating as traditional warlords, controlled most of the Mekong Delta south of Saigon. Then there was the Cao Dai sect—who practiced an amalgam of Confucianism, Buddhism, and Catholicism—with its pope presiding from a python-shrouded throne, a holy see, female cardinals, and its canonization of Victor Hugo. The Cao Dai controlled an army of some twenty thousand fighters. Lastly, there was the Binh Xuyen sect, composed of former bandits who had preyed during each harvest on the large landowners in the delta. They extended their power into Cholon, the Chinese city alongside Saigon, where they managed the gambling halls, brothels, and opium houses. Desperately short of manpower, the French had armed the sects so that they could keep the south quiet while the balance of the French forces fought the main war in the north. When the French withdrew from the hinterland, the sects remained the most formidable armed force.

In early September, the army's chief of staff, General Hinh, began a series of public attacks on Diem. He called for a "strong and popular" new government, openly boasting about the coup he was preparing. Diem ordered him to leave the country within twenty-four hours. Hinh brazenly defied the order, riding in shirt sleeves through Saigon's streets on his motorscooter to his supporters' glee. Next, "the warlords, gangsters, bordello owners, and dishonest sect leaders" issued a virtuous-sounding manifesto demanding a new government. When Diem publicly accused Hinh of rebellion, the general countered by sending tanks to surround Diem's headquarters, where Binh Xuyen-controlled police provided his only guards. The next day nine of fifteen members of Diem's government resigned, and Bao Dai recommended that Diem resign as well. Diem's fall seemed near.

In Washington, the director of the Central Intelligence Agency confirmed to the NSC that the power struggle in South Vietnam had reached the crisis stage. There was little agreement within the administration on what to do. Almost everyone believed that Free Vietnam faced two Communist threats, a direct military assault and internal subversion. Most also still believed that the threats were part of a worldwide Communist offensive. For some, China had replaced Russia as the archenemy. Admiral Radford, for example, now talked about a Chinese offensive against Southeast Asia featuring subversive and indirect aggression. Others still saw Indochina as a place "where Soviet-inspired international Communism is conspiring to achieve complete domination." No one seemed to think that Ho Chi Minh's brand of nationalism was operating according to Vietnamese imperatives.

Regardless of origins, the National Security Council staff had carefully studied what had happened in Indochina. It divined a master Communist program, initiated in 1949, that called for "national liberation armies" to conduct "armed struggle" throughout Southeast Asia. Indeed, these were terms used in Communist revolutionary doctrine and they had precise meanings. A new generation was to relearn them in the 1960s. In 1954, the planning staff told the National Security Council that the partition of Vietnam was "one step toward victory for international Communism," grimly warning that "armed struggle" would continue despite truce or peace agreements.

American indecision and disagreement, particularly between the Departments of State and Defense, persisted. The schism stemmed from a policy review undertaken after the Geneva Conference. The review did not try to disguise the magnitude of the defeat. It had been "a drastic defeat of key policies . . . and a serious loss for the free world." Having toppled the first domino, the Communists stood poised to apply pressure throughout Southeast Asia and imperil Japan. Moreover, in addition to the loss of northern Vietnam, the United States had lost prestige. The NSC concluded that the U. S. had backed the losing side, most of Asia now doubted American resolve to check further Communist advances. It cautioned that "U.S. prestige will inescapably be associated with subsequent developments in Southeast Asia."

A most basic question that required an answer before proceeding was whether the domino theory still held. Radford, Dulles, and formal NSC policy statements had long maintained that the loss of any part of Indochina would cause the loss of the balance of Southeast Asia. After Dien Bien Phu, when Giap sent his victorious legions toward the crucial Tonkin Delta between Hanoi and Haiphong, the administration reconsidered. The NSC posed the question: "If the Tonkin Delta is lost, is it militarily feasible to prevent Communist control of the rest of Indochina and of Southeast Asia." Radford, representing the JCS, now said that "if all or part of Indochina is lost, there is a reasonable possibility of holding the rest" by a policy of collective defense.

During the discussion of what policy to adopt, Secretary of State Dulles saw a silver lining where others found disaster. He said that henceforth, at least the United States would not be constrained by French colonialism. He wanted to draw a line in Indochina and make it known that if the Communists passed it, the U.S. would take action. Like a true believer whose strength of conviction only increases when prophecy fails, he still believed in the domino theory and said that if the rest of Vietnam was lost, the Pacific would become "a Communist lake," thus forcing American defenses back to the West Coast. By nimbly shifting their position, the domino theory partisans retained a dominant voice within the Eisenhower administration. The loss of Tonkin discredited neither them nor the domino theory.

Dulles framed the post-Geneva problem by asking whether there was a good Vietnamese whom both the United States and France could back. It seemed doubtful because Franco-American relations had plunged to a nadir. American intelligence reports indicated that Mendès-France and the Viet Minh were collaborating behind the United States' back. With the degree of French support unknown, one National Security Council plan called for a limited, sharply focused approach to the most likely Communist challenge: internal subversion. The American role should be "limited to strengthening the ability of local governments to maintain order and . . . to attract sufficient popular support to limit the effectiveness of the indigenous Communists." This plan did not envision a U.S. training role.

Secretary of Defense Wilson also offered a solution that would have avoided an expanded American role. During the debate over Dien Bien Phu, he had advocated the United States' noninvolvement and received heavy criticism from the President. With a new crisis peaking, he again declared that the "desirable course of action was for the United States to get completely out of the area. The chances of saving any part of Southeast Asia were nothing." Once more the President rejected his advice.

Rejecting one alternative did not answer the problem. Taking over the training of the Vietnamese military seemed to be a way to restore prestige and block "creeping subversion," but the Joint Chiefs of Staff continued to resist the training burden until there was a stable Vietnamese government. Dulles acknowledged that Diem was neither strong nor stable, noting that he had only been in power for a little over a month. He recognized that the training decision was "the familiar hen-and-egg argument as to which comes first," but argued that "one of the most efficient means of enabling the Vietnamese Government to become strong is to assist it in reorganizing the National Army and in training that army." The secretary of state submitted that the Vietnamese Army's mission would be merely to provide internal security and that defense against outside aggression would come from a new regional defense organization. In a power play move to assert direction over any new enterprise, Dulles maintained that since the Vietnamese Army would have a limited role and the greatest threats would be political, the State Department, not the JCS, should make decisions regarding that army's size and composition.

Although Dulles failed to obtain State Department control over the Vietnamese Army, he succeeded in his larger purpose. At a National Security Council meeting in mid-August, Eisenhower approved the NSC recommendation that the United States take primary responsibility for training Vietnamese military forces. The American inability to waken most Vietnamese to the Communist threat had long frustrated the President. He told the Vietnamese ambassador that "for some years the U.S. has found it exceedingly difficult to get through to the Vietnamese people." The need to operate through the French had tied the hands of the United States. Eisenhower believed that henceforth things would be different. On August 18, the State Department notified the French government of the watershed decision: The United States would authorize its military mission in Vietnam to train the Vietnamese. Two days later, Eisenhower approved a new NSC statement formally declaring that the United States would "make every possible effort, not openly inconsistent with the U.S. position as to the armistice agreements, to defeat Communist subversion and influence and to maintain and support friendly non-Communist governments" in Indochina.

The NSC reference to "armistice agreements," underscored a potential problem that only military men had considered. The Geneva Accords specified that no country could introduce additional military manpower over the number present when the agreement was signed. If the United States adhered to this constraint, it would have to make do with its 342 men currently serving in the Military Assistance Advisory Group. Yet, the military's first concrete estimate, formulated in May, specified that for the entire Associated States 2,270 men would be needed to augment existing MAAG personnel. The Joint Chiefs prophesied that given the unstable political climate, coupled with the manpower limitations imposed by the Geneva agreement, "U.S. participation in training not only would probably have but limited beneficial effect but also would assume responsibility for any failure of the program." Therefore, "from a military point of view" the JCS recommended against a training mission. "However, if it is considered that political considerations are overriding," the Joint Chiefs would go along.

On the surface, the JCS position was illogical. They seemed to be saying that training was impossible but the military would do it anyway if the politicians so decided. In reality, the JCS had employed the time-honored bureaucratic trick of going on record to shift the blame should failure ensue. Ridgway's assistant, General Gavin, recalled that "we in the Army were so relieved that we had blocked the decision to commit ground troops to Vietnam that we were in no mood to quibble" with what seemed to be a minor issue.

Without focusing on the manpower problem, the State Department looked at the JCS disclaimer and decided that political considerations were indeed "overriding." In making this decision, it also ignored the Central Intelligence Agency's predictions that Diem would not survive. The department presented its policy prescription to the National Security Council, proposing that the United States should support Diem by promoting internal security and political stability in "Free Vietnam," by helping him establish and maintain control, and by counteracting Viet Minh infiltration and paramilitary activities in the south. All of this would be done by immediately developing a crash training program for the Vietnamese Army, the initial emphasis of which was to break the political stalemate in Saigon by drawing top Vietnamese officers away from Hinh and into Diem's camp.

Admiral Radford had one last chance to explain the Joint Chiefs' objections regarding the absence of political stability. He acknowledged some merit in the State Department's "hen-and-egg" argument that in the absence of a strong military posture there could be no political stability. However, he maintained that the reverse was more true. Radford also objected to the cost. Not only would the United States have to pay to keep the French in Vietnam, if it undertook the training burden there would be substantial additional costs.

Since the beginning of the administration's assessment of the wisdom of assuming training duties, the Joint Chiefs held to its set of preconditions. Dulles tried both to persuade them to drop them and to recognize that more or less they had been met, even though this was not the case. Dulles experienced much more success with the Commander in Chief, who now made his decision. Addressing the National Security Council with great conviction, Eisenhower announced: "In the lands of the blind, one-eyed men are kings. What we want is a Vietnamese force which would support Diem. Therefore let's get busy and get one." He said his experience in the Philippines had shown that problems like this could be tackled quickly if clear orders were sent to the officer on the scene, in this case General O'Daniel. If the French continued to oppose Diem, the President proposed, the United States would "get rough" with them. The obvious solution to the problem in Vietnam was to authorize O'Daniel "to use up to X millions of dollars . . . to produce the maximum number of Vietnamese military units on which Prime Minister Diem could depend to sustain himself in power."

The Commander in Chief had spoken. Everyone at the meeting fell into line. As Admiral Radford said: "The time for rapid action was at hand." Dulles immediately informed the appropriate American embassies of the policy change. He summarized the President's thinking by explaining that time was running out for the Diem government and the President feared that without some immediate United States action it would collapse. By implementing an assistance program, the President hoped to establish a government of national union around Diem.

While the Department of State and the Joint Chiefs fenced over the details of the assistance program, diplomats cleared the way for the new American policy. For two days in late September, French and American officials met. Bedell Smith explained that the United States and the French shared the common goal of strengthening the non-Communist elements in Free Vietnam. In fact, Smith appreciated that this might not be a common goal at all, alluding to French factions that sought to undermine this policy and who might, he warned, go so far as "to abandon the nationalist anti-Communist groups and possibly even to make a deal with Ho Chi Minh." He believed these factions to comprise people who had investments in Vietnam and might be tempted to make the best deal available. Smith contended that the task at hand was to produce something constructive so that pressures to make accommodations with the Vietnamese Communists could be resisted.

Smith and Dulles believed they had accomplished their objectives by meeting's end. France abrogated previous agreements that had given her control over Vietnam's economy, trade, and finances. She transferred command of the National Army to Diem's government, gave Diem full control over American aid, handed over training responsibility to the MAAG, and agreed to withdraw her Expeditionary Corps whenever asked by the Vietnamese government. With these decisions, it was clear that henceforth South Vietnam's survival depended on the United States. But the meeting did not resolve the root source of French opposition to Diem, namely the Vietnamese leader's vocal anti-French attitudes. A powerful French colonial presence remained in the south and their interests would suffer if Diem's government succeeded.

Following the Geneva Conference, the Eisenhower administration had the opportunity to reevaluate its policies toward Southeast Asia. Here was a chance to disentangle itself from Vietnam or to begin a fresh approach. Several State Department officials mused about the chance to start with a clean slate, and observed that the United States "should not be maneuvered into a position any longer of supporting archaic, outmoded governments just because the communists are at the other extreme."

The Eisenhower administration had several options to choose from. Except for the secretary of defense, it did not consider withdrawal. Instead, Eisenhower sanctioned decisions that inextricably bound the United States to South Vietnam's fate. He accepted the premise that American prestige was at stake. He authorized the assumption of training responsibilities that put American servicemen in the forefront—guerrilla wars have no rear—of a future fight most experts expected to break out sometime. He directed Dulles to create an alliance, SEATO, that would require military intervention under a variety of likely occurrences. He did this open-eyed to risks and consequences.

As to the risks: Before the conclusion of the Geneva agreement, top-rank American and Allied military officers had examined the situation in Southeast Asia and concluded that if northern Vietnam fell to the Communists, "it would be extremely difficult to draw any other defense line in Indochina." Dulles had said the chance of success was one in ten. Yet because American prestige was in play, the United States had upped the ante in its high-stakes Vietnam gamble, which led John Foster Dulles to proclaim: "The stakes are so high that I feel confident that we shall succeed." However, even the secretary of state's confidence wavered as events unfolded. Two months later he told the Saigon embassy that "unless Diem receives unreserved U.S. and French support, his chances of success appear slight. With such support, his chances are probably better repeat better than even."

As to consequences, the NSC policy statement said that if a local government requested help in the event of Communist subversion or rebellion, the President should consider requesting congressional authority to use American military forces.

The day after approving an urgent program to assist Free Vietnam by training its army, Eisenhower asked the Joint Chiefs of Staff to prepare a concrete, long-range training program to enable Vietnamese forces to maintain internal security. The President wanted to determine the minimum Vietnamese force that could accomplish this task with bearable costs and a limited need for American personnel. Eisenhower recognized the perils of hastily prepared crash programs. He wanted a more considered longer view of the task in order to judge the adequacy of the United States prescription and its feasibility for curing the disease.

Eisenhower prepared another, more important correspondence that day. He wrote Ngo Dinh Diem to explain that the United States had been exploring ways "to make a greater contribution to the welfare and stability of the Government of Viet-Nam." He told Diem that he had instructed the American ambassador to confer with him on how "an intelligent program of American aid given directly to your Government can serve to assist Viet-Nam in its present hour of trial, provided that your Government is prepared to give assurances as to the standards of performances" it would maintain. Eisenhower specified that he expected Diem to undertake needed reforms to create "an independent Viet-Nam endowed with a strong government" responsive to nationalist aspirations.

Eisenhower's letter to Diem tackled anew the old aid-without-influence problem. He knew that Diem lacked realism and experience, and that his government needed a broader geographic representation. The American President expected these shortcomings to be rectified and intended to emplace certain performance standards in return for American aid. How it would work out in practice remained to be seen. Regardless, his letter violated the Geneva Accords in two ways. It put Free Vietnam in an alliance, and it elevated Free Vietnam's status from one part of a temporarily divided nation to a sovereign state.

♦ ♦ ♦

As early as the spring of 1953, Eisenhower had spoken out on the need for a collective arrangement to assure the security of Southeast Asia. About a year later, referring to the domino theory, he explained that some kind of treaty structure was needed to provide "a unifying influence, to build that row of dominoes so they can stand the fall of one." Ever an optimist—in public and private alike he was fond of saying, "Long faces and defeatism don't win battles"—he saw after the Geneva Accords an opportunity, untainted by French colonialism, to try again to create an alliance to defend the region from communism.

During the French-Viet Minh war, the United States had laid much of the groundwork for a regional defense organization. It was clear, however, that the problem was how to put teeth into such an organization. At a five-power military conference in the summer of 1954, involving the United States, United Kingdom, France, Australia, and New Zealand, military men agreed that to stabilize the situation in Indochina required three divisions and some three hundred aircraft. They further agreed that sending non-French forces would buttress flagging Vietnamese morale. However, none of the governments offered to send the necessary forces.

In early September the five powers met again in Manila. This time representatives from Pakistan, Thailand, and the Philippines joined them. They were there because Eisenhower specifically wanted Asian participation to avoid criticism of a "white man's" treaty. Eisenhower was willing to accept, however, criticism that a treaty would violate the Geneva Accords. The State Department's legal adviser had examined this question and concluded that the accords prohibited Free Vietnam from entering the type of treaty the United States desired. But to Dulles and Eisenhower, strategic necessity overrode treaty violations, particularly a treaty neither the United States nor Free Vietnam had signed. So the meeting proceeded with the conferees adopting a Pacific Charter that affirmed the right of self-determination and expressed the intent of the signatories to resist all Communist attempts in the treaty area to subvert freedom. A draft defense treaty formed the basis for what would become the Southeast Asia Treaty Organization (SEATO). It spoke exclusively to the problem of Communist aggression. Most of the participants had preferred a more general obligation dealing with all aggression but Dulles did not want to embroil American forces in border disputes that did not involve Communists. He managed to argue down the more general language. France and Great Britain had opposed language encouraging the aspirations of colonial people. On this issue as well, Dulles succeeded in persuading them otherwise. Still, it made for an uneasy alliance.

In the minds of many Americans, SEATO seemed to be another bedrock foundation akin to NATO. In fact, although the other treaty members had pushed for an alliance on the NATO model, Dulles had resisted both for domestic political reasons and to preserve American freedom of action. Consequently, SEATO was very different from its European counterpart. It lacked the obligations for action clearly stated in the NATO Treaty and had no standing military force. Instead it was a tepid arrangement calling on each signatory to meet Communist aggression in accordance with its constitutional processes. In the event of threats other than armed attack, internal subversion for example, the parties would meet to consult on measures for the common defense. A special protocol extended SEATO protection, such as it was, to Free Vietnam, Laos, and Cambodia.

In large part, the weak treaty language was due to incompatible American objectives. On the one hand, the United States wanted to use the treaty to deter Communist expansion. On the other hand, American negotiators did not want to undertake military commitments that would restrict future freedom of action. As an American military participant reported to the secretary of defense, the treaty was "in effect a reconciliation of these conflicting objectives . . . The area is no better prepared than before to cope with Communist aggression."

SEATO was another example of the American "engineering" approach to foreign policy. The United States built alliances, constructed treaty organizations, and prepared paper defensive lines of containment. The President judged it consistent with post–World War II policy designed to further collective security for the free world. It also allowed him to answer political criticism that the country was being forced to play policeman for the entire world by pointing to the treaty as an example of burden sharing. SEATO showed the extent to which, in spite of earlier administration and Republican party rhetoric, collective security had replaced united action as the guiding foreign policy principle.

In sum, Eisenhower and Dulles were pleased with SEATO, believing that "the dilemma of finding a moral, legal, and practical basis for helping our friends of the region need not face us again." It had been exactly these moral, legal, and practical obstacles that had prevented some form of Operation Vulture. In Eisenhower's mind, SEATO cleared the way for intervention the next time.

♦ ♦ ♦

While the Eisenhower administration considered the wisdom of taking over the training mission and the State Department polished the SEATO arrangement, a remarkable exodus was taking place in Vietnam. The Geneva Accords stipulated that for a ten-month period civilians would be free to resettle on either side of the 17th Parallel. During August, large numbers of Vietnamese thronged to Hanoi and Haiphong seeking passage south. Many were Catholics from the Tonkin Delta, people who had contributed the most manpower to the Vietnamese fighting force under the French. Joining them were civil servants, functionaries, hangers-on, collaborationists, and anyone who feared Communist retaliation. Their numbers overwhelmed the French capacity to move them.

The South Vietnamese government asked the United States to help. While French airplanes transported the well-to-do, the U.S. Navy began an emergency sealift for the peasant masses. Called Passage to Freedom, the Navy ferry operation began in Haiphong. There, silent, frightened refugees—the Communists had told them that the men would be dumped overboard and the women sold into brothels—arrived at the embarkation port to be herded at rifle point by French Foreign Legionnaires toward the ships. Carrying their few belongings in baskets or on bamboo balance poles, they moved through delousing stations amid white clouds of DDT dust. They boarded ships to encounter unprepared American sailors who just weeks before had been practicing assault landings. Unexpectedly the sailors had received emergency orders to sail to Vietnam. An officer recalls that although "the heat, crowding, disease, filth, and smell were awful and there was a deep, well-founded fear of contagion, most of the sailors overcame their natural aversions and treated the refugees kindly."

To ease the difficulties of what could only be a bewildering voyage for the Vietnamese, the Navy called for interpreters from all over the Far East. French-speaking sailors and marines of French-Canadian descent from New England or Cajuns from Louisiana volunteered. But the unfamiliar, archaic language of Canada and the baffling Cajun patois were as incomprehensible to the Vietnamese as English. At the disembarkation ports in Free Vietnam there was a woeful lack of resources to care for the refugees' basic needs, let alone enough to help them assimilate into their new surroundings.

In spite of all obstacles, the U.S. Navy transported over 300,000 refugees. A total of about 800,000 people fled south—some 60 percent of whom were Catholics—while the Viet Minh moved about 90,000 troops north along with 40,000 nonmilitary men and women. Eventually, the displaced northerners would be an important source of strength to the Catholic Diem. However, at the time they arrived they posed one more complex, expensive drain upon Diem's very limited resources.

While American propaganda teams delighted in the spectacle provided by hundreds of thousands of Vietnamese fleeing "Communist enslavement" aboard U.S. Navy ships, an operation of a very different sort was taking place in Hanoi. American agents tried a variety of clandestine activities to hinder the Viet Minh takeover of northern Vietnam. These covert operations followed a National Security Council recommendation "to make more difficult the control by the Viet Minh of North Vietnam." They stemmed from the fertile imagination of a recently arrived American officer, Air Force Colonel Edward G. Lansdale. Nominally an assistant air attaché, he actually led a special Central Intelligence Agency team stationed in Saigon. No other American was to have such influence over the early fate of Free Vietnam.

Like most of the important intelligence officers stationed in Vietnam, Edward Lansdale had served in the OSS during World War II, where he had used his background as an advertising executive to devise inventive psychological warfare tactics. Following the war, he joined the newly created U.S. Air Force. In the early 1950s, he worked for the CIA in the Philippines, where he helped the government suppress the Communist-dominated Huk rebellion. The close relationship he forged with the Philippine president had been the key to his success. He had accompanied General O'Daniel during that officer's trip to Vietnam in 1953. While O'Daniel reported optimistically on French progress under the Navarre Plan, Lansdale reached very different conclusions. He reported at the time that the West faced a new type of warfare that required learning new rules of combat and strategy. Both the French and O'Daniel seemed unsuited for this task whereas the "little guys, the rice paddy farmers, know far more than the policymakers. [Theirs] is the simplified wisdom of the victim."

The combination of his flair for unconventional warfare and his self-promotion abilities attracted the favorable attention of John Foster Dulles as well as the American ambassador in Saigon. Dulles told Lansdale to go to Vietnam and do what he had done in the Philippines. He arrived in Saigon the month after the fall of Dien Bien Phu.

Among the different American agencies trying to mold the new nation, there was competition and rivalry. The regular CIA station in the United States embassy regarded Lansdale as an uncontrollable wild man. The station chief called him "a stupid goddamned amateur" and told him to stay out of the way and "let us pros really move the pieces around on this chessboard." He reciprocated the dislike. He considered the regular CIA hidebound and unimaginative, preferring to get things done with a small group of dedicated staff. His behavior soon confirmed the regular establishment's worst fears that he was a loose cannon.

A vigorous man of action, Lansdale stood in a public street to assess the people's mood the day Diem entered Saigon. Diem's motorcade whizzed by and Lansdale judged it a missed opportunity for the new Vietnamese leader to mingle with the people and attract supporters. He headed for the American embassy to tell Ambassador Donald R. Heath that whoever was advising Diem had made a mistake. To prevent further mistakes, he wanted to meet Diem and suggest a series of actions to solidify his support. Heath told him to go ahead.

Capable of sleepless prodigies of work, Lansdale spent the remainder of the day and all night writing up a detailed set of recommendations. Accompanied by an aide who helped him translate his paper, the next day, only Diem's second in Vietnam after a four-year absence, Lansdale met with him to discuss generating popular support for the government. Diem took his paper and started to read. Lansdale later reported: "After a moment, he reached into a pocket and pulled out a small French-English dictionary of the type useful for shopping or asking when the trains are due—not in translating phrases concerning the political, social, psychological, economic, and military lifestream of a nation."

Lansdale offered the services of his translator only to learn that this gentleman had forgotten his glasses. Diem laughed, offered his own pair, and "listened intently, asked some searching questions, thanked me for my thoughtfulness," and put the paper in his pocket. It was the beginning of a close relationship that "developed into a friendship of considerable depth, trust, and candor." It featured ever more frequent meetings until the two met daily.

While Lansdale worked with great success to earn Diem's trust, his efforts to hamper the Viet Minh consolidation of power in the north proved much less effective. Beginning in 1953, two American special warfare experts had been stationed in northern Vietnam to handle equipment requests from anti-Communist guerrilla groups operating in Viet Minh territory in the hill country along the Laotian border. The overall program displeased Eisenhower. In June 1954, the President, referring to special warfare experts' attempts to support the guerrillas, complained that the French had rejected most American efforts "that would tend to keep our participation in the background, but could nevertheless be very effective."

By the time Lansdale arrived, the Americans had largely taken over from the French the support of the anti-Communist guerrillas in the north. As would be the case in the second Indochina war, America's Vietnam War, the French had recruited most of the fighters from tribesmen living in Laos. Also, as would be the case in the Vietnam War, there was no capability for long-term support for these commandos. Although the Geneva Accords had specifically stipulated that there be no Viet Minh reprisals against French-supported partisans, no one seemed to think this proviso would be honored. When the French evacuated the hinterland, they abandoned the tribesmen. Under cover of the French evacuation, the CIA managed to oversee some smuggling operations to get arms and explosives to them, but it was not nearly enough. Some of the French leaders stayed with the tribesmen to conduct lonely, futile fights that raged on two years after the Geneva Accords. One by one the Viet Minh eliminated the guerrillas until in 1956 a last radio message came over the airwaves from North Vietnam. A French-speaking voice pleaded: "You sons-of-bitches, help us! Help us! Parachute us at least some ammunition, so that we can die fighting instead of being slaughtered like animals." Two decades later similar messages could be heard, only this time the voices spoke English.

Unable to do much to help the anti-Communist tribesmen, Lansdale turned to other covert activities. He organized secret training for displaced northerners at a U.S. Navy base in the Pacific. He then infiltrated them back into North Vietnam to try their hand at disrupting Viet Minh rule. Within two years, all had been killed, captured, or exposed. He sent his chief lieutenant to conduct clandestine operations from Hanoi. Assisted by specially trained CIA technicians brought from Japan and Hawaii, this officer organized a series of sabotage missions. One mission sought to sabotage Hanoi's buses by having agents contaminate the fuel in a storage depot. Another laced coal piles used to fuel train engines with explosives disguised as coal bricks. According to the mission leader, when thrown into engine burners these bricks "would blow the hell out of a train."

Such efforts at direct action either amounted to annoying pinpricks or failed entirely. Lansdale did invent and implement some clever psychological warfare ploys. He directed that an authentic-looking manifesto be printed and distributed in Hanoi on the eve of the day the French would hand over control to the Viet Minh. The manifesto called for everyone to participate in a week-long celebration to honor the liberators. The manifesto was so well done that Communist party cadres believed it entirely, circulating it within the city to ensure a huge turnout. Lansdale hoped that the seven-day work stoppage would limit transportation, power, and communications services and thus "give the Communists an unexpectedly vexing problem as they started their rule."

Lansdale's covert activities accorded with the NSC call for

actions to hamper Viet Minh rule, but they could not address the larger challenge in the south where Diem's tottering government stood in dire peril. To meet that challenge, Eisenhower sent one of his most able World War II generals to Vietnam.

Part 3. ENTER LIGHTNING JOE

General J. Lawton Collins emerged from World War II with a tremendous reputation. He led the "Tropic Lightning" division in the Pacific with distinction, thereby earning his nickname Lightning Joe, although some claimed his nom de guerre derived from his hair-trigger temper. Transferred to the European theater, he commanded a spearhead mechanized corps with great verve and dash during the Normandy breakout. Arguably Eisenhower's most skilled corps commander, his abilities attracted the attention of Eisenhower's great rival, the British General Bernard Montgomery. During the bleak early days of the Battle of the Bulge, Montgomery accepted Eisenhower's order to clean up one side of the German breakthrough only after securing Collins's services. Few Americans found Montgomery easy to get along with, but Collins proved an exception, thereby displaying an unexpected diplomatic skill. Following the war, Collins rose to become Army Chief of Staff during the Korean War. More than most high-ranking American officers, Lightning Joe Collins had considerable experience in Asia, including a visit to Vietnam in 1951.

When Diem's new government fell afoul of plot and conspiracy, Secretary of State Dulles requested that a military man be sent to Vietnam to assess the situation "and see whether a viable military position could be created." Eisenhower's military adviser suggested Collins, the President agreed, and so Collins came out of retirement to serve as Eisenhower's special representative with the personal rank of ambassador. Eisenhower gave his old comrade broad discretionary powers subject to the guidance of basic United States policies. Collins needed them because he confronted an enormous task.

Before he departed for Vietnam, Collins, along with Admiral Radford, attended an informal meeting at Dulles's residence. Dulles explained that the situation reduced down to the character of one man, Ngo Dinh Diem. Dulles felt inclined to back Diem, whom, he explained, "has many essential qualities despite being weak in others. There is no real alternative." The secretary of state was blunt about Collins's chance of success. He told him it was about one in ten. To protect the President from probable failure, he told Collins that he did not want the President too closely associated with the mission. This stipulation was odd, because Eisenhower's informal instructions, given to Collins three days later, clearly specified that he was "authorized to speak with complete frankness and full authority on behalf of myself and the Government of the United States."

The President instructed Collins that in order to promote the United States' goals of supporting a friendly non-Communist government and eradicating Communist subversion and influence, the immediate requirement was to stabilize and strengthen Diem's government. While there would be economic and political programs designed to promote Diem's stability, Collins's main mission was military. The President's written instructions emphasized that "it should be understood that the overall problem with which you are confronted is essentially military in character." He was to concentrate on improving the Vietnamese military and make recommendations about "overall force which should be retained or developed."

There was a problem. The State Department's legal branch observed that the Geneva Accords prohibited a change in the status quo of foreign military missions in Vietnam. Sending General Collins to Saigon would violate this provision and, worse, provide a propaganda opportunity for the Communists. To finesse the issue, the State Department issued a news release explaining that Collins would embark upon a "diplomatic mission of limited duration."

With the State Department providing him with a diplomatic front, Collins prepared for his mission by reading the most recent compilation of American intelligence concerning Diem. It presented a bleak picture. Collins read that Diem confronted "inefficiency, disunity, and corruption in Vietnamese politics . . . extraordinary problems of a mass evacuation of the Northern population and the hostility of many French officials. Despite his qualities of honesty and zeal, he has not yet demonstrated the necessary ability to deal with practical problems of politics and administration." As for the future, everything since the Geneva Conference had increased the likelihood of the Viet Minh gaining control of the south without having to make large-scale military attacks.

Collins continued his reading and learned that the Vietnamese Army could be of little comfort to Diem. A MAAG evaluation found an absence of fighting spirit. It was incapable of planning and executing even minor police operations without French or American direction, in large part because it lacked officers. French policy had deliberately discouraged the formation of an officer corps for the very good reason that such a group might easily become a source of nationalist pride and ultimately anti-French subversion. The Vietnamese Army had only 650 officers ranked captain or higher to lead a force of 145,000 regulars and 35,000 auxiliaries. The MAAG reported it "lacks everything which makes a modern army: leadership, morale, training, and combat experience." Compared with the Viet Minh, its effectiveness was negligible. Regarding future prospects, the MAAG predicted that the "Vietnamese as [a] whole would not have shown any inclination to make individual and collective sacrifices required to resist Communist threat. Unless Vietnamese themselves are determined to fight aggressively against Viet Minh, no amount [of] external U.S. and/or French pressure and assistance can long delay complete Communist victory south of the 17th parallel."

Diem's rival, General Hinh, still controlled the Vietnamese Army. Perhaps worse, from the shadows the French continued to intrigue in an attempt to control events. French opposition to Diem was becoming increasingly apparent, yet American intelligence told Collins that Diem's only hope was to receive wholehearted French support. Collins's formal marching orders from the President underscored the seriousness of his mission: "The threat to the independence and security of Free Viet-Nam has reached such a critical stage that emergency measures are required to assist Free Viet-Nam

to maintain itself, and to promote United States policies regarding Viet Nam."

General Collins arrived in Saigon on November 8, 1954. He
found a Byzantine political environment. The Vietnamese
leader he was to support controlled little more than his own
office. Guarding the Presidential Palace were police controlled
by the gangsterlike Binh Xuyen. Army Chief of Staff Hinh
spoke openly of a coup while his massed tank force stood
poised only a few blocks from the Presidential Palace. The
head of the MAAG, General O'Daniel, and American Ambassador Heath disagreed vehemently about what to do. O'Daniel
thought Hinh a patriot who could be worked with, while
Heath believed that O'Daniel was naive and Hinh had to be
removed. In addition to friction within the official American
establishment in Vietnam, a third American, Colonel Lansdale, operated outside of official channels. Working from both
the shadows and through a blooming friendship with Diem,
Lansdale tried to promote American interests.

Lansdale believed that he had already thwarted one of
Hinh's coup attempts. While no one was ever sure about
Hinh's seriousness, one evening Lansdale visited his head-
quarters to find everyone abuzz with talk of an impending
coup. He told Hinh that this was too bad because he had come
to invite the general and his staff to a Philippine visit.
Wouldn't he like a visit to the nightclubs of Manila? he asked.
Hinh answered that "regretfully" he would be busy but that
Lansdale could take some of his staff. Lansdale picked several
key officers and whisked them off to Manila for a fun-filled
week devoted to pleasure. Leaving Hinh's staff to explore the
Manila fleshpots, Lansdale returned to Saigon where Hinh
told him he had called off the coup because of the absence of
key lieutenants.

The arrival of a new American ambassador threatened
Lansdale's freewheeling maneuvers and worried the French.
They had always gotten along well with Ambassador Heath
and took it as an important sign that Collins had arrived to
replace him. Consequently, General Ely would not even greet
Collins when he arrived, preferring to remain in his villa in
the highland resort of Dalat. Declining to take affront, Collins
flew to Dalat to meet with Ely. Collins's tact, candor, and excel-

lent command of French all worked to win Ely's confidence. By day's end the two were calling each other by their first names and exhibiting a hearty bonhomie. Better still, Ely agreed that the Diem-Hinh feud had to end and that the French would not support the various sects opposing Diem. From the American viewpoint, here was remarkable diplomatic success accomplished by skilled personal diplomacy.

Four days later Collins's work bore fruit. Responding to overwhelming French and United States pressure, Bao Dai—still maintaining his rule from the French Riviera—ordered Hinh to join him. Two weeks later Hinh complied. Having overcome the immediate crisis in short order, Collins turned to the military portion of his mission. Working with characteristic decisiveness, within a week he finished a plan calling for a smaller, but well-equipped and well-trained Vietnamese Army. He recommended a more than 50 percent reduction from its current manpower strength by mid-1955. Half of the remaining strength would be deployed to stop an invasion from the north, and the balance to provide internal security. Vietnamese officers would command the entire force. The Joint Chiefs of Staff and the State Department approved Collins's proposal. The only obstacle, which seemed slight after so many larger problems, was French reluctance. Because of French dislike of Diem, United States reluctance to fund fully the French military in Vietnam, and French pride, the French government did not formally cede training authority for the Vietnamese military until February 12, 1955. It was almost a full ten months after O'Daniel had proposed to begin the task, but Collins had achieved another success.

He and Ely also agreed to a seven-point program to support the Diem government. The military reorganization and training component was only part of one point. Other aspects included refugee resettlement, economic adjustments, and provisions for psychological warfare, Lansdale's specialty. The program also called for land reform, establishing a National Assembly as a step toward representative government, improving relations between military and civil authorities, and strengthening the Diem government by the inclusion of capable administrators. It was these recommended reforms, particularly the last, that created growing friction between Collins and Diem.

A good deal of the friction arose from the fact that when developing the program, and notably when making decisions about the future strength of the Vietnamese Army, once again American planners failed to take into account Vietnamese views on the subject. Furthermore, it turned out to be a matter of great importance to the survival of the Diem government. While Collins was calling for dramatic manpower reductions, Diem was trying to buy off sect opposition by integrating certain sect armed forces into his own regular army. Of necessity, this would increase the army's manpower strength.

Although after meeting with Diem, Collins compromised on the manpower issue, Diem's demands frustrated him. To Collins, Diem seemed keener on obstructing the American program than on cooperating to get the job done. A simple fact was emerging. As planners back in Washington noted: "Our ability to influence Diem is limited."

By the end of 1954, Collins developed strong misgivings about the Diem government. He began to doubt that the man he was supposed to support had the wherewithal to be saved. Furthermore, the Vietnamese president had enjoyed little respite following the removal of General Hinh. A new, more formidable challenge emerged from the three major sects. Writing about that challenge, Collins told the State Department that while he was not ready to give up on Diem, he was highly doubtful that Diem was an able enough leader to convince anyone outside his immediate Catholic-based supporters to subordinate their private interests to the common good. By implication, Diem could never be a true popular leader. This was very unwelcome news in Washington.

After Collins's departure for Saigon, planners for the National Security Council followed events with the keenest of interest. As a group, they recognized that to succeed, Diem must tap Vietnamese national sentiment, which heretofore only the Viet Minh had engaged. However, just as had been the case during the decision to assume training responsibilities, the Departments of State and Defense split over specific policy. Military officers wanted to proceed slowly, while State Department representatives felt that at a minimum further

immediate steps had to be taken to gain time. During this debate the Department of State continued to be the driving force
for an activist policy in support of Diem. Then the department received both news of Collins's attitude toward Diem
and an opposing view from Ambassador Heath. Heath reported that lacking "more useful alternatives . . . we will continue to support Diem, because there is no one to take his
place who would serve U.S. objectives any better."

Heath's judgment concurred with the secretary of state's
whereas Collins's doubts thoroughly alarmed and annoyed
Dulles. The day before Christmas, Dulles responded to Collins. He objected to his pessimism and observed that despite
everything, Diem had held on in the five months since Geneva. Moreover, the secretary was convinced that the Vietnamese people were "fundamentally anti-Communist." He
told Collins that there was ample enough justification for the
American investment in Vietnam "if only to buy time [to]
build up strength elsewhere" in the area. He warned that to
withdraw support now would begin a fatal toppling of the
dominos. Dulles concluded: "Under present circumstances
and unless situation Free Viet Nam clearly appears hopeless
and rapidly disintegrating, we have no choice but continue
our aid [to] Viet Nam and support of Diem."

The secretary of state had asked for a competent military
man to go to Vietnam to evaluate the situation from a military
standpoint. He had told Collins, Eisenhower's handpicked
personal ambassador, that his chances of success were only 10
percent. Yet, when Collins's field appraisal failed to support
Dulles's opinion, the secretary began to turn against him.

CHAPTER IX

▲▼▲▼▲▼▲▼▲▼

HIGH STAKES

Sometimes under pressure nations like people rise to unknown heights.
— KENNETH YOUNG, OFFICE OF PHILIPPINE AND
SOUTHEAST ASIAN AFFAIRS, 1955

Part 1. "50-50 CHANCE"

Colonel Edward Lansdale often ran afoul of more conventional thinkers, but also had an uncanny ability to charm those whom he hoped to influence. By his own admission he got off on the wrong foot with General Collins. Collins's predecessor, Ambassador Heath, had conducted the Saigon meetings of the American "country team"—the term referred to United States government representatives in Vietnam including members of the military, State Department, and CIA—in an open, informal manner. Collins insisted on a disciplined format in which members gave a brief oral report, "after which we would all shut up and sit there while he told us what the situation *really* was like and what each of us was to do about it." During Collins's first country team meeting, he paid scant attention to Lansdale's ideas.

The colonel had originally conceived some of those ideas

256

during his Vietnam tour with O'Daniel in 1953, and his on-the-scene experience matured his thoughts. Characteristically, although a mere colonel, he expressed them in a long letter to the famous General Collins before the latter's departure from Washington. He explained that the American commitment to Vietnam represented an even higher stake than was usually associated with the domino theory. Japan, the Philippines, and indeed all of Asia watched carefully to learn what was meant by American support, making Vietnam a test case. Lansdale wrote: "We have no other choice but to win here or face an increasingly grim future, a heritage which none of us wants to pass along to our offspring." He asked what it would "take to win," and then supplied the answer. Somehow, the United States had to instill in the Vietnamese a "willingness to risk all for freedom." He cited Mao Tse-tung's statement, that guerrillas must be like fish swimming in a sea of popular support, as indicative of the essential link between a guerrilla force and the masses. The Viet Minh had "learned this lesson well" and were now applying it to the political struggle south of the 17th Parallel. To compete, the American team in Vietnam had to convince the people that they and their children had a much more rewarding political, social, economic, and spiritual future under capitalism as opposed to communism. A critical piece in this future was "a truly representative government." Lansdale volunteered to coordinate efforts to accomplish these goals.

Now, at their first face-to-face encounter, Collins told Lansdale that he was out of order, and that he, Collins, as the President's personal representative, would set priorities. Did Lansdale understand?

"Yes sir. I understand. I guess there's nobody here as the personal representative of the people of the United States. The American people would want us to discuss these priorities. So, I hereby appoint myself as their representative—and we're walking out on you."

Lansdale expected to be court-martialed for his insubordination, but instead Collins called him to his office and in fatherly tones told him he was disappointed with his behavior. Lansdale explained that he wanted Collins to succeed in his mission, but that the general confronted an alien environment. He wanted to contribute information so that the general could make sound decisions. Boldly, Lansdale suggested that they have private meetings so he could "illuminate" important factors bearing on Collins's decisions.

Lightning Joe smiled at Lansdale's audacity but explained he did his "heaviest thinking" alone, during a brief rest after lunch. Lansdale asked if Collins napped during these sessions and Collins replied that he just stretched out and thought.

"Good," replied Lansdale. "I'll come over to your house right after lunch and join you in your room, sitting there quietly while you rest. If you want to talk, okay, we'll talk. If you want to rest, I'll not say a word. Let's find out if this will work."

Lansdale had neatly boxed the general in. Collins could not resist him and so for a short while the two met regularly. Although that gave Lansdale an opportunity to propound his theories on how to save Vietnam, the two remained in fundamental disagreement. Soon Collins concluded that the sessions were "a lousy idea" and put a stop to them. As one of the colonel's friends said, Lansdale had one hundred ideas each day, most of them useless. Yet one of them would be stunningly brilliant. His postlunch "thinks" with Collins proved to be in the first category. What he wanted was a farsighted policy at a time when most Americans performed tactical thinking by focusing on the crisis at hand. It recognized the subordination of military solutions to the political and economic, but the rapidly developing sect crisis distracted attention from Lansdale's plans and, indeed, prevented the colonel from focusing on them himself.

At the beginning of 1955, Collins set to work implementing the program he and General Ely had agreed upon. In the past, Americans had castigated the French for their colonial attitudes. French unwillingness to concede to the Vietnamese rights of self-government had prevented the French from effectively employing native soldiers to resist communism. For all the latent anticolonialism inherent in most Americans' attitudes, in a fundamental way Collins behaved very much like a French rubber plantation baron. He visited a few sites, listened to Western experts, and together with the French decreed the future for the Vietnamese.

His attitude is clearly revealed in a telegram to the State Department in early January. Noting that he never intended the memo formalizing the Ely-Collins deal to be shown to the Vietnamese government, he discussed how best to approach Diem with the news. He and Ely had agreed that presenting a *fait accompli* was inappropriate. Rather, the "agreed program of US and French support for reorganization and training of Vietnam forces should come from Diem himself in manner designed to enable him to get credit for enlisting French and US aid in strengthening Vietnam Armed Forces." In other words, Diem's role was to rubber-stamp a policy devised by Westerners. During the critical early days of a new era, the Americans, like the French, refrained from making the Vietnamese equal partners in important decision making. Rather, the Americans strived to be more clever than had been the French. By dispensing with the outward trappings of colonial rule, Collins presented plans in a way designed to bolster the facade of Vietnamese self-rule, something the haughty French had bothered with only to the extent of satisfying American demands. But, in the final analysis American officials, too, imposed their policy upon the Vietnamese. Collins would have argued with anyone who called him a colonialist, but in a very real way he and his staff were acting as master puppeteers directing the Vietnamese to accomplish United States goals.

♦ ♦ ♦

Collins's essay into Vietnamese politics had riled the secretary of state. The general accepted Dulles's response and its implied dressing down. Nonetheless, he continued to inform the State Department about the situation as he saw it. He believed the chances of success warranted an American effort, noting that "since complete withdrawal of US support would be unacceptable, we consider [the] problem to be not whether US should render aid, but rather how much should be provided." However, he maintained that the best he could do amid nearly incompatible objectives was to balance "somewhat conflicting aims."

Greatly complicating his juggling act was the unknown attitude of the French. United States strategists believed that the continued presence of the French Expeditionary Corps was vital to protect South Vietnam from invasion from the north although the French seemed unwilling to accept this mission. French officials at all levels doubted Diem's viability. Consequently, government-level Franco-American agreements, the type that Dulles and his French counterpart signed, had been ineffective in securing complete French cooperation. Moreover, French officials stationed in Vietnam tended to be more responsive to local French commercial interests than to direction from Paris. They seemed to undermine Diem's position by both encouraging the religious sects to oppose Diem and by still boosting General Hinh as a rival to Diem. Admiral Radford took an even darker view of French behavior. He said that they "were definitely working for all of Vietnam to fall to Ho Chi Minh, and to be attached to the French Union." His was a sobering attitude toward an ally American strategists, up to and including Dulles, believed indispensable if the United States was to succeed.

After an initial period of bracing progress, Eisenhower's personal representative confronted an extremely complex problem. He shared his feelings with his good friend, General Alfred Gruenther, at the beginning of the new year. Gruenther had written to complain about the military-diplomatic frustrations of trying to direct NATO, an experience he likened to trying to run a six-ring circus. Collins retorted by asking his friend to consider "our minor show down here," which lacked even a circus tent. If there was one, the performers would refuse to enter together. His show was an opera bouffe: "We have five separate armies . . . gambling houses and worse, all operated with the tacit, if not open, approval of the Chief of State; two religious sects with their own private domains; a pope; an active underground Viet Minh; a Foreign Expeditionary Force; and an absent emperor who still remains the only legal source of power."

In spite of all of this, Collins's successes to date encouraged the Eisenhower administration. Planners for the National Security Council declared their satisfaction that the "Diem government is making slow but steady progress toward establishing itself as a potent anti-communist regime." Still, the NSC had searching questions regarding the future. Could American objectives be obtained within the two-year span for which military and economic aid estimates had been made? What was the popular attitude toward United States support? What were the prospects that Diem would implement Collins's entire reform program? What should American policy be toward the elections authorized by the Geneva Accords? Given these questions, and the additional consideration that the U.S. Military Assistance Advisory Group would assume the direct training of the Vietnamese Army in mid-February, the President decided to recall Collins to Washington for consultation.

At the end of January, the general briefed the National Security Council on progress to date. He had only been in Vietnam for two months, but in the past he had earned Army-wide renown for his ability to comprehend complex military problems. Apparently Vietnam was somewhat different. Before his briefing he told Dulles that the situation in Vietnam "is most complex and difficult to fathom." Collins explained to the NSC and the President that French intentions remained unknown but their influence enormous. The sects wielded effective veto power over Diem's efforts to institute reform. Diem continued to exhibit integrity and tenacity and recently had shown increased self-confidence. Collins reported very little success in his efforts to encourage Diem to broaden the base of his government. The Vietnamese President was reluctant to accept anyone he viewed as a potential rival, a category that naturally included the best candidates.

Lightning Joe had learned from his unhappy experience at the end of 1954 that Dulles and presumably the President did not want to hear pessimistic reports. Accordingly, he concluded that while he wished to avoid seeming overly optimistic, if the NSC adopted his program "there was at least a 50-50 chance of saving South Vietnam from the Communists." This was apparently tremendous progress since his departure when Dulles had rated his chances of success as one in ten. More important, Collins gave a ringing endorsement to the domino theory. He said that however problematical was American success, the consequences of failure were a near mathematical certainty. The United States had to try to support South Vietnam—the label now entered official vocabulary to replace "Free Vietnam"—because it could not afford to let it fall by default, which would lead to further Communist advances throughout the Far East. Therefore, "on balance I believe that Diem's integrity, strong nationalism, tenacity, and spiritual qualities render him the best available Prime Minister to lead Vietnam in its struggle against Communism."

It seemed the corner had been turned. American diplomats in Saigon also expressed guarded optimism. They felt that United States efforts had caused the Vietnamese Army to support Diem's government and believed that Diem himself had demonstrated "unexpected personal popularity" as well as more confidence. While acknowledging Diem's weaknesses as a leader, the American embassy reported that the atmosphere in South Vietnam "has begun to lighten."

Naturally there were dissenters who did not join the chorus of optimism. One National Security Council staffer questioned whether Collins's difficulties with Diem were not due to his not appreciating Diem's outlook. Instead of an American general imposing United States positions upon Diem and then concluding that Diem's opposition stemmed from his incapacities, the staffer proposed another way to reach the Vietnamese leader. He suggested using an intermediary, a trusted Maryknoll missionary whom Diem had met during his years in the United States, to persuade Diem to accept American ideas. The staffer recognized his suggestion to use a nongovernment person was "bureaucratic heresy," but he cogently argued that despite recent optimism "American policy is definitely bungling along because there is no real sympathetic cooperation between the young inexperienced Viet Nam government and the U.S. Mission in Saigon." A nonconformist like Lansdale would have emphatically agreed with this analysis, but it truly was "bureaucratic heresy," so decision makers ignored it. Even during a period of relative calm in Vietnam and optimism about the future, clear-sighted officials detected important flaws in the American approach to Vietnam.

Another, perhaps less clear-sighted participant also offered some excellent advice at about this time. In times past, the United States had enthusiastically joined the French in supporting a Vietnam ruled by Bao Dai. Now that Diem was the man, American diplomats cast about for a way to remove Bao Dai from the political equation. It seemed simplest to buy him off. The once bright "Bao Dai solution"—a former linchpin of American policy—had been reduced to the level of a Chicago-style patronage bribe.

Although accorded the low respect due a figurehead who had been used by every dominant power in Indochina since the beginning of World War II, the emperor Bao Dai had a surprising capacity for lucid analysis. Interviewed by a State Department official while pursuing his life-style as a French Riviera playboy, he commented about Diem's difficulties with the sects. Sect activity had jeopardized his own rule in the past, so Bao Dai felt well able to understand Diem's problems. While empathetic, he worried that everyone in South Vietnam had lost sight of the real peril, the Viet Minh. The only way to survive the Viet Minh menace was to have all freedom-loving elements working together, and here Bao Dai severely faulted Diem. According to Bao Dai, Diem was not drawing upon capable men who had diverse viewpoints to form a truly national government. By relying almost exclusively on his Catholic base—which represented only a small percentage of the total Vietnamese population—Diem alienated the political and religious elements whose support he needed if South Vietnam was to survive. The emperor urged that his words be conveyed to General Collins so that Collins, in turn, could try to persuade Diem. Having unburdened himself, Bao Dai returned to his bittersweet pursuit of pleasure.

On the same day that Bao Dai warned about preoccupation with the sects, Secretary of State Dulles—who had decided to visit—and Collins, who had returned from his Washington trip, conducted a high-level strategy meeting with Diem in Saigon. As if to confirm Bao Dai's concern, the meeting concentrated on the sects' difficulties. Dulles was, however, well aware of Diem's need to broaden the base of his government. Dulles told Diem that the American government, and in particular its President, had a "great stake in him and in Vietnam." Now that American aid had given Diem a secure position, he could afford to admit men into his government who otherwise would be his political opponents. Dulles warned that continued congressional and public support for Vietnam might well depend on such a step and repeated how important the success of the Diem government was to the American strategic position worldwide.

Examining Dulles's somewhat convoluted effort at persuasion, it is apparent how the beleaguered Diem must have felt. In his mind Dulles's logic collapsed because it presupposed that Diem's position was secure. Manifestly, his position was not secure. He had been telling any American he encountered about the grave threat the sects posed, and he repeated this again to Dulles. The second message that came through loud and clear from Dulles was that both the top American leaders and America as a whole had a tremendous investment in his government. Diem must have reasoned that a powerful leader such as Eisenhower could keep his own house—Congress and American public opinion—in order to make good on this investment. Therefore, he concluded that any threat of an American cutoff of support could be safely ignored. So Diem replied that the security problem posed by the sects was the most important issue confronting his government and would be dealt with first. "Will you broaden the base of your government, Mr. President?" the American secretary of state asked. In diplomatic language, Diem's reply was as clear a no as a leader could express.

Dulles accepted Diem's response. He reported to Washington: "In Saigon I was favorably impressed by Diem. . . . He is not without defects, but his merits seemed greater than I had thought. . . . Great difficulties remain, but magnitude is less than six months ago."

Part 2. BATTLE FOR SAIGON

Unlike other sects that were religious groups with ethnic ties to specific areas in Vietnam, the Binh Xuyen represented no specific ethnic group. It had originated in the waterlogged Mekong Delta south of Saigon, where it acted as a brotherhood of river pirates and then expanded to control the vice activities in Saigon. Diem's planned reforms represented a mortal challenge to the Binh Xuyen's sources of illegal profits. Such a challenge would inevitably be resolved by force. Since the Americans considered the Binh Xuyen nothing better than a "gangster sect," Diem expected United States support for the pending contest while correctly anticipating French opposition. The French had encouraged the sects, including the Binh Xuyen, as part of their divide-and-rule policy in Vietnam. They retained close links with sect leaders and covertly aided sect opposition to Diem's rule.

So the rivals gathered strength for a showdown. On the one side stood President Diem. He could depend upon a handful of loyal, regular army troops whose real control did not extend beyond the perimeters' of their headquarters. Most of the army responded to their officers' guidance, and the majority of officers preferred to straddle the fence pending resolution of the sect crisis. The sects controlled organized military units numbering more than twenty thousand armed soldiers. Another twenty thousand had been nominally integrated into the regular Vietnamese Army. Through force and coercion they exerted nearly autonomous rule over large areas. The Binh Xuyen also controlled the capital's police.

There was one other powerful force to influence the balance of power, Colonel Lansdale. Lansdale decided to employ his unique brand of personal diplomacy toward the Binh Xuyen problem. He met with several of the lords of the Saigon-Cholon underworld and suggested that they consider how they would be remembered in Vietnamese history. Surprisingly, his unlikely appeal bore fruit. He negotiated a promising deal whereby the Binh Xuyen would enter mainstream Vietnamese society by financing the construction of a highway running south from Saigon. Since the highway's terminus would be in an area where the sect owned much land, the Binh Xuyen leaders would enjoy a legal profit. Furthermore, the highway would be named after the sect's leader.

But the perils of being an independent operator redounded to unravel Lansdale's scheme. He arranged a meeting between the Binh Xuyen leader and Diem without adequately briefing the Vietnamese president. Diem humiliated the leader, calling his scheme silly and implying that he was a scoundrel. Enraged, the leader departed, summoned the aide who had originally met with Lansdale to arrange the meeting, and shot him in the stomach. The shooting ended chances for a peaceful resolution between Diem and the Binh Xuyen.

When Diem refused to renew the Binh Xuyen's license to operate the Grand Monde gambling casino, the sect decided it had tolerated more than enough. On March 5, 1955, the Binh Xuyen leader hosted a meeting of leaders from all the sects. Together they plotted how to seize the government and divide the spoils. They formed a united front and issued democratic-sounding manifestos calling for thorough government reform. Lansdale, who normally maintained a work schedule that would have defeated two normal mortals, went into high gear. As he saw matters: "The United Sects Front was on a collision course leading to a civil war, unless its leaders could be persuaded to act rationally." He set his proven powers of persuasion to the task, but could not win over Ambassador Collins. Although Collins did authorize Lansdale to foment dissension within the sects, he had decidedly mixed feelings toward the sect challenge. He thought it might push the heretofore stubborn Diem toward broadening his government's base.

By the third week in March the sect front sent an ultimatum to Diem. Either he would accept sect members into key cabinet positions, a step that would effectively reduce him to a figurehead ruler, or else. Diem had five days to decide. The Binh Xuyen positioned mortars around Diem's Presidential Palace to back up the threat. The uneasy coalition supporting the president panicked and resigned. Only Diem, his family, and a handful of loyalists remained firm. In his palace, Diem spread out a large-scale map of Saigon and on it marked Binh Xuyen mortar positions. Remarking that the mortars should do little damage to the palace's thick walls, he calmly prepared the palace's defense. He ordered loyal military units to the capital and then answered the ultimatum by a dramatic action, the replacement of the Binh Xuyen chief of national police with one of his own men.

At midnight, March 29–30, Saigon awoke to the sound of explosions. In a tit-for-tat move, a band of Binh Xuyen troops responded to the ouster of the chief of national police with an assault on a police headquarters in Cholon that had been recently occupied by army troops. Simultaneously, other sect troops made probing attacks elsewhere. The sect leaders and some of their French supporters did not expect to meet much resistance. Nearly everyone in Saigon, most Americans included, believed the demoralized army troops would be no match for the "battle-hardened" sect forces, but the army repulsed the nocturnal attacks. The next day presented a sad spectacle to the officers of the American Military Assistance Advisory Group. The army they had hoped to train for battle against the Communist juggernaut lay deployed in battle positions against a gangster sect in the streets of Saigon. During the day General Ely, with Collins's approval, used his French soldiers to force a halt in the fighting. An uneasy truce ensued.

♦ ♦ ♦

By mid-March, intense American scrutiny of the sect crisis left most American officials convinced that Diem was not up to the challenge of leading South Vietnam. The French, well embarked upon an anti-Diem policy, reinforced this view at every opportunity. Worried about their crumbling influence, the French again promoted Bao Dai—whom they were confident they could manipulate, everyone including the Japanese, Viet Minh, and themselves having done so in the past—as the leader to resolve the sect crisis. The French warned particularly of dire consequences if Diem initiated military action against the sects. With that warning they hoped to take away Diem's only means for effective action.

Since first arriving in Saigon, General Collins had experienced doubts about Diem. At that time, Diem had opposed several of his key ideas regarding how to restructure the Vietnamese Army. By the end of March, French reports, coupled with the battles in the streets of the capital, prompted Collins to tell the State Department that "we must now squarely face [the] fact Diem is operating practically [a] one-man government." Collins went on to say that Diem had had a fair chance to establish an effective government and had failed to do so. His personality seemed to eliminate the possibility of a truly representative government. Collins strongly recommended beginning a search for an alternative to Diem.

His message caused an uproar in Washington. Just after midnight on April 1, Dulles phoned Eisenhower to brief him on Collins's message, expressing surprise at the general's attitude. Eisenhower replied that he did not see any alternative to telling Collins "not to give up on Diem . . . because we bet on him heavily." The following morning Dulles informed Collins that "we do not think that [a] switch would be desirable or practicable at [the] present time." Dulles also urged Collins to warn Diem again that should he fail to do a better job "we may have to cease U.S. support." It was another toothless warning that merely heightened Diem's anxiety and provided an outlet for the American government's concern without actually changing anything.

Meanwhile, Lansdale had uncovered good evidence that during the Binh Xuyen attack, French units had deliberately blocked the arrival of key Vietnamese Army reinforcements. To the outraged colonel, that was as shameful as if the U.S. Army had intervened in the 1920s "to help Al Capone and his gang take over the city of Chicago." But Collins did not see matters in the same light. Although he met with General Ely to ask about Ely's threat to arrest Diem if the disorder heightened, Collins did not fully appreciate the extent of French influence. Lansdale, on the other hand, was up to his ears in intrigue and was profoundly angered by French actions. Probably at this time he began to work at cross-purposes to Collins.

In only partial contrast, Collins continued, more or less, to represent loyally the official United States position. He explained to Ely that while recognizing Diem's serious administrative inadequacies and his inability to develop executive teamwork, the American government still supported the Vietnamese president. The United States believed that "Ho Chi Minh and his phony religion of Communism could best be met by the leadership, however inadequate from practical standards, of a man of spiritual qualities, high integrity, moral courage, and devoted nationalism, such as Ngo Dinh Diem. No other Vietnamese has these qualities to the same degree."

At this point another important American who backed Diem stepped forward, the influential Democratic senator from Montana, Mike Mansfield. Mansfield had a keen interest in the Eisenhower administration's Southeast Asian policy. The administration, in turn, courted the senator in order to obtain bipartisan support for its policy. Toward this end, Mansfield had accompanied Dulles to the formal signing of the SEATO Treaty. Mansfield also had a friendly, personal re-

lationship with Diem dating from the time the latter had lived
in a Maryknoll monastery in New Jersey. Back in the autumn
of 1954, when a coup by General Hinh seemed likely, Mansfield had told Dulles why American support for Diem was essential. In Mansfield's opinion, Diem faced opposition because
he wanted to end corruption and achieve genuine national independence, goals opposed by the sects and the French. The
senator told Dulles that most of Diem's opponents had a long
history of serving the French. To the senator, the issue was
"not can Diem form a worthy government but do the French
really want Diem and what he stands for to succeed?"

In light of Collins's increasing doubts about Diem during
the sect crisis, Dulles invited Mansfield for a personal discussion. He described the worsening situation and laid out alternatives to keeping Diem in office. In addition, the secretary
mentioned the possibility of pressuring Diem to broaden his
government. Mansfield replied that delivering lectures about
reform was extremely inappropriate at that time, emphasizing
his point by noting that if Diem quit or was overthrown, a civil
war would result and "Ho Chi Minh could walk in and take
the country without any difficulty." To give teeth to his position, Mansfield threatened to withhold congressional appropriations for Vietnam if the United States abandoned Diem.

The secretary of state, and ultimately the President, had to
choose between opposing viewpoints regarding the importance of political reform in South Vietnam versus the risk of
political instability. Just as had been the case in the French-
Viet Minh war, numerous NSC and Pentagon papers identified political reform—broadening the base of the government
—as a prerequisite for successfully defeating communism.
Collins's experience in Saigon independently confirmed this
position. On the other side stood Diem, strongly supported by
Mansfield, who said he first had to restore internal security by
defeating the sects before turning to political reform.

The Central Intelligence Agency agreed with Diem, pointing out that many Vietnamese associated the sects with French
rule. If the sects triumphed over Diem, or seemed to triumph
because the French and Americans forced Diem out, their success would indicate that the French retained their colonial authority. Any Diem replacement would then face an even

tougher challenge because he would inevitably be viewed as a French puppet. A South Vietnam divided among the sects and a weakened central government would not be able to resist Viet Minh infiltration. Although the French claimed that if Diem forcefully opposed the sects disaster would result, the CIA recognized risk but concluded "that Diem would have the capability, if given full US and French backing, of dealing with the present crisis in Saigon."

This line of reasoning swayed the President. He ordered Dulles to put the strongest pressure on the French to permit Diem to assert his authority over the Binh Xuyen. He said that failure would be too bad, "but it would be better to find out now rather than later whether the National army on which we were spending so much money was loyal." Later, the United States would attend to the problems of political reform.

On the eve of the showdown between Diem and the sects, Dulles sent Collins a heartfelt message: "I do not for a moment doubt your analysis of Diem in that he lacks many desirable qualities. On the other hand, I thought we felt when I was in Saigon that the decision to back Diem had gone to the point of no return and that either he had to succeed or else the whole business would be a failure."

In spite of Dulles's claim that the choice to support Diem had been made, Collins continued to argue for an examination of alternatives. A military man rather than a diplomat, trained to utilize American military flexibility as exemplified by the armored corps, he feared that the decision to back Diem, warts and all, was overly rigid and left no room for maneuver. In spite of Collins's objections, Dulles told the NSC and the President that in the current "extremely critical situation," there were no good alternatives to backing Diem. The main problem continued to be French refusal to cooperate with the United States in allowing Diem to unleash his forces against the sects. The secretary explained further that the Vietnamese Army had been organized and trained for the purpose of maintaining internal order, precisely the type of problem Diem faced in the streets of Saigon.

Accordingly, Dulles directed Collins to meet Ely again in order to learn the final French policy toward the sect crisis. Ely entered the meeting believing that he and Collins made a good team and shared the mission of barring Communist advance into Southeast Asia. He told Collins that Diem could only be preserved at enormous cost and that even if saved, "we shall have spared for Vietnam the worst Prime Minister it ever had." Ely noted that while the Americans considered Diem a strong nationalist leader, in fact Diem had very little popular support and "is more of a puppet than any of his predecessors." The French general understood that however close he and Collins were in their opinion of Diem, the American represented superiors in Washington who disagreed. Therefore, Ely concluded that he and Collins had to convince their governments to remove Diem.

On April 7, Collins gave the secretary of state his final judgment of Diem. Asserting that he had followed Eisenhower's orders and done everything in his power to assist Diem, he added: "The man lacks the personal qualities of leadership and the executive ability successfully to head a government that must compete with the unity of purpose and efficiency of the Viet Minh under Ho Chi Minh." He told the secretary of state that under Diem the country would fall to the Communists, making a change essential. He assured Dulles that he had reached his conclusion "with great regret, but with firm conviction."

Collins enumerated Diem's faults: his lack of practical political sense; his inability to compromise, or to cooperate with others; and his suspicion of anyone who disagreed with him. These were characteristics that others, including Dulles, had discovered; but Collins added a new and even more serious complaint, Diem's incapacity for creative thinking and planning. Collins observed that Diem had yet to offer a single constructive or original thought, which was a bit like a puppeteer blaming the puppet when the show failed to excite. Collins doubted that Diem understood the significance of the progressive programs he and Ely had devised, and was certain that Diem did not know how to implement them. Eisenhower had sent a fellow World War II warrior to serve him in an important role in Vietnam, and the trusted veteran's final judgment was that Diem had to go.

Dulles and Eisenhower recognized they had reached another critical juncture in their foreign policy. If the administration dumped Diem, it would have enormous political ramifications. Therefore, one of the first steps they took was to share Collins's telegram with Senator Mansfield. The senator's response was straightforward: "The US should stick to its guns in continuing to support Diem." Mansfield referred to Collins's earlier even-odds estimate that American policy could succeed and said that although Diem now had a smaller than 50-50 chance, the stakes were so important that the chance was worth taking. Unwittingly, Mansfield had echoed Dulles's earlier attitude during the Hinh crisis. Then, Dulles had shown himself to be an even greater risk taker. The secretary had estimated the odds at one in ten, but concluded the stakes were so high the United States simply had to win.

While Washington digested Collins's recommendations, the general elaborated upon his thinking for the future. No clearer indication of Collins's attitude toward colonialism is needed than this subsequent telegram outlining steps to be taken to replace Diem. He wrote, in part: "After France and U.S. have agreed on a man, Bao Dai's consent must then be obtained. This would have to be done through Paris." Here was a Western-imposed solution that gave the French the major role in determining the affairs of South Vietnam. Credit must go to General Ely, who performed superbly for France, playing an apparently lost hand so well that he had convinced Collins that France had to be intimately involved in orchestrating a change of head of state in South Vietnam. Heavily influenced by Ely, as well as possessing an Old World attitude toward colonialism, Collins still retained acute powers of observation. He examined Diem's popular support and the potential support for any successor, and concluded that except for Ho Chi Minh, no Vietnamese leader had "grass roots support."

After discussing Collins's recommendations for change with Eisenhower, Dulles informed Collins that the President was prepared to accept them, but that they first wanted the ambassador to reconsider. Dulles reminded Collins that the United States had backed Diem as the best available person and that "the only alternatives now suggested are the same persons who were regarded as unacceptable substitutes some months ago." To remove Diem would betray the continued heavy hand of France and would be interpreted in Asia as the "U.S. paying lip service to [the] nationalist cause." Finally, he told Collins, such an ouster faced heavy congressional disapproval.

Collins responded by contesting Dulles point by point. He doubted that his proposed substitutes for Diem had ever seriously been considered and felt that several candidates had excellent nationalist credentials. He believed the force of his argument would persuade congressional leaders of the need for change. He also noted the cost of continued indecision; because of the sect crisis, the MAAG had not yet had time to perform its mission to train the Vietnamese armed forces. Dulles, on Eisenhower's behalf, had begged Collins to change his mind. Instead, Collins stood firm.

The next day Dulles yielded and drafted a message telling Collins to go ahead and replace Diem. Then, at the proverbial eleventh hour, another change occurred. At a final meeting with Eisenhower to authorize the change in policy, a new voice spoke forcefully in dissent. The State Department's director of the Office of Philippine and Southeast Asian Affairs, Kenneth T. Young, argued that Diem should not be abruptly discarded. For appearance's sake, the change should be made gradually. At a minimum, Young asserted, a change should not occur until after an upcoming regional conference. Young's opinion regarding a small matter of tactics tilted the scale in favor of delay. A new draft cable did not authorize Collins to proceed. Instead, it read: "We have had in mind an intermediate solution which would not kick Diem completely out of the picture or keep him in his present status with full powers." While there was considerable disagreement about whether to replace Diem or not, parties on both sides shared the attitude that Diem was a pawn in the greater game of American statesmanship.

A man of action now becoming impatient, on April 12 Collins cabled Washington to urge the State Department to make some kind of decision. He feared that further procrastination would lead to reduced options. He also responded to specific departmental concerns about the consequences of Diem's removal and focused on one of these, potentially unfavorable American public opinion. Three days earlier he had explained how the United States and France would manage the transition. This day he advised: "American public opinion also would need some preliminary preparation. Care would have to be taken, however, to insure that if leaks did occur, the initiative for the projected change is properly attributed to the Vietnamese and not to either France or the U.S." With his comment, Collins introduced a new theme that was to become an enduring characteristic of American involvement in Southeast Asia. American public opinion would have to be "prepared"—in other words, manipulated—so that the public would approve controversial policies. Further, the truth would have to be disguised because the public would not support certain essential policies if the unvarnished truth became known.

Recognizing that Collins was slowly succeeding in shifting American support away from Diem, the beleaguered Vietnamese president's most stalwart American ally, Colonel Lansdale, worked frantically to reverse the course of United States policy. He provided the State Department with a much more optimistic appraisal of Diem's situation. Armed with conflicting analyses, Dulles shuttled south to Augusta where Eisenhower was enjoying a golf vacation. Having only been reluctantly convinced of the need to replace Diem, Eisenhower seized upon Lansdale's estimation and restated his preference to stand by Diem at least until a viable alternative emerged. Amid the confusing situation, the President and his secretary of state decided to summon Collins back home for a firsthand report.

Collins flew to Washington on April 21. Unbeknownst to him, President Diem had correctly interpreted the American ambassador's recall to Washington as a sign that Collins had turned against him. While Collins tried to explain to the Eisenhower administration and the Washington bureaucracy why Diem had to go, the Vietnamese president worked with equal vigor to save himself. The day after arriving, Collins lunched with Eisenhower. He described the situation in Vietnam in the bluntest possible words, referring to Diem as "this impossible fellow." He added that Vietnamese military men had told him that the Vietnamese Army had no desire to fight the sects. Eisenhower was dubious, telling Collins that he had received reports contradicting many of Collins's claims. Lightning Joe now revealed his true attitude toward Lansdale. He told the President that he did not want what he was about to say repeated outside this room, but that the colonel had been providing "inadequate and inaccurate intelligence," which Eisenhower should discount. Still Eisenhower remained unreceptive, emphasizing difficulties associated with Congress and with public opinion. He instructed the general to take his ideas to the foreign policy specialists and persuade them. For himself, he would withhold judgment.

Collins was up against a formidable challenge. Outside of the administration, Senator Mansfield made public the threat he had related to Dulles. He told *The New York Times* that if Diem was overthrown, the United States should suspend all aid to South Vietnam. Arrayed against Collins inside the executive branch were the two Dulles brothers and two of Foster Dulles's chief lieutenants. If he could convince them, the President would probably follow. During the next days, Collins had long meetings at the State Department. A participant summarized the proceedings by saying that the general firmly believed that Diem had to be removed but "State is reluctant to face the fact that they must admit a failure in U.S. policy." Slowly Collins advanced his case, but by and large the administration preferred to wait to see if Diem had the courage and determination to act against the sects. This attitude gave Diem his great opportunity.

In Saigon, the uneasy French-imposed truce had gone on for nearly two weeks. Soldiers of the Vietnamese Army and the Binh Xuyen confronted one another from sandbagged positions on opposite sides of the street. Armed and ready, their strongpoints dotted the city, but they confined themselves to posturing and hurling insults. French troops provided a third force as they positioned tanks in the middle of traffic circles and strung barbed wire along the boulevards. Lansdale and Diem could not help notice that within the French zones Binh Xuyen soldiers circulated freely while French roadblocks restricted Vietnamese Army movement. Behind one French-protected zone, only eight hundred yards from Diem's office and residence, the Binh Xuyen fortified a position at the National Security Police headquarters. Nearly everyone in Saigon believed Diem's fall imminent. Graham Greene wrote in *The*

New Republic that Vietnam was "about to retire behind the iron curtain."

Yet Diem, closely advised by his brother Nhu and bank-rolled by Lansdale's CIA funds, adroitly exploited his enemies' unnatural alliance. Using bribes and appeals to Vietnamese nationalism—two of the sects were strongly anti-Communist —Diem managed to weaken the United Sect front. He accepted that the leader of the Hoa Hao might join his government while retaining a young protégé in the countryside just in case. Diem understood such tactics and sensed that many of his opponents could be bought, having pledged allegiance to the United Sect front as a ploy to raise their price.

Lansdale spent more than $10 million in bribes to fracture the sect coalition. It proved worth the price. Most of the non-Binh Xuyen sect leaders either stood neutral or discreetly supported Diem. This was not apparent on April 23—the day after Collins lunched with Eisenhower—when the Vietnamese president made a national radio address. Most experts expected him to announce his resignation; but instead, in a brilliant stroke, he told the world that there would be general elections for the National Assembly in three to four months. He hoped that that announcement, a step toward representative government, would make it harder for the Americans to remove him.

The pace of events in Saigon and Washington now accelerated to a near bewildering speed. In Washington, Collins's arguments that Diem had to go had finally won over the secretary of state. From April 25 to 27, State Department officials worked on a long, complicated series of telegrams to Paris and Saigon preparing the way for Diem's removal. In Saigon on April 26, Diem decided to precipitate a crisis. The next day the State Department sent a message to the American embassy in Saigon alerting them that the administration had decided to remove Diem. Somehow Diem learned of Washington's decision, and the following day skirmishing between the Vietnamese Army and the Binh Xuyen in Saigon escalated to outright battle.

It began around noon, Saigon time, when mortar fire from an unknown source wounded French soldiers in a Binh Xuyen-controlled area of Saigon. The Binh Xuyen retaliated with what was initially called a "shelling of the Presidential Palace," although the CIA reported that only three shells struck the palace compound. Diem, who was at the palace, then phoned Lansdale and asked him to listen on the line while he told Ely that if the shelling did not stop, he would unleash the army. The French general dissembled. Then an audible explosion reverberated over the telephone. The Vietnamese president told Ely he had had enough and was ordering his army into action.

Everything about this incident remains shrouded in mystery. The CIA reported that one shell had been fired, followed by a pause and then two more shells, with Diem then phoning Ely to announce he was ordering his army to return the fire. Ely, a biased source, said that he did not know who was responsible but could not conceive of what advantage the Binh Xuyen hoped to derive from starting trouble at this time. Frank Melroy, a political officer in Saigon, accused Lansdale of trying to outflank Collins while Collins was away. Later, when Collins more completely understood what had taken place during his absence, he called Lansdale's actions mutinous.

In any event, news of the battle for Saigon took Washington by surprise. The administration thought it was about to install a new government in Saigon when events overtook its meticulously laid plans. The secretary of state reacted with speed by ordering the Saigon embassy to disregard the cables pertaining to a change in government. The NSC met that day and devoted most of its time to the crisis. CIA director Allen Dulles reviewed events, observing that although it was hard to know which side had been responsible for precipitating the fight, it seemed that Diem was forcing a showdown. Secretary of State Dulles said that he did not know if Diem was losing control. He added that unless the Vietnamese leader emerged as a hero, he would have to be removed. Collins predicted that "Diem's number was up." He also said that if Diem moved against the Binh Xuyen, civil war would result. The council recognized that the United States still might have to orchestrate a change of governments. CIA director Dulles said that in that case the fighting in Saigon was welcome, since changing a government was easier during the confusion of a civil war. However, with the secretary of state urging caution, the NSC decided to support Diem until the situation clarified. The President concluded he did not "see what else we could do at this time."

So the outbreak of fighting caused the Eisenhower administration to halt plans to remove Diem and to await events. In Saigon, Lansdale recognized opportunity. He began sending a series of on-the-spot appraisals emphasizing that in the streets Diem's army was winning. Interwoven with the "facts" was his advice that the Diem government still offered the best chance for success. Cleverly playing upon the administration's fears of communism, he noted that removing Diem at this time would only benefit the Viet Minh. To reinforce his message, he cooperated with General O'Daniel to send a follow-up report stating: "Any change in leadership or command at this time could result in chaos." This appraisal, coming at a time when Collins, the spokesman for the rival view, was in Washington and therefore out of touch with the situation, was decisive.

John Foster Dulles received one of Lansdale's messages while attending a dinner party. He discussed it with his brother and then departed to inform the President. On the strength of Lansdale's optimistic report, Eisenhower concluded that Diem had ably met the crisis and that the United States would continue to support him. That seemed a good choice when, over the next few days, the Vietnamese Army continued to gain ground. Combat exposed the vaunted, "battle-hardened" Binh Xuyen fighters as poorly motivated, indifferent warriors. They were better at extorting money from frightened casino owners than at defending barricades against determined army soldiers. Still, there was some hard fighting that consumed large areas of Saigon.

In the State Department, the clique of Diem supporters, including Kenneth Young, observed the events with satisfaction. Happily, Young wrote: "As this crisis develops we are being forced to take a more and more unequivocal and strong stand for Diem." From Capitol Hill came bipartisan support for the administration's decision to back Diem. Among many, Senator Hubert Humphrey said that Diem was America's "best hope" in South Vietnam and deserved "the wholehearted support of the American Government."

All of this caught General Collins in transit as he hastened back to Saigon. Two weeks earlier he had departed on a mission to remove the Diem government. Upon his return he found a message from the secretary of state announcing his failure: "Events in past few days have put Vietnamese situation in broader and different perspective than when you were here." No longer was it merely a question of how to alter the Diem government. According to Dulles, because of Diem's success against the Binh Xuyen, he had become both an American and an international symbol of the Vietnamese struggle against French colonialism. To now remove Diem "would not only be domestically impractical but highly detrimental [to] our prestige in Asia." Accordingly, Dulles passed on Eisenhower's instructions that Collins again support the "Diem Government to maintain its authority and to restore law and order." Collins summoned the country team. After caustically observing that somebody had fomented a revolution within the team, a remark Lansdale objected to, Collins described the new policy.

By May 2, the Vietnamese Army secured Saigon. Better still—and this made Diem's decision to confront the Binh Xuyen appear all the more marvelous to the Eisenhower administration—civil war did not erupt in the hinterland. Remnants of the Binh Xuyen armed horde fled to the swamps south of Saigon where those who resisted were eliminated during the summer. Eventually, army forces captured the sect's leader and publicly guillotined him.

The French and Americans had told Diem to avoid confronting the sects, warning that such a move would lead to civil war. Diem had ignored their advice and been rewarded with total support from the Americans. Equally good, his decision led to a large reduction in French influence. In sum, he had won, and he had done it his way. Among many consequences was the birth of a large measure of self-confidence in Diem. During the battle for Saigon, he had become very much a commander in chief of the national military. He ordered battalion maneuvers, kept track of logistical minutiae, and closely followed his officers' performance.

In 1963 a new crisis much like the confrontation against the sects would arise. Once again a significant group, this time Buddhists, began protesting Diem's rule, and rumors circulated about the cutoff of United States support. The Americans advised Diem not to confront the demonstrators in the streets. Recalling the events of 1955, Diem again ignored the American advice and relied upon his own judgment. This time he miscalculated and paid for it with his life.

During his time in Saigon, Collins had done his best to change American policy. He made an unpopular assessment and courageously stood by it. Unfortunately, during the crucial days when Diem attacked the Binh Xuyen, he had been in Washington. Then, as soon as he returned to Saigon, Dulles announced that he had missed out on important developments in Washington. Collins, a skilled soldier but a less adroit diplomat, probably would not have disagreed that in the battle of Saigon he had been masterfully outflanked by his opponents.

Many had doubted that Diem could survive the sect crisis. When he did, Dulles and Eisenhower felt surprise and relief. Overlooking Ho Chi Minh, Dulles exulted to the National Security Council that Diem had become "the national symbol of the break away from the French." Neither he nor the President understood that Diem's victory had been gained at steep cost. Diem's quarrel with General Hinh at the end of 1954 split an already ineffective national army. When most members of his cabinet, which at that time represented a cross-section of the nation and contained able men, resigned upon the formation of the United Sect front, Diem replaced them with family members and other northern-born Catholic loyalists. This had paved the way for his successful tactic of absorbing certain sects into the army while suppressing others. Although not immediately apparent, Diem's strategy worked only because he had replaced the United Sect front with a Catholic-based president's sect, and therein lay trouble. Finally, Diem's victory over the Binh Xuyen did more than remove a powerful rival faction, it captured the support of the American government. In mid-May the Eisenhower administration recalled Collins and replaced him with G. Frederick Reinhardt. Upon arriving in Saigon, Reinhardt publicly defined his mission as support for the government of Premier Ngo Dinh Diem.

Before the new ambassador arrived he had the opportunity to read the latest National Intelligence Estimate on Vietnam. It described a new and potentially revolutionary situation. Observing that Diem's success derived from his own initiative and resources, it predicted he would become more independent and less willing to follow American advice. Although the situation had improved, the estimate concluded, "it will still be extremely difficult, at best, for Diem or any Vietnamese government to build sufficient strength to meet the long-range challenge of the Communists."

Part 3. COLLISION COURSE

During the sect crisis the commander of the Military Assistance Advisory Group, General O'Daniel, continued with the important business of building a Vietnamese National Army. One of the MAAG's elementary chores was to determine the optimal size of that army, which in theory should have been based on an assessment of risk. It was not so simple, however; in the spring of 1955, numerous nonmilitary factors influenced the decision. They included the ability of the Vietnamese civilian economy to absorb discharges and their dependents, Diem's twin desires to integrate the military forces controlled by the fighting sects and to keep as many men as possible employed by the military, and the amount of money the United States was prepared to pay to maintain this army. So complex was the equation that when O'Daniel tried to put it all on paper, he almost completely ignored the threat posed by the Viet Minh. American planners did not tailor the army's strength to meet the Communist threat, but instead focused on overriding nonmilitary issues.

At this same time a Department of Defense staff study very cogently predicted the likely course of events should Diem's government succeed in pacifying and controlling South Vietnam. The study laid out a series of Communist countermeasures: psychological warfare and subversive penetration; sabotage and local terrorist actions; initiation of wide-scale guerrilla activity; reinforcement of this effort by infiltration from the north; and overt invasion. While the authors of this study intended it for short-range planning purposes, it proved a blueprint of events over the next twenty years.

Having received from Eisenhower a clearly defined policy to support Diem, Secretary of Defense Wilson wrestled with the problem of replacing O'Daniel, whose tour of duty was coming to an end. He called on Foster Dulles to help find a competent officer to lead the MAAG. Dulles listed the requirements for this post in their order of importance: first, previous success with Asians; then, the capacity to train men; and finally, French speaking ability. Wilson interjected that the candidate should also have executive leadership abilities as well. Dulles commented that he thought all military men at this rank had such capabilities. Dulles then said that in the State Department's view the training mission "is taking a gamble but it is Defense's responsibility."

It was a neat trick. All along, the State Department had pushed for more aggressive policies toward Vietnam than the Department of Defense wanted. Now that the policy was in effect, it became the Defense Department's concern. Wilson felt uncomfortable with this transfer of responsibility—he certainly feared a bureaucratic ambush—and mentioned that he did not consider the chances for success very good. He had said this before, directly to the President, and been shot down, so now he had little choice but to try to make the training program work. In accepting this responsibility, however reluctantly, the military role of the United States in Vietnam grew.

♦ ♦ ♦

An immediate consequence of Diem's success against the Binh Xuyen was an irretrievable Franco-American split over Western policy in Indochina. Heretofore, the French Expeditionary Corps had been counted on to protect South Vietnam during its perilous early days. Indeed, American military planners from the Joint Chiefs in Washington to the MAAG in Saigon had repeatedly maintained that French support for a Vietnamese government was a fundamental key to obtaining American goals. When the anti-French Diem defeated the sects, French leaders recognized they had failed in their ef-

forts to maintain a dominant influence in Vietnam. That failure, coupled with a new colonial war in Algeria, caused the
French to evacuate Vietnam much more quickly than American strategists had expected. When assuming the training burden, the American military had established a number of
preconditions. The premature French withdrawal undermined one of them. Remaining at issue was the other minimum criterion, the creation of a truly representative
Vietnamese government.

Lightning Joe Collins clearly realized this. In one of his last
recommendations before his recall, he informed the State Department that regardless of who led South Vietnam, it would
not be saved without sound political, economic, and military
programs and wholehearted cooperation among the Vietnamese, French, and Americans. Absent such cooperation, he recommended American withdrawal. But Diem's success had
discredited him and no one listened. However, nearly simultaneous with Collins's last plea, there was a diplomatic meeting
in Europe where the subject of American withdrawal also
arose.

It was another high-level encounter between France and the
United States, and the French entered it most unhappy.
Diem's show of independence and his subsequent support
from the Americans came just at a time when the French, acting through Ely, thought they had reached agreement with
the Americans to remove the Vietnamese leader. This startling change of policy reminded them of the experience with
the on-again, off-again Operation Vulture. They complained
bitterly to Dulles during a European visit the first week of
May. To smooth matters over, the conferees agreed that common interests between the two countries transcended the importance of Vietnam. It was simply not worth a major quarrel.
Nonetheless, the French prime minister explained, his country
could not support Diem since Diem had turned actively anti-
French. He inquired if the Americans could offer guarantees
regarding protection of French lives and property in Vietnam.

Dulles agreed that the United States and France could not afford to adopt competitive policies in Vietnam and that one or
the other should leave Vietnam. In an amazing turnaround, he
volunteered American willingness to depart. Eisenhower ap-

proved of this about-face, commenting that the "U.S. could not afford to have forces committed in such undesirable areas as Vietnam." In fact, ever a risk taker, Dulles was engaged in a high-stakes bluff, as were the French. Whoever successfully called the other's bluff won and stayed in Vietnam.

The Joint Chiefs of Staff offered their opinion on all of this during the second week of May. They stated that the decision to support any particular Vietnamese regime was outside their area of responsibility. The Chiefs confined their analysis to the military implications of the various alternatives being considered by Dulles and the French. They stated that the Vietnamese National Army currently could neither maintain internal security nor resist outside aggression unaided. Since the Geneva Accords prevented the United States from sending troops to Vietnam, by default only the French could offer the necessary foreign support. However, given the growing anti-French feeling in Vietnam, France could not succeed alone. The U.S. had to provide moral and material support for the Vietnamese Army to develop into an effective force. Accordingly, the JCS rejected the two alternatives of French or American withdrawal, concluding, as had General Collins, that the only viable strategy for preserving the south from communism was one of full cooperation among the Vietnamese, French, and Americans. For purposes of long-range planning, Admiral Radford said that American intervention under the auspices of SEATO could someday give South Vietnam the military security currently provided by the French.

Armed with the views of the Joint Chiefs, and after letting passions cool, Dulles met again with the French. After tortuous negotiation, he believed he had worked out a program for a progressive reduction of French forces consistent with the ability of the Vietnamese to take over the French role. There would also be a pause in the French withdrawal at some minimal force level. In effect, rather than either country calling the other's bluff, the participants agreed to call off the game itself. The United States would stay in Vietnam.

◆ ◆ ◆

Meanwhile, the clock continued to tick toward the Geneva-mandated general election. According to the Geneva agreement, representatives from the north and south were to meet in July 1955 to arrange the election mechanics. The voting would follow one year later. While neither the United States nor South Vietnam had signed the accords, the Americans felt bound by their requirements. However, prior dealings with the Russians had taught American statesmen that Communists had a very different idea about what constituted a "free" election. Experience also seemed to indicate that insistence upon a Western definition of free elections would be rejected by the Communists. From the American view, though, the problem with any general election was that the wrong side would probably win.

In the north, people had grown weary of sacrifice; although "the ration of rice, equal for all, had a nobility in the jungle," it lacked that quality in times of peace. A poor harvest, coupled with Viet Minh efforts to nationalize the economy, reduced the standard of living. Few motor vehicles cruised Hanoi's streets, cinemas showed nothing but propaganda films, and the handful of restaurants listed prohibitive prices. Most people had to attend endless compulsory lectures on communism and political meetings. The youth spent hours in rigorous physical training to prepare to join the military. Nonetheless, Ho Chi Minh remained a tremendously popular figure and no one doubted he would win a Vietnam-wide election.

In a statement made jointly with Winston Churchill in the summer of 1954, President Eisenhower had reaffirmed the nation's commitment to uphold the Atlantic Charter. Addressing the issue of countries divided against their will, a category presumably including Vietnam, the leaders pledged "to seek to achieve unity through free elections supervised by the United Nations to insure they are conducted fairly." Perhaps the President should have known better than to place the United States foursquare behind free elections. Given what Bedell Smith and others were saying, it might well lead to future embarrassment. Only a week earlier Smith had told Eisenhower that if there was an election, Ho Chi Minh would win 80 percent of the vote. That was clearly intolerable to the United States, and accordingly, Secretary of State Dulles began casting about for means to thwart the election.

Dulles's first idea was to delay. A month after the recommitment to the Atlantic Charter, he wrote the American ambassador in Paris that since it was "undoubtedly true that elections might eventually mean unification [of] Vietnam under Ho Chi Minh this makes it all [the] more important they should be only held as long after cease-fire agreement as possible and in conditions free from intimidation."

By the spring of 1955, the United States' attitude toward the election shifted. The new strategy relied upon suggesting conditions for a "free" election it knew the Communists would reject: One of those conditions was the placing of so-called electoral safeguards on the North Vietnamese. When the hoped-for rejection occurred, the north could then be blamed for blocking the elections. Unfortunately, from the American perspective, President Diem began to speak out against any election on the grounds that fair elections were impossible. His public utterances interfered with the more devious American plan. An American diplomat in the Saigon Embassy explained to the State Department: "Vietnam Government must agree [to] play the game at least in appearance and cease repudiating Agreement."

Although with difficulty the United States could manipulate Diem's attitude toward elections, the failure of the Viet Minh to respond as anticipated upset American plans. From the north came reasonable-sounding statements and an underlying moderate position that made it increasingly difficult to show "that the failure to secure free elections is the fault of the Communists." As one of Dulles's top deputies concluded: "As I see it, one of our basic objectives in Viet-Nam is to prevent the Communists from winning any kind of elections whereby they would take over control of all Viet-Nam by political and legal means."

Meanwhile, the Department of Defense had also examined the elections issue as part of a study intended to form the basis for military policy toward Southeast Asia. It recommended that the United States "make every effort to abolish or postpone indefinitely the elections." The department also warned of the perils of promoting truly free elections, since the Communists very well might win even them.

When the National Security Council met in June, its Planning Board presented a draft statement on United States policy toward the elections. A key phrase, "to prevent a Communist victory through all-Vietnam elections," explained the objective. The policy presentation contained a familiar prescription for accomplishing this goal: first, military strength to deter or defeat Viet Minh insurrections; and second, military strength to impose and sustain order. But the third recommendation was something new: to limit the election to the south so the Diem government could control the electoral process. The planning staff emphasized that blocking the elections was an "extremely delicate problem" but that the Geneva agreement was ambiguous enough to allow room for maneuver.

By 1955, while everyone liked the strategy of limiting elections to the south, which is what eventually occurred, the Joint Chiefs of Staff reacted very negatively to another aspect of the emerging policy. They understood that the American policy risked a strong Communist reaction. In essence, that policy sought to prevent through political maneuvering the victory the Viet Minh had earned on the battlefield. When the Viet Minh realized that the elections would not be held, they might resume military activity. Should they do so, they would defeat their much weaker southern cousins since the French could not be counted on to stop them. Therefore, the National Security Council planners recommended that the United States "should be prepared to oppose any Communist attack with U.S. armed forces . . . consulting the Congress in advance if the emergency permits—preferably in concert with the Manila Pact allies of the U.S., but if necessary alone." In response, the Joint Chiefs of Staff wanted the clause authorizing unilateral American action deleted. The State Department disagreed, believing that the U.S. had to be prepared to act alone. Here was an issue for the President to decide.

In preparation, Dulles met with his top Asian experts. He suggested that if the country was unprepared to use its military to help Diem, then perhaps the policy of opposing elections was flawed. He and his advisers could not make up their minds what to do and so recommended deferring a decision until events became more clear. The secretary of defense was only too glad to postpone the decision as well and so the NSC decided to have the Planning Board again look at the critical paragraph of the official strategy document that was relevant to American military intervention.

In mid-August the board gave its conclusions: It had examined the exact nature of the likely American response in case of overt aggression from the north. Predictably, the board called for further detailed study; however, the operative assumptions governing such study revealed its thinking. Intervention would be swift and decisive on a scale best calculated to prevent hostilities broadening into general war. Contingency planning had to be based upon both the use and the nonuse of nuclear weapons. The board would also consider whether merely to repulse the aggressor or to proceed by conquering North Vietnam. In either event, the Planning Board wanted the Joint Chiefs to prepare a detailed operational plan specifying the nature and duration of operations, as well as the forces and logistic support required. Not since Ridgway's report during the Dien Bien Phu crisis had such a comprehensive review of American military policy in Vietnam been conducted.

A serious subject warranted serious study. It took until the fall for the Joint Chiefs to respond. Then, they explained how the nation would repulse and punish overt Viet Minh aggression. The Navy and Air Force would attack immediately, while on the ground the Vietnamese Army, supported by American air power, would fight as best it could. As soon as possible, United States mobile forces would arrive in Vietnam to conduct joint operations and missions beyond the capabilities of the Vietnamese forces. The Joint Chiefs concluded: "The success of intervention by U.S. forces . . . is believed dependent on the military energy and solidarity of the Vietnamese, the extent of warning and preparations made before an attack, the restriction imposed on U.S. military operations, and the season of the year." While the JCS's concern over weather proved largely misplaced—the introduction of helicopter warfare would provide nearly weatherproof mobility—the other factors cited were crucial to the outcome when America really did go to war in Vietnam.

The Joint Chiefs doubted that overt aggression was the

main threat anyway. Rather, they believed that the true peril continued to be guerrilla subversion. In contrast, the overt threat attracted the most attention from the State Department. The department believed that if the United States clearly demonstrated that it would resort to armed intervention in the event of overt aggression, such aggression was very unlikely. The drawback was that if America committed its resources to deter aggression and then the aggression occurred anyway, the country would have no choice but to fight. To do otherwise would greatly erode American prestige, render the Manila Pact and SEATO useless, and give the Chinese Communists tremendous inroads throughout Southeast Asia.

The end of 1955 provided an opportunity for review and reflection. On balance, the Eisenhower administration was pleased. Because of its actions there was in place "a government determined to resist accommodation to the Viet Minh." Diem had been able to consolidate power. The United States had helped him "avoid international pressures for face to face consultations with the Viet Minh on all Vietnam elections." Although Diem's position remained far from secure, the situation warranted "sober optimism."

In the year following the battle of Dien Bien Phu, President Eisenhower made several critical decisions regarding Vietnam. He decided to accept the burden to train the Vietnamese military. He authorized the creation of the SEATO alliance. He overruled his personal representative's advice and aligned the country with the flawed leadership of Ngo Dinh Diem. He accepted his Defense and State departments' plans that called for involvement in a ground war in Asia. Finally, he endorsed a policy to resist general elections. Neither he nor anyone else perceived that this last decision to oppose elections, and thus resist a final settlement to the problem of an unnaturally divided country, meant there would be an inevitable challenge to the American presence in Vietnam. Because of the decisions made in this watershed year, that challenge would result in war.

CHAPTER X

THE MAKING OF AN AUTOCRAT

There is nothing but drift, indecision and confusion on our side.
  —Kenneth Young, director of the Office of Philippine and Southeast Asian Affairs, July 1955

Part 1. PROGRESS AND DOUBT

One of President Eisenhower's gifts was the capacity to make a decision and then allow others to execute it. He had clearly defined the American mission in Vietnam as the promotion of internal security and political stability. Henceforth, all of the many United States military and economic aid programs aimed at one or both of these goals. No one in the administration was happy about the loss of the northern half of Vietnam, and while some military contingency plans continued wistfully to prepare for the liberation of the north, the President accepted North Vietnam as a fact of life. Once having established American policy toward Vietnam, after mid-1955 he played a diminished role. The implementation of his chosen policy depended upon the government bureaucracy and the military. His influence would still be felt in that his appointees held key posts within that bureaucracy and as

290

Commander in Chief he also had ultimate authority over the military, but actual implementation was the task of the embassy in Vietnam and the Military Assistance Advisory Group. Much now depended on how well they performed.

The complex personality of the South Vietnamese leader dominated the American effort. Except for Lansdale, no American had worked as hard to secure Diem's position as John Foster Dulles. The secretary of state appreciated that he had created an ambiguous American relationship with Diem. On the one hand, the United States had bountiful advice for the Vietnamese leader and felt enormous frustration when he failed to heed it. On the other hand, Dulles maintained, "if Diem were the kind of man who would do our bidding in this way, he would not be the kind of man who could do what was required to save the situation in Vietnam." He elaborated on this view in a telegram to the embassy in Saigon: "Future of Vietnam depends on having a nationalist government which is not subservient to foreign demands but which will be receptive to proper suggestions." Baldly stated, he wanted an independent government open to American manipulation.

The new United States ambassador to Vietnam, Frederick Reinhardt, had to grapple with this policy's inherent inconsistency. Because Diem was a poor administrator, there were numerous opportunities for American advisers up to and including Reinhardt to meddle. For example, when Diem drew up a statement on elections, Reinhardt was full of advice about how to change it. Similarly, Diem's plan to convene a National Assembly upset his American backers. Although they frequently urged him to broaden his government's base, the State Department worried that an "unruly" assembly would weaken Diem's central authority. With unintended humor, Reinhardt assured Washington that the "Diem government can be depended on not to permit such [a] situation to arise."

Indeed, soon after the election of the National Assembly, Diem confronted the reality of what had happened. He summoned Lansdale for a talk and told his favorite American that he worried that the assembly was full of dilettantes, men who did not know what needed to be done. Worse, they would resist his plans. Lansdale replied that every democratic leader experienced problems with his legislature. He explained that the art of politics was making deals in order to get one's way, noting that "even Franklin Roosevelt had to manage his Congress."

Diem seemed to have gained the wrong impression from this discussion. He concluded that the National Assembly was a necessary democratic facade to satisfy the Americans. It was something he could and should manipulate, or in other words a puppet assembly. As an American official later observed, with considerable understatement: "There was undoubtedly slippage in these lessons in democracy as you tried to translate them into an Asian framework."

The State Department's director of the Office of Philippine and Southeast Asian Affairs, Kenneth Young, headed a special Vietnam task force. In the spring, he had been an influential supporter of Diem, his recommendation for delay proving pivotal when Eisenhower and Dulles considered replacing Diem. By the summer, he began to have misgivings. He saw "nothing but drift, indecision and confusion on our side." While the United States had exhibited a tremendous amount of activity, some of it with good results, he concluded: "I am more and more uncertain of the outcome in the long run." By the fall, he came to realize that Diem's successes stemmed largely from the fact he faced no organized political opposition. In spite of this, Diem's forces had failed to pacify outlying regions where Viet Minh sympathy remained strong.

When Young looked to another area of intense and expensive American activity, the field of economic reform, he found little to dissuade him from his somber conclusions. The South Vietnamese economy presented several near intractable problems. By providing monetary aid, the United States hoped to foster economic growth based on American-style capitalism. The common Vietnamese would see that he could better improve his lot by supporting Diem than by supporting the Communists. Congress authorized the aid in dollars, but it was used to finance piaster expenditures in Vietnam, producing a tremendous inflationary impact on the already weak, struggling Vietnamese economy. Rising prices threatened to undo all of the economic aid programs. If rampant inflation caused by increasing the amount of dollar aid to support a large Vietnamese military blocked a peasant's economic progress, he had little reason to back Diem.

The embassy in Saigon received detailed reports on economic progress, or the lack thereof, from Wolf I. Ladejinsky, the land reform adviser to the United States mission. Ladejinsky was one of the rare types of "experts" on Vietnam who took frequent field trips to the hinterland. While officials at the top, including most importantly Dulles, spoke glowingly of Diem's increasing popularity with the people, Ladejinsky sent gloomy reports describing Diem's lack of political, administrative, and military backing at the all-important provincial and village levels. Although Kenneth Young touted him as "a wonderfully perceptive and reliable observer," the State Department largely ignored Ladejinsky's reports.

Ladejinsky met with Diem—the two had become acquainted during Diem's stay in the United States—at the beginning of June 1955. The American explained to Diem the weak link between the national government and the peasant farmers. Appealing to his vanity, Ladejinsky stressed that Diem was the only Vietnamese who could give them a stake in making the new government work. In the long run, Ladejinsky stressed, giving the peasants such a sense of participation in the government would be the most effective weapon against the Viet Minh and the best tool for government stability. Diem listened with unconcealed discomfort, leading Ladejinsky to observe: "As in earlier conversations, Diem continued to give the impression of viewing the various economic, social, and administrative programs discussed as subordinate to the immediate political and military problems with which he was engaged."

Diem was advancing the old argument that no reforms could be undertaken until he tackled the more fundamental problem of security. To outflank Diem's obstinacy, the country team tried a variety of programs to strengthen support for the central government. Typical of these endeavors was Project Action. Project Action recognized that many rural people were apathetic toward Diem's government and retained a strong fear of the Viet Minh. To combat these attitudes, the project tried to teach "the Vietnamese the concepts of the Free World Way." Planners intended that Project Action's concepts be presented in such a way as to be readily understood, accepted, and spread by Vietnamese peasants, but few Americans had any experience in dealing with rural Vietnamese. Furthermore, those who went into the field spoke French, the language of colonialism, and not Vietnamese. Regardless of the merits of the myriad programs the country team launched, most were doomed because of the inexperience and lack of language skills of those charged with implementing them.

The danger of such efforts as Project Action lay in the way officials far from the field, in Saigon and particularly in Washington, perceived them. Officials designed programs to advance American goals and allocated money and manpower for those programs. Over time they received program reports indicating progress toward realizing the goals, but such reports did not describe accurately the reality of a Project Action team visiting a village, giving a lecture or showing a film about the benefits of the "Free World Way," and eventually departing having changed very little, if anything. Officials could feel confident that something was being done, but too often Vietnamese peasants remained as unconnected as ever to the distant central government.

The obstacles confronting Project Action similarly hampered the activities of American military advisers. Because of the Geneva Accords, no shooting was taking place in Vietnam. Instead there was a Geneva-mandated, phased Viet Minh evacuation of South Vietnam, leaving a void in the war-devastated hinterland. South Vietnam lacked civilian administrators—the French had always provided them—who could oversee pacification and reconstruction. Lansdale convinced Diem that the army had the only available executive talent for the chore. However, the army also had a well-deserved reputation for intimidating and stealing from the population. American military advisers therefore tried to instill new attitudes within the army by stressing so-called civic action. Its first test, Operation Liberty, came with the reoccupation of the country's southern tip, the Camau Peninsula. It had been a Viet Minh stronghold during the French war. Departing Communist cadres instructed the villagers not to cooperate with Saigon government forces.

Ably stage-managed by Lansdale, the transfer of control

proved a successful propaganda exercise. The army set to work repairing roads, distributing food, and holding medical clinics. Normal economic life slowly returned. When Lansdale invited Diem himself to visit, the people turned out waving government-provided placards displaying his picture. Such demonstrations boosted Diem's morale and reports reaching Washington went a long way toward convincing the Eisenhower administration that Diem enjoyed true popular support. In the coming months, American advisers happily reported progress as measured by miles of roads improved, tons of rice transported, and numbers of patients treated. However, even here in Camau, where a highly visible pacification effort took place against no active opposition, beneath the facade were ominous signs.

The core Viet Minh bastion was in a mangrove swamp known as the U Minh Forest. Lansdale's intelligence reports, based upon information received from Viet Minh deserters, said that some one hundred soldiers remained behind in the swamp. Although government soldiers "sealed off" the swamp, they did not enter it; the Communist underground government structure and cadre of guerrillas remained intact. Moreover, once the spotlight of attention shifted elsewhere, it would become clear that the effect of civic action upon the population was minimal. It "produced no lasting effect, for the political and social conditions which had long generated support for the Viet Minh remained virtually unchanged." When the Viet Minh, soon to be called the Viet Cong, returned to active combat, the elite U Minh battalion would spearhead attacks from its impenetrable base in the swamp.

The National Army's return to the Camau Peninsula revealed Viet Minh strategy for South Vietnam. The Viet Minh intended to preserve a guerrilla capability in the south. The experience in Camau, where civilians occasionally led government soldiers to hidden Viet Minh arms caches or exposed stay-behind soldiers, repeated itself as the National Army occupied new territory. It was very hard for United States intelligence to measure the extent of the Viet Minh presence. In late summer 1955, Ambassador Reinhardt sent a message to Washington that underscored the lack of concrete intelligence, saying that Viet Minh circumspection regarding the Geneva

Accords "has permitted Viet Minh to operate so covertly and unobstrusively that probably only they themselves can accurately estimate their capabilities." He could not describe satisfactorily the Viet Minh paramilitary and stay-behind regular military organization.

The inability to assess enemy intentions would plague all subsequent American efforts in Vietnam. It contributed to the creation of another enduring characteristic of the American presence, a statistical approach that would tend to quantify progress. It began with yet another of Lansdale's suggestions. He recommended that each province in South Vietnam be categorized according to its receptivity to government control. A national security province was one judged too lawless for effective civil administration. It required troops to impose order before all else, and a military commander would serve as province chief for civil matters. At the opposite end of the spectrum was a civil province where peace reigned under the civilian rule of a province chief.

This rating scheme seemed like a good idea because in theory appropriate mixes of military and civil programs could be targeted to a province depending upon its status. However, there was an inherent possibility for abuse of the system. A military man serving as province chief might become accustomed to the benefits accruing from his position. If he reported too rapid progress, his province would be regraded and he himself replaced by a civilian. On the other hand, since promotion came with accomplishment, an officer with greater ambition might be tempted to claim his province had progressed to civil rule status while in fact this was not so. Finally, under a host of circumstances, as progress reports passed up a chain of command, an air of unreality could easily begin to intrude. Even the well-intentioned knew that optimism and reports of progress enhanced promotion opportunities, which might color judgment and analysis. In the end, when an officer or diplomat in Saigon, at Pacific headquarters in Honolulu, or in Washington examined a map purporting to show which provinces were under government control, he might be gazing at something that bore little resemblance to the true situation on the ground.

In sum, the situation demanded adept administrators who

also had a receptive and responsive ear within their government, which meant that Diem had to create an able, representative government where none previously existed. For the Americans, it meant that 342 men—the number authorized by the Geneva Accords—belonging to the Military Assistance Advisory Group would be spread exceedingly thin.

In spite of all problems, compared with the recent past the situation in Vietnam appeared much improved. The American ambassador in Saigon spoke for many when he told Washington that "the relative power ratio is moving in [a] favorable direction." Better still was information provided by an American senator who visited Diem in mid-August 1955. Senator Mike Mansfield reported that Diem said that for the past year he been forced to deal in negatives such as consolidating his government and rooting out dissidents. "Now he felt Viet Nam was entering a new and constructive phase."

Part 2. ARRESTS IN THE NIGHT

The consulate in Hanoi was closing. There would now be only one American diplomatic presence in Vietnam, the Saigon embassy. Since the United States did not accord the Communist regime in China formal diplomatic recognition, the principle of consistency seemed to demand the same for North Vietnam. Regardless of the advantages of adhering to a principle, there were manifest disadvantages flowing from this decision. It eliminated one avenue for diplomatic discussion. At a minimum, a diplomatic presence in an enemy country provided glimpses into the way that enemy worked. During the time the United States had retained its Hanoi consulate, American officials behaved according to instructions and acted as had Dulles in Geneva by studiously avoiding all contact with the Viet Minh. Still, consular officials did gather some useful intelligence. For example, they learned that the Chinese were helping the Vietnamese build railroads and airports. The American consul reported to Washington that this was the apparent beginning of a Chinese effort to replace the French in Vietnam.

The consul's report described exactly the kind of activity

most administration officials expected and feared. It served as
further confirmation for their monolithic view of communism.
The Chinese were on the move and the Viet Minh were Chinese puppets. Although Washington's analysis might be faulty,
it overlooked the historic animosity between the Chinese and
the Vietnamese; at least it was based on firsthand observation
of something concrete. When the consulate closed in the fall
of 1955, it severed a source of direct information. It was a
self-inflicted wound. In the future, if the United States was to
know its enemy, such knowledge would not come from face-
to-face encounters.

Assessing Viet Minh intent was very much on the mind of
Americans involved in implementing the President's decision
to support Diem. Such an assessment influenced everything
from the type of training a South Vietnamese infantryman received to contingency plans for American military intervention to the number of millions of dollars the United States
spent for assistance to Vietnam. Ambassador Reinhardt tried
his hand at predicting the future and concluded that there
were simply too many "unknown factors." In his opinion,
whether the South Vietnamese military could cope with all-out
insurrection depended upon the Viet Minh's underground
strength and the fighting ability of the South Vietnamese armed
forces. Neither was known.

Following the ambassador's effort, the head of the MAAG,
Iron Mike O'Daniel, provided his estimate of Viet Minh capability. He predicted that from mid-1955 on, the Viet Minh
could conduct raids with units up to battalion size and also
perform terrorist attacks throughout Vietnam. The Viet Minh
could dominate the rough terrain in central Vietnam and hold
trails leading into Vietnam from neighboring Laos, allowing
the rapid increase of their underground forces. O'Daniel believed that they would await the outcome of elections, still
scheduled for the summer of 1956, before exercising these
capabilities. As events turned out, he had done a very good
job at forecasting what the Viet Cong would do.

In Washington, American intelligence agencies reviewed
Reinhardt's and O'Daniel's opinions. The State Department's
Intelligence Branch observed that the Communists had un-
doubtedly maintained hidden arms caches and "in the past,

Vietnamese Communists have displayed ability to transform apparently peaceful civilians into trained guerrillas and suddenly to initiate large-scale guerrilla fighting in supposedly 'pacified' areas." Historically, they had been able to do this because of popular support. The State Department analysts added that although Diem's political standing had risen, the Communist apparatus retained considerable power to control the people in many areas, spread propaganda, form front groups, and infiltrate and subvert the Diem government. Communist "shadow governments" probably controlled many rural villages at night. It was a remarkable piece of intelligence work, particularly given the paucity of hard data with which to work. It too offered an accurate descriptive outline of what was to come.

Finally, there was the National Intelligence Estimate, which combined all other sources to present an intelligence estimate at the highest level, the National Security Council. It predicted that the Communists would concentrate on the political struggle leading up to the July 1956 elections. It further anticipated "that unless they effectively challenge the position of the Diem government," the government would gradually strengthen and stabilize its position. At that point, the Communists "might therefore decide to initiate guerrilla warfare in the south, provided such action was consistent with over-all Bloc policies and provided they estimated that such a course would not provoke Manila Pact counteractions." Unlike the more assertive estimates made at lower levels, this was a much diluted warning full of conditional statements and hedges.

With the sect crisis over and Diem ascendant, Eisenhower no longer kept track of the details of what was happening in Vietnam. Thus he did not know about the very specific problems and threats described in reports delivered to deputies. What he read was the National Intelligence Estimate and it contained nothing to alter his views. He understood that a challenge from the north was likely and knew United States-sponsored programs were in place to meet that challenge. Having set the course, he did not meddle in the actual sailing of the ship.

♦ ♦ ♦

The ever active Edward Lansdale had an idea. In September of 1955 he listened to one of Diem's lengthy monologues about politics. The Vietnamese leader's family, upon whom he had begun to rely more heavily, had organized a political movement to support Diem called the Can Lao party. Diem's Catholic constituency comprised only some 15 percent of the population. Diem's brother, Nhu, sought to broaden support for the president by employing heavy-handed tactics. Lansdale cautioned the Vietnamese leader not to use authoritarian methods to oppose the authoritarian Communists, maintaining that the people should choose. Diem reflected upon this and the next month announced a referendum to determine who would lead South Vietnam. It was an unprecedented step, but a decision made easier by Lansdale's and Diem's choice of opponents. The election, to be held less than three weeks hence, would pit Diem against Bao Dai, who conveniently still lived in France.

Taking no chances and knowing the power of superstition in Vietnam, Lansdale advised that Diem's ballot be printed in red, the Asian color for happiness and good luck. Bao Dai's ballot was green, the color of misfortune. In the subsequent election, Diem received nearly 99 percent of the votes. His overwhelming victory finally removed Emperor Bao Dai from the political scene. Cut off from his people and his source of funds, Bao Dai went on to lead a lonely life of increasing poverty. Having disposed of his rival, three days later Diem proclaimed the birth of the Republic of South Vietnam.

After vanquishing his French-supported rival, Diem turned against the French themselves. In December he formally terminated South Vietnam's economic and financial agreements with France. It was through those agreements that France had hoped to retain influence. Diem next requested France to denounce the Geneva Accords and sever relations with North Vietnam. To irritate the French further, the South Vietnamese Army exchanged French-patterned uniforms for those resembling American ones, adopted the American salute, and staged a ceremonial burning of French-style rank insignias. All of this, symbolic and real, proved too much for the French. Slighted by her former colony, needful of troops for the growing troubles in her North African possessions, France recalled her expeditionary force. By late spring of 1956, the

French abolished their high command for Indochina. Shortly thereafter, her last troops departed, her one-hundred-year experiment in Asian colonial rule over, her onetime crown jewel colony abandoned to its fate.

In a sense what Ho Chi Minh and Vo Nguyen Giap had begun at Dien Bien Phu, Ngo Dinh Diem had completed. He had experienced an incredible first year in office, fraught with peril and full of conflict. He now had an opportunity. The Viet Minh were granting his new republic a breathing spell since they would not undertake aggressive action for at least another year until the passage of the Geneva-mandated election date, leaving him without immediate external threats. Internally, he faced no serious political opposition. His war-weary people might welcome enlightened leadership. The world's greatest power stood ready to pour out riches for his benefit. All of this was not to underestimate the serious problems he confronted, but relative to the prior year's crisis piled atop crisis, calm prevailed and consequently opportunity.

More than most, Edward Lansdale appreciated this situation. Thus, when the relatives of some prominent politicians appeared at his door one morning bringing stories of midnight arrests of their menfolk, the news surprised and dismayed him. He knew armed men calling themselves special police could not circulate without authority from the top. His investigation led him to the conclusion that the arrestees were victims of political reprisal by the Can Lao party. Government officials and army officers were being pressured to join the party. Supposedly membership involved a secret initiation ceremony where new members kissed a picture of Ngo Dinh Diem and swore undying fealty to him. Those who refused received nocturnal visits from the special police.

Lansdale went to Diem with his news. Diem seemed embarrassed and laughed at allegations of some secret initiation. Regarding the arrests, he consulted with his brother Nhu and then said there had been a mistake. Diem ordered the detainees released. He explained that the Can Lao party was indeed attracting new members, but that it was because his brother was building a political group to support the newly elected president of the Republic of Vietnam. The situation was anal-

ogous to the United States where Presidents enjoyed support
from a political party.

Lansdale argued that Vietnamese nationalists supported
Diem because they believed he would give everyone a fair
chance to participate in national political life. If instead a clandestine political organization led by Diem's brother and en-
forced by secret police squashed opposition, it could only
benefit the Communists. Until now, Diem had counted Lansdale as his closest American friend, but this encounter
changed their relationship. There was a marked cooling between the men. Gone were the days of regular, candid meetings. Gone were the days when an American colonel molded
the destiny of an entire country.

This change was not immediately apparent when Lansdale,
following his meeting with Diem, went to the United States
embassy to discuss the Can Lao party with Ambassador Reinhardt. He received his second surprise when Reinhardt told
him that official American policy supported the Can Lao. The
embassy's political staff explained that it was desirable to have
a strong nationalist party supporting Diem and rejected Lansdale's arguments about the evils of the Can Lao. The colonel
responded in typical fashion by going over their heads and
appealing to Washington. He would travel home to explain
what was happening and why it was wrong.

Around this time, others also detected disquieting signs. In
Washington, State Department analysts observed that after
one year Diem's "regime has given the impression of moving
desperately from one crisis to another with little attention to
basic reforms necessary to improve the administrative operations of the government." Still, viewed from a different perspective, concerns about Diem's failings as an administrator
were a sign of real progress. They compared so favorably with
the problems of the past year, when American leaders and
Diem alike had been preoccupied with survival.

Lansdale must have been influenced by Washington's air of
optimism, because when he arrived in the capital in November
to report to the various Southeast Asian foreign policy groups,
he did not talk about the Can Lao after all. Instead, what he
described contributed to the administration's confidence that
it was embarked upon the right course. He explained that the

United States' effort in Vietnam aimed to unite the Diem government and the general population, "to offset any attraction the communist Viet Minh state might have for the people." American training programs sought to end unruly army behavior, typified in the past by a unit sweeping into a "liberated" village and looting it. Under American guidance, the army marched into areas vacated by the Viet Minh and built roads, distributed rice, and dug wells. Lansdale concluded that "when the people saw the Vietnamese Army behave better than the communist army, the populace gave them their loyalty and every possible support." Furthermore, the South Vietnamese Army was also being trained to fight and this too was paying dividends. In their campaign against the Binh Xuyen, they had succeeded in the swamps of the Mekong Delta where the French had failed. Consequently, their morale was soaring and they were becoming positively "cocky." Whatever his original intention to fly to Washington as the bearer of bad tidings, Lansdale's visit reinforced the prevailing optimistic attitude.

The next month the head of the Joint Chiefs of Staff, Admiral Radford, gained a very different sense of what was taking place when he met with Diem in Saigon. Radford found Diem to be a leader who, though lacking military training, held strong views on all military matters ranging from the small to the large. Diem explained his plan for arming villagers in order to oppose the widespread Viet Minh terrorism. Radford interrupted with surprise. Referring to Diem's electoral triumph over Bao Dai, he told the South Vietnamese leader "that the election results seemed to indicate that he had a wide basis of population support," theoretically making it very difficult for the Viet Minh to operate. The admiral noted that a very difficult feature of the French war had been the ability of the guerrillas to disappear into the villages where the French could not separate them from the innocent locals. He wondered how such a thing could be going on today. Diem replied that the people were politically naive and this made them incapable of effectively opposing Viet Minh terrorism. For this reason, the Vietnamese leader wanted to arm a militia group in every village. Radford wondered, but did not ask, how Diem could arm the loyal militia from a population of uncertain loyalties.

Strategically, Diem fixated on the potential for overt aggression from the north. Diem complained that his forces needed more transport to counter the anticipated Viet Minh thrusts. Radford asked why the Viet Minh had cross-country mobility on foot while the South Vietnamese Army did not. Diem explained that the Viet Minh were trained and organized for missions in difficult terrain while his forces were organized to utilize vehicles. Neither Diem nor Radford completely appreciated that, like the French, Diem's forces were becoming roadbound.

Radford was struck by Diem's emphasis on the threat of conventional invasion. So serious was this threat that he wanted to free the armed forces from internal security tasks so they could man defensive positions facing north. Radford believed that the country's lack of internal stability was the real threat and was disappointed and surprised by his conversations with Diem. He had thought things were better than Diem claimed they were. He also felt that the Vietnamese president did not grasp the true nature of his problems and could only do so by listening to American advisers. Radford did not realize that in many ways that was already exactly what Diem was doing. Much later, General Samuel Williams would say that Diem never disputed his military advice. That was true; Diem's focus on invasion from the north reflected Williams's fears.

General O'Daniel had served a long and difficult tour in Vietnam, and now that things seemed to be proceeding smoothly he was coming home. He met with Eisenhower at the end of February 1956 to give the President a final report outlining events since 1945. He explained developments in Vietnam in terms of an international Communist conspiracy. Nonetheless, he concluded that Diem was making steady progress under difficult circumstances. His upbeat report encouraged the President, who later told Secetary of State Dulles that it was "a very refreshing account of conditions in Indochina, of United States prestige there, and the good progress made by Prime Minister Diem."

O'Daniel's words were "refreshing" because they contrasted

with the sobering report CIA director Allen Dulles had given the President the previous month. He had told Eisenhower that Diem was having serious troubles, that the Viet Minh had increased infiltration into South Vietnam, and that Diem had not yet increased his government's base of support. When weighing the contrasting assessments, the President might have reflected that Iron Mike O'Daniel had once been confident about Dien Bien Phu as well, but he was a strong believer in the advantages of positive thinking. Any doubts he may have had decreased when his secretary of state met with Diem in Saigon in mid-March 1956. Dulles informed Eisenhower: "I leave Saigon greatly impressed by the immense improvement which has occurred over the past year."

So the two men who mattered most, John Foster Dulles and Eisenhower, believed the troubles in Vietnam were coming to an end under Diem's admittedly flawed but, in their view, fundamentally sound leadership. Formal National Security Council policy reflected their attitudes. Regarding political considerations, the NSC described the refined objective of American assistance to Vietnam as the development of more effective Vietnamese political organizations and the fostering of "greater allegiance" to the central government. The Can Lao party thereby grew unchecked by the United States, increasingly acting against dissent, filling the prisons with political opponents, driving many nationalists underground, and providing a favorable environment for resurgent communism.

Part 3. 350 MORE

There had been a Lightning Joe and an Iron Mike. It may have seemed that colorful nicknames were a requirement for high-ranking service in Vietnam when the new head of the MAAG arrived. Lieutenant General Samuel T. "Hanging Sam" Williams was the rarest of generals, a man who had risen from the ranks after enlisting as a private in the Texas National Guard. He was a veteran of both world wars and had led a division in Korea. He acquired his nickname because he insisted on stern punishment for a child rapist in a regiment he commanded. It also well suited his character, that a strong disciplinarian intolerant of slackness.

As soon as he arrived in Saigon, he set about shaping up the MAAG by issuing fierce tongue-lashings toward all he deemed sloppy. His roars echoed in the halls as he charged one after another officer with performing "like the Texas militia." Beneath this bluster was a keen student of guerrilla warfare. He had studied guerrilla operations in Korea and had come to certain conclusions. To be successful, guerrillas had to have the support of a portion of the civil population and access to supplies from friendly bases of a sponsoring power. Using a small, well-led force, they tied down large numbers of conventional forces. They terrorized the population into passive inaction. They mobilized popular support by claiming their operations were revolution against colonialism, corruption, and oppression.

Williams believed that the Viet Minh were emulating Korean tactics whereby guerrilla operations pulled large forces into unimportant areas in order to pave the way for a conventional cross-border invasion. Therefore, he recommended that any regular South Vietnamese troops sent on pacification missions against guerrillas quickly complete their task, hand over responsibility to local defense forces, and return to confront potential conventional threats. He said that military operations alone were insufficient for success since there were two objectives: destroying the guerrillas and eliminating their influence on the civil population. A combined political, psychological, economic, administrative, and military effort was needed. Williams concluded that "the major political and psychological mission is to win the active and willing support of the people."

Regarding military operations, Williams emphasized that troops could not sit in garrison and await raids before reacting. Rather, they had to sweep the terrain and screen the population to eliminate guerrillas. The general stressed that the mobility of antiguerrilla forces was more important than firepower. He was not in favor of sending American advisers into the field to accompany South Vietnamese units. If this were to occur, he predicted, the guerrillas would seize upon it to make effective propaganda by telling both civilians and the Vietnamese soldiers that they were American pawns. In addition, he warned that harsh, unjust mass punishment of innocent people for the misdeeds of a few would drive more people into the guerrilla ranks.

He concluded that guerrillas could be destroyed—as had occurred in Korea, Greece, the Philippines, and Iran—if fast, aggressive action was taken. It had to be a coordinated political, economic, psychological, and military effort and had to apply relentless pressure to maintain the initiative. Success required active help from the civilian population. Therefore, the people needed a reason to support the government as opposed to the guerrillas. Finally, the guerrillas could not be defeated until cut off from the source of supply of the sponsoring power.

Williams's comprehensive analysis of guerrilla warfare contained a great deal of wisdom. However, his Korean experience had taught him to believe that the Communists utilized guerrillas to draw defenders away from the crucial national borders. Once the defenders vacated the borders, the real blow would fall. His first experience in Vietnam strengthened his belief. He spent the holiday season at the end of 1955 along the demilitarized zone between North and South Vietnam. Receiving reports of North Vietnamese troops, equipped with Soviet tanks and artillery, massing along the border, he wondered if invasion was imminent and so went to the front. As he inspected the South Vietnamese defenses along the border, he decided that important changes were needed to defeat an invasion. Then and thereafter, this general with many good ideas about how to defeat guerrillas set about preparing for a possible conventional invasion from the north because it appeared the most likely and most dangerous threat.

When the Joint Chiefs of Staff originally accepted that the proposal that the United States should undertake the training of the Vietnamese military, they gave only conditional agreement. Arguably, one of the salient prerequisites had been met: A strong, stable government ran the country. The second condition required a French presence. The JCS had believed the French necessary as a shield to defend against an invasion from the north, and all American planning had assumed the presence of French forces. These plans became invalid following Diem's victory against the sects because after that point the French forces in Vietnam ceased to cooperate

with either the South Vietnamese or the Americans. Angered
by Diem's anti-French attitudes, the French had accelerated
the pace of their withdrawal. Consequently, the MAAG shifted
its training emphasis from pacification and antiguerrilla operations to more conventional instruction so that the Vietnamese
military could step into the vacuum created by the earlier than
expected French departure. Thus, American concerns and
French pique, coupled with General Williams's strategic assessment, conspired to produce in South Vietnam a conventional
army capable of conducting a Korea-style defense against a
conventional invasion from the north.

At its inception, the American training effort had been intended to be a partnership with the French. The French abdi-
cation of any training role increased the American burden.
Moreover, the American effort quickly ran afoul of the Gene-
va-imposed 342-man ceiling limiting the size of the American
military team in Vietnam. During their heyday, the French
had committed nearly 5,000 men to the training job. American military men in Vietnam united in the belief that the
French had performed instructional duties poorly, but it was
asking too much for 342 United States trainers to replace
them and achieve results. Recognizing the extreme difficulty
of accomplishing its mission with so few men, the military began a campaign to increase its presence.

Admiral Radford told Secretary of Defense Wilson that
"military personnel restrictions for MAAG Vietnam have become an increasingly serious handicap to the attainment of
U.S. objectives in Vietnam." Radford complained that the 342-
man limit came from the State Department's interpretation of
the Geneva Accords and that this number had never been
considered adequate by MAAG or the Commander in Chief,
Pacific. Radford endorsed the Pacific Command's view that
the adverse consequences of receiving international criticism
over a technical violation of the manpower ceiling had to be
weighed against the consequences of a second failure in Indochina.

In a strange juxtaposition, the State Department opposed
the Department of Defense. The military had been less than
eager to become involved in Vietnam, but in order to accomplish the mission it needed more men to train the Vietnamese.

The State Department had pushed strongly for an American military presence in Vietnam but wanted to adhere strictly to the Geneva Accords. In January of the new year, 1956, Secretary of State Dulles vetoed Radford's request to raise the MAAG ceiling. He suggested that alternatives be considered, such as greater use of civilians and putting military men in civilian clothes.

A high-level meeting between Defense and State department officials convened at the beginning of February 1956 to explore ways to circumvent the manpower ceiling. Responding to the military claim that the size of MAAG needed to be doubled, a State Department official asked if it was necessary for military men to wear uniforms. A military representative hastened to inform him that this was indeed the case. No one could come up with a compromise until, a week later, the secretary of state saw his way clear to a solution. It was a neat approach that made a virtue out of a problem. One consequence of the French departure was the abandonment of a tremendous amount of American-supplied military equipment. There was no better display of why expensive United States aid to the French had such small impact than the thirty-two acres of vehicles and parts strewn in open fields at a central depot near Saigon or the mountains of ammunition left to the elements in unprotected dumps throughout the country. In total, an estimated $500 million worth of American-supplied equipment lay moldering in the tropical weather. To an American government struggling to reduce the deficit and a military strapped for funds, it was an upsetting spectacle. Dulles saw opportunity and suggested that the "necessity [of] protecting [these] material assets creates extraordinary situation in respect our self-imposed restraints under Geneva Accords." He recommended dispatching additional United States military personnel on a "temporary" basis to recover this equipment. When told of the plan to increase the MAAG in Vietnam, the President responded favorably.

To sell the idea to the International Control Commission, the group charged with overseeing the Geneva Accords, the State Department presented it as a peace-promoting measure. Officials told American allies and the world community that the temporary mission would recover United States equipment and ship it out of the country. Department officials explained that it was a peaceful mission leading to an important net reduction in the amount of armaments in Indochina. Although the two non-Communist members of the Control Commission gave provisional approval, the commission never formally endorsed the mission. Regardless, the first of 350 extra American servicemen went to Vietnam in June 1956.

From the beginning the MAAG welcomed the equipment recovery team as reinforcements for its overextended training effort. Nominally, the new men attended to their overt mission. Yet by the end of 1957, only 7 of the 350 personnel worked full time on equipment recovery. The rest trained the South Vietnamese military. Over time their extended presence led to complaints from the International Control Commission. The American embassy observed in mid-1957: "It [is] increasingly difficult and embarrassing to maintain indefinitely a mission, mainly engaged in training, under guise of a temporary mission solely concerned with recovery and out-shipment [of] equipment." Undaunted, the Eisenhower administration determined that to double the number of advisers in Vietnam was well worth some degree of international opprobrium.

Something else that was increasing was the cost of aid to Diem's government. No sooner were estimates prepared than they became outdated because of unexpected expenses. An example occurred toward the end of 1955. Diem, having accepted another of Lansdale's ideas, proposed the creation of a Self-Defense Corps intended to operate at the village level against infiltration and subversion. Naturally, he wanted the United States to finance it. Initially American planners saw it as an emergency measure only and authorized $6 million for 1956. The Self-Defense Corps expanded yearly—it proved to be the precursor to a bewildering array of irregular armed forces in Vietnam—and became another dependent fixture requiring American money.

During the years 1955–60, Vietnam received more than $2 billion in aid, 80 percent of which went toward providing security for Diem's government. It was the third-ranking non-NATO recipient and the seventh-ranking worldwide. The economic aid mission in Vietnam was the largest anywhere. Only in Saigon was a Military Assistance Advisory Group commanded by a lieutenant general. Whatever occurred would not happen for want of money or lack of top-rank attention.

In February 1956 the State Department's Office of Intelligence Research evaluated the situation in Vietnam. While it believed matters much improved compared with the previous year, new stresses were beginning to appear. Apparently the Communists had stepped up their campaign against the Saigon government. Examining internal security, the office believed that some ten thousand guerrillas were in South Vietnam. They gave the Communists the capability to disrupt and possibly immobilize the regime through a terror campaign featuring assassination, a capability they had not yet chosen to use.

The South Vietnamese military, on the other hand, remained ill prepared. An early spring 1956 Joint Chiefs of Staff assessment described a serious lack of adequate officers and an absence of logistical support. The army could maintain internal security against dissidents but not against the Viet Minh, the report concluded. "In event of organized full-scale guerrilla and subversive activity by 'planted' Viet Minh elements, control of relatively large undeveloped areas of Free Vietnam would likely pass to the Viet Minh." If confronted by a conventional invasion, the army could probably hold for a mere sixty days. In sum, nearly two years after the fall of Dien Bien Phu, although after only one year of American training, the South Vietnamese Army remained incapable of meeting the likely threats.

The Eisenhower administration and the President himself still held to the tenets of the domino theory, although some details had changed. No longer was North Vietnam a Moscow-supported puppet; now it was "Communist China's main satellite regime in the area." But that did not change Vietnam's strategic value. South Vietnam was an exposed free world outpost checking the march of communism through Southeast Asia. Given the South Vietnamese Army's incapacity, United States security demanded the willingness to send the American military to defend Vietnam. Accordingly, the JCS refined a plan specifying how this would take place. The strategy had its roots in a plan originally prepared in mid-1955. At that time the Joint Chiefs had examined military responses to a renewal of fighting in Vietnam. They envisioned two approaches—punishing the aggressors and reconquering North Vietnam—either of which required immediate American naval and air intervention supported by ground forces. The passage of a year had not fundamentally changed their views.

Unlike previous such exercises during the French war, planning assumed that the Chinese would not be involved. The war would begin with a North Vietnamese invasion across the 17th Parallel. The U.S. Air Force and Navy would immediately provide extensive support for the South Vietnamese. Nonetheless, it would not be enough. Within a few days of the outbreak of hostilities, American forces would have to arrive. However, the "fight should be won by Vietnamese backed as much as possible by other Asians." In detail, the plan called for the Vietnamese Army to conduct a fighting retreat from the 17th Parallel to favorable terrain where they would be joined by twenty-five hundred specially trained U.S. Army advisers. Regular American forces, including two Marine Corps regimental combat teams and an Army battalion, would be air- and sea-lifted to Saigon and Cam Ranh Bay. While the study considered both the use and nonuse of nuclear weapons, it doubted there would be many worthwhile targets for nuclear strikes. All in all, here was a detailed military plan representing the most specific blueprint for intervention yet. Most important, it called for ground intervention by United States troops on the Asian mainland. President Eisenhower's signature made the plan official American policy on September 5, 1956. A Communist invasion would not automatically trigger the plan. The President would still have to give final authorization. The Joint Chiefs estimated he would make the decision "within a matter of hours so that forces could begin deployment almost immediately."

Like all contingency plans, it was subject to refinement. The Commander in Chief, Pacific, Admiral Felix Stump, reviewed the plan and found it wanting; he doubted that the South Vietnamese Army could make any effective defense. It had no experience fighting at higher than the battalion level and would require American advisers at the company level and up. He felt that it was too optimistic to expect SEATO nations to do any more than provide an equivalent of one American division. Stump also doubted the wisdom of overly relying upon United States naval and air support; their effectiveness fighting guerrillas in Vietnam's rough terrain would be limited. Similarly, ground operations would be hampered by the inability to use heavy weapons and equipment, including nuclear artillery units. Instead, Stump recommended that planning consider an American amphibious invasion north of the 17th Parallel into North Vietnam to cut the enemy's lines of communication. It was an idea American strategists would turn to again and again in response to battlefield difficulties in the coming decade.

Since Stump's plan called for many more ground troops than did the JCS plan, he considered its domestic political implications. He said he thought Congress would resist sending Army troops to Vietnam but they would permit the dispatch of Marine forces. In conclusion, Stump reiterated that without American ground forces, the United States could not accomplish its stated objectives. Furthermore, he recommended against an incremental buildup, noting: "If US ground forces are committed to the defense of Vietnam they must be in numbers sufficient to ensure the early defeat of the Viet Minh."

The problem with these plans was that they required a scarce commodity, troops. United States strategy, embodied in the New Look, had been based upon nuclear deterrence. In order to fight smaller wars, official policy called for the creation of a highly mobile force with atomic capability but not dependent upon use of atomic weapons. In reviewing the latest defense plan for Vietnam, analysts questioned whether enough resources had been allocated to create this mobile force. To answer this question, they recommended that the Department of Defense make a special presentation of American capabilities for fighting a limited war. For planning purposes Vietnam served as a test case.

Radford presented to the National Security Council the military view regarding its ability to deal with local aggression in Vietnam. Responding to Stump's earlier criticism and recognizing the global manpower shortage, this plan required the Vietnamese to do the brunt of the fighting while American forces would provide security for key bases. Importantly, in contrast with French operations, the defense would be carried out "in the presence of a friendly population." Since the local population would support the American presence, there would not be a need to commit so many troops for static, rear-area defense. It had been that commitment to guard duty that had so restricted the French effort. Radford concluded that the military could fulfill the mission without seriously disrupting security elsewhere and "with good prospects of success." These conclusions delighted Secretary of State Dulles. He elaborated on them by listing the international assistance through SEATO the United States could expect: contingents of Thai, Filipino, Australian, New Zealand, and Pakistani armed forces. He was more doubtful about help from the French and British.

Following Radford's presentation, the President asked about contingency planning with Diem. Radford replied that none had been done so far and that the Vietnamese seriously doubted whether the United States would send combat troops to Vietnam. Apparently many Vietnamese officials, including Diem, feared the Americans would not intervene. Instead the United States would take the attitude that the conflict was a civil war. The admiral hastened to say that "such a notion had never even occurred to him." Radford recommended that American officers visit the potential battlefields in Vietnam. Eisenhower asked if General Williams could not arrange for this to be done. The difficulty, Radford answered, was that such visits could not be kept secret. Eisenhower replied that that was for the good since it gave some additional evidence of the strength of the United States' concerns regarding Vietnam. Radford agreed, but added that the Geneva Accords prevented sending in additional manpower. The President joked, "Take out an orderly temporarily and put a colonel in his place." When NSC members began to seriously discuss this, Eisenhower had to say he was being facetious, but that he felt it important to demonstrate discreetly American resolve in Southeast Asia.

In his final review of the military aspects of the plan, Eisenhower said he doubted the Viet Minh would attack across the 17th Parallel. Rather, if they invaded, he expected a flanking movement through Laos. With this statement, Eisenhower showed that he retained his keen strategic sense. An aide inquired whether the President wanted a formal Record of Action authorizing joint defense planning with the Vietnamese. Here the President balked, preferring "a series of little things." He wanted to avoid making commitments that the United States could not carry out. Eisenhower's hesitation revealed a certain inconsistency. He participated in and endorsed contingency planning for American intervention, but his instinctive aversion to a military ground commitment in Asia led him to authorize "little things" instead of giving final approval.

Eisenhower asked Dulles to what extent the Administration could intervene under the SEATO Treaty without congressional authorization. Dulles replied that it could be done without Congress, but strongly recommended that Congress be consulted if it were in session. Eisenhower agreed. He felt that the SEATO arrangements gave the military leeway to plan, but that "we must carefully guard against the spread of any idea that we are sitting down to plan a war with our friends in Vietnam."

In Saigon, General Williams received a copy of the plan and gave his critique. He enthusiastically concurred with the concept that the fight should be won by Vietnamese backed by other Asians. However, he believed it unrealistic. Given current forces, the Viet Minh would outnumber the South Vietnamese by two to one. Regardless of SEATO, in the event of war he doubted that large-scale Asiatic support from other Asian nations would be forthcoming. Tactically, like Eisenhower, Williams questioned the effectiveness of holding a line along the 17th Parallel since the Viet Minh would outflank this position by debouching through Laos. The limited commitment of United States ground forces did not alter this. The plan also entertained the possibility of conquering the north but called for only one American division; while Williams felt that six to eight divisions was much more realistic. Williams then turned to an important issue he believed strategists in Washington had overlooked. Vietnam was xenophobic, and intervention by "Western colonialists" would weaken southern fighting spirit while inflating northern morale. It would, according to Williams, let Ho Chi Minh "again claim to be fighting to drive out the foreigners and Diem will be called the 'puppet' of the West."

Williams's critique was poorly received by Radford. He had been proud of his presentation. He had talked it over with retired General O'Daniel, the officer he considered to have the greatest expertise on the subject, and Iron Mike had endorsed it. Admittedly, Army Chief of Staff Maxwell Taylor had also found fault, but Radford had little use for Taylor anyway. He spoke scathingly of Taylor's assessment, but he saved his most barbed criticism for Williams, declaring that "if this really represents his considered thinking on the military aspects of this area, I have grave doubts as to his ability and as to his being a proper representative in this important area." Again, Washington and the man in the field seriously disagreed about fundamental strategy.

But the controversy and indeed the detailed plan for military intervention appeared to be moot in the summer of 1956. The National Intelligence Estimate, issued in mid-July, looked at events for the coming year and gave the most optimistic assessment yet. It doubted the Viet Minh would invade or resort to large-scale guerrilla warfare, predicting that in the south the trend toward political stability and popular support for Diem would continue. As the army was released from internal security missions and began "proper," conventional training, it too would improve.

General O'Daniel confirmed this estimate. Following his retirement he had become chairman of the American Friends of Vietnam. Retaining a deep interest in the country, he toured Vietnam for three weeks beginning in mid-August. Upon his return he reported to the State Department that in his view "Free Viet-Nam was now entirely pacified and secure."

In the White House, President Eisenhower rested easy in the belief that the United States had saved a country from communism.

CHAPTER XI

▼▼▼▼▼▼▼▼▼

DRIFTING WITH DIEM

Today the interests of the United States and of the free world, as well as the aspirations of the Vietnamese people, repose to a perilous degree in the person of President Ngo Dinh Diem.

—VIETNAM EVALUATION REPORT, 1959

Part 1. THE FRIENDS OF VIETNAM

In the mid-1950s, many Americans in Vietnam felt a sense of mission. They were in the midst of a new nation's birth. They were of the nation that had won World War II and believed that they represented a system of government without peer. It was a time when foreign service—whether in the military, State Department, or CIA—was prestigious. To serve the United States overseas was the dream of many. They were eager to export their form of government to Vietnam.

Once in Vietnam, the country itself exerted a powerful charm. An officer with the CIA recalls the environment:

There was that sense of a young country, which was very inspiring. . . . There was a very graceful, traditional culture, an enormously pleasant way of life. Saigon was an elegant city. The beautiful tropical foliage, the flamboyant trees, the cabarets, the lovely slim women in those gorgeous ao dais. The whole thing was just elegant and romantic as hell.

For many advisers it was a dream assignment, so alluring the entire country could have been staffed by volunteers. The advisers were the good guys, participating in a race against time. They had to build a strong military before it met the inevitable challenge from the bad guys to the north. Often they fell in love not only with the country but with their Vietnamese unit and their jobs. At tour's end many did not want to leave. As one tried to explain, life in Vietnam was like living in a full-color movie; return to the States was like living in black and white. So, by and large, Vietnam in the mid-1950s attracted dedicated, idealistic men with a sense of mission who liked a life of adventure in an exotic land. A French journalist described how they seemed to "very sincerely believe that in transplanting their institutions, they will immunize South Vietnam against Communism."

The commander of the Military Assistance Advisory Group in particular believed that exposing the Vietnamese to American methods would resolve many of the South Vietnamese Army's problems. Beginning in mid-decade, the MAAG had emphasized laying a sound basis for the future through a military school system. Vietnamese officers and specialists attended schools both in Vietnam and in the United States. Before they could study tactics, they had to learn the language, so much of the training involved language instruction as thousands of Vietnamese studied English. Their efforts helped bridge the language barrier. There was no reciprocal effort on the part of the Americans. Fewer than a dozen military men in the MAAG possessed any Vietnamese language facility. The U.S. Army did not have a Vietnamese language school, which made training difficult. One American instructor tried to teach some Vietnamese recruits the simple drill command "About face!" The order puzzled his interpreter who nonetheless passed it on, and a recruit left the ranks and went over to a pail of water to wash his face. The American tried two more times with the same results. After the third attempt the recruit rebelled, saying, "There was nothing wrong with his face, that it was clean because he had washed it three times." While such miscommunication was trivial, it underscored the frequent mutual lack of comprehension that plagued training efforts.

Even when language was not an obstacle, cultural differences, baffling to most advisers, arose. Another adviser observing a South Vietnamese mortar practice, saw vendors circulating through the class selling soup while the commanding officer was dressed in nonregulation style. The scene affronted the American who questioned the officer at day's end. The Vietnamese officer had attended mortar instruction in the United States, and the adviser asked him how it compared with what had just taken place; the Vietnamese officer answered it had been "much better" in the States. When pressed as to why, he replied, "Well, sir, that was Fort Benning and this is Vietnam." These types of incidents easily led to feelings of contempt toward the Vietnamese. Many grew to think of them as primitive. The U.S. Army recognized this tendency and issued an order banning reference to the Vietnamese as "the natives," but it was easier to issue orders than to change attitudes.

The heart of the United States training program was the adviser system. The adviser's tour of duty was one year, the length of time the Department of the Army deemed reasonable for a man to be away from his family in an unhealthy, distant land. Those fortunate enough to be stationed in Saigon experienced an easy life. Their duties entailed mostly paperwork. At the end of the day they returned to comfortable quarters, ate in a common mess, and could spend the evening on the town. The advisers stationed away from the capital had a slightly less pleasant life-style. But they too had their vehicles complete with Vietnamese drivers, as well as hired orderlies, cooks, and servants, and the conveniences and pleasures available to all Westerners.

Professionally, most of their work sought to persuade the South Vietnamese to adopt American military procedures. Their success depended upon their skills and on the willingness of their counterparts to accept their ideas. In an army where many did not obey their superiors, it was all too easy for the Vietnamese to ignore advisers. The short tour of duty frequently contributed to ineffectiveness. If he so chose, a Vietnamese officer could outwait his American counterpart.

He knew the American did not know the language, could not be everywhere all the time, and would be gone within a year. Since the adviser relationship had to be recast each year, there was a natural tendency toward redundancy, with a new adviser thinking he had to start with the basics. That caused even dedicated South Vietnamese officers to feel like they had heard it all before. Too often, what a South Vietnamese learned was how to manage his adviser.

There was one other pitfall in the adviser system. The adviser had to worry that should he report problems or failures, it would reflect adversely upon himself. At a Senior Advisers' Conference in late 1959, a participant was "shocked to hear some advisers reporting on a world I had never seen." The optimistic tone contrasted with his own experience. When his report came up, General Williams reacted angrily: "And his reason, I feel, was that since he had been there from the very beginning he felt any criticism was a failure on his part. . . . People were scared to death of General Williams. . . . People were afraid to speak." From the earliest, candor proved dangerous. From the beginning, perceptions of progress were very much a matter of perspective.

◆ ◆ ◆

In addition to actual face-to-face instruction, a large part of the MAAG task was to organize the Vietnamese military in an appropriate way to confront likely threats. The new nation had an embryonic air force of limited capability. Its small navy could undertake river patrols and minor coastal operations. The army was the key. General Williams believed, as had O'Daniel before him, that one major French blunder had been scattering forces in small units. The Viet Minh, on the other hand, fielded division-size units. To compete, the South Vietnamese needed units of equal size, so Williams organized their army into divisions. The MAAG devised a training cycle for these divisions, that once completed, would enable them to confront Communist divisions from the north.

Williams considered pacification duties and the like as distractions from this training cycle and its attendant preparation for defense against invasion. For similar reasons, he opposed certain organizational steps undertaken by his predecessors. At one time the so-called light divisions had been a promising idea underwritten by great amounts of American money. Designed for internal security duties, these units lacked artillery and logistical capacity for extended combat against regular enemy formations. Williams wanted to upgrade both the light divisions and similar territorial formations into regular combat units.

President Diem heartily concurred. He equated larger, more heavily armed units with power and security. Yet before authorizing the new organization, Williams insisted on extensive studies to determine optimum size and structure. So slowly did those studies proceed that it was not until 1959 that actual reorganization began. In Vietnam, the region deemed to have the highest priority of any American advisory effort, three years passed from the time Williams decided reorganization was necessary until it commenced. For this delay military men had no one to blame but themselves. In large part indecision stemmed from the dual nature of what they expected the South Vietnamese Army to accomplish. It had to counter insurgents, an antiguerrilla style of war, and defend against conventional invasion. Moreover, as new American officers arrived in Vietnam, thinking evolved and perceptions of threats changed. Consequently, thought about the optimum structure of the Vietnamese Army kept reversing.

General Williams considered the desired end result of the American training effort to be a unit capable of accomplishing both conventional and antiguerrilla missions. The South Vietnamese division would have firepower superior to its North Vietnamese counterpart while maintaining, he claimed, "the same foot mobility" as a guerrilla unit. His assertion was a bit disingenuous, as the new South Vietnamese units trained according to American doctrine that stressed reliance upon artillery support. While its soldiers could march through jungle and swamp, the artillery could not. Experience would show South Vietnamese officers reluctant to move beyond range of their artillery. Regardless of its theoretical mobility, this reluctance tethered the new South Vietnamese Army to its artillery, rendering it just as road-bound as had been the French.

♦ ♦ ♦

In 1951 a thirty-four-year-old congressman from Boston's Eleventh Congressional District toured Vietnam. He dined with colonial authorities and visited combat zones where Foreign Legionnaires fought the Viet Minh. Like all Americans who came into contact with the French Union fighting men, he admired their valor; but unlike many he was not swayed by the standard tour showcasing white men assisting devoted natives to resist communism. Congressman John F. Kennedy wrote in his trip report: "We have allied ourselves to the desperate effort of a French regime to hang onto the remnants of an empire. There is no broad, general support of the native Vietnam government [by] the people of that area." Yet this insight seemed to wane over the years. During congressional discussion about intervention, he endorsed the Eisenhower administration's policy. He spoke favorably of "united action," fully recognizing that it might require some commitment of American manpower. For him, Diem's government "is our offspring—we cannot abandon it."

Given his strong interest in Vietnam, it was natural that Kennedy attended the gathering of a prestigious, powerful group in Washington on the first day of June 1956. They had no political affiliation, drew members belonging to both parties, and called themselves simply the American Friends of Vietnam. Retired General O'Daniel was chairman. Following dinner, they pushed their chairs back from the table and listened to a speech by the now senator from Massachusetts. Kennedy described Vietnam as "the cornerstone of the Free World in Southeast Asia," a place where the "fundamental tenets" of United States foreign policy rested. It represented "a proving ground of democracy in Asia" and a "test of American responsibility and determination." He concluded that any new outbreak of trouble in Vietnam inevitably would involve American security.

Following Kennedy came the administration's assistant secretary of state for Far Eastern affairs, who reviewed the government's goals and accomplishments. First and foremost, American efforts sought to sustain South Vietnam's internal security forces. Toward this end, the United States devoted eight out of every ten aid dollars to security, a priority that accorded with President Diem's perceptions of what his country most needed. Unable to attend, Diem sent a letter explaining that South Vietnam had "arrived at a critical

point in our national life." Indispensable to a peaceful outcome, he explained, was support for the army. He concluded: "Economic aid can be only effective once security
is restored."

The American Friends of Vietnam represented bipartisan
politics in action: citizens and politicians working in harness
with the Eisenhower administration to accomplish what all regarded as a crucial job. Many of its members had participated
in Southeast Asian program development and policy implementation since before the French war. Careful reflection
might have revealed an eerie parallel between Diem's message
and the French approach to military victory first, reform later.
If anyone thought of this they did not speak up. A wave of
optimism washed through the White House and the bureaucracy, encountering and reinforcing a similar wave
spreading from Congress and the American Friends of Vietnam. If danger lurked in the eddies, no one realized it.

Part 2. VISITOR FROM SAIGON

The time for the Geneva-mandated, Vietnam-wide election
came and passed. The United States' efforts to thwart it succeeded, and there was no election. This was a cruel blow to
those Communists who had remained in the south in the expectation that soon Vietnam would be one country. Northern
Communists faced the daunting task of building a socialist
state in North Vietnam. It required most of their attention, so
northern leaders decided it should precede efforts to reunify
Vietnam. In the meantime, southerners could continue to lay
the foundation for a future armed uprising against Diem. Not
only did the elections fail to take place, but something else
American strategists had greatly feared did not occur. Once it
became apparent that there would be no election, the dreaded
Communist response, invasion, did not happen.

The ensuing lull enabled Ngo Dinh Diem to return to the
United States for the first time since his self-imposed exile
from Vietnam. Five years earlier he had led a retiring life in
East Coast Maryknoll seminaries. Now, flying aboard a plane
personally provided by President Eisenhower, he returned as
the savior of Southeast Asia.

The Eisenhower administration had long ago decided to accept the Vietnamese leader, warts and all. Two of his most noticeable flaws, from the American viewpoint, were his unwillingness to broaden his government's base and his tendency to resist American-conceived policies. Since the time of Diem's success against the sects, Secretary of State Dulles rationalized American support for an autocrat by saying that one-man rule was customary in Asia. Moreover, in contrast with the chaotic situation prevailing in ex-colonial areas in other parts of Asia and Africa, or with the corrupt governments running Latin America, Diem's rule shone bright. He remained untarnished by the mischief of his friends and family because he himself was incorruptible. Dulles similarly endorsed Diem's independent streak, saying that if he were an American puppet he could not succeed in rallying national support. South Vietnam's progress seemed to vindicate the secretary of state's judgment. A National Security Council report in mid-March 1957 said quite simply that United States policy was working. In fact, it was working so well that no policy review was even required.

Under Diem's leadership South Vietnam had become a well-established sovereign state recognized internationally by numerous non-Communist nations. It had at least the form of a representative government complete with a constitution and elected National Assembly. Diem himself was pledged to extensive land reform and improving public health and education; and he commanded an apparently modern army that, combined with police and rural security forces, controlled the country.

However, the same forces that, in the eyes of the Eisenhower administration, were imposing desirable internal security looked different to an analyst writing in *Foreign Affairs* at the beginning of 1957: "South Vietnam is today a quasi-police state characterized by aribitrary arrests and imprisonment, strict censorship of the press and the absence of an effective political opposition."

The United States embassy in Saigon did not describe things quite so baldly, but its assessment did not fundamentally disagree. It reported that while Diem was an undisputed, respected leader, he did not enjoy nationwide popularity.

Moreover, because he considered himself and his country imperiled, he focused on centralization of power and internal security, which emphasis made him ever more intolerant of dissent and reliant upon his small circle of loyal advisers and family. Diem had never understood national economics, which was unfortunate because, as the embassy assessment concluded, the ultimate strength of his regime depended upon its ability to better the lot of his people. Ambassador Reinhardt had been promoting this idea, and at last the Vietnamese president seemed to understand, leading the American ambassador to declare: "He has repeatedly stated in [the] past year that north-south contest [is] moving from phase of military propaganda to one of economic competition."

This news was both good and bad. It was a sign of progress that economic concerns had begun to replace military ones, but according to an evaluation of economic progress undertaken for the National Security Council, there remained the persistent problem of the inflationary impact of American monetary aid. Added to it was the realization that South Vietnam would, for the indefinite future, devote far too much of its struggling economy to pay its military bills. American economic aid policy had been based on the "showcase concept," which held that a strong, stable, and constitutional government coupled with a growing economy would demonstrate to all Vietnamese the palpable advantages of a close association with the free world. Unfortunately, American economic experts concluded that the showcase concept was not working, explaining that South Vietnam would be able neither to produce nor in the foreseeable future to pay for "the military hardware which the two countries consider it in the mutual interest" for Vietnam to possess. The United States would have to continue to pump aid into the country, thus creating a state of dependency that in the long run would be counterproductive. If South Vietnamese leaders always had to look to Washington for handouts, they would fail to develop either national self-sufficiency or personal ability to make decisions.

Therefore, the economists explained, American policy needed a major readjustment. They submitted that there were only two ways to do it, reduction of South Vietnam's military budget, and/or higher taxes. Regarding the former, analysts explored every possibility and concluded that South Vietnam's present level of force could not be reduced without jeopardizing military security. It was equally difficult to see how substantial revenues could be extracted from South Vietnam's infant economy. Quite simply, the economists described a conundrum: an entrenched problem of economic dependency that belied the showcase concept, and one for which they had no solution.

The economists could clearly see problems caused by President Diem's ignorance of economic matters. They were less insightful about certain contributions to the problem made by General Williams and the MAAG. About one half of the United States' nonmilitary aid to South Vietnam underwrote one of Diem's cherished projects, the construction of a secondary road system connecting the remote Central Highlands with the coast. The Central Highlands had long been dominated by the Viet Minh. Diem hoped that a road system would spur economic development, in turn attracting the people away from communism, but expected that, at a minimum, it would provide access for his military to root out Viet Minh remnants. It was an expensive plan of dubious merit, yet Williams enthusiastically supported it because it created roads that could carry American forces called for by military contingency plans, if and when they were needed. Aid money also went to improve Tan Son Nhut airfield outside Saigon, enabling the field to accommodate jet aircraft, something both the fledgling South Vietnamese Air Force and the civilian air service lacked, but something very useful to United States contingency plans calling for immediate air intervention by American jets if North Vietnam invaded. Finally, at General Williams's insistence, a twenty-mile section of highway linking the capital and Bien-hoa—the future site of an immense American military logistical complex—received more American economic aid than the total spent on community development, social welfare, health, and education in the years 1954–61.

Most of the details of South Vietnam's economic problems were not passed up the Eisenhower administration's chain of command. The President had defined the mission, expected difficulties, but was interested in results. What he and his National Security Council learned through mid-1957 was that substantial progress was being made. Eisenhower had much larger problems to address than the wisdom of road construction plans in the Central Highlands. One of the President's main problems was, however, linked to the construction activities taking place in Vietnam. The United States too faced budgetary difficulties as defense and foreign aid consumed a tremendous amount of money; and, adhering to the Republican ideal of a balanced budget, Eisenhower sought to reduce the deficit. As one of the principal recipients of foreign aid, South Vietnam was one place the administration considered cutting costs for 1958. Diem learned of this and it greatly alarmed him. It was a catalyst in moving him to do something he did not enjoy: to undertake a journey, not to the distant Camau Peninsula or a remote market town in the Highlands but even farther, to Washington to meet the American President.

He flew to the United States in May 1957. In preparation for his visit, President Eisenhower had done some studying, reading among other things a list of the issues the Vietnamese leader was likely to raise. Foremost on the list was internal security and stability. The recommended response was for Eisenhower to agree that it remained "a serious problem" requiring "extreme vigilance." Eisenhower intended to tell Diem that the United States would "exchange information on this problem" with both the South Vietnamese government and SEATO countries and then strive to develop effective countermeasures.

When the two leaders met, internal security proved indeed to be Diem's major concern. At their first formal session, Eisenhower invited him to outline his principal problems. Diem began graciously by thanking the United States for its support, saying his country would not have been able to resist pressure from the north without it. He explained that the danger was not over and that Communist leaders had anticipated South Vietnam's collapse in the year following the Geneva Conference. Since that had not occurred, they stood ready to invade with the four-hundred-thousand-man North Vietnamese Army. To oppose them, Diem wanted to increase the size of

his own army and pleaded for the United States to maintain
its current level of support.

Eisenhower reminded him that SEATO protected his land,
but Diem replied that he had carefully considered this issue
and that while SEATO constituted a good deterrent, he seriously doubted that any significant numbers of troops would
arrive to help defend South Vietnam. Diem also showed that
he had done some studying of his own. He appreciated that
nuclear weapons were a key element in United States military
strategy and told Eisenhower that tactical nuclear weapons
would be of little help for the defense of Vietnam, since the
nature of the terrain and the dispersed tactics of the enemy
mitigated against their effectiveness. Consequently, it came
down to a question of ground forces. President Diem then
took his message to Capitol Hill. Speaking before Congress, he
again thanked the United States for its generous and unselfish
assistance and pledged to continue to fight communism. Then
he went to New York City, where Mayor Robert Wagner predicted that history would judge him one of the century's great
leaders. Almost everywhere he went the reaction was the
same. Congress and the national press responded warmly to
his personality and his message. *The Saturday Evening Post*
praised him as "the mandarin in a sharkskin suit who's upset-
ting the Reds' timetable." *The New York Times* described him as
"an Asian liberator . . . devoted to his country and to his God."
In sum, Ngo Dinh Diem's visit was a huge success, marking
the high-water point of his relationship with the United States.

Following their discussions, Eisenhower hosted a dinner for
President Diem. While such occasions frequently were all style
and form, the brief speech and formal toast given by the
American President were sincere, encapsulating Eisenhower's
true feelings. Like most of those who had met the Vietnamese
leader, Eisenhower was impressed by Diem's integrity. In his
speech he referred to Diem's ability to resist overwhelming
Communist forces and attributed it to his understanding of
"how much moral values and the concept of human dignity
could count for in the minds of men." Because of Diem's leadership, South Vietnam had become an international symbol of
the ability of a small country to resist with courage Communist
imperialism. President Eisenhower concluded with a toast to

President Diem, the Vietnamese people, and "the great and lasting friendship between our two countries."

Officials in Washington were always at least one beat behind their subordinates in the field. Even as they publicly lauded Diem, the American country team in Vietnam, led by the new United States ambassador, Elbridge Durbrow, was developing profound doubts about the future. Then a stunning act of violence in Saigon focused thinking on a new threat. Five months after Diem's triumphal American tour, a series of dynamite explosions heralded a new phase in the competition for Southeast Asia. A bomb detonated in an American barracks in Saigon; ten minutes later, another destroyed an army bus; later in the day a third bomb exploded at the United States Information Services library. The day's terrorist actions wounded thirteen American soldiers. A new Communist resistance movement had proclaimed its opposition to the American presence in Vietnam.

Part 3. THE VIET CONG

The years 1957 and 1958 were very hard on the stay-behind Communist cadres in South Vietnam. Nineteen fifty-four had seemed to mark the end of a long period of sacrifice. The Communists, southerners and northerners alike, had anticipated bloodless final victory in the elections of 1956. The post-Geneva resettlement had moved the majority of the active Viet Minh fighters north. Left behind were some 5,000 to 10,000 trained men. The northern-based Communist leadership intended these "stay-behinds" to serve as a cadre around which the party could rebuild if necessary. In the meantime, the leadership ordered many of them to return to their homes, reenter civilian life, and await further instructions. A select handful received orders to undertake political actions in preparation for the forthcoming nationwide elections but to avoid military activities.

It was a disheartening blow when elections did not take place and instead Diem's government grew stronger. In the north at least, Communists could devote themselves to nation building and enjoy some of the fruits of victory. Such was not the case in the south, where gradually the euphoria of victory gave way to despair. The government of South Vietnam instituted an Anti-Communist Denunciation Campaign that drove the remaining Viet Minh underground. The Diem government decreed an expansive security order by which "individuals considered a danger to the state" could be detained at reeducation centers. Slowly the government located and arrested numerous cadre members in an effort marked by indiscriminate brutality. Hounded mercilessly, the Communist cadre diminished as one after another comrade disappeared into government jails. A veteran Party member since 1936 who experienced French persecution recalled the years 1955 to 1959 as the most difficult of the entire revolution.

The handful of surviving Communists worked to expand their ranks. Since they had freed the country of the hated French, they enjoyed some degree of respect and admiration among the peasants. As Diem's repressive measures increased and his government's disregard for rural people became apparent, the Communists employed the time-tested appeals to nationalism and social justice. They began to refer to the government as the *My-Diem*, or "American Diemists," a term nicely calculated to capture rural xenophobia and dislike of Diem. In addition, they began to intimidate former Viet Minh, through threats and terror, to join the new resistance. By 1956, the Saigon press coined a name for the new resistance to distinguish it from the Viet Minh: A contraction of *Viet Nam Cong-San*, or "Vietnamese Communist," the name was *Viet Cong*. Although the Diem government used *Viet Cong* to refer without distinction to both southern and northern Communists, in the belief that the latter controlled their southern brethren, more accurately it referred to the indigenous Communists in the south, and the label entered common usage.

Compared with the past few years, Americans considered the first half of 1957 to be a year in which peace had finally returned to Vietnam. So apparently secure was the situation in Vietnam that a March 1957 progress report concluded that the South Vietnamese Army had successfully restored internal security. The Viet Cong terrorist bombings in Saigon in the autumn of 1957 gave pause to such optimism. Furthermore, during a single month that fall, the Viet Cong killed or wounded twenty-two village notables or local officials, killed six village chiefs and eleven militiamen, and kidnapped fourteen others.

It was part of a new campaign launched by the Viet Cong without formal authorization from the north. The guerrillas avoided the South Vietnamese Army and instead worked on securing village-level support. Central to the policy was a program of intimidation of local officials and leaders. If they refused to desist from supporting the central government, the Viet Cong kidnapped or killed them to make an example. A party leader explained: "In principle, the Party tried to kill any official who enjoyed the people's sympathy and left the bad officials unharmed in order to . . . sow hatred against the government." The pattern of assassination proved notable to one perceptive observer.

Bernard Fall had served as a combat reporter during the French war. Like so many, something about Vietnam charmed him, drawing him to visit it again and again. A staunch anti-Communist, he also had scant patience for officials who directed affairs from air-conditioned comfort with little knowledge of and less concern for what was happening in the field. Having observed the French failure, he was keenly interested in how the Americans proposed to tackle Vietnam's problems. When he arrived in Saigon, no official he talked to expressed particular concern over Communist activities. However, he found the number of newspaper reports of deaths and assassinations in the rural hinterland striking. Visiting a South Vietnamese military headquarters, he saw that the violence was occurring in the same places the military map marked as having active Communist cells. He realized that the Communists were following the successful pattern of their operations against the French by assassinating village chiefs in rural areas and reached the inescapable conclusion that the Communist insurrection far exceeded official American reports about the extent of the violence in South Vietnam.

In March 1957, a new ambassador, Elbridge Durbrow, had arrived in Vietnam. A career Foreign Service officer, in the 1930s and 1940s he served in the United States embassy in Moscow, an experience that solidified his attitude that communism had to be contained. In Vietnam, Durbrow offered a fresh, and somewhat unwelcome, perspective. To begin with, he and the head of the MAAG, General Samuel Williams, simply could not tolerate one another. Officially the ambassador outranked the general, but Williams did not like it and tried to run the MAAG without regard to the ambassador. In addition, Durbrow, unlike Williams, held expectations for South Vietnamese progress that went well beyond the military. He understood that the Eisenhower administration hoped 1957 would see something more than mere security and survival. A half year's presence in Vietnam dashed Durbrow's expectations, and by year's end he reported to the State Department increasing signs indicating all was not as it should be. When he talked this over with Diem, the Vietnamese leader replied that he himself worried that people in the United States felt he had performed a miracle in the past three years and that now all problems were solved. He asked Durbrow to help enlighten Washington that the Communist threat remained alive. Durbrow recognized that the Viet Cong had increased terrorism, but maintained that Diem would be better off if he paid more attention to nonmilitary issues. To rationalize his impression and Diem's claims, Durbrow had his country team prepare an assessment designed to take the current pulse of the country.

The assessment found discernible problems that, "if disregarded, might lead to a deteriorating situation in Viet Nam within a few years." Diem had concentrated on building up the military to the exclusion of "the economic and social foundations necessary to secure Viet Nam's future independence and strength." His suspicious nature and authoritarian style also hindered progress, and his regime's popular base remained narrow. At the moment, Diem was procrastinating by declining to make fundamental decisions regarding his country's development, and there was a growing lag between the people's expectations and the government's ability to show results. The country team urged strong pressure on Diem to make decisions but recognized that Diem habitually resented such pressure.

The country team evaluation also looked at the state of the South Vietnamese military. It found substantial progress and concurred with earlier reports that Diem's army could maintain internal security, while noting that in the rural west and south certain traditional Viet Minh strongholds continued to show signs of unrest. The peasants basically went along with whomever carried the guns, allowing the Viet Cong to continue operations. Currently, government forces were engaged in large-scale sweeps in the Mekong Delta, which the country team hoped would help to increase Diem's standing and prestige. Durbrow concluded by noting that Williams disagreed with any implication that Diem was failing or that there should be any cuts in his military support. On this the ambassador deferred to the general, maintaining, however, that simultaneous progress could be made on fronts other than military. In the ambassador's view, the most important task was to persuade Diem to make decisions to promote economic and social development. He ended with the lament that the United States had to find ways to make its influence more effective.

Although most members of the country team, including the military attachés from the three armed services and the CIA station chief, agreed upon the major trends that the assessment described, Williams dissented. In heated discussions the general argued against any claim that Diem was heading for trouble. Williams had toured the country with Diem and seen apparent spontaneous popular expressions of support for the Vietnamese president. He did not realize he had been duped. For example, the American consul at Hue reported that the villagers who paraded to ceremonies honoring Diem had no concept of what they were doing. A journalist writing in *The New Republic* said: "Diem holds the fort through the Army and the police force provided by U.S. [money]." He remained in power only because the Communists had not yet decided to evict him.

Except at times of crisis, when President Eisenhower paid attention to even the details of a given policy, the National Security Council provided most of Eisenhower's information about Vietnam. It took time for field assessments to enter NSC reports. Thus, official NSC policy in November of 1957 continued to be based on perceptions of progress. The President and his top advisers learned that "many surface developments in the area seemed to favor the free world," including progress toward a representative government as evidenced by the first ever submission of a national budget "to a constitutionally elected body," the National Assembly; Diem's continued "strong" executive leadership; and "significant improvement" in the Vietnamese armed forces. Regarding the threat to internal security, the South Vietnamese government "has neutralized Communist capabilities for armed resistance in South Vietnam." The only inkling of the rising tide of Viet Cong violence reported to the NSC came in a statement that "dissident and bandit elements" had become active in the Mekong Delta and along the Cambodian border.

The White House was not alone in believing that the situation continued to improve. For every warning of danger from any source in or outside the government, there were at least an equal number of reports describing substantial progress. A highly respected British expert toured Vietnam in 1958 and wrote that after three years of relative calm, it was now possible to travel safely anywhere in the country. He concluded that the army and the security forces had triumphed. So, among many and in the face of decidedly mixed evidence, General Williams stoutly maintained that there was no significant problem within Vietnam. Actually, he believed there was one major problem, but that it was eminently solvable. In his opinion, the State Department and its representative on the scene, Ambassador Durbrow, caused unnecessary difficulties by agitating for Diem to reform his government, which had no effect except to jeopardize the Vietnamese president's confidence in the United States.

By the end of 1957, the great rivalry between the Departments of Defense and State had seen a nearly 180-degree shift in positions. Whereas a Pentagon precondition for assuming the burden of training the South Vietnamese military had been a stable, democratic regime, while the State Department had argued for stability before democracy, the positions now reversed. The result was a growing divergence between the two departments' representatives in Vietnam that occurred simultaneously with the Viet Cong's emergence from hiding.

At the time that General Collins had wanted to remove him, Diem learned a lesson from his mentor, Edward Lansdale, about American bureaucratic turf fights. He was by now an experienced hand at playing off rivalries among American of-

ficials, and understood the discord between Williams and Durbrow and their respective agencies. Diem considered General
Williams a friend who agreed with him about what needed to
be done, but saw in Ambassador Durbrow an enemy who
urged idealistic reforms at a time when heightened Communist pressure made them unrealistic. He knew that Williams
supported the current level of United States aid to South Vietnam, while Durbrow seemed to be looking for ways to cut that
aid. He tried to explain to Durbrow that the Communists were
responding to his army's success by resorting to tactics of desperation. Diem argued that to combat effectively the increasing terrorism, he needed the military budget to remain as it
was. He later told Williams that if he had to find savings, he
would cut from his economic development budget rather than
from military expenditures.

The new year, 1958, brought further signs of deterioration.
South Vietnamese officials, on whom the United States was
almost entirely dependent for intelligence—just as it had at an
earlier time relied upon the French—told the MAAG that the
Viet Cong were improving an extensive trail system along the
Vietnam-Laos border in the west. It would grow to become
the famous Ho Chi Minh Trail. When Durbrow met with
Diem early in February, the Vietnamese president described
in detail stepped-up Viet Cong subversive activity. Durbrow
"expressed surprise at his new view of the situation." He had
thought that the subversive problem was well in hand.

Because the Viet Cong still avoided contact with large South
Vietnamese units and refrained from attacking well-fortified
defenses, the extent of their strength remained largely hidden
from American observers. Recalling his Korean experience,
General Williams believed that the Viet Cong operated according to a plan conceived in Hanoi whereby guerrillas
sought to draw South Vietnamese units into the hinterland.
The general reasoned that if South Vietnamese troops went
chasing the guerrillas in remote areas, they would be playing
into Giap's hand since they would be out of position to defend
against a conventional invasion. Therefore, he still resisted
having the government army combat the insurgency. Moreover, the newly created South Vietnamese divisions needed to
continue their training cycle. Not only did pacification duties

interrupt the cycle, but dispersing the division for guard duty "around bridges and market places" caused them quickly to "go to pot."

By the middle of the year, President Diem told the Americans that he possessed intelligence that international communism planned a campaign to reunify Vietnam. The country team disregarded his claim. Increasingly alarmed, Diem ignored Williams's advice and sent his forces against the guerrillas. Although often slow and ponderous, the army achieved surprising results. In large part this was due to the fact that the Viet Cong fought unaided by their northern comrades. They were weak and poorly equipped and suffered heavy casualties. Official Communist party historians would write that it was "the darkest period," a time when Party membership plummeted by two thirds. Such was the pressure exerted by the Diem government that in one typical province Party membership declined from about 1,000 at the time of the Geneva Accords to 385 in mid-1957 to 6 stalwarts in mid-1959.

In desperation, the surviving Communists in the south took an enormous gamble. In violation of doctrine, and again without authorization from Hanoi, they escalated the struggle from armed propaganda and assassinations to outright company- and battalion-size military activity. That they were able to recruit enough manpower to flesh out these units had much to do with some misguided policies undertaken by Ngo Dinh Diem.

President Diem's father had been a mandarin administrator and Diem had never learned very much about the peasant masses who made up the majority of his country. Rural Vietnam was a collection of self-governing villages. An ancient Vietnamese edict said: "The emperor's rule ends at the village wall." During a century of colonial rule, villagers learned to think of the government as a remote body that collected taxes, demanded unpaid labor, and conscripted young men for the military. Largely through ignorance Diem made a series of decisions that reinforced this lesson. To extend his authority, Diem decreed that a system of appointed leaders replace the custom of village self-government. District and province chiefs named the village leaders. Diem, in turn, appointed the chiefs, most of whom lacked any qualification except loyalty. In 1958, one third of the province chiefs were military officers, but two years later the military component had doubled. In this manner Diem gained the dubious loyalty of numerous officers but at a terrible price. His system stifled local initiative and, worse, transgressed the custom of village autonomy. It provided a powerful recruiting tool for the Viet Cong. Henceforth, the Viet Cong blamed whatever went wrong in a village on the Diem-appointed leader. It proved a most effective argument in turning villagers against Diem.

Some of the evils of this system might have been redressed had Diem successfully implemented meaningful land reform. In spite of much American advice, here too was colossal failure. Over three quarters of South Vietnam's population lived in rural areas. Absentee landlords controlled great holdings, made no investment in seed or fertilizer, and extracted up to half a peasant's annual yield. The Viet Minh had driven off many landlords and given their land to the poor, but when Diem came to power, his government restored property to the landlords and then passed laws limiting the extent of their holdings and regulating the landlord-tenant relationship. Ambassador Durbrow proudly told a Senate hearing in 1959 that it was the "largest land reform program in Asia." Whatever it was, a 1960 census found that less than one fourth of the population of the Mekong Delta, Vietnam's fertile rice basket, owned any land at all. In lieu of ownership was a system of red tape and legalisms ripe for abuse, giving the Communists another unmistakable target for their propaganda arrows.

Diem's catalog of blunders was diverse: abusive, discriminatory policies toward ethnic minorities, particularly Montagnard tribesmen living along the western border among the soon to be important supply trails heading north; Can Lao party excesses that appalled non-Communist nationalists; reliance upon his family and a northern-born, Catholic elite to direct affairs from positions of authority; and an inept Civil Guard. Charged with maintaining internal security, the Civil Guard was torn between the State Department's efforts to make it a police force responsive to civil rule, the MAAG's efforts to make it a military reserve force, and Diem's desires to create a loyal counterweight to the army. Nonetheless, the

Communists were apparently so weak in 1958 and the first half of 1959 that no one expected what would come.

◆ ◆ ◆

In early summer 1958, the National Security Council's planning organ, the Operations Coordinating Board, submitted an updated plan for Vietnam. It was a compromise, a reconciliation between the Departments of State and Defense, which differed over the significance of Diem's authoritarian leadership and his methods of ensuring internal security. The State Department thought Diem "heavy-handed" and that his squashing of dissent "posed dangers," while the Department of Defense considered Diem's actions merely "stern," but justified by Communist pressure. They only agreed upon the continuing need to stop Communist advances in Southeast Asia.

Secretary of State Dulles was well aware of the deteriorating situation, although as always he thought in terms of tactical modifications, not strategic policy changes. He reasoned that if the internal security situation was worsening, then the internal security forces, the Civil Guard, had to be strengthened. Owing to General Williams's insistence, the regular armed forces had changed missions from internal security to resisting invasion from the north, placing the burden of fighting the Viet Cong on the poorly trained and equipped Civil Guard. Diem wanted to place the Civil Guard under military authority so that they would become eligible for MAAG assistance; however, not yet appreciating the seriousness of the Viet Cong challenge, many at the American embassy in Saigon thought this was a subterfuge to increase the size of his standing army. Against this background, Dulles asked that the embassy reconsider.

Edward Lansdale had been reassigned to the Pentagon's Office of Special Operations in 1956. From his position as an adviser on unconventional warfare, Lansdale supported Dulles's position. He compared the militarization of the Civil Guards with the right of Americans to bear arms, observing that this right contributed to the successful founding of America during the Revolutionary War. In a similar manner, he claimed, arming more Vietnamese civilians would be in keeping with the American goal to broaden the base of support for Diem's government.

While the Departments of State and Defense argued about the proper role of the Vietnamese Civil Guard, the erosion of Diem's popular support continued. By 1959, his three-year-old Anti-Communist Denunciation Campaign had expanded and thereby greatly increased dissatisfaction with the Saigon government. Under its mandate, arrests of former Viet Minh—as well as people who never had been Communists—became common. Many families of those who had gone north received the heavy-handed attention of Diem's security forces. New, increasingly harsh laws, such as those that allowed roving military tribunals to conduct on-the-spot trials of "terrorists" or authorized jail sentences for anyone caught in a rebel district, coupled with curfews that hampered fishermen and farmers and compulsory labor for the government, all stoked popular resentment. Although Diem's policy had eliminated much of the Communist cadre, a hard core remained. Moreover, a restive population provided a fertile recruiting ground for the Viet Cong.

In January 1959, the Communist Party Central Committee convened its fifteenth plenum. Many years later Vo Nguyen Giap would say: "Perhaps we should have acted sooner, but our people were tired after a long war, and they might not have responded to a call for yet another armed struggle." By 1959, northern leaders had no choice because their southern cadre was fast disappearing. Therefore, the Central Committee adopted a resolution endorsing the use of force to overthrow the My-Diem regime. Specially trained former guerrillas who had moved north after Geneva began to reinfiltrate South Vietnam. In the Laotian panhandle, a newly created Communist unit, Group 559, began to improve the supply corridor to facilitate movement south. Group 559 reinforced the trail-building efforts that South Vietnamese intelligence had detected the previous year, marking the formal beginning of what would become the Ho Chi Minh Trail. The Diem government was about to confront Communist-inspired "armed struggle." North Vietnam, however, was a backward, poor country unable to arm and equip a large guerrilla force overnight and infiltrators heading south moved no faster than their feet carried them. It would take time for the significance of the Central Committee's decisions to be felt.

The year 1959 brought the continuing MAAG effort to accomplish its training mission to a critical point. Since its inception, it had labored under the Geneva agreement and its manpower ceiling. It had managed to double its strength through the subterfuge of the "temporary" equipment-recovery team, the group ostensibly concerned with shipping out war material left over from the French war. After four years, its "temporary" mandate had worn thin in the eyes of the International Control Commission. In the spring the Commission ordered the team to finish and depart by the end of June. Such a departure would cripple the MAAG just as the Viet Cong were intensifying the struggle. The United States had already done everything it could conceive of to increase the effective size of the MAAG including transferring the personnel slots for forty-four military men who served the American community in Saigon at the post exchange, commissary, and communications office to the embassy roll so that forty-four replacement advisers could enter the country. There was no way to compensate for the loss of the manpower associated with the equipment-recovery team.

Looking for a long-range solution of the problem, one of Dulles's deputies suggested the abandonment of the policy of compliance with the Geneva Accords. He argued it would be worth international censure in order to have a permanent organization unfettered by international scrutiny. Dulles, in one of his last decisions regarding Southeast Asian policy, rejected this idea. He wanted to preserve the facade of compliance. The State Department asserted that at the time of the Geneva agreement there had been some 888 French and American advisers in Vietnam. Substituting permanent advisers for the "temporary" personnel would still keep the total American presence within that limit. The State Department carefully prepared the diplomatic groundwork for this substitution and then broached it to the International Control Commission. Twelve months later, during which time the United States retained its working complement of advisers intact, the commission approved. By that time John Foster Dulles was nearly a year in the grave. For some time his health had been noticeably failing. After a brave effort to work until his health collapsed completely, he died of cancer in May 1959.

About the same time, the Military Assistance Advisory Group began a transformation that radically changed the nature of the United States presence in Vietnam. According to a long-standing practice, American advisers had been prohibited from operational planning or accompanying Vietnamese troops into the field. By the end of March 1959, this restriction had begun to frustrate General Williams enormously. He felt that recent South Vietnamese missions had been failures because of inadequate planning, logistical snarls, lack of aggressiveness, but he had no firsthand information. Arguing to his superior officer that this prevented him from carrying out his mission to train the Vietnamese, Williams requested permission to allow Americans to accompany Vietnamese units on combat operations.

In reply came the following: "It is likely that we can get the necessary U.S. authority for you to have your people participate in operational planning, and perhaps even to accompany units in the field if there is some way we can throw a block at the direct participation which seems to be such a sensitive subject in Washington." Williams assured the Pentagon that he neither desired nor felt it appropriate for advisers to enter combat. At the moment most were stationed at fixed headquarters. He wanted them to join their units during field operations but to stray no further. There they could monitor daily events and provide on-the-spot advice on tactical and logistical matters. The advisers would be able to inform Williams more accurately of the military situation, thereby permitting him, as the top adviser serving Diem, to offer better advice.

While Williams reiterated that he did not want advisers to get involved in firefights, his request overlooked the fact that in a guerrilla war a field headquarters could be the target of enemy attack. If the advisers sortied into the field, some would inevitably become casualties. On May 25, 1959, Williams received the orders he wanted. Henceforth Americans could accompany their units into the field and provide tactical advice as long as they stayed at field headquarters. It was a significant escalation of the American advisory effort. Back in 1954, the French General Ely had pointed out that if the Americans pursued their concept for training Vietnamese, they would "have to accompany units into battle." This would lead, he warned, to the central question whether the United States was prepared to participate in combat operations. Ely's question was about to be answered.

Part 4. TREMORS

Since Diem's triumph over the sects, Vietnam had receded from the forefront of President Eisenhower's awareness. The Soviet invasion of Hungary, Sputnik, test-ban talks, the Berlin blockade, and numerous other events had overshadowed Southeast Asia. In his last years in office, President Eisenhower had two major objectives. In the field of foreign affairs, he sought to create a better atmosphere for disarmament and peace, while domestically, he emphasized reducing federal expenditures and balancing the budget. Eisenhower did not ignore what was taking place in Vietnam, but it was very much a secondary consideration.

When the President did attend to Southeast Asia, his principal source of information continued to be the Operations Coordinating Board progress reports submitted to the National Security Council. Regarding Vietnam, they described Diem's problems in weak, hesitant language laden with qualifications and conditions. For example, in the summer of 1958—at a time when United States intervention in Lebanon and Chinese pressure against Quemoy and Matsu demanded presidential attention—Eisenhower read that Diem's political and economic policies had caused a "certain amount of internal dissatisfaction," hardly the language of crisis. The report continued by suggesting that "should" Diem's behavior worsen, "there may be danger" that "might" lead to problems. The President, beset with difficult and diverse concerns, found nothing unduly alarming in this tepid warning.

So, too, Eisenhower's principal deputies remained optimistic, an attitude nourished by numerous favorable reports emanating from Saigon. At the beginning of 1959, the recently retired head of the United States aid program in Saigon met with State Department officials in Washington. He described "excellent" progress during the past four years and summarized the current situation as "good." Other, lower-ranking

American economists disagreed; they could not see an end to Vietnamese economic dependency. The American land reform specialist, Wolf Ladejinsky, also was pessimistic. Ladejinsky approached his mission with the same zeal Lansdale applied to military problems. Like Lansdale, he loved the country and appreciated Diem's positive characteristics, which only heightened his despair when he reported to the American ambassador conversations he had had with high-ranking Vietnamese officials including the South Vietnamese vice president. They had expressed great concern over Diem's exclusive reliance on military methods to suppress the Communists. When they had tried to persuade Diem of the value of winning over the peasants, he responded the same way he responded to American pressure for reform, saying that military security came first. After listening to Ladejinsky, Durbrow commented that peasant discontent made fertile soil in which the Viet Cong could plant the seeds of insurrection.

Six months after writing a vague warning about a worsening situation, in the first month of 1959 the Operations Coordinating Board submitted a much more alarming Vietnam progress report to the National Security Council. For the first time it announced that the Communists had begun "a carefully planned campaign of violence" against Diem using tactics reminiscent of the war against the French. To make matters worse, the report described growing discontent in the South Vietnamese Army and government over Diem's authoritarian leadership and the suffocating power of his family. One thing had not changed, but this too was bad news: United States influence on Diem remained "greatly limited" owing to Diem's "extreme sensitivity."

At about the same time the OCB issued its report, one newly arrived American intelligence official quickly gained firsthand confirmation of the problems caused by Diem's family. William E. Colby came to Saigon during the beginning of 1959 to serve as the CIA station chief. He found Saigon peaceful and calm, "a gracious colonial city," with the Diem family "operating as a feudal monarchy amid the trappings of a constitutional republic." Acting as a mandarin administrator, Diem forced his ideas of development upon the people. He employed the French-trained bureaucracy to do his bidding, all the while complaining about them. As soon as possible, he intended to replace them with the first Vietnamese graduates in public administration from American universities. As Colby probed deeper, he discovered that people still loyal to the sects or aligned with regional chiefs were filling the vacuum caused by Diem's relentless repression of all opposition. They tended to ignore central direction from Saigon if it interfered with their main motive of lining their own pockets. The diffusion of authority left South Vietnamese wondering who really ran things. The country was full of rumors and conspiracy theories about what took place behind the Presidential Palace's facade. Many believed that Ngo Dinh Nhu, and Nhu's wife—the immaculately lacquered, bejeweled, and exotic Madame Nhu—controlled matters of state through their secret service.

Colby found the CIA's Far East Division populated with gifted professionals. Present were old China hands, men who had fought the Huks in the Philippines, agents who had shared in the failed revolt against Sukarno in Indonesia, and some who had cooperated with the British in the long but eventually successful campaign against the Malaysian Communists. All in all, it was a team with as much Asian experience as any American field organization could muster. In spite of this expertise, the CIA team played a decided second fiddle to the MAAG. In Colby's mind, the military dominated even the ambassador. He believed that two factors accounted for this relationship: The Army and Navy had won the war in the Pacific only fifteen years earlier, and then had managed the Japanese occupation and fought the Korean War; thus, by recent tradition they prevailed in policy discussions. Furthermore, official American policy emphasized the military mission in South Vietnam over the economic and political. Accordingly, the MAAG, led by its irascible boss, General Williams, dominated planning in both Saigon and in Washington. It was another reason that warning signs detected by the CIA and the embassy went unremarked.

On July 8, 1959, the Viet Cong attacked a MAAG billet housing thirteen American advisers at Bien-hoa, about ten miles north of Saigon. Security at Bien-hoa was poor. A two-strand barbed-wire fence surrounded the advisers' quarters with two South Vietnamese Army soldiers standing guard at the front entrance. Each evening at 7:00 P.M., the Americans screened a movie in the mess hall. On the evening of July 8, while the guards watched the movie through the windows, the Viet Cong struck. A six-man team infiltrated into the compound. Three positioned themselves at the mess hall windows and opened fire. In the resultant hail of shots five men died: a Vietnamese mess attendant; a South Vietnamese Army guard; one Viet Cong attacker; and two American advisers. They were the first advisers to die by enemy action in Vietnam.

In the ensuing investigation it emerged that two young women who had occasionally attended the movies were Viet Cong agents. Their reports, coupled with simple observation of the advisers' and guards' routines allowed the raid to take place smoothly. The raid startled the entire MAAG into the realization that the Viet Cong had perhaps initiated a new phase of the struggle for Vietnam and also had ramifications for the bureaucratic rivalry over who gained the ear of Washington decision makers. During the critical years 1957–60, American intelligence groups waged fierce internecine battles to control intelligence activities in Vietnam. The CIA had had no advance warning of the attack, an intelligence failure that tarnished the Agency. Its detractors, rival Army intelligence officers, used the incident to discredit all subsequent Central Intelligence Agency estimates.

Viewed with hindsight, no American intelligence group correctly judged the extent of rural disaffection in Vietnam or correctly estimated the strength of the Viet Cong. The United States judged that the Viet Cong were gaining strength by activating their stay-behind network and through the return of soldiers who had moved north after the Geneva Accords. In fact, the Communists were experiencing great success in rebuilding their armed units by recruiting from the discontented rural population. Because of this ample manpower source, Viet Cong ranks swelled much more quickly than Americans thought possible. At the same time, intelligence overestimated the combat ability of the South Vietnamese military. As important as these matters were, they were merely tactical details in contrast with strategic intelligence, which consistently provided sound information between 1955 and

1960. Since Diem's arrival in Vietnam, the National Intelligence Estimates had predicted that accumulating popular grievances would cause trouble. The estimate of May 26, 1959, stated that the South Vietnamese military would remain incapable of withstanding an invasion from the north and "will not be able to eradicate . . . guerrilla or subversive activity in the foreseeable future." Furthermore, Diem's repressive measures would cause opposition to grow. Such bleak forecasts did nothing to change American policy, largely because President Diem continued skillfully to perform the minimum activities needed to impress his benefactors.

At the end of August 1959, South Vietnam held its first national elections since 1956. The Communists urged their followers to vote for the more leftist candidates. When the CIA and South Vietnamese intelligence learned of this directive, Diem went all out to see that his supporters won. Can Lao party members or their supporters won a total of 121 of the 123 seats in the National Assembly, and the assembly then convicted the 2 successful opposition candidates of electoral fraud and prevented them from taking their seats. Nonetheless, to most officials in Washington the election of 1959 seemed to be another indication of South Vietnam's strong, stable government.

Another reason United States policy did not change as Viet Cong violence increased was the still optimistic reports Washington received from General Williams, who was sufficiently confident that in late 1959 he predicted that by 1961 the South Vietnamese defense budget could be reduced and that American advisers could begin to return home. Even his enemy, Ambassador Durbrow, testified to the Senate in the summer of 1959 that Vietnam's internal security was not in jeopardy.

A year earlier, the Senate had become concerned with the ever increasing cost of foreign aid. Much of this aid was channeled to countries like Vietnam through something called the Mutual Security Act. Its stated objective was to assist recipients "to achieve economic stability and maintain self-government and independence." The Senate had heard tales of inefficiency and waste connected with Mutual Security expenditures. In particular, it had received testimony about adverse effects on developing countries when military aid received too much emphasis as opposed to technical assistance and "self-liquidating economic assistance." A group of senators, including Mike Mansfield and John Kennedy, argued that "overemphasis" on military assistance caused the United States to support regimes lacking broad popular support. The Eisenhower administration recognized this issue as a potentially very hot political potato. Accordingly, the President appointed a high-level group, the Draper Committee, named after the retired general who chaired it, to provide an objective, non-partisan analysis of the American military assistance program. It sought to estimate long-term prospects and to propose needed changes. One subcommittee, led by Dillon Anderson, had the broad mandate to evaluate the progress of the Mutual Security Act in Southeast Asia.

The group charged with visiting Vietnam included two experts who were old adversaries, General J. Lawton Collins and Colonel Edward Lansdale. Typically, the latter fell afoul of his fellow committee members. While most members enjoyed a whirlwind tour of exotic places—spending a mere two days in Vietnam, many members, including the Commander in Chief, Pacific, managed to find time for a sightseeing trip to the famous Cambodian temples at Angkor Wat—Lansdale tried to tap his ubiquitous sources to learn what was really happening. He largely failed, in part because the rupture in his once close relationship with Diem had never healed. He and other committee members listened to a parade of experts and specialists who hustled through all too brief testimony. They received a VIP tour of a showcase resettlement project in the Central Highlands, which worked as it was supposed to, and many, including General Collins, who began the tour skeptical, came away impressed.

Sensitive to Eisenhower's political problems in connection with the projected $12 billion budget deficit, Dillon Anderson explained to Ambassador Durbrow that all aid had to be carefully scrutinized. One way he believed savings could be made was by refusing to finance an increase in the size of the Vietnamese military. Durbrow replied that it would have an adverse psychological impact throughout Southeast Asia given the recent recognition of Communist China by Cambodia,

Viet Cong movements into Laos, and increased subversion inside South Vietnam. Durbrow argued that aid should be maintained at its current level for at least another year in order to whip the Vietnamese Civil Guard, a group increasingly taking on the brunt of combat against the Viet Cong, into shape. Once the Civil Guard became effective, aid could be reduced. Anderson retorted that experience showed that if reductions in aid were put off in 1960, there would be a new set of "valid" reasons for not reducing aid in 1961. Durbrow acknowledged the justice of this observation but "reiterated that we definitely planned to cut military aid as soon as the Civil Guard became a more effective organization."

Collins questioned the American ambassador about the size of the South Vietnamese Army. He believed that it was impossible for the country to become economically self-sufficient with such a large army and wondered if a reappraisal of American strategy in Southeast Asia was in order. As Collins saw matters, in an all-out world war Indochina would not see any significant action; in a brush fire war, well-trained friendly armies would be of some help but planning still called for United States intervention. He doubted the point of spending such vast sums for such limited gains.

The Draper Committee was the last chance during the Eisenhower administration for a major change in Vietnam policy. Of all the committee members who went to Vietnam, only Collins saw this opportunity. Everyone else, including Lansdale, left Vietnam with the impression that there was a need for tinkering at the margins of the ongoing American assistance program but no need for major changes. The Draper Committee reported that "the vitality and effectiveness of the Vietnamese armed forces" was impressive. The committee recognized that Vietnam's military budget dominated the economic sector and distorted economic development, but emphasized the compensating advantages, saying that South Vietnamese Army operations were contributing to development in much the same way that the U.S. Army had contributed to the opening of the American West. It saw the beginning of a most desirable "pioneer spirit." Although it could not escape the conclusion that Vietnam's economy was faring poorly, the committee concluded that a military assistance program was not necessarily an obstacle to a recipient's economic development. All that was needed, the Draper Committee suggested, were a variety of technical and administrative fixes to ameliorate conditions.

In the short run, the Draper Committee's visit to Vietnam focused United States attention on the financial implications of the American commitment to Vietnam to the exclusion of much else. So, in the month following the committee's visit, when Diem reported serious military skirmishes with the Viet Cong, Durbrow largely dismissed them as part of the premier's "usual spring offensive to influence volume of US aid." In addition to blinkering field analysis, the committee unwittingly laid the groundwork for a tremendous expansion of the military assistance program to Vietnam by basically endorsing existing policy. Moreover, among many recommendations made, the committee suggested a series of preparatory steps to be taken just in case the situation required American forces.

The committee's findings had one other significant impact upon what was to come. Senator Mansfield, one of the senators whose probing questions had led to the formation of the Draper Committee in the first place, was keenly interested in reading the sections of the report on Vietnam. Eisenhower was equally interested in keeping them confidential, and a tremendous row ensued. Eisenhower wrote to Mansfield to tell him that he was not withholding the report to prevent disclosure of its findings but rather because sharing it would set a bad precedent. He argued that "under the historic doctrine of the separation of powers," he had the right to withhold information in the national interest—claiming the constitutional right of executive privilege. While the information Eisenhower sought to keep confidential was neither embarrassing to him nor of great importance, his line of reasoning would be shared by future Presidents, who would employ this device for darker motives.

CHAPTER XII

▼▲▼▲▼▲▼▲▼▲

ON THE BRINK

I can't remember one time that President Diem ever did anything of importance concerning the military that I recommended against.

— GENERAL WILLIAMS, 1964

Part 1. DEBACLE AT TAY NINH

For Vietnamese Communists fighting in the south, the months following the January 1959 declaration of armed struggle witnessed gratifying progress and hinted at the possibility of complete success in the near future. There were a succession of national and international meetings that pledged ever firmer support for their cause. In May 1959, the Communist party's Central Committee in North Vietnam "called for a strong North Vietnam as a base for helping the South Vietnamese to overthrow Diem and eject the United States." At a political meeting on January 1, 1960, North Vietnam condemned the United States and established the reunification of Vietnam as a national objective. But it was a national congress in September 1960—a gathering that featured speeches by Ho Chi Minh and Vo Nguyen Giap—that committed North Vietnam to the support of the Viet Cong. At that meeting the

350

Communist leadership took the historic step of establishing a unified front to lead the struggle against My-Diem. The next month, a Moscow conference of Communist parties added its support for the struggle, identifying the United States as the major colonial power. The conference declared that Communists everywhere were obligated to fight colonialism.

In the south, within twelve months of the declaration of armed struggle, the new National Liberation Front quadrupled its strength. Viet Cong units began to challenge Diem's army in open combat. They demonstrated the ability to seize and hold provincial capitals for short periods of time. The Communists formally activated the depleted stay-behind net. Many had been fighting a battle for survival already, and many had fallen to Diem's Anti-Communist Denunciation Campaign. They now received reinforcements from the ranks of those men and women who had migrated north in 1954. In addition to the infusions of manpower, substantial amounts of war material began to be shipped by land and sea across South Vietnam's porous borders. All of this greatly increased the size and effectiveness of their guerrilla forces and led to an increase in assassinations, terrorist strikes, and kidnappings.

American officials, military and diplomatic alike, remained largely ignorant of the sea change in North Vietnamese strategy. They did see the tremendous upsurge in Viet Cong activity but perversely attributed it to the success of the South Vietnamese government. This view held that the violence represented a last gasp, a final desperate effort by the insurgents, who found themselves on the brink of defeat. Diem explained: "The strategic battle against the VC [Viet Cong] has been won." What remained was the tactical battle to clean out the remaining enemy. Although Williams and Durbrow agreed on very little, they agreed on this.

An air of heady optimism held sway in Washington, and it seemed that all that was needed was to perfect the details of the American advisory effort. Toward this end, in the first week of July the new secretary of state, Christian A. Herter, told the Saigon embassy that the Department of Defense was considering detailing U.S. Army Special Forces teams to Vietnam and asked the embassy for a way to introduce them without exceeding the MAAG manpower ceiling.

Herter's question came in response to a Diem initiative requesting expert assistance in antiguerrilla tactics. In spite of General Williams's emphasis on combatting the conventional threat and in contrast to his claim of strategic victory, the Vietnamese president judged the situation so serious—his brother Nhu was telling the American ambassador that his country faced virtually full-scale war—he disregarded Williams and asked for this extra help. His old friend, Edward Lansdale, learned of Diem's request and provided Secretary of State Herter with his appraisal. In it he asked how acts of terrorism and sabotage occurred. If, as he suspected, locally established Viet Cong organizations perpetrated these acts, then they had to have local support. The correct counter was political and economic action coordinated with military security to win sympathies away from the Viet Cong. The Viet Cong organization would be isolated, exposed, and then destroyed.

Lansdale predicted that the Saigon country team would suggest that it respond to Diem's request by offering to undertake the role as "anti-guerrilla" advisers to the South Vietnamese, cautioning that the United States "has remarkably few experienced officers in this category." He discounted experiences in Greece and Korea—where Williams felt he had learned so much about how to counter guerrillas—because in Vietnam, unlike Greece and Korea, the guerrillas received great popular support. Lansdale recommended that the Army Special Warfare School dispatch teams to Vietnam. He wanted them to observe small-unit combat before proffering advice, thereby gaining experience to enrich American tactical doctrine.

Lansdale's concern about the U.S. Army's antiguerrilla capabilities was well founded. The combination of the New Look's emphasis on massive retaliation and the Army's focus on conventional threats in Europe and Korea left it unprepared to wage guerrilla warfare. The Army had developed neither counterinsurgency training methods nor doctrine. Not until 1961, and only then at the State Department's insistence, did Fort Bragg's Special Warfare School introduce lecture courses about the economic, social, and related factors that created revolutionary conditions. Whatever antiguerrilla resources the Army had were concentrated in the Special Forces, the force that would evolve into the "Green Berets." At this time the Special Forces were ready to conduct ranger-style operations behind enemy lines in the event of a conventional war. They were not yet oriented toward fighting guerrillas or training others how to fight them.

Against this background, the Pacific Command examined Herter's query about introducing the Special Forces into Vietnam for seven months. In mid-February 1960, it recommended the idea be "shelved." Ambassador Durbrow vehemently disagreed, asserting that the situation required extraordinary measures and flexibility in interpreting the Geneva Accords. Lansdale endorsed Durbrow's views stating: "This is a real opportunity to assist the Vietnamse [to] meet a Communist threat and to gain valuable experience in a type of warfare which is still too-little understood by Americans." For the time being their arguments failed. Not until the debacle at Tay Ninh would this issue resurface.

As 1959 drew to a close, and after nearly five years of pressing Diem to broaden the base of his government, Durbrow sent a country team assessment reviewing events at the end of a decade of American involvement in Vietnam. It reported: "The Diem Government is continuing the creation of democratic facades which have so far been imbued with little life, but which provide a skeletal framework for eventual political evolution in Vietnam." Reviewing progress, Durbrow reported that the government had made major advances in internal security, particularly compared with five years ago. Bandit gangs operated from remote jungle hideouts and no longer presented a substantial threat. The Communists were "now more a clandestine and underground problem rather than a danger to the security of the state." Durbrow felt that the lack of Communist disruptions in the recent National Assembly elections was dramatic evidence of improved security. The country team report stated that Diem's "somewhat authoritarian government" was compatible with United States interests in Vietnam as long as it continued to work to improve the conditions of the Vietnamese people. It deserved full American diplomatic and material support both because it was strongly anti-Communist and because of its sincere efforts "to remove conditions which breed Communism from within." Given what was really taking place, it was a remarkably naive assessment.

The end of a decade gave Edward Lansdale an opportunity for reflection as well. He suggested the need to "take a hard look at this problem while it still permits solution within our present scale of effort" and maintained that the fundamental problem was political. Since the United States had created the present political organization and military of South Vietnam, it was responsible for the outcome. The official National Security Council objective was a "strong, stable, and constitutional government." However, the way to obtain such a government was not so clearly stated. Therefore, Lansdale recommended "a clear U.S. appreciation and definition of the way to reach the political objective the U.S. desires for Vietnam." Toward this end, he urged the selection of American officials whose task would be to promote political development in cooperation with Diem. Again he said military assistance should be subordinated to this goal.

♦ ♦ ♦

During the autumn of 1959 and through the first month of a new decade, President Diem assured American officials that the internal security situation was improving. On January 26, 1960, a stunning refutation came when the Viet Cong launched their most audacious assault to date. In the past they had avoided combat against regular troops in general and those manning fortified positions in particular. Early in the morning, some two hundred Viet Cong guerrillas overran outlying guard posts before an alarm could be given and bore in against a South Vietnamese regimental headquarters located in a town in Tay Ninh Province northeast of Saigon. The American advisers assigned to the headquarters were not present, which was probably a blessing given what transpired. The attackers caught about three hundred South Vietnamese soldiers unaware in their barracks. Enjoying the fruits of their typically superb intelligence, one Viet Cong detachment went straight for the battalion arms room to seize weapons while another headed for the building housing the officers. During the hour-long battle, the Viet Cong blew up two large barracks and the headquarters building while inflicting sixty-six casualties. Moreover, they carried off a bountiful harvest of about 350 rifles, 30 automatic rifles, 150 carbines, 40 pistols, 2 machine guns, 2 mortars, and abundant ammunition. It was a shocking setback to five years of United States aid and training.

The country team closely investigated what had happened. The Americans learned that just as had been the case in the Bien-hoa raid, in which American advisers had been killed, at Tay Ninh the Viet Cong had operatives within the target base with the local population providing support. The attackers had ably planned and coordinated the operation and then carried it out with aggressive tactics. In contrast, the defenders, in spite of advanced warning, had not been alert and had not fought effectively. The MAAG's evaluation of South Vietnamese Army operations characterized them as plagued by security leaks, inadequate planning, lack of aggressive leadership, failure to coordinate troop movements, and unwillingness to close for combat. In other words, in virtually every category of military significance the Viet Cong displayed skills while the South Vietnamese exhibited deficiencies. In sum, the country team assessment was a comprehensive indictment.

The Tay Ninh attack made waves that traveled up the chain of command all the way to Washington. As commander of the entire training endeavor, General Williams received his share of criticism. He became angry when critics said that the MAAG did not train the Vietnamese in antiguerrilla operations; he argued that it was an established military fact that well-trained soldiers could fight successfully in any type of terrain against any type of opponent, a belief underlying official U.S. Army doctrine. Therefore, the MAAG had concentrated on training good soldiers. In Williams's opinion, a major problem was that Vietnamese officers found too many excuses not to listen to American advice. He concluded: "I'm sure that now since the Viet Cong operations have been intensified and all too often with complete success against Vietnamese troops that are better armed and equipped than they are themselves that commanders will begin to pay more attention to the training of themselves and their troops." It was as if he were a teacher blaming his students and saying that now that their failures were obvious they would of course start to pay more attention.

The attack convinced the country team that the North Vietnamese official statement in May 1959, claiming the struggle to reunify Vietnam would be carried out by all appropriate means, in fact reflected Communist intentions. The team also reassessed a North Vietnamese diplomat's comment to a Canadian International Control Commission official, repeated on two occasions, that they would drive the Americans into the sea. Agents informed the country team that Communists who had left after the Geneva Accords were now returning south, and one source reported that their mission was to establish a headquarters, including a general staff, supply bases, logistical network, and a political section. All of this could only mean the Viet Cong were preparing for the type of all-out guerrilla war that had been fought against the French.

While reassessing Communist intentions, the team also came to the realization, echoing numerous similar past conclusions beginning with the French war, that "it is highly unlikely that any final solution can be found to the internal security situation in South Vietnam if the GVN [government of South Vietnam] does not enjoy the support and cooperation of the rural population." At the moment, the combination of distrust, apathy, and fear of the Viet Cong put an enormous distance between the peasants and the government.

In Washington, the Tay Ninh debacle prompted the State Department to request a special embassy report on the internal security situation. This report, also prepared by the country team, acknowledged that once again internal security had become Vietnam's number one problem. Assassinations, ambushes, and intensified Viet Cong attacks culminating with the Tay Ninh incident had brought home "the full impact of the seriousness of the present situation." Searching for the silver lining, the report paraphrased Williams's observation that recent attacks had the salutary effect of alerting Diem and his government to the gravity of the situation, claiming further that "there is no reason to become alarmist if prompt steps are taken to correct the situation."

From the Pentagon, Lansdale realized that the Tay Ninh

incident and the country team report would cause a major policy reevaluation. Interested in protecting the military from any criticism, and wanting firsthand information for any bureaucratic infighting, he asked Williams to provide his assessment. Williams could offer little more insight than the country team. Predictably, he suggested organizational and training refinements, acknowledging the importance of social, economic, and political policies in the areas of major Communist activity. He observed that current policies did not seem to be working: "This is not my field but appears some GVN policies in action in the Delta are not palatable to populace," a clear statement underscoring the military's lack of understanding about anything except strictly military matters.

At the Pentagon, a special meeting of high-ranking United States experts met to discuss the situation in light of Tay Ninh. Specifically, they examined the political situation in relationship to the guerrillas' success. Noting that the Communists were creating a popular base, they predicted: "As the situation worsens, the military will be pitted more and more against the Vietnamese people." However, all the experts could suggest was the policy refinement of assigning American advisers to those Vietnamese government officials, the province chiefs, who dealt with civilians. The implication was that merely involving American advisers would straighten out any problems.

By the third week in March, Tay Ninh had penetrated to the halls of the Joint Chiefs of Staff. The Chief of Staff of the U.S. Army, General Lyman L. Lemnitzer, proposed that the people of South Vietnam had to be physically and psychologically separated from the Viet Cong, allowing the Viet Cong to be hunted down. This was the method successfully employed by the British in Malaysia. He then addressed the recurring proposal to initiate special antiguerrilla training for the South Vietnamese. Citing the views of the Commander in Chief, Pacific, Admiral Harry D. Felt, who believed that a change in training emphasis could accomplish this goal, Lemnitzer said that the Army agreed but also wanted to introduce Army Special Forces to conduct specialized training. He recommended that the JCS concur in the decision to send them to Vietnam and adjust the troop ceiling upward in whatever way necessary to accomplish this.

First a request had to be extracted from the Vietnamese leader. In light of the Tay Ninh disaster, that proved easy. On April 4, 1960, the South Vietnamese government officially asked for American Special Forces. The Pentagon dispatched three 10-man teams to Saigon, telling them to wear their uniforms only while on duty to avoid arousing the International Control Commission. They arrived in May, the first of a team whose special abilities would so attract President Kennedy—he would award them their trademark green berets in 1961—and whose men would carry the brunt of the American fighting commitment to Vietnam through 1965.

In Saigon, the Tay Ninh incident prompted Diem to agree with his brother and call the serious internal security situation a war. Having had six weeks to reflect, Diem again met with Durbrow. Like the French, he responded to Communist military success by asking the Americans for more military help. Like the French, his list of urgently needed equipment featured those items—aircraft, helicopters, all-terrain vehicles—intended to overcome terrain problems and force the Viet Cong to fight a conventional battle. Diem also wanted to increase the size of his standing army.

Durbrow expressed doubt that more troops were the answer, telling Diem it was more important to win the confidence of the population. His response drove a wedge further between the embattled Diem and Durbrow. On April 6, Williams asked Diem how long it would be until the country was pacified; in other words, how long until victory? Diem evaded the question, responding that the problem could be solved by military means and that what he needed was about five thousand more Civil Guards. He, like most strategists in Washington, believed that what the situation demanded was refinement in existing policies.

Part 2. THE FIRST COUP

In the early spring of 1960, Ambassador Durbrow wrote about one of his "perennial problems," General Williams. Diem was pressuring Durbrow to support antiguerrilla training for the South Vietnamese Army. When, in turn, the ambassador raised this question with Williams, the general replied that not much of this training had been done because conventional training subsumed specialized training for fighting guerrillas. Durbrow explained that for almost a year he had worried that the MAAG's training emphasis was more relevant to fighting "another World War II" than to the conflict in Vietnam. Yet Williams continued to recommend against antiguerrilla training because he believed it interfered with the more important conventional instruction.

In Williams's view, Durbrow was meddling in a subject he knew nothing about. Back in 1959, he had reluctantly given the ambassador copies of the latest U.S. Army training manuals regarding guerrilla operations. These manuals were Williams's bibles. When he gave them to Durbrow, he observed they could "mean little to other than an Army officer," but Durbrow studied them closely. He comprehended that fundamental American doctrine for fighting guerrillas relied on something called advanced individual training and basic unit training. Both were conventional, and, armed with this information, in April 1960 Durbrow hoisted Williams on his own petard. Williams rejected special antiguerrilla training, relying instead on conventional American doctrine. By this standard, the Vietnamese were still inadequately trained since, as Durbrow pointed out, only three of seven South Vietnamese divisions had received a full course of individual and basic unit training. By skillfully attacking Williams on his own ground, Durbrow scored debating points while also ensuring that a large, disruptive schism would occur within the country team.

In spite of Williams's and the MAAG's focus on a conventional invasion and conventional training, by late spring no one could continue to ignore Viet Cong activities inside of South Vietnam. It would not matter if South Vietnamese troops were properly stationed to defend against a conventional invasion if, behind their defenses, the nation fell to the guerrillas. Under Williams's leadership, the MAAG had taken great pride in organizing and training a South Vietnamese Army complete with many modern trappings suitable for conventional warfare. Now it was apparent this was not enough. Therefore, in a major strategic reversal, the Joint Chiefs of Staff proposed special measures to fight an antiguerrilla, or counterinsurgency, war. The Central Intelligence Agency had urged such measures in mid-1958, but had been overridden by the MAAG. Two years later, with egg on its face, the Army had to agree with the correctness of the CIA's recommendations.

The Joint Chiefs of Staff ordered the MAAG to shift its training emphasis for selected South Vietnamese units "from conventional to anti-guerrilla warfare." Accordingly, the MAAG prepared a training plan designed to teach selected officers and noncommissioned officers how guerrillas fought and how to fight back. The American Army, despite little or no experience in guerrilla warfare, believed it could instruct soldiers whose ranks included veterans of fifteen years of guerrilla warfare. At no time did the Americans try to seek out outstanding Vietnamese to learn lessons based upon their experience. Instead, fresh-faced, eager Americans would tell them how to do it.

On April 21, the State Department presented Eisenhower with a short memorandum on Vietnam. It began by stating that the Communists had markedly intensified their subversive activities in the south, warning the President that plans to counter the Viet Cong might call for increased American assistance in counterguerrilla training as well as additional specialized equipment. There was no mention of any need for political, economic, or social reforms. In a similar vein, the OCB's "Operations Plan for Vietnam," dated April 29, 1960, provided a clear statement of the American response to Communist aggression in Southeast Asia. The United States would invoke the UN Charter and/or the SEATO Treaty, and, if requested by the South Vietnamese government, take the necessary military action. It would be contingent upon prior congressional approval unless the President determined that a crisis situation required immediate action.

On May 9, 1960, Eisenhower delivered his views on the deteriorating situation to the National Security Council. Although he stressed American military initiatives, the President also addressed nonmilitary measures. Mentioning that he had received numerous reports about South Vietnam, he observed: "Heretofore we have been proud of Diem and had thought he was doing a good job. Apparently he was now becoming arbitrary and blind to the situation." Told that Diem seldom ventured into the countryside and was out of touch with the people, Eisenhower asked whether any Americans were trying to persuade Diem to develop closer ties with his people. His question reveals how out of touch Eisenhower himself was with the situation, for, as was explained to him, Williams and Durbrow had constantly worked on this problem. Eisenhower concluded: "We had rescued this country from a fate worse than death and it would be bad to lose it at this stage." He recalled that during the sect crisis, he had received recommendations to oppose Diem, and he hoped that in the current situation everyone would pull together to try to save the Diem regime.

In Saigon, such cooperation was not happening. The American embassy featured "barely civil" meetings among Williams, Durbrow, the CIA, economic experts, and State Department officials. While the ambassador and Williams feuded bitterly about the nature and effectiveness of MAAG training, in the countryside the Communists continued to expand their power base, and, regardless of success or failure, the bureaucracy charged with distributing the funds to support the American effort churned out more of the same. As the Defense Department's program summary explained: The "FY 1960 program provides training to maintain the current effectiveness and improvement of the Army."

For the second half of 1960, everyone labored on a "Counterinsurgency Plan for Vietnam." It was not completed until January 1961, just in time to be examined by a new President. By this time a new general commanded the MAAG. Until the end of his tenure, Hanging Sam Williams believed he just about had the problem licked, even predicting in mid-1960 that the MAAG could "work itself out of a job" and begin to withdraw from Vietnam the following year. He would not be around to see it happen. In September, Lieutenant General Lionel C. McGarr replaced him.

McGarr's perspective was different from William's; he believed that counterinsurgency required special doctrine and techniques. However, he had a delicate mission—to build upon the MAAG's accomplishments while instilling an entirely new orientation. As he explained it to the American advisers in Vietnam: "Our hunter-killer teams of 'antiguerrilla guerril-las' . . . must find a better way [not] only to counter the Viet Cong guerrilla in the swamps, the canal-gridded, inundated Mekong River delta, and the rugged mountains and jungles of both the high plateau and the entire land border re-gion—but to crush him!"

Williams's departure enormously pleased the State Depart-ment. At last there would be a shift in military thinking. The secretary of state for Far Eastern affairs, J. Graham Parsons, optimistically believed that the new counterinsurgency train-ing would allow the South Vietnamese to perform much more effectively. Caught up in this thinking, he seemed to pay mere lip service to the nonmilitary aspects of the problem: "Of course, we all recognize that there is a political and social as-pect to this whole problem . . . and which we continue to hope Diem is taking some steps to correct." Conversely, Wolf Lade-jinsky felt near total despair. He bemoaned Diem's fate, a leader whom he felt had brilliant talents but had fallen into arrogance, love of power, and belief in his own infallibility. The only positive factor Ladejinsky saw was that the United States could exert strong influence because Diem absolutely depended upon American aid. He would undoubtedly resist such advice, but in the end he "had no place else to go" and so would be ultimately susceptible to American influence.

When Edward Lansdale stepped back from the bureau-cratic politics of the recurring State Department–Department of Defense feuds, he analyzed the situation in Vietnam with great insight. He proferred advice to the chairman of a Spe-cial National Intelligence Estimate dedicated to reexamining Vietnam policy. Lansdale felt the essential first step was to un-derstand accurately the nature of the enemy. The Viet Cong were "far more formidable than [just] some guerrillas and ter-rorists skulking about the swamps and jungles." Their ranks included skilled and dedicated individuals who understood the importance of political, psychological, and economic fac-tors in the conflict with Diem's government. Their years of fighting the French had taught them how to perfect their co-vert organization. In Lansdale's view, the Viet Cong were a committed, professional, and formidable foe, and the pending Special National Intelligence Estimate should so describe them. He also urged that the estimate be based upon firsthand accounts from people who had been out into the countryside and lived among the peasants, because he had observed a large discrepancy between many official reports and the informal personal reports he received from acquaintances living in Vietnam. All of this was wise advice.

But Lansdale's pro-Diem feelings interfered with his analysis. He firmly believed Diem retained popular support and so told General McGarr. He also said that the Communists simply wielded more effective propaganda. He recommended to McGarr that a starting point to redress this imbalance was to sell the merits of Diem's agroville concept to the people. Agrovilles were designed to solve the problem of rural support for the guerrillas. The policy relocated isolated peasants to "prosperity and density centers" located along major roads and canals. The idea was that the regrouping of peasants into fortified villages would eliminate the guerrillas' source of supplies, manpower, and intelligence. It was very much in accord with the views of Army Chief of Staff Lemnitzer regarding the need to isolate the people from the guerrillas. The program also appealed to Americans both because it involved things they were good at—building entire villages complete with electricity and medical clinics—and because it seemed to improve the peasants' lot by giving them the wherewithal to better their lives. It did not address the underlying grievances of the villagers and was a reversal of centuries-old social and economic patterns by violating traditional attachments to ancestral homes. Although the agroville program would fail by early 1961, derivatives would reemerge throughout the 1960s. At its inception, it was just one more counterproductive initiative consuming resources while playing into enemy hands.

The Special National Intelligence Estimate for which Lansdale provided his ideas came out near the end of August 1960. It warned that current adverse trends, while not irreversible, if unchecked would cause the collapse of Diem's regime. Absent substantial changes, the estimate believed, the Viet Cong would continue to expand their control over the countryside and a political crisis would result. From Saigon, Ambassador Durbrow concurred, stating: "It [is] thus now quite clear we are in for prolonged battle with Communist guerrillas with survival Free Viet-nam at stake." Echoing Eisenhower's words from the early summer, he concluded that the United States must support Diem to "back up our investment."

The Military Assistance Advisory Group also responded to the Special National Intelligence Estimate. It began by noting what it perceived to be a paradox: After five years of slow and steady national growth, the threat to Diem's stability had increased. Unwittingly, it also answered this paradox by observing that despite national economic growth, the peasants' economic status was no different than it had been under the French.

The anticipated Viet Cong expansion of control happened faster than anyone thought possible. By mid-September, Durbrow told the State Department about Communist influence over demonstrations in Saigon. He felt the situation so serious that it called for drastic action. Aware that in the past Diem had shown astute judgment contrary to American advice and thus survived serious crises, he realized that the Vietnamese president would resent frank talk. Nonetheless, the ambassador believed the situation called for administering a psychological shock to change the trend of events, recommending a carrot-and-stick approach. The carrot would be provided by Eisenhower, whom he recommended should write a letter pledging continuing American support on the occasion of the Republic of Vietnam's fifth anniversary. The ambassador also concluded, for the first time, that if Diem's position continued to erode, the United States might have to consider alternative courses of action and other leaders to accomplish national objectives. Aware of Durbrow's growing criticism of Diem, Lansdale argued that regardless of Diem's failings, he was an American-supported leader in a combat situation and asked if this was the appropriate time to threaten and distract him.

The ambassador ignored Lansdale's counsel. In mid-October, Durbrow met with Diem to make a carefully considered presentation designed to move Diem toward significant reform. In particular, Durbrow addressed the tricky, sensitive question of Diem's brother Nhu and his wife's influence upon internal affairs in Vietnam. Many State Department officials had spent much time weighing the impact of each word Durbrow spoke, yet it merely produced the familiar response that as much as Diem wanted to do what the Americans advised, Viet Cong activities made initiatives at this time most difficult. Then came Eisenhower's letter conveying good wishes, admiration, and promises of unending support in the struggle ahead. The secretary of state believed the letter would balance Durbrow's strong and unpalatable advice. Viewed from Diem's perspective, it must have seemed another example of divided American counsel, another mixed signal he could ignore.

Professor Wesley R. Fishel was an American who counted himself as a friend of Diem. He had worked in Vietnam until the spring of 1958. Thereafter, he stayed well informed about events in Vietnam and corresponded several times a year with Diem. When he had departed in 1958, Diem had been ascendant, the Communist threat apparently shrinking. Now, some two years later, because of profound American uneasiness in both official and business circles, Fishel wrote candidly to Diem. He addressed four factors that contributed to American unease. First was the weakness of leadership displayed by Diem's ministers and civil servants, who as a group continued to be unwilling to show initiative and accept responsibility. Second was the slowing of democractic development. Fishel assured Diem that he understood otherwise, but that to the so-called experts who did not have the same close understanding and relationship with Diem it appeared that Diem's rule was a dictatorship. Third was the security situation. The professor's Washington friends wanted to know if the apparent deterioration was staged by Diem to attract more United States aid or whether it represented a weakening of Diem's power. Observing that Diem's critics seemed easily able to marshal statistics on assassination rates and the like to support their view that Diem's government was slowly disintegrating, Fishel gently requested that Diem provide concrete information to rebut this view. The fourth and final factor Fishel addressed concerned administrative reform and reorganization. Washington was rife with reports of Vietnamese administrative snafus that fatally delayed effective response to Viet Cong actions. High-ranking State Department officials told Fishel that the provincial and district chiefs remained out of touch with the population. Meanwhile, military units such as the South Vietnamese marines behaved brutally toward civilians. Fishel informed Diem that all of this added up, in the view of State Department critics, to Diem's reliance upon repressive measures to assert his authority. His was a blunt warning from a close friend.

The combination of warnings and advice from diverse sources seemed to have an effect. At the beginning of November, Durbrow reported cautious optimism to the State Department. He believed he saw evidence that Diem understood the gravity of the situation and was making a serious effort to regain popular support. Diem's state of the union message, which for the first time acknowledged government failings, excited the American embassy. Durbrow acknowledged that this apparent change might be designed to fool critical Americans and dissident Vietnamese, but he saw real hope that Diem finally understood what he had to do.

Just when the embassy began to believe it had moved Diem along the path toward reform, events intervened. On November 11, 1960, a small group of disgruntled South Vietnamese paratroopers staged a coup attempt. The coup plotters had several objectives. They were unhappy with Diem's promotion policy based upon personal loyalty rather than military competence, and they worried about losing the war to the Communists. Apparently hazy in their understanding of the American electoral process, they timed the coup for just after the United States elections, hoping to present the new President with an in-place alternative to Diem. Telling their troops that Diem's presidential guards had betrayed the president, officers led the paratroops in an attack against the Presidential Palace. During the fighting a stray machine-gun round narrowly missed Diem himself. The coup troops seized some objectives in Saigon including the national radio station. Broadcasts denounced Diem's "feudal totalitarianism." In the end the paratroops failed to capture Diem himself, who managed to summon loyal reinforcements from the hinterland in time to suppress the plotters.

Amid the confusion the American embassy narrowly avoided a serious misstep. Durbrow's sources seemed to indicate that the coup leaders had made an arrangement with Diem whereby the president would continue to hold office in a titular role only. Durbrow prepared a draft statement recognizing the new government. He explained his haste to the State Department on the grounds that rapid action would be needed to keep the new government from considering a tilt away from the United States toward neutralism and to convince the Communists that the crisis had been quickly resolved and did not represent an opportunity for them. In fact, Durbrow's action demonstrated his mounting willingness to abandon Diem. Furthermore, one of Colby's CIA operatives, overtly a member of the embassy staff, was present at rebel headquarters. Although he maintained a strictly neutral stance, his presence could be construed as indicating American support for the coup. Coup leaders had also worked closely in the past with MAAG officers. All of this might make even a secure person skeptical about American support. It did make a great impression upon the suspiciously inclined Vietnamese leader. Seeking reassurance, Diem phoned Durbrow, but the ambassador was noncommittal about American support. This carefully guarded, neutral response convinced Diem that at least the United States ambassador supported the coup. Diem's resentment of Durbrow hardened.

The coup attempt taught Diem one other hard lesson. He realized that, more than ever, his rule depended upon the loyalty of the South Vietnamese military. He had to keep them happy even if this meant diminished resources for nonmilitary purposes. In Diem's mind, the type of reforms his American backers believed so important had always been second to the military contest against the Communists. Now that elements within his own security forces had revealed themselves as threats, his attention to reforms all but disappeared.

In Washington, Lansdale wrote to the secretary of defense to question what to do next. He believed that Diem would turn for comfort to the MAAG and that this would make McGarr's role vitally important. He wished McGarr to be unshackled from embassy control as he conferred with Diem. While normally the task of pushing Diem in the direction the United States wanted him to go was the job for an ambassador, Lansdale doubted that Durbrow had any personal stature remaining with Diem, thinking that Diem must feel that the ambassador had sided with the rebels. Lansdale's description of the dynamics of the Diem-Durbrow relationship was perceptive. His letter to the secretary of defense had the additional purpose of using the coup attempt to pursue his turf battle with the Department of State over who would guide policy in Vietnam. Regarding this conflict, many Pentagon officers shared his view. One noted that "the sooner we get . . . Durbrow out of S.E. Asia the better."

The schism between the Departments of State and Defense now pervaded all analysis. On November 12, Secretary of State Herter cabled the embassy that the department believed "the regime's prestige has suffered seriously" as a result of the coup attempt. In the department's view, the attempt indicated a serious lack of support for Diem within the military and among the people. In contrast, the next day McGarr told Lansdale that "Diem has emerged from this severe test in position of greater strength with visible proof of sincere support behind him both in armed forces and civilian population."

A few days later, one of Lansdale's subordinates reported from Saigon that the situation was rapidly deteriorating and that the United States' ability to influence events was diminishing at a similar rate. Furthermore, he told Lansdale that the Viet Cong held a much stronger position than policymakers in Washington realized.

Something else was happening in Saigon that had not happened before. Anti-American leaflets, which seemed to have Diem's tacit approval, began circulating. This activity coincided with a searching reappraisal by the United States government unit charged with providing economic aid to South Vietnam. It was another opportunity for a radical change in American policy.

Dr. D. A. FitzGerald served in the International Cooperation Administration. He brought a fresh and, more important, an open mind to a problem that had received so much study. He did no original research; rather, he looked at the most current reports from Vietnam. His unique contribution was to separate optimistic statements from the hard predictions concerning the likely course of future events, and to consider what would happen if the predictions came true. He began by observing that American intelligence had arrived at a consensus, although they did not realize it, that absent prompt, decisive improvement in Diem's government, South Vietnam would collapse. He cited the most recent Special National Intelligence Estimate as a prime example of this conclusion. Next, he noted that in spite of major economic progress and intensified South Vietnamese military efforts, the Viet Cong were achieving startling military and political inroads, and that American analysts had concluded that political changes were required. Accordingly, Durbrow had pushed as strongly as possible for such changes. FitzGerald continued: "President Diem has chosen, with active U.S. support, to concentrate almost exclusively upon the strengthening of the Vietnam military organization to sustain his collapsing regime," observing that Diem was, as some State Department officials had anticipated, taking inadequate half-measures instead of making the dramatic reforms the situation demanded. In this situation, FitzGerald said, providing economic assistance with the strong probability that it would be ineffective was unwise. He concluded: "We believe that the urgency of the situation requires an immediate and drastic re-evaluation of United States policy toward Vietnam." The reevaluation should address whether further efforts to influence Diem could be effective. If not, it was time to "consider the alternatives that exist to the present leadership."

Even while FitzGerald's report worked its way up the chain of command, Diem sensed, possibly because Lansdale alerted him, the new and equivocal attitude of the United States toward him. For the first time since the coup attempt, he summoned the new head of the MAAG, General McGarr, to an urgent meeting. So anxious was the president that he did not wait for an interpreter before beginning to speak, which was unprecedented. McGarr observed that Diem was obviously troubled and hurt. In his monologue, Diem indirectly attributed the coup to foreign influence, which, in turn, had led to the anti-American activities witnessed recently in Saigon. Amid all this trouble, Diem told McGarr, his one consolation was MAAG's steadfast support. It was a clever ploy ensuring McGarr's unstinting help.

Although Diem won over the all-important MAAG, State

Department officials at the United States embassy in Saigon remained unimpressed. The influential embassy counselor annotated McGarr's report of his conversation with Diem. In the margins next to a sentence where Diem described his critics as demagogues without constructive suggestions for reform, the counselor wrote: "Look in the mirror, Diem." He added at the end of the report that Washington seemed to be losing patience with Diem, but that no one had any other suggestions. Therefore, he recommended: "We must first give Diem a chance for 6–12 months to take steps needed in his own interest; if he doesn't start things going shortly he'll be lost no matter what we want. More troops aren't the only answer."

Preparation for locating an alternative to Diem caused the Central Intelligence Agency to report on prominent Vietnamese politicians who might lead the nation. It bleakly observed that Diem's continued domination of Vietnamese politics made it very difficult for an alternative to emerge through constitutional processes.

By year's end, many in the Eisenhower administration recognized the enormous schism between the Departments of State and Defense. While everyone in both organizations claimed to agree that there were two fundamental, interrelated problems, the defeat of the Viet Cong and the winning of popular support for the government, the relative weights assigned to the tasks separated the camps. From his vantage point in Washington, a State Department official described this to Durbrow:

> The Pentagon warmly supports Diem and, I think, tends to feel that if he could only beat the insurgents, his other problems would disappear. On the other hand, there is a fairly vocal school of thought around here which has little regard or hope for Diem, and tends to feel that Viet-Nam's current problems can only be licked under a government more responsive to the people.

Durbrow responded with his grimmest forecast yet. He predicted a "drawn-out full scale guerrilla war" that very well might lead to American intervention.

The Military Assistance Advisory Group in Vietnam had a different idea. It strongly believed that more South Vietnamese troops were at least part of the answer, describing the South Vietnamese situation as unique because the country faced active guerrilla warfare combined with a conventional external threat. To avoid SEATO intervention, the Communists fomented internal revolution through subversion. It was vital to defeat this stratagem because "here in Vietnam a preview in miniature of world conquest is being conducted." MAAG continued with a detailed, point-by-point refutation of Durbrow's opposition to a troop increase and concluded:

> It is the professional judgment of this MAAG that, regardless of the obstacles which must be overcome, there is a clear and urgent need for an increase in military force to assure the restoration of internal security in the degree necessary to the development of political and economic stability. Further, the time to move in this direction is now and not later when the situation is out of hand and training will be both impossible and too late.

On December 1, 1960, staffers for the Department of Defense examined what the United States could do to help the defense of Indochina given the Viet Cong successes. They reached the same conclusion that analysts in the past had reached when confronted with a "crisis" or "emergency" in Vietnam. They too recommended a technical adjustment, in this case the dispatch of eleven more helicopters. What is notable is that the President of the United States, charged with overseeing an immense budget and handling the foreign policy of the country, felt the question of eleven helicopters important enough to warrant his own attention. For three years, since Diem's triumphal tour of America, Eisenhower had been relatively uninvolved with Vietnam policy; but by the end of 1960, he realized that the situation had gone so sour that it demanded his own attention. Accordingly, he read the relevant material regarding the eleven helicopters and added a marginal note. Referring to the question whether or not to provide helicopters, he wrote: "If we do—then now!"

One major reason the President had been distracted from events in Vietnam was because of a new emerging crisis in an obscure country called Laos.

Part 3. "THE CORK IN THE BOTTLE"

Military training remained the heart of United States policy toward Vietnam, yet after three solid years of adviser-directed training, the South Vietnamese Army's inefficiency was becoming harder to ignore. This army failed time and again against outnumbered, outgunned opponents. For a long time General Williams had countered criticism that the troops received inappropriate training by saying that the real problem was lack of training. He cited the frequency with which units interrupted their training cycle to engage in security operations. Partially justified, his opinion overlooked the fact that even when units completed training, major weaknesses remained.

One adviser commented that he would not trust his platoon leaders to undertake operations without American assistance, declaring, "They'd be lucky to be able to march down a straight road." Another adviser set himself the modest goal of keeping his men from slinging boots, equipment, and the occasional chicken from their rifles. By tour's end, it seemed he had succeeded. However, delayed at the airport for several days, he returned to spy on his unit as they marched by. Slung from the rifles were the familiar accoutrements. A third adviser observed with disgust that he had no doubt that given the freedom to do so the South Vietnamese would "revert quite happily to what they were familiar with in the past."

No army can be better than its noncommissioned and junior officers. For a variety of reasons, perhaps the most important being a lack of military tradition after a century of colonial rule coupled with a pervasive patronage system that discouraged initiative, at this level the South Vietnamese Army remained deficient. Among Vietnamese officers a common joke held that promotion stemmed from the "three Ds": "*Dang*," or party, meaning membership in the Can Lao; *Dao*, or religion, meaning Catholicism in a country 85 percent Buddhist; and *Du*, a vulgar term for Diem's home region. In addition, too many experienced men served in comfortable rear-area headquarters and support units. Too often, the rawest conscripts carried out combat duties. Too many operational reports contained deliberate falsifications intended to make a unit appear combat-effective.

Serious flaws in the advisory system also contributed to the ineffectiveness of the training. The advisory role in a guerrilla war was a new concept largely unconnected with past United States military experience. An American soldier whose professional life revolved around receiving and issuing orders found himself giving advice. Since he neither spoke the language nor comprehended the culture, he could hardly assess the effectiveness of this advice. The advisory effort was failing because it reflected the American emphasis on the quantifiable activities of building agrovilles, roads, and ports; providing weapons and equipment; and increasing the amount of training or the number of advisers. Conversely, to try to influence underlying social and economic conditions—which had created the insurgency—involved things uncountable, unquantifiable, and maybe unknowable to Americans who did not understand the culture they were dealing with.

In any event, the combination of the nebulous role of the adviser and the increasing signs of failure prompted the Pentagon to look harder at Edward Lansdale's recommendation that the MAAG shift from a training and advice-giving function to a new role more appropriate for the crisis, "on-the-spot advice and assistance in the conduct of tactical operations against the Viet Cong." President Eisenhower had always resisted the idea of putting Americans into combat on the Asian mainland, however, and the idea hung fire.

One of Lansdale's astute roving observers arrived in Saigon in late 1960. He reported that the situation had markedly worsened since his previous visit one year ago. He concluded: "Vietnam exemplifies the fact that we have not yet, after so many bitter years of experience, developed the necessary capability for assisting foreign armed forces in dealing with Mao-type guerrilla warfare."

♦ ♦ ♦

Laos had been one of the French-controlled Associated States. The Geneva Accords of 1954 had dealt with Laos in much the same way as with Vietnam except that the accords did not formally divide the country. When the Vietnamese Communists assented to the accords, they sold out their wartime allies, the Pathet Lao. To the Eisenhower administration,

Laos possessed unique strategic importance. Not only did it have long borders alongside both North and South Vietnam, it also bordered the behemoth to the north, Communist China. Ideally, the administration wished to contain China by supporting anti-Communist regimes all along its borders. Laos was one place it wanted to implement this strategy, but a Vietnam-style American military aid program was not tried in Laos since the French retained a training monopoly there until late 1958. So sparsely populated and undeveloped was Laos that it stood no chance of defending itself should either of its Communist neighbors decide to invade.

At the end of 1957, an uneasy three-faction alliance formed a neutral coalition government. Since the government included the Pathet Lao, the Eisenhower administration opposed the coalition as best it could. Nonetheless, Laotian elections seemed to promise a peaceful future when two things occurred: The right-wing Royal Laotian Army began a program to resist communism and the United States withheld aid payments that propped up the neutral government. The head of the government resigned to be replaced by the CIA-backed General Phoumi Nosavan. A series of amazingly convoluted political-military maneuvers ensued, resulting in Phoumi establishing one government and the neutralist Prince Souvanna Phouma heading another. American military aid flowed to the militarist Phoumi while economic aid went to Prince Souvanna. Although some American officials sought to rationalize this schizophrenic approach, others backed one or the other faction. So muddled was Washington's direction that a Laotian leader complained: "Since so many voices are heard, it is impossible to tell which has an authoritative ring."

When North Vietnam decided to resume armed struggle against the south in January 1959, it also decided to increase its aid to the Pathet Lao and within a month arms shipments began. Shortly thereafter, select North Vietnamese military units entered Laos. This contributed to the American decision to have its ambassador pressure Prince Souvanna to renounce neutrality and accept Phoumi into his government. Souvanna's reluctance convinced American officials that he must be removed. Meanwhile, Prince Souvanna learned of Washington's intentions. To verify his hunch, he asked the United States for special assistance to relieve specific shortages in Laos. When the United States refused, he turned to the USSR, which enthusiastically agreed and established a mission in Hanoi to coordinate the aid. At the end of 1960, large Russian planes were leaving Hanoi to deliver food and later weapons to Souvanna.

By this time, however, Souvanna had been driven from his capital by an American-planned attack conducted by Phoumi. It was to prove one of the few "victories" ever achieved by Phoumi. Not only did the attack drive the prince from his capital, it drove him into alliance with the Communist Pathet Lao. This, then, was the situation by the end of 1960, the end of President Eisenhower's term of office. Moscow and Peking recognized and supported Prince Souvanna as the Laotian leader. The Communist Pathet Lao provided most of Souvanna's military assets. In January 1961, they spearheaded an attack that overran the Plaine des Jarres in central Laos. Countering the attack was Washington-supported Phoumi, who controlled a poorly organized, poorly motivated military force that made the South Vietnamese seem an army of titans. It was a sign of progress, one American Army briefer explained, that the Laotian Army who had abandoned their weapons when they retreated only a few months before, now "take their weapons with them when they run away."

At the end of 1960, official American policy, as described by the National Security Council, foresaw "a grave danger of a most serious threat . . . in the coming days and weeks" in Laos. So bad was the situation that when Eisenhower briefed the new President about Southeast Asia it was Laos, not Vietnam, toward which he directed attention.

Vietnam had played a minor role in the presidential campaign of 1960. As Eisenhower later said: "At that time the only trouble we had in Vietnam of any consequence" was Diem's nepotism. To the extent that the candidates discussed foreign affairs, they addressed Cuba, Chinese Communist pressure on the Offshore Islands, and Laos. Republican candidate Richard Nixon alluded to South Vietnam in a speech at the Veterans of Foreign Wars convention, saying that there had been a civil war raging there, but "as a result of our taking the strong stand we did" it was ended. Democratic candidate

John Kennedy's contribution to the topic was to criticize Nixon's views on intervening to help the French in 1954, saying, "If ever there was a war where we would have been engaged in a hopeless struggle without allies, for an unpopular colonialist cause," that was the war. In the fall of 1960, Kennedy asked his audience rhetorically whether other Southeast Asian countries besides Laos were to be lost. Regarding the region, he asked, "What contribution can we make to the cause of freedom?" answering with a pledge for "new solutions." He was not more specific.

On January 19, 1961, the day before he took office, President-elect Kennedy met with Eisenhower to receive a last briefing. The deteriorating situation in Southeast Asia dominated discussion. Back in 1953, Eisenhower had concluded that Laos occupied an important strategic location. At that time he had said its loss would trigger the fall of the rest of Southeast Asia and imperil places as distant as India, and the passage of time had not altered his opinion. Eisenhower told Kennedy that Laos was in jeopardy. Kennedy respected the older man and asked him which he would prefer, a coalition with the Communists or intervention through SEATO. Eisenhower replied, "It would be far better to intervene through SEATO," and explained why. Since his explanation was a last chance to influence policy toward Southeast Asia, a last chance to justify the immense American expenditure in Vietnam, a last chance to ensure that all of his attention and effort had meaning, his words represent a pure distillation.

Eisenhower explained that the United States should try to persuade SEATO or the International Control Commission to help defend Laos. Unfortunately, neither the British nor the French wanted SEATO to act there. But Eisenhower had concluded that Laos was so vital to American interests that it justified direct intervention, and that "our unilateral intervention would be our last desperate hope in the event we were unable to prevail upon the other signatories to join us." He elaborated by explaining that Laos was vital to the national interest, "the cork in the bottle," a place whose loss would begin the toppling process leading to the "loss of most of the Far East."

Eisenhower's words had great impact upon the young, impressionable President-elect. Here was a great world leader who had finished eight years of responsible service to the country. The Eisenhower administration comprised men who had long familiarity with the "facts" bearing on the issue, and now they were warning that the United States must not permit a Communist takeover of Laos. Neither Kennedy nor his advisers had any reason to challenge this assessment even had they been inclined to do so. Instead, the President-elect asked how long it would take to position an American division in Laos. Eisenhower's secretary of defense replied twelve to seventeen days if the troops came from the continental United States and less if they came from forces already stationed in the Pacific. The secretary concluded that Laotian political support for intervention was problematic, but that he was confident about the capability of the American military to fight in Laos. And that was all. The discussion then turned to economic matters.

As Eisenhower handed over the country to the new President, his Vietnam legacy was clear. He had kept the country out of another Asian war but he had ordered American advisers into Vietnam and permitted them to edge toward active combat. Moreover, until his last day in office, he retained a firm belief in the domino theory. He bequeathed it to his successor.

CHAPTER XIII

THE CAUSE OF FREEDOM

We begin to understand that in a far-off corner of the globe is an agony of conflict, where no matter how it started, has become again a testing ground between dictatorship and freedom.

—DWIGHT D. EISENHOWER, 1954

This is the worst yet. . . . You know Ike never briefed me about Vietnam.

—JOHN F. KENNEDY, 1961

Part 1. DECADE IN REVIEW

When the 1950s began, few Americans, inside or outside the government, paid any attention to far distant Southeast Asia. Vietnam penetrated American consciousness in mid-decade when the gripping saga of Dien Bien Phu received national attention. The likelihood of war loomed large, and the Eisenhower administration set to educating the public about why United States security hinged on what took place there. The President employed the analogy of a row of dominos to describe what might happen. As suddenly as it entered national awareness, Vietnam receded into the backwaters of public attention. In this the nation mirrored its leader. Once partition became a fact of life and Ngo Dinh Diem seemed established, President Eisenhower turned to other affairs. During the decade's second half, Vietnam occasionally received national scrutiny—when Diem made his triumphal tour in 1957 and when the first United States advisers died in combat in 1959—but, by and large, the decade ended as it had begun. Compared to ten years earlier, more government officials were aware and anxious about what was taking place, but theirs was the concern of the specialist. Neither did the presidential candidates address Vietnam in the 1960 campaign nor did Eisenhower mention it to the President-elect in his last briefing; and so the public followed.

Yet, during the decade two Presidents molded a strategy from which all else followed. Their strategy held that Southeast Asia was vital to American security. Vietnam's loss to the forces of communism would begin a toppling process involving a long row of strategic countries. To prevent this, the United States had to prop up the first domino, no matter how shaky its foundation.

Given the earliest history of the United States' relationship with Ho Chi Minh, had there been a plausible alternative to the policy adopted by Truman and continued by Eisenhower? Because of the enormous human misery and the terrific strategic impact of what did take place, this question still haunts. While the temptation is to hedge on any response, the answer must be yes.

As we have seen, from the time he first encountered Americans during World War II, Ho Chi Minh took great pains to establish a relationship with the United States. He was absolutely consistent in what he told OSS officers regarding his hopes for his country. He wanted Vietnam to receive the same type of treatment the United States accorded the Philippines: a formal status that would eventually lead to full sovereignty. He peppered American diplomats in China with letters intended for higher officials. These messages reinforced his spoken words. While writing impassioned letters to the President, secretary of state, and the U.S. Senate may not be the usual method to conduct foreign policy—today the letters read as painfully naive—given Ho Chi Minh's circumstances he had no other way to communicate his hopes.

Yes, he was a Communist—an orientation that in 1945 he periodically sought to hide from Americans—but he, at any rate, did not think his political philosophy precluded a close relationship with the United States. His communism was an obstacle, but it did not have to be an insurmountable one. It is when examining the circumstances of 1945 and 1946 that the case for a plausible alternative most weakens. It is unreasonable to expect any President, let alone one like Truman, new to his office and in the midst of world war, to pick out from the blizzard of messages a single flake that might be important. Furthermore, recall that Truman never saw Ho Chi Minh's letters. He only saw related documents that contained allusions to them. However, in this regard it is useful to remember the words of Napoleon Bonaparte, a national leader who daily confronted a deluge of reports ranging from the strategic to the minute. Referring to the need to analyze all relevant information before making policy, Napoleon said: "Whatever has not been profoundly meditated in all its details is totally ineffectual."

Unlike the President, Secretary of State Stettinius received from subordinates in Asia reports about Ho Chi Minh's desires to establish a relationship with the United States. Arguably, the same line of reasoning excusing Truman accounts for the secretary—also a busy man with diverse pulls upon his time—and his inattention. Accept for the moment that the American leaders at the top were blameless in their disregard for a minor guerrilla leader in an obscure country. Still, the Department of State and the OSS both had offices charged with attending to precisely such matters. Those offices too received myriad bits of information. It was their responsibility to separate the wheat from the chaff and to make sure their superiors saw that which was important. Somewhere along the line that did not occur. Ho Chi Minh's messages, as well as the reports of OSS agents who met with him, reached Washington, where they disappeared into the bureaucracy. In Washington was a system that permitted the State Department's Southeast Asian desk to respond to one of Ho Chi Minh's telegrams in November 1945 with the directive "that no action should be taken." It allowed the assistant chief of the Division of Southeast Asian Affairs, Kenneth Landon, to file Ho's letters away because "our government was just not interested."

The fact that a mid-level bureaucrat felt comfortable making such a determination points back to the men at the top. They set the tone, the guiding philosophy governing the daily

workings of the government. Concern for France as an ally
in the postwar world superseded Roosevelt's legacy regarding
Vietnam, his search for an international mechanism to express
the historic American antipathy toward colonialism. Truman
had opportunities to reconsider. For example, the American
ambassador in China warned him about dire consequences
flowing from the growing Asian perception that the United
States supported colonial powers. Truman, with open eyes,
weighed the matter and stuck to his decision. His rejection
of Ho Chi Minh and the Viet Minh version of Vietnamese
nationalism marks a historic turning point.

In early 1954, John Foster Dulles reviewed the history of
the United States involvement in Indochina, concluding that
the decisive blunder occurred in 1945 when the United States
permitted the French to return. He noted that Roosevelt had
promoted his idea of trusteeship against the opposition of the
British and French at the Cairo and Teheran conferences.
Then, Roosevelt had opposed any French presence in Southeast Asia. The British and French capitalized upon the inattention of the Truman administration to return forces to
Vietnam. Dulles acknowledged that Truman had been under-
standably preoccupied by other matters but still believed that
he had committed a grave error.

Until the Korean War, President Truman paid little attention to Indochina. Clark M. Clifford, who served in his administration, recalls that Truman never had to focus on Southeast
Asia. It "was regarded by our government as a French problem." When North Korea invaded across the 38th Parallel, the
Truman administration perceived that it confronted a choice
between a policy of anticolonialism, an ideal that arguably
even Roosevelt had abandoned in the breach, or anticommunism. When it chose the latter, it took a decisive step along a
path that led to Dien Bien Phu, Ngo Dinh Diem, the Gulf of
Tonkin Resolution, and the ugly flight from the rooftop of
the Saigon embassy in 1975. At the time it was one rather
minor decision among myriad other more pressing presidential decisions.

In addition to this connection between the Korean War and
the American involvement in Vietnam, two more should be
highlighted: The specter of Chinese intervention in Indochina

clouded the Truman administration's deliberations about the region. Secretary of State Dean Acheson never recovered from accusations that his neglect had caused the Korean War in the first place. To protect himself from similar blame, he spent more time worrying about what the Chinese might do in Vietnam than about the wisdom of the basic United States position that supported the French.

The Korean War, the first American conflict in the nuclear age, also established the precedent that the United States would fight future wars without necessarily using its entire arsenal. This evolved into an acceptance of "limited wars," conflicts full of battlefield constraints. The United States showed the world that it would tolerate enemy use of sanctuary areas adjacent to the war zone. This precedent greatly impeded the American war effort in Vietnam, particularly the self-imposed reluctance to violate Cambodian and Laotian "neutrality" at a time when those countries served as the principal Communist logistical centers.

♦ ♦ ♦

Once the United States had made the initial decision to ignore Ho Chi Minh's appeals, it is much more difficult to see how the decision could have been reversed. It is a historical tragedy that steps taken by Marshal de Lattre in 1951 toward Vietnamese independence were not taken in 1946 at Fontainebleau during Ho's negotiations with France. They might have led to a peaceful transition. Sainteny, the main French negotiator, quoted Ho as saying: "Although we wish to govern ourselves and insist that you withdraw your administrators, I do need your professors, your engineers and your funds with which to build a strong, free Vietnam."

The Fontainebleau agreement signed by the French and Ho Chi Minh is one of the most puzzling aspects of this period. Did either or both parties enter the agreement in good faith or did they sign for tactical reasons? Both sides prepared for war at the same time that they talked peace, but this was mere prudence given past history. Even Ho's enemies believed he might have been sincere in his desire for peace. On the other hand, no one doubts that Admiral d'Argenlieu returned to Indochina and set about deliberately undermining the agreement. He took successive steps that forced Ho Chi Minh either to compromise to the extent that he would be considered a traitor to the nationalist cause or to strike back in open war. After mid-1946, the French refused to negotiate or even to talk with the Communist-dominated Democratic Republic of Vietnam, an attitude the United States emphatically endorsed. What remained were the Vietnamese nationalists outside of Ho's movement, who enjoyed only tepid popular support. By negotiating with the French and opening themselves to charges of collaborating with the colonial oppressors, these groups further reduced their credibility. By limiting talks to the feeble splinter groups, French policy ensured that officially recognized nationalism remained weak.

The United States having turned its back on Ho Chi Minh, the dominant American diplomatic concern was to find and back a non-Communist alternative. In theory this was an attainable goal. Edmund Gullion, who served as second-in-command in the U.S. embassy in Saigon from 1950 to 1953, believed that in the early 1950s, while all Vietnamese celebrated Ho's success against the French, he was "a long way from being the national choice of the Vietnamese," particularly those in the south. The problem then and thereafter was the lack of alternatives, a consequence of the previous French policy to stifle nationalism. Any Vietnamese leader who was a product of the French was fatally tarred by that association. Later, the same would be true of those leaders who closely associated with Americans. The intractable problem was that any Vietnamese nationalist found it extremely difficult to coalesce the forces of nationalism while depending militarily upon France or the United States.

When Dulles and Eisenhower chose to back Diem, the choice represented the best available alternative to Ho Chi Minh. In 1967 General Collins, the man who first wanted to replace the Vietnamese leader, described Diem as "staunchly anti-Communist, honest, courageous, and determined to establish the unity and independence of his country." But it was as if the stars in their courses conspired against him. From day one, Diem was literally under siege by opponents. He was never able to escape from under this crushing burden, and thus to utilize his manifest talents. Had circumstances been different, he might still be celebrated as Vietnam's national hero.

The history of the Eisenhower administration's relationship with Diem is a continuation of the problem policymakers faced when dealing with the French. The United States provided massive aid, first to France then to South Vietnam, but it was always aid without real influence. Neither American diplomats nor military officers found a way to translate assistance into political influence. If they provided aid before desired reforms occurred, the recipient had no incentive to carry out the reforms; but if aid was withheld contingent upon reform, it might arrive too late. This conundrum plagued the Truman and Eisenhower administrations and was apparent when the Kennedy administration entered office. Secretary of State Dean Rusk commented in 1961 about the frustrating problems facing diplomats in Vietnam, saying: "They were caught between pressing Diem to do the things he did not wish to do and the need to convey to him American support." Even ten years further into the American involvement in Vietnam, this problem persisted. A decorated combat veteran, Colonel David H. Hackworth, identified as a fundamental policy flaw the fact that by 1970, "while all along we paid the bills for the war effort and kept our toys and boys coming, we had little real control . . . over the Viet leaders on the receiving end."

From the military assistance program's inception, United States officials recognized the pitfalls of providing aid, and they tried to establish performance standards. Two examples, among many, occurred at key times in the program's development. Mindful of the unhappy history of military aid to Chiang Kai-shek, the Joint Chiefs of Staff reviewed Truman's proposed first package of military aid to the French in Indochina, expressing a strong antipathy toward unconditional aid. Instead, they wanted it to "be carefully controlled" and "integrated with political and economic programs."

Four years later, when looking at the disintegration in the south following the surrender at Dien Bien Phu, American diplomats in Saigon recommended an immediate aid program for "Free Vietnam." But they wanted this aid tied to performance in "instituting needed reforms." It was a recurring refrain. Although many recognized the underlying need for extensive political reform and pointed out that the absence of such reform provided the rallying point for the Communists, Americans proved largely powerless to influence political change inside South Vietnam. Absent reform there was not enough popular support for the American-backed government. Absent sufficient popular support, the South Vietnamese could not suppress the Communists.

Not only was the United States unable to promote reform effectively; perversely, as aid increased, American leverage decreased. When the United States expanded assistance to France, the American stake in the outcome increased. The French realized this and so felt better able to resist pressures for reform. This applied equally to the American relationship with South Vietnam. Also, and perhaps more important, once a large, visible assistance program became evident, American prestige became engaged.

American leaders, most importantly Eisenhower himself, believed prestige—by which he meant the value the world placed upon the United States' word and the reliability with which the nation honored its commitments—to be an invaluable resource. During the debate over intervention at Dien Bien Phu, prestige had been a cautionary factor. "The President said that if we were to put one combat soldier into Indochina, then our entire prestige would be at stake, not only in that area but throughout [the] world." Yet, a year later prestige pulled in the opposite direction, when Secretary of State Dulles said: "We do have a tremendous stake in the future of Vietnam . . . from [the] viewpoint of our national security and prestige." Senator Kennedy, speaking to the American Friends of Vietnam in 1956, picked up on this theme when he warned that if the United States failed to support South Vietnam "our prestige in Asia will sink to a new low."

Beginning with Eisenhower, perceptions of prestige joined with assessments of national security and desires to justify sunk costs to bring leaders to conclude that the effort had to continue. No one looked at it through the eyes of the opponent. At any decision point—1950, 1954, 1956, 1961, 1964—the Vietnamese Communists had more at stake—having expended more effort, scarce treasure, and blood—than did the United States. However much prestige, national security, and the imperative to recoup an investment drove American decision makers, these factors drove the Vietnamese Communists even harder.

♦ ♦ ♦

One of the striking features of American policy toward Vietnam during the Eisenhower administration is the consistent emphasis on the need to enlist the support of the native peoples. A single three-week span in 1954 highlights this fact. The day after the fall of Dien Bien Phu, Eisenhower lamented that it was clear the native population was far from "won over" to the French. Their reluctance to resist communism was "heartbreaking." Sixteen days later the Operations Coordinating Board echoed the Commander in Chief's views, reporting to the National Security Council: "The essential problem or task is to clarify the issues in the minds of the Vietnamese people and to convince them that the civil war is being exploited by international Communism which is capturing the legitimate nationalist movement."

By the end of May, Eisenhower concluded that popular support was absolutely necessary to attain the United States' goals. He told the National Security Council that without such support "no purely military victory would prove worth having."

Statesmen and military men alike appreciated that the root cause of failure was French inability to motivate the Vietnamese people. Nearly every American individual or group, military or diplomatic, who visited Vietnam during the French war, including Vice President Nixon and Congressman Kennedy, understood and reported this. When the Eisenhower administration decided the United States should replace France in Vietnam, it invested a great deal of effort to avoid repeating the errors of the past. Despite all, it failed.

Many Americans came to Vietnam with reasonable-sounding ideas that somehow did not work when they tried to implement them in an alien environment. Edward Lansdale believed that a large part of this problem stemmed from the fact that "words meant one thing to an American in Washington and something very different out in Saigon." Even worse, according to Lansdale, many American officials maintained superior airs much like colonial masters. Referring to both Collins and Maxwell Taylor, he said that "their talk with Diem was the country squire looking down his aristocratic nose at a bumpkin. . . . Let's cut out the American self-delusion. We lose 'people's wars' that way." William Colby said much the same thing when he reflected upon what had gone wrong, maintaining that "the underlying reason, I believe, was the American difficulty in understanding that alien culture, and its insistence that the Vietnam problem could be handled by concepts and solutions that we Americans prescribed."

After World War II, the American approach to foreign policy was that of an engineer. In the Truman and Eisenhower administrations, the secretaries of state erected structures—treaty organizations and alliances—to contain communism. This was done in the belief that the deterrent effect of the structure would keep Communists at bay. In places it worked. The Russians never challenged NATO, and neither the Russians nor the Chinese attacked a SEATO country. SEATO also acted as a check against a conventional North Vietnamese invasion, although the major problem in Vietnam was neither international communism nor conventional attack from the north. Just as the prime architect for SEATO, John Foster Dulles, warned when he spoke about the Communist ability to "burrow under" any defensive line utilizing subversive tactics, it was internal subversion that fatally undermined the elaborate structure the United States conceived and built in Southeast Asia. Dulles had intended SEATO only as an emergency stopgap measure, but those who followed tried to make it more than it could be. When Congress adopted the Tonkin Gulf Resolution by vote of 504 to 2 in 1964, it stated that the United States was prepared "to take all necessary steps" to assist in the defense of a SEATO country. The edifice Dulles erected to deter the Communists at a delicate time in 1954, a structure supposedly designed to ensure an international response to threat, became, ten years later, the rationale for unilateral American intervention.

How does a nation end a mistaken commitment? Any bureaucracy has enormous difficulty reversing a position. Along with the factors already cited, vested bureaucratic interests become attached to specific programs, propelling them ever onward. Within the government, individuals have trouble criticizing an existing policy since they recognize the importance of an optimistic outlook. Promotions are based on perceptions of progress, the extent to which someone has advanced a program toward its stated goal.

Harry S. Truman pondered this problem. He recognized that top military and political leaders receive most of their facts from their staffs, and that staffers provide this information in condensed form, usually via briefings. Truman believed that the system worked for the President because his staff comprised people from a variety of backgrounds who could argue policy without fear that it might end their careers. In a worst case, they could return to their previous employment, which was often outside government. Truman worried that this was not the case in the military, where staffers' futures depended upon the efficiency reports given them by their superiors, a substantial disincentive for argument against their superiors' notions. While there is much truth in Truman's reflections, it is notable that the military did not simply rubber-stamp the American drift into Vietnam. Time and again in the 1950s, key military men objected strongly to a growing involvement. They proposed fundamental preconditions for American success that have stood the test of time. Civilians just as often chose to ignore their advice.

In view of the enormous obstacles impeding radical adjustments to an ongoing policy, let alone the abandonment of a commitment entirely, it is essential to take steps to ensure that policies are built on firm ground from the start. Here the experience of a military commander who was never defeated on the battlefield and later rose to become head of state is applicable. Arthur Wellesley, the first duke of Wellington, developed and employed a system utilizing men he called "exploring officers." They were handpicked, active, intelligent young men who rode about the countryside talking to all, observing everything, and sending digests back directly to Wellington himself. Quite simply, they were an extension of the general's eyes. Updated to modern times, the United States would be well served by a small corps of similar people who would be assigned to Third World, backwater places; precisely the locales that have bred every trouble requiring American military intervention from Korea to Vietnam through Panama to the Persian Gulf. Without constricting bureaucratic ties, these modern "exploring officers" would be free to mingle with the people and assess the pulse of the country. They must report directly to someone important, so the intelligence they glean is not lost to bureaucratic impediment.

In Vietnam in the 1950s, Americans were first dependent upon the French and then upon the South Vietnamese for information about what was taking place in the all-important hinterland. Lack of language skills forced the United States into this perilous dependency. At a minimum, to prepare for the future the United States should promote foreign language literacy. The government could target obscure but potentially critical languages. There are some 128 languages spoken in the Soviet empire. If that empire disintegrates, the ability to communicate with the fragments would be invaluable. This is perhaps even more important in the Persian Gulf, where lack of language skill and cultural understanding interfered with embassy intelligence gathering in Iran before the Shah fell and contributed to the confrontation with Iraq.

♦ ♦ ♦

When North Vietnam finally conquered the South in 1975, the domino theory received its acid test. Instead of triggering a collapse, as the theory had predicted, the fall of the first domino resulted in the others turning inward on themselves. Vietnamese fought Cambodians, who defended themselves with Chinese assistance. China attacked Vietnam. The glue that had bonded Communist solidarity, Western occupation, dissolved once the last Western power left and Vietnam became whole. The domino theory proved a fallacy.

The domino analogy more correctly fits the way successive administrations made decisions regarding Southeast Asia. Once Truman determined to support the French, each subsequent decision to expand the American effort inexorably fell into place. In the future, when American leaders question whether the nation may be entering into a mistaken commitment, they will undoubtedly reflect upon the same issues of consistency, prestige, and justification for spent resources that influenced presidential decisions about Vietnam. These issues overwhelmed objective evaluation of the likelihood of success in Vietnam, pushing leaders toward the next escalation. Vietnam, the first domino, showed that the ultimate cost of defeat is much higher than perceptions of inconsistency, lost prestige, and wasted effort.

Part 2. THE CONTINUING VEIL OF SECRECY

Dwight D. Eisenhower died on March 28, 1969, a day when some 440,000 American fighting men were on the ground in Vietnam. At the beginning of the month soldiers of the 101st Airborne Division helicopter-assaulted into the A Shau Valley to begin an extended campaign against this Communist bastion. It would produce a battle that seared the American consciousness, the battle of Hamburger Hill. Over a nine-day period the North Vietnamese defenders bloodily repulsed four assaults before a fifth captured the hill. The American infantry suffered heavy losses for an insignificant objective they abandoned soon thereafter. The battered soldiers represented exactly the ground commitment in Asia the former President had so feared. Their presence produced two grand strategic questions relevant to the Eisenhower period: Would he have made the decisions that his successors made? and How did he evaluate his administration's role in the American involvement to Vietnam? From the time he left office until his death, there were Americans fighting in Vietnam. Eisenhower's refusal to do anything to jeopardize servicemen in combat caused him to neither speak nor write with complete candor regarding the war.

After leaving office he had set to work on the first volume of his memoirs, *Mandate for Change*. The draft chapter devoted to Indochina kept growing longer even while it became apparent that Vietnam was to figure prominently in his successor's foreign policy. Pressed by a looming publication date and the desire to avoid interference with President Kennedy's handling of a difficult situation, Eisenhower ruthlessly slashed his text until the chapter entitled "Chaos in Indochina" was reduced to a manageable forty-four pages. At that, it remained the longest chapter in the book. But the shortened chapter left to his confidants and biographers the task of explicating much of what had occurred during his presidency and of assessing to what extent, if any, Eisenhower believed he had misstepped.

The starting place for an examination of this tantalizing what-if has to be Eisenhower's briefing given to Kennedy on the day before the latter's inauguration. The participants' recollections, first revealed in Arthur M. Schlesinger's biography of Kennedy and elaborated upon by another who was present, Clark M. Clifford, in a 1969 article reappraising the American role, largely match the declassified archival record of the conversation. There is no avoiding the fact that Eisenhower told Kennedy that Laos was vital to American interests and, if all else failed, justified American combat intervention. One could only conclude that if Eisenhower believed intervention in Laos necessary, then he believed the same about Vietnam itself, unless Eisenhower's words should not be taken at face value. This latter is the idea sympathetic biographers have developed.

William Bragg Ewald, Jr., who served as the former President's research chief during the writing of his memoirs and later wrote his own biography of Eisenhower, advances the theory that Eisenhower said conflicting things about Laos, just as he had done during the parallel crisis in Indochina in 1954 and the Formosa Strait in 1955 and 1958. He claims that Eisenhower's special assistant for national security affairs, Gordon Gray, "vividly recalls Eisenhower's vehement insistence that landlocked Laos would be the last place where he'd want to commit U.S. troops." Ewald concludes that when Eisenhower left office he had not resolved what to do but chose deliberately "the line of ambiguity, between capitulation and intervention—that had long been a central characteristic of the Eisenhower performance." But, Ewald continues, Eisenhower believed Kennedy was badly inexperienced and that he had a tendency to "tilt soft." Therefore, to stiffen the new President's resolve toward Southeast Asia, he described the situation in a hawkish way.

This theory overreaches. Eisenhower did feel that Kennedy

was inexperienced, and he had also learned that obfuscation was the art of deterrent diplomacy. However, throughout his career Eisenhower proved a shrewd judge of character and ability. Surely he would know that his complex approach toward deterrence, involving a mixture of subtle warning and threatening bombast—the John Foster Dulles method—would be lost on the inexperienced new President. Given that he wanted to share his experience with his successor, either he should have realized that Kennedy would take his words at face value, or these words reflect his true belief. The Eisenhower historians who try to frame his words in a favorable light in view of what was to come are too uncritical. They do not want him seen as the architect of the country's greatest post-World War II foreign policy and military disaster.

Eisenhower did not authorize Americans to serve as combat troops in Vietnam, although he tolerated an advisory role that increasingly approximated combat. The crucial factor influencing his decision was the appearance that the American-sponsored government was winning. His successors confronted an entirely different situation, one in which it appeared that the South Vietnamese government was losing.

In *Mandate for Change,* Eisenhower observed that even after Dien Bien Phu's fall the French had sufficient forces to win if they could induce their Vietnamese forces to fight and the population to support that fight. He wrote a conclusion that should have been pondered deeply by later American strategists who devised plans designed to "win the hearts and minds" of the Vietnamese people, stating: "But guerrilla warfare cannot work two ways; normally only one side can enjoy reliable citizen help."

During the Dien Bien Phu crisis, both Eisenhower and his Vice President emphasized the importance of defeating the Viet Minh guerrilla tactics lest the Soviets export them to other places. Nikita Khrushchev's January 1961 speech supporting wars of national liberation made real the threat. By that time a different leader sat in the White House, but he reacted in much the same way: President Kennedy wanted the Green Berets to go to Vietnam to defeat a war of national liberation because he considered Vietnam a showcase conflict. Kennedy believed that American success was necessary to prevent the Communists from employing these tactics elsewhere.

There can be little doubt that had Eisenhower been President once Americans entered combat in Vietnam, the war would have been fought much differently. In *Mandate for Change* he stressed that the United States should not fight future "brush-fire" wars as it did in Korea, stating: "We would refuse to permit our adversary to enjoy a sanctuary from which he could operate without danger to himself; we would not allow him to blackmail us into placing limitations upon the types of weapons we would employ." He further revealed his attitude toward the use of nuclear weapons, when, in the 1960s, an interviewer asked if American bombing at Dien Bien Phu had been seriously considered. He answered that only an atomic weapon could have been effective.

On July 2, 1965, Eisenhower and President Lyndon Johnson discussed the situation in Vietnam. Johnson was about to attend a pivotal meeting to decide the future of the American role in Vietnam. Three top advisers—Secretary of Defense Robert McNamara, Chairman of the Joint Chiefs of Staff General Earle G. Wheeler, and the commander in Vietnam, General William Westmoreland—all recommended sending more troops to Vietnam. An alternative, promoted by General James Gavin—the paratroop general who had helped Matthew Ridgway keep the Army out of Indochina in 1954—was the "enclave" strategy. It proposed that Americans would help the South Vietnamese hold key cities and ports, but not challenge the Communists in the hinterland. Johnson supposed he would agree with the escalation policy and that he would have to call up the reserves. Before deciding what to do, he wanted to hear from the man he called his "best Chief of Staff." So, he asked Eisenhower for his opinion: "Yes, when you go into a place merely to hold sections or enclaves you are paying a price and not winning. When you once appeal to force in an international situation involving military help for a nation . . . you have to go all out! This is a war, and as long as they [the enemy] are putting men down there, my advice is do what you have to do."

Plaintively, Johnson inquired, "Do you really think we can beat the Vietcong?"

Eisenhower replied that it was "hard to say" because no one

seemed to know how many of the Viet Cong came from the north and how many from within South Vietnam.

Johnson told him that "we had killed 26,000, 300 yesterday and 250 the day before."

After discussing numbers, Eisenhower repeated that it was his feeling that the United States should go ahead and escalate as quickly as possible. He concluded, "We are not going to be run out of a free country that we helped to establish."

As time passed and criticism of the war increased, Eisenhower's brother Milton talked with Johnson about the course of events. The President kept saying that he was carrying out the policy of Truman, Eisenhower, and Kennedy. Milton Eisenhower replied, "President Johnson, you're making a terrible mistake. President Eisenhower was bitterly opposed to any participation in the Vietnam war. He was importuned by the Air Force and everybody else, and he declined time and again." Johnson expressed surprise, saying that the former President had never criticized the war to him. Milton Eisenhower pointed out that his brother would never undermine the military and said, "You just remember that Truman gave monetary help, Eisenhower put in a few men as advisers, but Kennedy put the first men in to start shooting, and you're the one that expanded the war."

♦ ♦ ♦

When Daniel Ellsberg leaked United States government documents to *The New York Times* in 1971, the American public learned in unprecedented detail about the origins of their country's involvement in Vietnam. The classified documents that became known as the Pentagon Papers provided tremendous illumination of what had taken place. For example, both in response to journalists' questions and in his autobiography, Edward Lansdale vehemently denied using CIA bribe money to lure Vietnamese leaders away from the United Sect front in 1954 and 1955. In fact, as we have seen, his $10 million expenditure proved to be instrumental in maintaining Diem during the sect crisis. When the Pentagon Papers revealed that his diary clearly mentioned these payments, he had to retreat saying, "If I did, it has gone from my memory and worries me that it has . . . I wonder why in hell I would do such a thing. I presume it was to help Diem at his request."

One could suppose that under the intense scrutiny generated by the Pentagon Papers, almost everything of importance
became accessible. It is startling to learn how much history
about the United States involvement in Vietnam remains
shrouded by the government's continuing veil of secrecy. Numerous important documents written thirty-five to forty-five
years ago and stored in the National Archives are not open to
the public. Others contain blank spots, ranging from a few
words to several pages. Why is this so?

When queried in 1990, the National Security Council and
Central Intelligence Agency explained the policy guiding their
decisions to declassify records held in the United States archival system. The Department of State did not respond. By executive order, national security information pertaining to nine
categories may be classified. Of these, six are relevant to the
American involvement in Vietnam: military plans, weapons,
or operations; foreign government information; intelligence
activities, sources, and methods; foreign relations or U.S. foreign activities; a confidential source; and other national security categories "that require protection against unauthorized
disclosure as determined by the President or by agency heads
or other officials who have been delegated original classification authority by the President." In sum, virtually the entire
historical record could legally be classified.

The fact that much is available is testament to a vital democracy. The continued classification of some material can be understood in light of the government's legitimate need to retain
certain secrets. As we have seen, Eisenhower's Cabinet seriously considered using atomic bombs to relieve the French at
Dien Bien Phu. Details of the debate remain unknown to the
historian. Similarly, it is conceivable that an agent who, in the
critical year of 1954, was thirty years old, is now alive in 1990
and is leading a reclusive retirement in China, Vietnam,
France, or the United Kingdom. His story too must be a
secret.

Do the categories that can be comprehended as requiring
closely guarded government silence account for the quantity
of still classified material? The answer is most definitely no.
Background papers, policy papers, briefings, memoranda of

conversations, are all intermittently absent from the historical record. Much material has been examined as recently as the early 1980s by the appropriate government agency and yet retains its secret classification. A file folder marked "Indochina, April 1954" may appear on an index at a presidential library. The researcher requests the folder and it arrives empty, with an attached card inside that informs that the document has been removed at the request of a government agency, most commonly the National Security Council or the Central Intelligence Agency. More frequent than completely empty files are those from which up to half the documents have been removed. By reading those related documents that are available, one can surmise that much of the still secret material cannot be connected to espionage activities, nuclear secrets, or the other types of information that still should require secrecy.

Archival material is subject to review for possible declassification under what can only be called an obtuse law regulating national security information. It does provide a researcher with certain procedures by which to try to obtain the classified material. Provided that it has not been evaluated within the past two years, a researcher can request that a classified document be reviewed for possible declassification. The agency that created the document performs the review, and three outcomes are possible: The material can be declassified; the request can be refused; or the document can be "sanitized" (its still classified material deleted) so that it may or may not be comprehensible. In any event, the review process takes a minimum of about one year.

The word from National Archives staffers in 1990 is that currently the CIA in particular is very chary of declassifying anything. Apparently, ever since the investigation into the arms for hostages dealings with Iran, the so-called Iran-gate affair, the agency has held on to past secrets with great tenacity.

From a practical standpoint, the continuing classification of numerous documents dating from as early as 1945 seriously interferes with historical research into the American involvement in Vietnam. The careful researcher can learn a great deal about the origins of that involvement. He can uncover numerous examples of mistaken assumptions, omissions, miscalculations, and worse. He can only speculate about what remains concealed. All too often both individual and government agency reputations remain concealed by one of the enduring legacies of the Vietnam War, the government's continuing veil of secrecy.

Part 3. TO BEAR ANY BURDEN

Edward Lansdale, now promoted to the rank of brigadier general, wangled yet another trip to Vietnam four days after Christmas, 1960. He met with the CIA station chief in Saigon, William Colby. It was a difficult meeting for Colby, who had received instructions to treat his visitor with kid gloves because the Washington rumor mill believed that President-elect Kennedy would appoint Lansdale ambassador to Vietnam. Lansdale was indeed straining every nerve to gain this appointment. Colby and Lansdale discussed the situation and found themselves in fundamental agreement that the conflict in Vietnam was "essentially a guerrilla war and that the military approach was not the answer." Lansdale also met briefly with his old friend, President Diem. He asked for a loan of a helicopter. When Diem inquired why, he replied, "I want to see what this war's all about you started. I don't think you're fighting it right."

Following his tour of the hinterland, Lansdale returned to meet again with Diem. As always, Lansdale was full of ideas. In times past he had shared them with the Vietnamese president during one-on-one talks; however this time, the two did not meet alone. Diem's brother Nhu participated, and his malevolent presence dominated. When Lansdale asked Diem a question, Nhu gave the answer. Exasperated, Lansdale snapped at Nhu, "I am talking to your brother, not to you." It did not seem to make any difference and Nhu continued to interrupt with his ideas while Diem merely nodded assent. Nhu's influence cemented Lansdale's despair that events were spiraling out of control.

Upon his return to the United States, he wrote a long trip report for the Defense Department. The report began: "1961 promises to be a fateful year in Vietnam." He described how the Viet Cong were much closer to conquering the country than people in Washington realized. The MAAG needed to make drastic changes in its methods, as only "an inspired and determined effort" could keep Vietnam free. Typically, Lansdale made numerous recommendations including the suggestion that American advisers be allowed to work in combat areas. Lansdale submitted his report to the Defense Department two days before the new administration entered office. The secretary of defense thought it contained much wisdom and personally gave it to incoming Secretary Robert McNamara. It impressed McNamara as well, who passed it on to Kennedy's foreign policy adviser.

Simultaneously, from Saigon, Ambassador Durbrow sent to Washington the completed draft of a counterinsurgency plan. The plan rested on the assumption that for the moment Diem remained the "best hope" for success in Vietnam, provided his government undertook "necessary corrective actions." It called for American funding for an expanded South Vietnamese Army and Civil Guard. The quid pro quo from Diem's government was the expectation that he undertake a list of political reforms.

The counterinsurgency plan was the first of its type President Kennedy had ever seen. He could not know how similar it was to a host of other United States proposals dating back to the Truman administration. Ten days after his inauguration, Kennedy endorsed the "Counter Insurgency Plan for Vietnam." Its mission was quite simple: to defeat the Communist insurgency. Toward this end, he authorized over $41 million in new aid, but Kennedy doubted it would be enough. He wrote on the planning document: "Why so little?" Five days later the new President read Lansdale's report. It stunned him. He turned to his aide and said: "This is the worst yet. . . . You know Ike never briefed me about Vietnam."

Kennedy's Cabinet discussed what to do. Weighing heavily in their thinking was a recent speech Nikita Khrushchev had delivered in Moscow. He said that the coming decade would lead to the triumph of world communism and considered ways that it would happen. The Soviet leader rejected conventional warfare since it inevitably led to nuclear holocaust. Instead, national liberation wars, "which began as uprisings of colonial peoples against their oppressors [and] developed into guerrilla wars" would provide the means to triumph. Khrushchev cited Vietnam as an example and concluded that Marxists everywhere should support such wars. Khrushchev's bellicose confidence that subversion and guerrilla war would result in worldwide Communist victory greatly alarmed Kennedy.

Eisenhower's warning about the Laotian crisis, the Military Assistance Advisory Group's counterinsurgency plan, Lansdale's Vietnam trip report, and Khrushchev's speech supporting wars of national liberation all occurred during Kennedy's first weeks in office. His secret responses were dramatic and decisive. As a stopgap measure, he immediately directed the head of the CIA to prepare covert operations against North Vietnam. He assigned an aide the task of evaluating the status of the U.S. Army's antiguerrilla capability. In short order this would lead first to his acquaintance with and then romantic admiration for the Army Special Forces. Soon he directed a tremendous expansion in their numbers. He would restore the green beret to them as a symbol that these warriors served as the shock troops in the war against Communist guerrillas.

At the end of January 1961, Kennedy offered his public response to Khrushchev's speech. In his first State of the Union Message he spoke of relentless Communist pressure in Asia and described his unswerving resolve to resist it: "We seek in all Asia, and, indeed, in all of the world—freedom for the people and independence for the government. And this nation shall persevere in our pursuit of these objectives."

From his first days in office Kennedy received briefings on Asian affairs that "supported the assessment of the previous Administration." The new President concurred with Eisenhower's conclusion that the United States should not withdraw from Southeast Asia. It was a position from which he never wavered.

John F. Kennedy made a promise in his inaugural address. To assure the survival of liberty, the nation would "pay any price, bear any burden." That burden would be the Vietnam War.

NOTES

CHAPTER I: DATELINE TO CONFLICT

Epigraph: George F. Kennan, *Russia and the West Under Lenin and Stalin* (Boston: Little, Brown & Co., 1960), p. 5.

15. "well-being of Annam": *United States-Vietnam Relations, 1945–1967*, U.S. Department of Defense, 12 vols., study (Washington, D.C.: Government Printing Office, 1971), Vol. 1, p. B-13. Hereafter cited as *US-VN Relations*.
17. "Rich people, soldiers": *US-VN Relations*, Vol. 1, p. B-20.
17. "no matter what obstacles": Quoted in Layton, Edwin T. *"And I Was There"* (New York: William Morrow & Co., 1985), p. 118.
18. "further offense": *US-VN Relations*, Vol. 1, p. A-11.
18. "respect the right": Joint Statement by President Roosevelt and Prime Minister Churchill, 14 August 1941, in *Foreign Relations of the United States, Diplomatic Papers 1941*, Vol. I (Washington, D.C.: Government Printing Office, 1958), p. 368. Hereafter *FRUS*.
19. "preserve for the French": *US-VN Relations*, Vol. 1, p. A-12.
20. "we'd ask our allies": Quoted in Harry Maurer, *Strange Ground: Americans in Vietnam 1945–75, an Oral History* (New York: Henry Holt & Co., 1989), p. 37.
20. "in all the greatness": Murphy to Giraud, 2 November 1942; *US-VN Relations*, Vol. 7, part VB, p. 16.
21. "the British Empire system": *US-VN Relations*, Vol. 1, p. A-19.
21. "France has milked it": Roosevelt to Stettinius, 24 January 1944, in *US-VN Relations*, Vol. 7, part VB, p. 30.
21. "the white man's rule": Quoted in Edward R. Stettinius, Jr., *Roosevelt and the Russians: The Yalta Conference* (Garden City, N.Y.: Doubleday & Co., 1949), p. 237.
22. "within the sphere of interest": William D. Leahy, *I Was There: The Personal Story of the Chief of Staff to Presidents Roosevelt and Truman Based on His Notes and Diaries Made at the Time* (New York: McGraw-Hill, 1950), p. 244.
23. "foreclosing the Americans": "Recent Developments in Relation to Indochina," 2 November 1944, in *US-VN Relations*, Vol. 7, part VB, p. 39.
23. "no final decisions": Roosevelt to Stettinius, 3 November 1944, in *US-VN Relations*, Vol. 7, part VB, p. 40.
24. "It is a matter for postwar": *US-VN Relations*, Vol. VII, part VB, p. 45.
25. "good policy": State Department telegrams of 2/2/45 and 2/18/45; file 800, Box 74; RG84, National Archives. Hereafter NA.
25. "While there is life": Leahy, op. cit., p. 313.
26. General Wedemeyer: Albert Wedemeyer, *Wedemeyer Reports!* (New York: Henry Holt & Co., 1958), p. 350.
26. "slaughtered in the jungle": Claire Lee Chennault, *Way of a Fighter: The Memoirs of Claire Lee Chennault* (New York: G.P. Putnam's Sons, 1949), p. 342.

27. "inadvisable": Memorandum for the Secretary of State, 17 March 1945, in *US-VN Relations*, Vol. 1, p. A-18.

27. Patti-Ho Chi Minh meeting: Archimedes L.A. Patti, *Why Vietnam?* (Los Angeles: University of California Press, 1980), p. 86.

28. "Vive la France": Translation of speech reported to American embassy in China; file 800, box 74; RG84, NA.

28. "disappointment to both sides": Debriefing at Department of State, 30 January 1946, in *US-VN Relations*, Vol. 1, p. B-45.

29. "seemed relieved": *US-VN Relations*, Vol. 1, p. A-21. And see: Embassy Chungking to Washington, 11 May 1945; file 800, Box 74; RG84, NA.

29. "The real trusteeship": Landon to secretary of state, 21 May 1945; file 800, box 74; RG84, NA.

30. "civil liberties": *US-VN Relations*, Vol. 1, p. A-21.

30. "outside intervention": Melby Papers: "Communist Activities in Southeast Asia," Southeast Asia File, 1948–49, Box 8, Harry S. Truman Library. Hereafter TL.

31. WELCOME: Maurer, op. cit., p. 29.

31. "Why not help us?": Quoted in Rene J. Defourneaux, "A Secret Encounter with Ho Chi Minh," *Look*, Vol. 30, No. 16 (9 August 1966), p. 32.

31. Anti-French sentiment: Quentin Roosevelt letter of 18 August 1945; file 800, Box 74, RG84, NA.

31. Ho Chi Minh's Headquarters, Summer 1945: Quoted in Defourneaux, op. cit., p. 33.

33. Bao Dai letter: Rose Conway File: "Memorandum for the President," 21 August 1945; OSS Chronological File, June–August 1945, Box 15, TL.

33. Donovan's report: Rose Conway File: "Memorandum for the President," 22 August 1945; OSS Chronological File, June–August 1945, Box 15, TL.

34. "They seem to have no knowledge": Rose Conway File: "Memorandum for the President," 31 August 1945, OSS Chronological File, June–August 1945, Box 15, TL.

35. "the fundamental issue": White House Map Room File: Incoming Messages, 12 September 1945; Top Secret File, Box 1, TL.

35. "we can still be friends": Quoted in Maurer, op. cit., p. 37.

36. "We are touched": Ho to Truman, 29 September 1945; file 800, Box 74; RG84, NA.

37. Kennan's report: Kennan to secretary of state, 26 September 1945; file 800, Box 74; RG84, NA.

37. Patti-Ho conversation: Patti, op. cit., p. 473.

38. "effort to please": Hale to Holland, 4 October 1945; file 800, Box 74; RG84, NA.

38. "The Soviet Union": R&A 1346; file 800, Box 74; RG84, NA.

39. "the struggle will be long and bloody": Sprouse to secretary of state, 24 October 1945; file 800, Box 74; RG84, NA.

39. "I beg to express": Ho to Byrnes, 1 November 1945; file 800, Box 74; RG84, NA.

40. "no action": Moffat to Vincent, 15 November 1945; file 800, Box 74; RG84, NA.

40. Indochinese Communist party: Central Committee Indochinese Communist Party, 11 November 1945, *US-VN Relations*, Vol. 1, p. B-42.

40. "babying the Russians": Quoted in Walter Isaacson and Evan Thomas, *The Wise Men: Six Friends and the World They Made* (New York: Simon and Schuster, 1986), p. 346.
41. "You don't tell a guy": Quoted in Maurer, op. cit., p. 40.
41. "the usual kind of guff": Quoted in ibid., p. 42. Landon's telegram informing the secretary of state about Ho's letters is in *FRUS 1946*, Vol. VIII, *The Far East* (Washington, D.C.: Government Printing Office, 1971), pp. 26–27.
42. "limits of Soviet power": Isaacson and Thomas, op. cit., p. 353.
42. Ho's treaty with French: Joseph Buttinger, *Vietnam: A Political History* (New York: Frederick A. Praeger Publishers, 1968), p. 242.
42. "sell our country": Quoted in ibid., p. 243.
43. "prefer to negotiate": *US-VN Relations*, Vol. 1, p. A-31.
43. "no question of imposing": Ibid.
43. "ambushed at San Jay": Ibid., p. A-25.
44. "our moral obligations": Quoted in Isaacson and Thomas, p. 373.
45. "Turkey must be preserved": Quoted in ibid., p. 370.
45. "world conquest": Quoted in ibid., p. 371.
45. "The language of military power": Quoted in ibid., p. 376.
46. "There is no reason": Quoted in ibid., p. 374.
46. "use all means": Quoted in Edwin Bickford Hooper, Dean C. Allard, and Oscar P. Fitzgerald, *The United States Navy and the Vietnam Conflict*, Vol. I, *The Setting of the Stage to 1959* (Washington, D.C.: Naval History Division, Department of the Navy, 1976), p. 120.
46. Haiphong incident: It is exceedingly difficult to learn the exact truth of these events. In November there were neither French nor international newspaper correspondents in North Vietnam so the truth must be deduced from official, and obviously biased, reports from both sides.
46. "Assume you will see Ho": Acheson to Reed, 5 December 1946, in *FRUS 1946*, Vol. VIII, pp. 67–68.
47. "intransigence and violence": Ibid., p. 68.
47. "against all whites": Byrnes to Certain Missions Abroad, 17 December 1946, in *FRUS 1946*, Vol. VIII, p. 72.
47. "basic Vietnam powers": Ibid., p. 73.
48. "France does not intend": *US-VN Relations*, Vol. 1, p. A-33.
48. "Before any negotiations": Quoted in Buttinger, op. cit., p. 284.
48. Vincent's report: Vincent to Acheson, 23 December 1946, in *US-VN Relations*, Vol. 1. p. A-43.
49. "The hour for national salvation": Quoted in Hooper et al., p. 122.

CHAPTER II: A DIRTY WAR

Epigraph: Kennan, op. cit., p. 8.
51. "The best interests": Quoted in Harry S. Truman, *Memoirs by Harry Truman*, Vol. I, *Year of Decisions* (New York: Doubleday & Co., 1955), pp. 14–15. Hereafter Truman.
52. "pent-up fanatical nationalisms": Ibid., p. 237.
53. "rightful and eminent place": 201 A Endorsements, file O.F. 203 (1945–49), Box 769, TL.
54. "and drink Coke": Quoted in Isaacson and Thomas, op. cit., p. 348.

54. "scare the hell out": Quoted in ibid., p. 395.
54. "support to free peoples": Ibid.
54. "no hedging": Truman, Vol. II, *Years of Trial and Hope: 1946–1952* (New York: Doubleday & Co., 1956), p. 105.
54. "expansion of Communism": Quoted in Isaacson and Thomas, op. cit., p. 400.
55. "except in cases": *US-VN Relations*, Vol. 1, p. A-44.
55. "we have no solution": Ibid., p. A-45.
56. "in same boat": Ibid., p. A-46.
56. "Moscow-directed conspiracy": Ibid., p. A-50.
56. "a puppet government": Ibid., p. A-48.
56. "The Soviet acknowledgment": Ibid., p. A-59.
57. "suffered a rout": Quoted in Ronald H. Spector, *Advice and Support: The Early Years of the U.S. Army in Vietnam 1941–1960* (New York: The Free Press, 1985), p. 99.
58. "does not justify": Quoted in ibid., p. 99.
59. "an obviously Russian": White House Confidential File, "Military Assistance for Indochina," Mutual Defense File, Box 25, TL.
60. "United States insisted": Quoted in Spector, op. cit., p. 103.
61. "in grave hazard": Papers of Harry S. Truman: NSC 64, 27 February 1950. NSC Records, Box 212. *TL.*
62. "pursue their peaceful": Secretary of State Statement, 8 May 1950, in *US-VN Relations*, Vol. 7, part V, p. A-2.
62. "I have similarly directed": "Statement by the President on the Situation in Korea," 27 June 1950, in Harry S. Truman, *Public Papers of the Presidents of the United States: Harry S. Truman 1950* (Washington, D.C.: Government Printing Office, 1965), p. 492.
63. "We cannot honestly": Papers of Dean Acheson, Kennan to Acheson, 21 August 1950; August file, Box 65, TL.
64. "in order to avoid": Papers of Dean Acheson, "Truman-Attlee Talks," 4 December 1950, Memoranda of Conversation; October file, Box 65, TL.
64. "hated colonial regimes": Papers of Dean Acheson, "Report of Senators Green and Ferguson on Their Round-the-World Trip," 9 January 1951; January file, Box 66, TL.
64. "a monstrous conspiracy": President's Radio Report to the American People on Korea and on U.S. Policy in the Far East, 11 April 1951, in *US-VN Relations*, Vol. 7, part V, p. A-2.
65. "We could not deny": Truman, Vol. II, p. 437.
66. "to pacify the area": Confidential File: Truman to Auriol, 17 August 1950; State Department Correspondence, Box 41, TL.
67. "the annexation": 201 A Endorsements, file O.F. 203f (Cambodia-Laos/Vietnam), Box 771, TL.
67. "The Bao Dai regime": NSC Records, "Intelligence Memorandum No. 231," 7 October 1949; NSC/CIA file Dec. 48–Dec. 49, Box 2, TL.
67. "the Bao Dai experiment": Papers of Dean Acheson, 12 October 1949; October–November file, Box 64, TL.
67. "the demonstrated inequity": Papers of Dean Acheson, 10 March 1950; Memoranda of Conversation, March 1950, Box 64b, TL.
68. "the United States is convinced": Spector, op. cit., pp. 96–97.
68. "better off with Bao Dai": "Speech Delivered by William S.B. Lacy Before the Institute of Public Affairs University of Virginia," 11 July

1950. Papers of John S. Melby, Box 9, TL. Lacy spoke on behalf of the deputy assistant secretary of state for Far Eastern affairs.

69. "a bunch of second raters": Quoted in Spector, op. cit., p. 112.
69. "It was a bit of a shock": Papers of John F. Melby, "The Situation in Indochina," 12 December 1950; MDAP file, Box 9, TL.
70. Melby's private report to Rusk: For this very candid appraisal, see Melby to Lacy and Rusk in the Melby Papers, Chronological file, unedited documents, Box 12, TL.
70. "the keystone": Melby Papers: "Report by the Military Group of the Joint State-Defense Survey Mission to Southeast Asia," Southeast Asia File, Box 9, TL.
71. "I will never agree": Quoted in Hooper et al., op. cit., p. 174.
72. MacArthur comments: Papers of Dean Acheson, "Addendum to Notes on Wake Conference October 14, 1950"; Memoranda of Conversation, October file, Box 65, TL.
74. "The French have a knotty problem": Robert H. Ferrell, ed., *The Eisenhower Diaries* (New York: W.W. Norton & Co., 1981), p. 190.
75. "Not true!": *US-VN Relations*, Vol. 1, part II, p. A-19.
75. "The menu": Maurer, op. cit., p. 70.
76. "marked the turning of the tide": Acheson Papers, "Interview with General de Lattre de Tassigny Regarding Indochina," 14 September 1951; Memo of Conversation, Box 66, TL.
77. "the remnants of an empire": *US-VN Relations*, Vol. 1, part II, p. A-26.
77. "somewhat surprised": American Legation to Department of State, 29 November 1951, Box 3696; RG59, NA.
77. "propaganda project": Sturm to State Department, 22 November 1952, Box 3696, RG59, NA.
78. "the JCS": Stephen Jurika, Jr., ed. *From Pearl Harbor to Vietnam: The Memoirs of Admiral Arthur W. Radford* (Stanford, Calif.: Hoover Institution Press, 1980), p. 291.
79. "had been wrong": Anthony Eden, *Full Circle: The Memoirs of Anthony Eden* (Boston: Houghton Mifflin Co., 1960), p. 93.
80. "The central problem": Quoted in Truman, Vol. 2, p. 519.
81. "Communist domination": Office of the Special Assistant for National Security Affairs (OSANSA) NSC Series, Policy Paper Subseries: NSC 124/2, 5 August 1953; Box 8, Eisenhower Library. Hereafter EL.
82. "France had done all": Acheson Papers, Memorandum of Conversation, 15 April 1952; April file, Box 67, TL.
83. "kidding ourselves": Tannenwald Papers, "Trip to S.E. Asia," Subject file, 12 January 1953; Box 9, TL.
83. "lesser of two evils": Dulles to Laubach, 31 October 1950; John Foster Dulles Papers, Princeton University.
83. "The fundamental causes": NSC Records: "Possible Future Action in Indochina," 28 November 1950; Box 212, TL.
83. "What is it worth": Papers of John F. Melby, "The Situation in Indochina," 12 December 1950; MDAP file, Box 9, TL.

CHAPTER III: PRESIDENT EISENHOWER

Epigraph: Eisenhower's inaugural speech, 20 January 1953; Public Papers, Eisenhower, 1953.
86. "a bunch of screwballs": Truman, Vol. 2, p. 513.

86. "added little": Dwight D. Eisenhower, *Mandate for Change 1953–1956* (Garden City, N.Y.: Doubleday & Co., 1963), p. 85.

87. "shielded traitors": Stephen A. Ambrose, *Eisenhower: Soldier, General of the Army, President-Elect* (New York: Simon and Schuster, 1983), p. 543.

88. "with his great grin": Max Hastings, *The Korean War* (New York: Simon and Schuster, 1987), p. 315.

89. "survival of Western civilization": Quoted in Ambrose, *Eisenhower*, op. cit., p. 496.

90. "We have learned to expect": DDE diary: December 27, 1935–July 20, 1937; EL.

90. "the Oriental mind": Quoted in Sherman Adams, *Firsthand Report: The Story of the Eisenhower Administration* (New York: Harper & Bros., 1961), p. 101.

91. "lawfully constituted": Eisenhower, *Mandate for Change*, op. cit., p. 83.

92. "to assume its true complexion": Ibid., p. 167.

92. "America's influence": State of the Union Message, 2 February 1953; Public Papers, Eisenhower, 1953, p. 12.

92. "regardless of consequences": Eisenhower, *Mandate for Change*, op. cit., p. 130.

93. "the responsibility": Adams, op. cit., p. 87.

93. "Foster has been": Quoted in ibid., p. 89.

94. "old politico-economic": Quoted in Ronald W. Pruessen, *John Foster Dulles: The Road to Power* (New York: The Free Press, 1982), p. 502.

94. "appeasement": Louis L. Gerson, *The American Secretaries of State and Their Diplomacy*, Vol. XVII, *John Foster Dulles* (New York: Cooper Square Publishers, 1967), p. 43.

94. "strike back where it hurts": Ibid., p. 72.

97. "a reassessment": Jurika, op. cit., p. 326.

97. "An outstanding impression": Maxwell Taylor, *The Uncertain Trumpet* (New York: Harper & Bros., 1959), p. 15.

100. "All right then.": Quoted in Stephen A. Ambrose, *Eisenhower: The President* (New York: Simon and Schuster, 1984), pp. 92–93.

101. Korean casualties: Recall the analogous situation in 1968: more American fighting men died after the Paris "peace talks" opened than before they began.

101. "would be a fraud": Address "The Chance for Peace," 16 April 1953, in *Public Papers, Eisenhower 1953*, p. 184.

101. "it was known in advance": Bernard B. Fall, *Hell in a Very Small Place* (New York: Vintage Books, 1968), p. 295.

101. "The Chinese Communists": Eisenhower, *Mandate for Change*, op. cit., p. 338.

103. "the best hope for France": Eden, op. cit., p. 91.

103. "But that's not the way": Hendrick Papers, "Mission to North Vietnam"; Mutual Security Administration, Box 6, TL.

104. "no French initiative": Bernard B. Fall, *Street Without Joy*, 4th ed. (Harrisburg: The Stackpole Company, 1967), p. 63.

CHAPTER IV: STEADY AT THE HELM

Epigraph: Quoted in David Douglas Duncan, "The Year of the Snake," *Life*, Vol. 35, No. 5, 3 August 1953.

107. "The rapid creation of": Acheson Papers, "Memorandum of Conversa-

tion with Mr. Jean Monnet," 6 May 1952; May file, Box 67, TL.

107. "Who in hell": Quoted in Spector, op. cit., p. 131.

107. "greater concessions": Melby Papers, Unedited Documents file, Box 12, TL.

107. "French-Viet combination": Hendrick Papers, "MSA Mission to North Vietnam," 17 February 1953; Box 5, TL.

111. "he evaded": Eisenhower, *Mandate for Change*, op. cit., p. 168.

111. "When the French win": Quoted in Hooper et. al, op. cit., p. 204.

111. "a 100 degree change": Quoted in Spector, op. cit., p. 171.

112. "could not stand aloof": Eisenhower, *Mandate for Change*, op. cit., p. 168.

112. Eisenhower on Mutual Security Program: Special Message to the Congress on the Mutual Security Program, 5 May 1953, in *Public Papers, Eisenhower 1953*, pp. 256–59.

113. State Department views on Mao: For these views see the State Department study of 3 April 1953 in White House Central Files, Confidential File, Subject Series, Department of State; Box 67, EL.

113. "to find out why": Jurika, op. cit., p. 309.

114. "if Laos were lost": Ann Whitman File, NSC Series: 141st Meeting, 28 April 1953; Box 4, EL.

115. "if we had to supply": Jurika, op. cit., p. 311.

116. "down a rathole": Ann Whitman File, NSC Series: 143rd Meeting, 7 May 1953; Box 4, EL.

116. "It is your duty": Quoted in Jules Roy, *The Battle of Dienbienphu* (New York: Harper & Row, 1965), p. 6.

117. "loyal, aggressive": "Proposed Terms of Reference for the Chief of the U.S. Military Mission to Indochina," in *US-VN Relations*, Vol. 9, p. 62.

117. Navarre's temperament: Cited in Fall, *Hell in a Very Small Place*, op. cit., p. 27.

118. "My principal aim": Quoted in Roy, op. cit., p. 17.

118. "to see this war through": Spector, op. cit., p. 175.

119. Bradley's opinion: See Bradley to secretary of defense, 11 August 1953, in *US-VN Relations*, Vol. 9, pp. 134–35.

119. "make the same mistakes": Roy, op. cit., p. 21.

120. "reached the crossroads": "Further United States Support for France and the Associated States of Indochina," 5 August 1953, in *US-VN Relations*, Vol. 9, p. 126.

120. "the Laniel government": Ibid., p. 128.

120. "perfect their independence": Quoted in Spector, op. cit., p. 175.

121. how many men: Mark Perry, *Four Stars* (Boston: Houghton Mifflin Co., 1989), p. 54.

122. "a political climate": Radford to secretary of defense, 28 August 1953, in *US-VN Relations*, Vol. 9, p. 138.

122. "really, why": Remarks at the Governors' Conference, 4 August 1953, in *Public Papers, Eisenhower 1953*, p. 541.

123. Eisenhower speech to governors: Ibid., pp. 540–41.

124. "has become corrupt": Duncan, op. cit., p. 79.

124. "'other nations'": Ibid., p. 81.

124. "go very rapidly": "Probable Developments in Indochina Through Mid-1954," 4 June 1953, in *US-VN Relations*, Vol. 9, p. 46.

126. "concessions necessary": *US-VN Relations*, Vol. 1, part II, p. A-27.

127. "light at the end of a tunnel": *Time*, Vol. LXII, No. 13, 28 September 1953.

127. "We should fully support": Quoted in Spector, op. cit., p. 180.
127. "overly optimistic": Ibid., p. 181.
127. "the disdain they felt": Quoted in ibid., p. 123.
128. "fall like husks": Richard M. Nixon, *RN: The Memoirs of Richard Nixon* (New York: Grosset & Dunlap, 1978), p. 125.
128. "little or no effect": Jurika, op. cit., p. 336.
128. "no Westerner really knows": Ann Whitman File, NSC Series: 173rd Meeting of the NSC, 3 December 1953; Box 5, EL.
128. "We salute": Joint Statement . . . Following the Bermuda Conference, 7 December 1953, in *Public Papers, Eisenhower 1953*, p. 813.

CHAPTER V: CRISIS AT DIEN BIEN PHU

Epigraph: Quoted in Fall, op. cit., p. 51.
133. "You must repair": Quoted in Roy, op. cit., p. 74.
133. "the passing of 1953": Eisenhower, *Mandate for Change*, op. cit., p. 170.
133. 1954 State of the Union Message, in *Public Papers, Eisenhower 1954*, pp. 7–8.
134. Heath's report: Heath to secretary of state, 23 January 1954; Box 3696; RG59, NA.
134. "The only purpose": Ann Whitman File, NSC Series: 179th Meeting, 8 January 1954; Box 5, EL.
135. "With continued U.S. economic": "Statement of Policy by the National Security Council," 16 January 1954, in *US-VN Relations*, Vol. 9, p. 225.
135. NSC meeting: The discussion regarding Southeast Asia is in the Ann Whitman File, NSC Series: 181st Meeting, 21 January 1954; Box 5, EL. Much of Eisenhower's criticism of French strategy remains classified.
136. "Will the U.S. employ": OSANSA, NSC series, Policy Paper Subseries: NSC 177, 6 January 1954; Box 8, EL.
137. "commitment of *large* U.S. forces": Ibid.
137. "even to global war": President's Secretary File: from Enclosure B "Analysis," Memo for the Secretary of Defense, 28 November 1950; file NSC Meeting No. 88, Box 212, TL.
137. Acheson on limited intervention: Acheson Memos, no title, 17 June 1952; June file, Box 67, TL.
138. Air interdiction: American military experts studying this and similar French operations drew many conclusions about faulty French tactics. Comparing their own resources to the paltry French efforts—a United States F-105 fighter-bomber typically carried three tons of bombs; a single B-52, thirty-one tons of bombs—planners predicted that the answer to blocking Communist supply lines was greater firepower. While the resultant barrage did greatly increase target damage to and suffering by the munitions and men marching south, it was as devoid of strategic significance as had been the French effort.
139. "Look at my plan of fire": Quoted in Roy, op. cit., p. 123. Piroth commanded twenty-four 105-millimeter howitzers, a single 155-millimeter battery, and sixteen heavy mortars.
139. "can withstand any kind": OSANSA, NSC Series, Briefing Notes Subseries, Indochina: "Report of U.S. Special Mission to Indochina," 5 February 1954; Box 11, EL.
139. American approval of Dien Bien Phu: Fall, *Hell in a Very Small Place*, op. cit., pp. 108–9.

140. "However, a force": OSANSA, op. cit.
140. "lack of enthusiasm": The President's News Conference of 3 February 1954, in *Public Papers, Eisenhower 1954*, p. 227.
140. "two or three percent": Ann Whitman File, NSC Series: 183rd Meeting, 4 February 1954; Box 5, EL.
140. O'Daniel's optimistic report: OSANSA, op. cit.
141. "despite the confidence": Quoted in Spector, op. cit., pp. 187–89.
141. Collapse of Vietnamese Army: For Navarre's assessment of the decline in morale, see Ann Whitman File, Dulles-Herter Series: McClintock to secretary of state, 24 April 1954; Box 2, EL.
142. "medals, women, money": Quoted in Roy, op. cit., p. 230.
142. "alarmist interpretations": Spector, op. cit., p. 189.
142. "O'Daniel's most recent": Ann Whitman File, Dulles-Herter Series: Eisenhower to Dulles, 10 February 1954; Box 2, EL.
143. "First we send them planes": William Bragg Ewald, Jr., *Eisenhower the President* (Englewood Cliffs, N.J.: Prentice-Hall, 1981), p. 107.
143. "we must not lose Asia": Hagerty Papers, Diary Entries, NLE Transcriptions: 8 February 1954; Box 1, EL.
143. "no one could be more bitterly opposed": The President's news conference, 10 February 1954, in *Public Papers, Eisenhower 1954*, p. 250.
143. "a greater tragedy": Ibid., p. 253.
143. "in a darkened room": Ibid., p. 254.
146. "The ravines are deep": Quoted in Roy, op. cit., p. 129.
146. "What of it?": Quoted in ibid., p. 136.
147. "as at Verdun": Quoted in ibid., p. 142.
147. "he is done for": Quoted in ibid., p. 143.
147. "Dien Bien Phu was chosen": Quoted in ibid., p. 145.
147. "The Commander in Chief": Quoted in ibid., p. 144.
148. "who has the power": Report by the secretary of state, 24 February 1954; Executive Sessions of the Senate Foreign Relations Committee (Historical Series), Vol. VI, 83rd Cong., 2nd sess., 1954 (Washington, D.C.: Government Printing Office, 1977), p. 163.
148. "patently obvious": Ibid., p. 169.
149. "with your Scotch-Irish up": Ibid., p. 183.
149. "the big job": Ibid.
149. "probability of salvaging": Ann Whitman File, NSC Series: Dulles to Nixon, 1 March 1954 re 186th Meeting of the NSC; Box 5, EL.
149. "over to Ho Chi Minh": OSANSA, NSC Series, Policy Paper Subseries: NSC-177, 8 January 1954; Box 8, EL.
150. "no real military disaster": Ann Whitman File, NSC Series: 186th Meeting, 26 February 1954; Box 5, EL.
150. "Indo-China is considered": "Report by the President's Special Committee on Indo-China," 2 March 1954, in *FRUS 1952–54*, Vol. XIII, *Indochina*, part 1. (Washington, D.C.: Government Printing Office, 1982), p. 1109.
150. "give promise of leading": Ibid., p. 1116.
151. "Winning the battle": Quoted in Roy, op. cit., pp. 156–57.
152. "We are all surprised": Quoted in Fall, *Hell in a Very Small Place*, op. cit., p. 137.
152. "We're done for": Quoted in Roy, op. cit., p. 172.
153. "Colonel Piroth died": Quoted in ibid., p. 175.
154. "getting graver": Hagerty Papers, Diary Entries: 20 March 1954; Box 1, EL.

154. Radford opinion: For Radford's recollections, see Jurika, op. cit., p. 390.
154. "If the United States sent": Ann Whitman File, Dulles-Herter Series: Memorandum for the President, 23 March 1954; Box 2, EL.
155. "Next General Ely asked": Jurika, op. cit., p. 394.

CHAPTER VI: THE FALLING-DOMINO PRINCIPLE

Epigraph: Quoted in Adams, op. cit., p. 118.
157. "Resolved": John M. Taylor, *General Maxwell Taylor* (New York: Doubleday & Co., 1989), pp. 180–81.
158. "The measures taken": "Memorandum for the President," 24 March 1954, in *US-VN Relations*, Vol. 9, p. 290.
158. "did not wish to be free": Ann Whitman File, NSC Series: 190th Meeting, 25 March 1954; Box 5, EL.
159. Destroyed contingency plan: This was the Special Annex to NSC 177.
159. NSC meeting: Ann Whitman File, NSC Series: 190th Meeting, 25 March 1954; Box 5, EL.
161. "would be a grave threat": Ewald, op. cit., p. 113.
161. Dulles's speech: John Prados, *The Sky Would Fall: Operation Vulture: The U.S. Bombing Mission in Indochina, 1954* (New York: The Dial Press, 1983), p. 89.
163. "essential to Western": "The Decisive Moment," *Newsweek*, Vol. XLIII, No. 15, 12 April 1954.
163. "in opposing": *Chicago Tribune*, 1 September 1953; cited in Leslie H. Gelb with Richard K. Betts, *The Irony of Vietnam: The System Worked* (Washington, D.C.: The Brookings Institution, 1979), p. 205.
164. NSC meeting: Ann Whitman File, NSC Series: 191st Meeting, 1 April 1954; Box 5, EL.
164. "we'd have to deny it": Hagerty Papers, Diary Entries: 1 April 1954; Box 1, EL.
164. JCS members' views on intervention: JCS to Wilson, 31 March 1954, in *FRUS*, Vol. XIII, *Indochina*, part 1, pp. 1198–1199.
164. JCS rebuke of Radford: Memorandum by Chief of Staff Army, 2 April 1954, in *FRUS*, Vol. XIII, *Indochina*, part 1, pp. 1220–21.
165. "could expect no": Spector, op. cit., p. 202.
165. "You could take all day": Quoted in Prados, *The Sky Would Fall*, op. cit., p. 92.
165. Draft resolution on war powers: Draft Joint Resolution, 2 April 1954, in *FRUS*, Vol. XIII, *Indochina*, part 1, pp. 1211–12.
166. "sent as gladiators": Caroline F. Ziemke, "Senator Richard B. Russell and the 'Lost Cause' in Vietnam, 1954–1968," *The Georgia Historical Quarterly*, Vol. LXXII (Spring 1988), p. 38.
166. "If you're in an airplane": Quoted in Doris Kearns, *Lyndon Johnson and the American Dream* (New York: New American Library, 1976), p. 149.
166. "like telling children": Quoted in ibid., pp. 161–62.
167. "no more Koreas": "Memorandum for the File of the Secretary of State," 5 April 1954, in *FRUS*, Vol. XIII, *Indochina*, part 1, p. 1224.
167. "The President knew": Adams, op. cit., p. 118.
169. "for good or evil": Dillon to Department of State, 5 April 1954, in *FRUS*, Vol. XIII, *Indochina*, part 1, p. 1237.

170. "We failed to halt Hirohito": Eisenhower, *Mandate for Change*, op. cit., pp. 346–47. The entire message is in *FRUS*, Vol. XIII, *Indochina*, part 1, pp. 1239–41.

170. "unconstitutional": "Memorandum of Presidential Telephone Conversation," 5 April 1954, in *FRUS* Vol. XIII, *Indochina*, part 1, p. 1242.

170. "As I personally": Dulles to Dillon, 5 April 1954, in *FRUS*, Vol. XIII, *Indochina*, part 1, p. 1242.

171. "tremendous tensions": Hagerty Papers, Diary Entries: 5 April 1954; Box 1, EL.

171. "military disadvantages": "Army Position on NSC Action No. 1074-A," in *US-VN Relations*, Vol. 9, p. 332.

172. "had backed down": A diary entry made at the time and cited in Nixon, op. cit., p. 151.

172. NSC meeting: For the discussion related, see the Ann Whitman File, NSC Series: 192nd Meeting, 6 April 1954; Box 5, EL.

175. "'enemy of the people'": Quoted in Congressional Record, Vol. 100, pt. 4; 83d Cong., 2nd sess. (1954); 6 April, pp. 4671–81.

175. Eisenhower on domino theory: The President's news conference of 7 April 1954, in *Public Papers, Eisenhower 1954*, p. 383.

176. "not follow": Memorandum by the Chief of Staff, 6 April 1954, in *FRUS*, Vol. XIII, *Indochina*, part 1, p. 1269.

177. "really getting rough": Hagerty Papers, Diary Entries: 7 April 1954; Box 1, EL.

178. "part of his anatomy": Prados, *The Sky Would Fall*, op. cit., p. 113.

179. Eden's opinion: Eden, op. cit., p. 100.

180. "French cannot lose": Aldrich to Dulles, 6 April 1954, in *US-VN Relations*, Vol. 9, p. 366.

180. Eden on compromise at Geneva: Eden, op. cit., p. 102.

181. Dulles on atomic balance: For Dulles's relevant comments to the British ambassador, see *FRUS*, Vol. XIII, *Indochina*, part 1, p. 1217.

182. B-29 bombers: Fall claims that B-29s with French markings, the tricolor bull's-eye insignia, could be seen standing ready at Clark Field in the Philippines. See *Hell in a Very Small Place*, op. cit., p. 304.

183. "two atomic bombs": Ibid., p. 307.

184. "three laughable squares": Ibid., p. 278.

184. "headed for disaster": Prados, *The Sky Would Fall*, op. cit., p. 138.

184. "defending the cause": Exchange of Messages . . . Concerning the Defenders of Dien Bien Phu, 16 April 1954, in *Public Papers, Eisenhower 1954*, p. 399.

184. "putting our boys in": Spector, op. cit., p. 210.

185. Reaction to Nixon's statement: For details of this incident, see *FRUS*, Vol. XIII, *Indochina*, part 1, pp. 1346–48.

186. "the lead B-29": Quoted in Fall, *Hell in a Very Small Place*, op. cit., p. 306.

186. "to wage war here": Message quoted in note 1, *FRUS*, Vol. XIII, *Indochina*, part 1, p. 1348.

187. "real air power": Message quoted in *FRUS*, Vol. XIII, *Indochina*, part 1, p. 1349.

187. "Americans may think": Eden, op. cit., p. 110.

188. "I am bound to say": Smith to Dulles, 23 April 1954, in *FRUS*, Vol. XIII, *Indochina*, part 1, p. 1367.

189. "Staff on an hour's call": Ewald, op. cit., p. 110; quoting Hagerty Papers.

189. "a troubled man": Eden, op. cit., pp. 113–14.
189. For Franco-American conversations, see Dulles to Department of State, 24 April 1954, in *FRUS*, Vol. XIII, *Indochina*, part 1, note 1, p. 1391. Also see Ann Whitman File, Dulles-Herter Series: Incoming telegrams, Department of State, 23 April 1954; Box 2, EL.
190. U.S.-French-British meeting: Among the many difficulties in sorting out what really took place is Radford's claim that when Ely mentioned Operation Vulture on 24 April, Radford responded he had not heard of it. See *FRUS*, Vol. XIII, *Indochina*, part 1, p. 1397.
191. "first-class importance": Eden, op. cit., p. 116.
191. "You have to educate": Hagerty Papers, Diary Entries: 22 April 1954; Box 1, EL.
191. "just a funny sounding name": Address at Transylvania College, Lexington, Ky., 23 April 1954, in *Public Papers, Eisenhower 1954*, p. 420.
192. "The French have asked": Quoted in Adams, op. cit., p. 123.
192. "In short we must": Dillon to Department of State, 25 April 1954, in *FRUS*, Vol. XIII, *Indochina*, part 1, p. 1403.
192. "token British participation": Eden, op. cit., p. 117.
193. "assist in misleading Congress": Ibid., p. 117.
193. Dulles's Geneva telegram: Ann Whitman File, Dulles-Herter Series: Dulles to Smith, Department of State, 25 April 1954; Box 2, EL.
193. "the world on our back": Quoted in Adams, op. cit., p. 123.
194. "We just can't stand it": Hagerty Papers, Diary Entries: 26 April 1954; Box 1, EL.; and Ewald, op. cit., p. 105.
194. "visibly collapsing": Ann Whitman File, Dulles-Herter Series: Dulles to Smith, Department of State, 23 April 1954; Box 2, EL.
194. "As you know": Eisenhower, *Mandate for Change*, op. cit., p. 352.
194. "For more than three years": Ewald, op. cit., p. 116.
195. "The question resolves": "Memorandum for the Joint Chiefs of Staff," 27 April 1954, in *US-VN Relations*, Vol. 9, p. 393.
195. "The Geneva Conference": Eisenhower, *Mandate for Change*, op. cit., p. 351.

CHAPTER VII: CONFERENCE IN GENEVA

Epigraph: Ann Whitman File, International Meeting Series, Indochina: Message from the President to Bao Dai on the Fall of Dien Bien Phu, 7 May 1954; Box 28, EL.
196. "a two of clubs": Quoted in Prados, *The Sky Would Fall*, op. cit., p. 176.
197. "leaped over situations": Ann Whitman File, NSC Series: 194th Meeting, 29 April 1954; Box 5, EL.
198. "Genghis Khan": Ibid.
198. "plenty of people in Asia": Hagerty Papers, Diary Entries: 26 April 1954; Box 1, EL.
200. "The fight continues": Fall, *Hell in a Very Small Place*, op. cit., p. 422.
200. Victory proclamations: Ibid.
201. "What is American policy": Quoted in Fall, *Street Without Joy*, op. cit., p. 417.
202. "We have the military means": Quoted in Prados, *The Sky Would Fall*, op. cit., p. 177. For a detailed discussion about using atomic weapons in Vietnam, see: OSANSA, NSC Series, Briefing Notes Subseries, In-

dochina: Memorandum for General Smith, 30 April 1954; Box 11, EL.

202. "never start a war": Ewald, op. cit., p. 114.

203. "the principal sources": Prados, *The Sky Would Fall,* op. cit., p. 187.

203. "loss of Asia to Communism": Bonesteel to secretary of defense, 9 May 1954, in *US-VN Relations,* Vol. 9, p. 442.

203. "I am becoming": Stevens to Wilson, 19 May 1954, in *US-VN Relations,* Vol. 1, part IV A.2, note 55, p. 24.

204. "explodes the myth": Stevens to secretary of state, 19 May 1954, in *US-VN Relations,* Vol. 9, p. 476.

204. "a thousand questions": Matthew B. Ridgway, *Soldier: The Memoirs of Matthew B. Ridgway* (New York: Harper & Bros., 1956), p. 276.

204. Survey team report: A situation Westmoreland confronted when ground forces did go to Vietnam. He had to dedicate the first year to building base areas to enable offensive operations.

205. "stuck to our guns": Quoted in Spector, op. cit., p. 209.

205. NSC on Chinese intervention: "Statement of Policy by the National Security Council," 16 January 1954, in *US-VN Relations,* Vol. 9, p. 230.

206. "We were well prepared": Jurika, op. cit., pp. 424–25.

206. "a declaration of war": OSANSA, NSC Series, Briefing Notes Subseries, Indochina: Conference in the President's Office, 2 June 1954; Box 11, EL.

206. "half-way measures": Ibid.

206. "I want you to carry": Quoted in Ambrose, *Eisenhower: The President,* op. cit., p. 206.

206. "approaching a fork": Ewald, op. cit., p. 117.

207. "Indochina is devoid": Radford to secretary of defense, 26 May 1954, in *US-VN Relations,* Vol. 9, p. 487.

207. "United States to stand alone": Ann Whitman File, NSC Series: 200th Meeting, 3 June 1954; Box 5, EL.

207. "date of expiry": Dulles to American consul in Geneva, 14 June 1954, in *US-VN Relations,* Vol. 9, p. 558.

207. Opinion polls: White House Central Files, Confidential File, Subject Series, Department of State: "Current Popular Opinion Bearing on U.S. Indochina Policy," 26 May 1954; Box 69, EL.

209. "Developments": Dulles to Department of State, 29 April 1954, in *US-VN Relations,* Vol. 9, p. 397.

210. "This department": Davis to Johnson, 15 April 1954, in *US-VN Relations,* Vol. 9, p. 384.

211. "on the boil": Quoted in Eden, op. cit., p. 127.

211. "cheated the Americans": Quoted in Prados, *The Sky Would Fall,* op. cit., p. 176.

212. "both had allies": Eden, op. cit., p. 131.

212. "an interested nation": "Draft Instructions," 10 May 1954, in *US-VN Relations,* Vol. 9, p. 444.

213. "big fish on the hook": Ann Whitman File, Dulles-Herter Series: Smith to Dulles, 20 May 1954; Box 2, EL.

213. "spinning things out": Eden, op. cit., p. 144.

213. "hastily recovered": Chester L. Cooper, *The Lost Crusade: America in Vietnam* (New York: Dodd, Mead & Co., 1970), p. 77.

216. "Yalta business": Ann Whitman File, NSC Series: 206th Meeting, 15 July 1954; Box 5, EL.

216. dividing the free world: Hagerty Papers, Diary Entries: 8 July 1954; Box 1, EL.

216. "sold down the river": Hagerty Papers, Diary Entries: 9 July 1954; Box 1, EL.
216. "threat or use of force": "Statement by the Under Secretary of State at the Concluding Plenary Session of the Geneva Conference," 21 July 1954, in *US-VN Relations*, Vol. 9, p. 671.
217. "a backward people": Hagerty Papers, Diary Entries, NLE Transcriptions: 26 March 1954; Box 1, EL.
218. "the umbilical cord": Ann Whitman File, Dulles-Herter Series: McClintock to secretary of state, 15 June 1954; Box 2, EL.
219. "President Eisenhower": Jurika, op. cit., p. 449.
219. "Foster Dulles": The President's news conference of May 5, 1954, in *Public Papers, Eisenhower 1954*, p. 456.
220. "go to the brink": Quoted in Prados, *The Sky Would Fall*, op. cit., p. 201.
220. "We make strong statements": Quoted in Jurika, op. cit., p. 420.
220. Churchill's comment: See Ann Whitman File, International Meeting Series: Bermuda Report, 7 December 1953; Box 1, EL.
221. "draw the line": Adams, op. cit., p. 124.
222. "those who resist": *US-VN Relations*, Vol. 1, part II, p. A-7.
223. "The struggle will be long": Quoted in Gerson, op. cit., p. 189.
223. "not to mourn the past": Quoted in ibid., p. 188.
224. "lose it all": Nixon, op. cit., p. 122.

CHAPTER VIII: PASSING THE BATON

Epigraph: The President's news conference, 12 May 1954, in *Public Papers, Eisenhower 1954*, p. 472.
226. "Niagara Falls in a barrel": Quoted in Prados, *The Sky Would Fall*, op. cit., p. 200.
226. "atomic forces": Quoted in Perry, op. cit., p. 54.
227. JCS voting: The commandant of the Marine Corps voted only on matters pertaining to the Marine Corps.
228. "cities were in ruins": Quoted in Ewald, op. cit., p. 243.
228. "the trouble with Ridgway": Ibid.
228. "directed verdict": Ridgway, op. cit., p. 289.
228. "Despite all the new": Ibid., p. 290.
229. "between the silent march": *US-VN Relations*, Vol. 2, p. 1.1.
230. "a practical solution": Melby Papers: Army Summary Report dated 15 November 1950 to Major General Graves B. Erskine; Southeast Asia File, Southeast Asia Regional Conference; Box 9, TL.
230. Vietnamese language skills: For the state of American knowledge about Vietnamese language and culture see White House Central Files, Confidential File, Subject Series, Department of State: Pruett to Edman, 5 August 1953; Box 67, EL.
231. "General Ely was": "Memorandum for the President's Special Committee on Indo-China," 29 March 1954, in *US-VN Relations*, Vol. 9, p. 280.
231. "I do not say": Quoted in Jurika, op. cit., p. 428.
232. "it is hopeless": Quoted in Spector, op. cit., p. 224.
232. "We do not wish": White House Office, NSC Staff Papers, 1948–61, OCB Central File Series: Dulles to American embassy, Paris, 2 August 1954; Box 38, EL.

233. "the warlords": Buttinger, op. cit., p. 393.
233. Views in Washington: OSANSA, NSC Series, Briefing Notes Subseries, Indochina: Memorandum of the Joint Chiefs of Staff on the Defense of Southeast Asia, 28 May 1954; Box 11, EL.
234. "Soviet-inspired": White House Office, NSC Staff Papers, 1948–61, OCB Central File Series, Indochina: "Sino-Soviet Direction and Nature of the Indo-China Conflict," 19 May 1954; Box 38, EL.
234. "one step toward victory": Ibid.
234. "a drastic defeat": OSANSA, NSC Series, Policy Paper Subseries: "Summary of Progress to 21 July 1954"; Box 9, EL.
234. "U.S. prestige": "Review of U.S. Policy in the Far East," in US-VN Relations, Vol. 10, p. 731.
235. "If the Tonkin Delta": OSANSA, NSC Series, Policy Paper Subseries: NSC 5405(2), 19 May 1954; Box 9, EL.
235. "if all or part": OSANSA, NSC Series, Briefing Notes Subseries, Indochina: Memorandum of the Joint Chiefs of Staff on the Defense of Southeast Asia, 28 May 1954; Box 11, EL.
235. "a Communist lake": Hagerty Papers, Diary Entries: 23 June 1954; Box 1, EL.
235. "limited to strengthening": OSANSA, NSC Series, Briefing Notes Subseries, Indochina: Paper of 17 May 1954; Box 11, EL.
235. "desirable course": Ann Whitman File, NSC Series: 215th Meeting, 24 September 1954; Box 6, EL. The response to Wilson's provocative proposal is deleted by authority of the NSC, dated 1985. Possibly the censored text is another strong attack on Wilson's judgment.
236. "hen-and-egg argument": Collins Papers, Briefing Book 3: Dulles to Wilson, 18 August 1954; Box 24, EL.
236. "for some years": White House Central Files, Confidential File, Subject Series, Department of State: Memorandum of Conversation, 16 August 1954; Box 69, EL.
236. "make every possible effort": Spector, op. cit., p. 228.
237. "U.S. participation": Memorandum for the secretary of defense, 19 October 1954, in US-VN Relations, Vol. 10, pp. 773–74.
237. "we in the Army": Quoted in Spector, op. cit., p. 230.
238. "The time for rapid action": Ann Whitman File, NSC Series: 218th Meeting, 22 October 1954; Box 6, EL.
239. "a deal with Ho Chi Minh": Collins Papers, Briefing Book 5: "Minutes of Opening Political Session," 30 September 1954; Box 24, EL.
240. "archaic, outmoded governments": White House Central Files, Confidential File, Subject Series, Department of State: Todd to Shanley, 7 July 1954; Box 69, EL.
240. "defense line": Ann Whitman File, NSC Series: 202nd Meeting, 17 June 1954; Box 5, EL.
240. "The stakes are so high": Collins Papers, Briefing Book 3: Dulles to American embassies, 18 August 1954; Box 24, EL.
240. "unless Diem receives": Collins Papers, Briefing Book 5: Department of State to Saigon embassy, 21 October 1954; Box 24, EL.
240. NSC policy: See "Statement of Policy by the NSC on Review of U.S. Policy in the Far East," in US-VN Relations, Vol. 10, pp. 736–37.
241. "an independent Viet-Nam": Collins Papers, Monthly Papers, November 1954 (1): Eisenhower to Diem; 23 October 1954; Box 25, EL.
241. "a unifying influence": The President's news conference, 12 May 1954, in Public Papers, Eisenhower 1954, p. 473.

242. "white man's" treaty: A concern first expressed at the 195th Meeting of the NSC. See Ann Whitman File, NSC Series: 195th Meeting, 6 May 1954; Box 5, EL.

242. Eisenhower view on Geneva Accords violation: OSANSA, NSC Series, Policy Paper Subseries: Phleger to Dulles, NSC 5429/1, 27 July 1954; Box 8, EL.

243. "a reconciliation": Davis to secretary of defense, 14 September 1954, in *US-VN Relations,* Vol. 10, p. 747.

243. President on free world security: OSANSA, Special Assistant Series, Briefing Notes Subseries, Indochina: Conference with the President, 5 May 1954; Box 11, EL.

243. "the dilemma": Eisenhower, *Mandate for Change,* op. cit., p. 374.

244. "the heat, crowding": Daniel M. Redmond, "Getting Them Out," *Proceedings, U.S. Naval Institute,* Vol. 116/8/1,050, August 1990.

245. "to make more difficult": "Statement of Policy by the NSC on Review of U.S. Policy in the Far East," in *US-VN Relations,* Vol. 10, p. 737.

246. "little guys": Quoted in Cecil B. Currey, *Edward Lansdale: The Unquiet American* (Boston: Houghton Mifflin Co., 1988), p. 135.

246. "a stupid goddammed amateur": Ibid., p. 141.

247. "developed into a friendship": Edward Geary Lansdale, *In the Midst of Wars: An American's Mission to Southeast Asia* (New York: Harper & Row, 1972), p. 159.

247. "that would tend to keep": John Prados, *Presidents' Secret Wars* (New York: William Morrow & Co., 1986), p. 118.

248. "You sons-of-bitches": Quoted in Fall, *Street Without Joy,* op. cit., p. 278.

248. "blow the hell out": Quoted in Currey, op. cit., p. 164.

248. "give the Communists": Lansdale, op. cit., p. 225.

249. "a viable military position": Quoted in Spector, op. cit., p. 232.

250. "has many essential qualities": OSANSA, NSC Series, Briefing Notes Subseries, Indochina: "Memo of Conference at Residence of Secretary of State," 31 October 1954; Box 11, EL.

250. "authorized to speak": White House Central Files, Confidential File, Subject Series, Department of State: Eisenhower to Collins, 3 November 1954; Box 69, EL.

250. Eisenhower's instructions to Collins: Ibid.

250. Eisenhower's supplemental instructions are in White House Central Files, Confidential File, Subject Series, Department of State: October–November file; Box 69, EL.

250. "overall force": Collins Papers, Briefing Book 3: Smith to Anderson, 7 September 1954; Box 24, EL.

250. "diplomatic mission": See press release in October–November file in White House Central Files, Confidential File, Subject Series, Department of State: 3 November 1954; Box 69, EL.

250. "inefficiency, disunity": Collins Papers, Briefing Book 4: "Current Trends in South Vietnam," 15 September 1954; Box 24, EL.

251. "Vietnamese as [a] whole": Collins Papers, Briefing Book 7: USARMA Saigon to DEPTAR, 23 October 1954; Box 24, EL.

251. "The threat": Collins Papers, Monthly Papers, November 1954 (1), Briefing Book 8: Eisenhower to Collins, 3 November 1954; Box 25, EL.

254. "ability to influence Diem": NSC Council Staff Papers 1948–61, OCB Central File Series, Indochina: Draft OCB Progress Report, 19 January 1955; Box 38, EL.

254. State-Defense debate: See OCB meetings of 1 November and 7 December 1954 in White House Office, NSC Staff Papers, 1948–61, OCB Central File Series: August–December 1954 (2); Box 38, EL.
255. "more useful alternatives": Heath to Robertson, 17 December 1954, in *US-VN Relations,* Vol. 10, p. 825.
255. "Under present circumstances": Collins Papers, Monthly Papers, December 1954 (3): Dulles to Collins, 24 December 1954; Box 25, EL.

CHAPTER IX: HIGH STAKES

Epigraph: Young to Collins, 15 December 1954, in *FRUS 1955–1957,* Vol. I, *Vietnam* (Washington, D.C.: Government Printing Office, 1985), p. 2. Hereafter *FRUS 1955–57.*

256. "we would all shut up": Lansdale, op. cit., p. 203.
257. Letter on importance of Vietnam: Lansdale to Collins, 3 January 1955, in *FRUS 1955–57,* pp. 4–7.
257. "Yes sir": Quoted in Lansdale, op. cit., p. 204.
258. "I'll come over": Quoted in ibid., pp. 205–6.
258. "a lousy idea": Currey, op. cit., p. 171.
259. "agreed program": Collins to Department of State, 3 January 1955, in *FRUS 1955–57,* p. 9.
259. "conflicting aims": Collins to Department of State, 8 January 1955, in *FRUS 1955–57,* p. 26.
260. "were definitely working": Department of State Memorandum of Discussion, 14 January 1954, in *FRUS 1955–57,* p. 35.
260. "We have five": Collins Papers, Gruenther Series: Collins to Gruenther, 4 January 1955; Box 17, EL.
260. "Diem government": White House Office, NSC Staff Papers, 1948–61, OCB Central File Series: Draft Progress Report, 19 January 1955; Box 38, EL.
261. "most complex": Collins Papers, Monthly Papers: Collins to Dulles, 20 January 1955; Box 25, EL.
261. "a 50-50 chance": Ann Whitman File, NSC Series: 234th Meeting, 27 January 1955; Box 6, EL.
262. "on balance": Collins Papers, Monthly Papers: Collins to Dulles, 20 January 1955; Box 25, EL.
262. "personal popularity": Kidder to the Department of State, 7 February 1955, in *FRUS 1955–57,* p. 78.
262. "bungling along": NSC Staff Papers, 1948–61, OCB Central File Series: Lilly to MacDonald, 21 January 1955; Box 38, EL.
263. "great stake in him": Dulles to Department of State, 1 March 1955, in *FRUS 1955–57,* p. 102.
264. "In Saigon": Dulles to President, 1 March 1955, in *FRUS 1955–57,* p. 97.
266. "United Sects Front": Lansdale, op. cit., p. 253.
267. "we must now squarely": Collins to Department of State, 31 March 1955, in *FRUS 1955–57,* p. 169.
267. "not to give up": Memorandum of telephone conversation between President and secretary of state, 1 April 1955, in *FRUS 1955–57,* p. 176.
268. "switch would be desirable": Dulles to Collins, 1 April 1955, in *FRUS 1955–57,* p. 179.

268. "may have to cease": Ibid.

268. "to help Al Capone": Lansdale, op. cit., p. 264.

268. "Ho Chi Minh and his phony religion": Collins to Dulles, 2 April 1955; *FRUS 1955–57*, p. 188.

269. "can Diem form": Collins Papers, Briefing Book 4: Mansfield to Dulles, 24 September 1954; Box 24, EL.

269. "Ho Chi Minh could walk in": Memorandum for the Record, by Senator Mike Mansfield, 1 April 1955, in *FRUS 1955–57*, p. 177.

270. "Diem would have": Kent to Dulles, 4 April 1955, in *FRUS 1955–57*, p. 202.

270. "better to find out now": Note 2, in *FRUS 1955–57*, p. 197.

270. "point of no return": Dulles to Collins, 4 April 1955, in *FRUS 1955–57*, p. 196.

270. "extremely critical": Ann Whitman File, NSC Series: 244th Meeting, 7 April 1955; Box 6, EL.

271. "more of a puppet": Collins to Dulles, 7 April 1955, in *FRUS 1955–57*, p. 215.

271. "the man lacks": Ann Whitman File, International Meeting Series, Viet Nam: Collins to Dulles, 7 April 1955; Box 50, EL.

271. "with great regret": Collins to Dulles, 7 April 1955, in *FRUS 1955–57*, p. 219.

272. "stick to its guns": Memorandum of a conversation between the director of the Office of Philippine and Southeast Asian Affairs and Senator Mike Mansfield, 8 April 1955, in *FRUS 1955–57*, p. 221.

272. "Bao Dai's consent": Collins to Department of State, 9 April 1955, in *FRUS 1955–57*, p. 224.

272. "grass roots support": Ibid., p. 227.

272. "unacceptable substitutes": Dulles to embassy in Vietnam, 9 April 1955, in *FRUS 1955–57*, p. 229.

273. "paying lip service": Ibid., p. 230.

273. "not kick Diem completely out": Dulles to Collins, 11 April 1955, in *FRUS 1955–57*, p. 241.

274. "American public opinion": Collins to Department of State, 12 April 1955, in *FRUS 1955–57*, p. 243.

275. "inaccurate intelligence": OSANSA, Special Assistant Series, Chronological Subseries: "General Joe Collins's Comments," 22 April 1955; Box 1, EL.

275. "State is reluctant": Davis to Hensel, 25 April 1955, in *FRUS 1955–57*, p. 287.

276. "the iron curtain": Graham Greene, "To Hope Till Hope Creates," *The New Republic*, Vol. 130, No. 15, 12 April 1954.

278. "what else we could do": Ann Whitman File, NSC Series: 246th Meeting, 28 April 1955; Box 6, EL.

278. "Any change": O'Daniel to Carney, 29 April 1955, in *FRUS 1955–57*, p. 325.

278. "As this crisis develops": Young to Robertson, 30 April 1955, in *FRUS 1955–57*, p. 338.

278. "best hope": *US-VN Relations*, Vol. 2, part IV A.5, tab 2, p. 12.

279. "Events in past few days": Dulles to Collins, 1 May 1955, in *FRUS 1955–57*, pp. 344–45.

280. "the national symbol": Ann Whitman File, NSC Series: 247th Meeting, 5 May 1955; Box 6, EL.

281. "challenge of the Communists": "The Current Saigon Crisis," 2 May 1955, in *FRUS 1955–57*, p. 350.

281. Department of Defense study: "Program for the Implementation of U.S. Policy Towards South Viet-Nam," in *US-VN Relations*, Vol. 10, undated (the attached cover letter is 22 April 1955), p. 933.

282. "taking a gamble": "Memorandum of Telephone Conversation," 4 May 1955, in *FRUS 1955–57*, p. 355.

284. "such undesirable areas": Note 5, *FRUS 1955–57*, p. 377.

285. "the ration of rice": Graham Greene, "Last Act in Indo-China," *The New Republic*, Vol. 132, No. 20 (16 May 1955), p. 10.

285. "unity through free elections": "Joint Declaration by the President and the Prime Minister of the United Kingdom," 29 June 1954, in *Public Papers, Eisenhower 1954*, p. 600.

286. Dulles on elections: OSANSA, NSC Series, Briefing Notes Subseries, Indochina: "Outline of General Smith's Remarks," 23 June 1954; Box 11, EL.

286. "undoubtedly true": Dulles to Dillon, 7 July 1954, in *US-VN Relations*, Vol. 9, p. 616.

286. "play the game": Kidder to Department of State, 3 March 1955, in *FRUS 1955–57*, p. 105.

286. "failure to secure": Sebald to Dulles, 8 June 1955, in *FRUS 1955–57*, p. 437.

286. "As I see it": Sebald to Dulles, 14 June 1955, in *FRUS 1955–57*, p. 449.

286. "make every effort to abolish": "Programs for the Implementation of U.S. Policy Towards South Viet-Nam," in *FRUS 1955–57*, p. 280.

287. "extremely delicate": OSANSA, Special Assistant Series, Chronological Subseries: "Draft Statement of U.S. Policy on All-Vietnam Elections," 9 June 1955; Box 1, EL.

287. "but if necessary alone": "Draft Statement of U.S. Policy on All-Vietnam Elections," in *FRUS 1955–57*, p. 412.

288. Planning Board conclusions: "U.S. Policy in the Event of a Renewal of Aggression in Vietnam," in *FRUS 1955–57*, p. 516.

288. "The success of": "Memorandum from the Joint Chiefs of Staff to Secretary of Defense," 9 September 1955, in *FRUS 1955–57*, p. 537.

289. "sober optimism": OSANSA, NSC Series, Policy Paper Subseries: NSC 5405, 23 December 1955; Box 9, EL.

CHAPTER X: THE MAKING OF AN AUTOCRAT

Epigraph: Young to Robertson, 5 July 1955, in *FRUS 1955–57*, p. 477.

291. "if Diem were": Ann Whitman File, NSC Series: 249th Meeting, 19 May 1955; Box 6, EL.

291. "Future of Vietnam": Dulles to embassy in Vietnam, 19 May 1955, in *FRUS 1955–57*, pp. 416–17.

291. "Diem government": Reinhardt to Department of State, 14 October 1955, in *FRUS 1955–57*, p. 562.

292. "even Franklin Roosevelt": Quoted in Maurer, op. cit., p. 88.

292. "slippage in these lessons": Quoted in ibid., p. 88.

292. "more and more uncertain": Young to Robertson, 5 July 1955, in *FRUS 1955–57*, pp. 477–78.

293. Young on Diem's success: Young to Robertson, 2 September 1955, in *FRUS 1955–57*, p. 533.
293. "wonderfully perceptive": Young to Reinhardt, 2 June 1955, in *FRUS 1955–57*, p. 429.
293. "As in earlier conversations": Reinhardt to Department of State, 15 June 1955, in *FRUS 1955–57*, p. 455.
293. "the Free World Way": OCB Central File Series, Indochina No. 4 (7) April–September 1955: "Application of Project Action Vietnam"; Box 39. EL.
295. "no lasting effect": Spector, op. cit., p. 243.
296. "has permitted Viet Minh": Reinhardt to Department of State, 31 August 1955, in *FRUS 1955–57*, p. 530.
297. "relative power ratio": Reinhardt to Department of State, 13 July 1955, in *FRUS 1955–57*, p. 482.
297. "Now he felt": Memorandum of a conversation, Saigon, 18 August 1955, in *FRUS 1955–57*, p. 521.
298. "unknown factors": Reinhardt to Department of State, 13 July 1955, in *FRUS 1955–57*, p. 482.
298. O'Daniel's predictions: OSANSA, NSC Series, Policy Paper Subseries: NSC 5405, 11 July 1955; Box 9, EL.
299. "shadow governments": Research and Analysis Branch Report 7045, 15 September 1955; RG59, NA. Hereafter R&A.
299. "would not provoke Manila Pact": Howe to the acting secretary of state, 26 October 1955, in *FRUS 1955–57*, p. 564.
302. "moving desperately": R&A 7045, 15 September 1955; RG59, NA.
303. "when the people saw": Memorandum of discussion at a meeting of the OCB's Special Working Group on Vietnam, 7 November 1955, in *FRUS 1955–57*, pp. 573–74.
303. Radford-Diem meeting: Memorandum for the Record, by Chairman of the Joint Chiefs of Staff, 27 January 1956, in *FRUS 1955–57*, p. 612.
304. "very refreshing account": Editorial note, in *FRUS 1955–57*, p. 647.
305. "I leave Saigon": Dulles to Department of State, 15 March 1956, in *FRUS 1955–57*, p. 658.
305. "greater allegiance": OSANSA, NSC Series, Policy Paper Subseries: "U.S. Policy in Mainland Southeast Asia," 5 September 1956; Box 18, EL.
306. "Texas militia": Lansdale, op. cit., p. 335.
306. "political and psychological mission": Paper prepared by the chief of the Military Assistance Advisory Group in Vietnam, 28 December 1955, in *FRUS 1955–57*, p. 608.
308. "military personnel restrictions": Radford to Wilson, 9 December 1955, in *FRUS 1955–57*, p. 598.
309. "self-imposed restraints": Dulles to embassy in Vietnam, 9 February 1956, in *FRUS 1955–57*, p. 640.
310. "recovery and out-shipment": *FRUS 1955–57*, p. 781, note 2.
311. "guerrilla and subversive activity": Defense Information Relating to the U.S. Aid Program for Vietnam, 13 April 1956, in *FRUS 1955–57*, p. 673.
311. "main satellite regime": NSC Council Staff Papers, 1948–61, OCB Central File Series: "Outline Plan of Operations with Respect to Vietnam," 1 November 1956; Box 39, EL.
312. JCS plan: See: OSANSA, NSC Series, Policy Paper Subseries: "U.S. Policy in the Event of a Renewal of Aggression in Vietnam," 9 September 1955; Box 9, EL.

312. "fight should be won": Burke to Stump, 30 May 1956, in *FRUS 1955–57*, p. 687.

312. "within a matter of hours": OSANSA, NSC Series, Policy Paper Subseries: Radford to secretary of defense, 21 December 1956; Box 18, EL.

313. "If US ground forces": Stump to Burke, 1 June 1956, in *FRUS 1955–57*, p. 691.

314. "a friendly population": Broad Outline Plan for U.S. Military Participation in the Event of Viet Minh Aggression in Viet Nam, 7 June 1956, in *FRUS 1955–57*, p. 705.

314. "with good prospects": Memorandum of Discussion at the 287th Meeting of the NSC, 7 June 1956, in *FRUS 1955–57*, p. 697.

314. "such a notion": Ibid., p. 698.

314. "Take out an orderly": Ibid., p. 699.

315. "plan a war with our friends": Ibid., p. 702.

316. "the 'puppet' of the West": Williams to Stump, 7 June 1956, in *FRUS 1955–57*, p. 710.

316. "grave doubts as to his ability": Radford to Stump, 14 June 1956, in *FRUS 1955–57*, p. 713.

316. "pacified and secure": Memorandum of a conversation, 25 September 1956, in *FRUS 1955–57*, p. 739.

CHAPTER XI: DRIFTING WITH DIEM

Epigraph: White House Central Files, Confidential File, Subject Series, Mutual Security and Assistance (1959): "Evaluation Report Viet-Nam"; Box 40, EL.

317. "There was that sense": Quoted in Maurer, op. cit., p. 85.

318. "very sincerely": Quoted in Spector, op. cit., p. 282.

318. "About face": Ibid., p. 288.

319. "that was Fort Benning": Quoted in ibid., p. 285.

320. "And his reason": Quoted in ibid., p. 295.

321. "foot mobility": Quoted in ibid., p. 298.

322. "remnants of an empire": Quoted in William J. Rust, *Kennedy in Vietnam* (New York: Charles Scribner's Sons, 1985) p. XV.

322. "our offspring": Quoted in ibid., p. xvi.

322. "proving ground of democracy": 1 June 1965, in *US-VN Relations*, Vol. 2, part IV A.5, tab 1, p. 31.

323. Diem letter: Ibid., p. 32.

324. Dulles's rationalization of support for Diem: Ann Whitman File, NSC Series: 249th Meeting, 19 May 1955; Box 6, EL.

324. "South Vietnam is today": *US-VN Relations*, Vol. 2, part IV A.5, tab 2, p. 45.

325. "north-south contest": White House Central Files, Confidential File, Subject Series, Department of State: Saigon embassy to secretary of state, 29 April 1957; Box 73, EL.

325. "military hardware": White House Central Files, Confidential File, Subject Series, Mutual Security and Assistance (1959): "Evaluation of Viet-Nam Program," International Cooperation Administration, 15 August 1957; Box 40, EL.

326. Airfield building program: Durbrow to Department of State, 5 August 1958, in *FRUS 1958–60*, p. 67.

327. "exchange information": White House Central Files, Confidential File, Subject Series, Department of State: Ngo Dinh Diem Visit, 8 May 1957; Box 73, EL.

328. "mandarin in a sharkskin suit": Quoted in Spector, op. cit., p. 304.

328. "an Asian liberator": Chester L. Cooper, *The Lost Crusade: America in Vietnam* (New York: Dodd, Mead & Co., 1970), p. 153.

329. Eisenhower's toast to Diem: Ann Whitman File, International Meeting Series: Diem Visit, 9 May 1957; Box 2, EL.

330. "a danger to the state": *US-VN Relations*, Vol. 2, part IV A.5, p. 45.

330. Progress report: See White House Office, NSC Staff Papers, 1948–61, OCB Central File Series, Southeast Asia (File No. 6) February–May 1957: "Progress Report on U.S. Policy in Mainland Southeast Asia," 14 March 1957; Box 81, EL.

331. "the Party tried to kill": Quoted in Spector, op. cit., p. 312.

332. "if disregarded": "Evaluation of Situation in Viet Nam: December 1957," in *FRUS 1955–57*, p. 872.

333. "Diem holds the fort": Quoted in Spector, op. cit., p. 305.

334. "bandit elements": OSANSA, NSC Series, Policy Paper Subseries: NSC 5612/1, 6 November 1957; Box 18, EL.

335. "expressed surprise": Durbrow to Department of State, 8 February 1958, in *FRUS 1958–60*, p. 12.

336. "go to pot": Quoted in Spector, op. cit., p. 326.

336. "darkest moment": Ibid.

337. "largest land reform program": Ibid., p. 309.

338. "heavy-handed": Operations Plan for Vietnam, 4 June 1958, in *FRUS 1958–60*, p. 47.

339. "tired after a long war": Quoted in Stanley Karnow, "Giap Remembers," *The New York Times Magazine*, 24 June 1990.

341. "accompany units in the field": Riley to Williams, 9 April 1959, in *FRUS 1958–60*, p. 180.

341. "accompany units into battle": Ann Whitman File, Dulles-Herter Series: Dillon to secretary of state, 27 May 1954; Box 2, EL.

342. "internal dissatisfaction": *US-VN Relations*, Vol. 2, part IV A.5, tab 4, p. 20.

343. Alarming OCB report: OSANSA, NSC Series, Policy Paper Subseries: NSC 5809, 7 January 1959; Box 25, EL.

343. "a gracious colonial city": William Colby and Peter Forbath, *Honorable Men: My Life in the CIA* (New York: Simon & Schuster, 1978), p. 142.

343. "a feudal monarchy" Colby and Forbath, op. cit., p. 156.

346. "will not be able to eradicate": Prospects for North and South Vietnam, 26 May 1959, in *FRUS 1958–60*, p. 202.

346. "achieve economic stability": White House Central Files, Confidential File, Subject Series, President's Committee to Study U.S. Military Assistance (5): "Statement Related to Southeast Asian Countries Visited," 3 March 1959; Box 51, EL.

347. "self-liquidating": Draper Committee: Vol. I, Composite Report, Reference Attachment, p. 185, 25 August 1959; Box 1, EL.

348. "as soon as the Civil Guard": Durbrow to Robertson, 16 February 1959, in *FRUS 1958–60*, p. 139.

348. "pioneer spirit": White House Central Files, Confidential File, Subject Series, President's Committee to Study U.S. Military Assistance (5): "Initial Draft," 27 February 1959; Box 51, EL.

349. "usual spring offensive": Durbrow to Department of State, 28 March 1959, in *FRUS 1958–60*, p. 177.
349. "separation of powers": White House Central Files, Confidential File, Subject Series, Mutual Security and Assistance (1959) (13): Eisenhower to Mansfield, 10 November 1959; Box 40, EL.

CHAPTER XII: ON THE BRINK

Epigraph: *US-VN Relations*, Vol. 2, p. 4.1.
350. "eject the United States": Hooper et al., op. cit., p. 375.
351. "against the VC": Quoted in Spector, op. cit., p. 334.
352. "remarkably few": Lansdale to O'Donnell, 4 June 1959, in *FRUS 1958–60*, p. 206.
353. "shelved": Felt to Office of the Secretary of Defense, 15 February 1960, in *FRUS 1958–60*, p. 282.
353. "a real opportunity": Lansdale to Irwin, 19 February 1960, in *FRUS 1958–60*, p. 288.
353. "a skeletal framework": Durbrow to Department of State, 7 December 1959, in *FRUS 1958–60*, p. 255.
353. "underground problem": Ibid., p. 259.
354. "breed Communism from within": Ibid., p. 269.
354. "take a hard look": Lansdale to Douglas, 12 February 1960, in *FRUS 1958–60*, p. 279.
354. "a clear U.S. appreciation": Ibid., p. 281.
355. "I'm sure that now": Williams to assistant secretary of state for national defense of the Republic of Vietnam, 29 February 1960, in *FRUS 1958–60*, p. 292.
356. "highly unlikely": Special Report on Internal Security in Vietnam, in *FRUS 1958–60*, p. 311.
356. "become alarmist": Durbrow to Department of State, 7 March 1960, in *FRUS 1958–60*, p. 300.
357. "This is not my field": Williams to Lansdale, 10 March 1960, in *FRUS 1958–60*, p. 324.
357. "As the situation worsens": Memorandum of a conversation, 18 March 1960, in *FRUS 1958–60*, p. 339.
359. "another World War II": Durbrow to Parsons, 19 April 1960, in *FRUS 1958–60*, p. 396.
359. "an Army officer": Durbrow to Williams, 19 April 1960, in *FRUS 1958–60*, p. 401.
360. "from conventional": *US-VN Relations*, Vol. 2, part IV A.5, tab 4, p. 83.
360. "arbitrary and blind": Memorandum of Discussion at the 444th Meeting of the National Security Council, Washington, 9 May 1960, in *FRUS 1958–60*, p. 447.
361. "fate worse than death": Ibid.
361. "barely civil": Colby, op. cit., p. 160.
361. "FY 1960 program": Paper prepared by the Operations Coordinating Board, 29 April 1960, in *FRUS 1958–60*, p. 422.
361. "out of a job": *US-VN Relations*, Vol. 2, part IV A.5, tab 4, p. 81.
362. "Our hunter-killer teams": Ibid., p. 85.
362. "political and social aspect": Parsons to Durbrow, 9 June 1960, in *FRUS 1958–60*, p. 493.

362. "no place else to go": Memorandum of a conversation between Fine and Ladejinsky, 11 July 1960, in *FRUS 1958–60,* p. 517.
362. "skulking about the swamps": Lansdale to Kent, 10 August 1960, in *FRUS 1958–60,* p. 527.
363. "in for prolonged battle": Durbrow to Department of State, 30 August 1960, in *FRUS 1958–60,* p. 544.
368. "Durbrow out of S.E. Asia": *FRUS 1958–60,* p. 653, note 1.
368. "the regime's prestige": Herter to embassy in Vietnam, 12 November 1960, in *FRUS 1958–60,* p. 655.
368. "Diem has emerged": McGarr to Lansdale, 13 November 1960, in *FRUS 1958–60,* p. 660.
369. "his collapsing regime": FitzGerald to Bell, 7 November 1960, in *FRUS 1958–60,* p. 674.
369. "consider the alternatives": Ibid., p. 676.
370. "Look in the mirror": *FRUS 1958–60,* p. 678, note 3.
370. "he'll be lost": *FRUS 1958–60,* p. 679, note 5.
370. "The Pentagon warmly supports": Steeves to Durbrow, 20 December 1960, in *FRUS 1958–60,* pp. 737–38.
370. "drawn-out": Durbrow to Department of State, 24 December 1960, in *FRUS 1958–60,* p. 745.
371. "preview in miniature": MAAG Comments on Recommended 20,000 Increase in RVNAF Force Level, undated in, *FRUS 1958–60,* p. 697.
371. "It is the professional": Ibid., p. 703.
371. "then now!": *FRUS 1958–60,* p. 705, note 2.
372. "revert quite happily": Quoted in Spector, op. cit., p. 345.
372. "three Ds": Ibid., p. 347.
373. "on-the-spot": *US-VN Relations,* Vol. 2, part IV A.5, tab 4, p. 53.
373. "Vietnam exemplifies": French to Erskine, 6 December 1960, in *FRUS 1958–60,* p. 715.
374. "an authoritative ring": Quoted in Arthur M. Schlesinger, Jr., *A Thousand Days: John F. Kennedy in the White House* (Boston: Houghton Mifflin Co., 1965), p. 326.
375. "when they run away": Quoted in Cooper, op. cit., p. 171.
375. "a grave danger": OSANSA, NSC Series, Policy Paper Subseries: NSC 6012, 17 December 1960; Box 29, EL.
375. "the only trouble": Post-Presidential Papers, Gettysburg, Indochina: Malcolm Moos's interview with Eisenhower, 8 November 1966; Box 2, EL.
375. "the strong stand we did": Quoted in Cooper, op. cit., p. 161.
376. "the cause of freedom": Quoted in ibid., p. 162.
376. "far better": Post-Presidential Papers, Gettysburg, Indochina: 19 January 1961; Box 2, EL.
376. "unilateral intervention": Clark M. Clifford, "A Viet Nam Reappraisal," *Foreign Affairs,* Vol. 47, No. 4 (July 1969), p. 604.
376. "the cork on the bottle": Post-Presidential Papers, Gettysburg, Indochina: 19 January 1961; Box 2, EL.

CHAPTER XIII: THE CAUSE OF FREEDOM

Epigraph: Address at Transylvania College, 23 April 1954, in *Public Papers, Eisenhower 1954,* p. 420. Kennedy: *US-VN Relations,* Vol. 2, part IV A.5, tab 4, p. 96.

379. Ho Chi Minh's letters: See Chapter I: Moffat to Vincent, 15 November 1945; file 800; RG84, NA; and Maurer, op. cit., p. 42.
380. "just not interested": Quoted in Maurer, p. 42.
381. "a French problem": Clifford, op. cit., p. 603.
382. "I do need your professors": Quoted in Graham Greene, "To Hope Till Hope Creates," *The New Republic,* Vol. 130, No. 15 (12 April 1954), p. 11.
383. "the national choice": Maurer, op. cit., p. 64.
383. "staunchly anti-Communist": Collins Papers: Box 47, EL.
384. "They were caught": Rust, op. cit., p. 26.
384. "toys and boys": David H. Hackworth and Julie Sherman, *About Face: The Odyssey of an American Warrior* (New York: Simon and Schuster, 1989), p. 713.
384. "political and economic programs": *US-VN Relations,* Vol. 1., part IV A.2, p. 9.
384. "needed reforms": Collins Papers, Briefing Book 3: McClintock to undersecretary of state; Box 24, EL.
385. "our entire prestige": Hagerty Papers, Diary Entries: 26 April 1954; Box 1, EL.
385. "national security and prestige": Dulles to Saigon embassy, 4 April 1955, in *FRUS 55,* p. 198.
385. "new low": Quoted in Rust, p. xvi.
386. "heartbreaking": Ann Whitman File, NSC series: 196th Meeting, 8 May 1954; Box 5, EL.
386. "the civil war is being exploited": White House Office, NSC Staff Papers, 1948–61, OCB Central File Series, Indochina: report of 24 May 1954; Box 37, EL.
386. "no purely military victory": OSANSA, NSC Series, Briefing Notes Subseries, Indochina: Conference in President's office, 28 May 1954; Box 11, EL.
386. Lansdale's beliefs: Quoted in Currey, op. cit., p. 170.
387. "alien culture": Colby, op. cit., p. 286.
391. "vividly recalls": Ewald, op. cit., p. 316.
392. "work two ways": Eisenhower, *Mandate for Change,* op. cit., p. 358.
393. "blackmail": Ibid., p. 454.
393. Eisenhower-Johnson conversation: Post-Presidential Papers, Gettysburg, Indochina: Memorandum of telephone conversation, 2 July 1965; Box 2, EL.
394. Milton Eisenhower's comments: Quoted in Stephen Ambrose, *Ike's Spies* (Garden City, N.Y.: Doubleday, 1981), p. 263.
394. Lansdale's recollection: Quoted in Currey, op. cit., p. 173.
395. classification of national security information: Federal Register, Vol. 47, No. 66, 6 April 1982: Executive Order 12356—National Security Information.
397. "essentially a guerrilla war": Currey, op. cit., p. 218.
397. "fighting it right": Quoted in ibid., p. 219.
397. Lansdale-Diem conversation: Quoted in ibid., p. 221.
398. "inspired and determined effort": *US-VN Relations,* Vol. 2, part IV A.5, tab 4, p. 66.
398. "best hope": Quoted in Spector, op. cit., p. 371.
398. "Why so little?": Quoted in Rust, op. cit., p. 26.
398. "The worst yet": *US-VN Relations,* Vol. 2, part IV A.5, tab 4, p. 96.

399. Khrushchev's speech: Schlesinger, op. cit., p. 303.

399. "We seek in all Asia": President Kennedy's State of the Union Message, 30 January 1961, in *Public Papers of the Presidents of the United States: John F. Kennedy 1961* (Washington, D.C.: Government Printing Office, 1962), p. 23.

399. "supported the assessment": Clifford, op. cit., p. 605.

399. "bear any burden": President Kennedy's Inaugural Address, 20 January 1961, in *Public Papers, Kennedy 1961.*

BIBLIOGRAPHY

DOCUMENTS

Dwight D. Eisenhower Library (National Archives and Records Administration) collections:

  Ann Whitman File: Dulles-Herter Series
  Ann Whitman File: International Meeting Series
  Ann Whitman File: NSC Series
  J. Lawton Collins Papers
  James C. Hagerty Papers
  Post-Presidential Papers
  U.S. President's Committee to Study the U.S. Military Assistance Program (Draper Committee) Records
  White House Central File: Subject Series
  White House Office: National Security Council Staff: Papers 1948–61: OCB Central File Series
  White House Office: Office of the Special Assistant for National Security Affairs (OSANSA): NSC Series
  White House Office: OSANSA: Policy Paper Subseries
  White House Office: OSANSA: Special Assistant Series: Chronological Subseries

Seeley G. Mudd Manuscript Library, Princeton University:

  John Foster Dulles Papers

Harry S. Truman Library (NARA) collections:

  Dean Acheson Papers
  John F. Melby Papers
  President's Secretary's File: General File
  President's Secretary's File: NSC Meetings File
  Records of the National Security Council: CIA File
  Rose Conway File
  Theodore Tannenwald, Jr., Papers
  White House Central File: Confidential File

Congressional Record, Vol. 100, pt. 4; 83rd Cong. 2nd sess. (1954).
Executive Sessions of the Senate Foreign Relations Committee (Historical Series), Vol. VI, 83rd Cong. 2nd sess. 1954. Washington, D.C.: Government Printing Office, 1977.

426

BOOKS

Adams, Sherman. *Firsthand Report: The Story of the Eisenhower Administration.* New York: Harper & Bros., 1961.

Ambrose, Stephen A. *Eisenhower: Soldier, General of the Army, President-Elect.* New York: Simon and Schuster, 1983.

———. *Eisenhower: The President.* New York: Simon and Schuster, 1984.

———. *Ike's Spies: Eisenhower and the Espionage Establishment.* Garden City, N.Y.: Doubleday & Co., 1981.

Buttinger, Joseph. *Vietnam: A Political History.* New York: Frederick A. Praeger Publishers, 1968.

Byrnes, James F. *All in One Lifetime.* New York: Harper & Bros., 1958.

Chennault, Claire Lee. *Way of a Fighter: The Memoirs of Claire Lee Chennault.* New York: G.P. Putnam's Sons, 1949.

Colby, William, and Peter Forbath. *Honorable Men: My Life in the CIA.* New York: Simon and Schuster, 1978.

Cooper, Chester L. *The Lost Crusade: America in Vietnam.* New York: Dodd, Mead & Co., 1970.

Currey, Cecil B. *Edward Lansdale: The Unquiet American.* Boston: Houghton Mifflin Co., 1988.

Eden, Anthony. *Full Circle: The Memoirs of Anthony Eden.* Boston: Houghton Mifflin Co., 1960.

Eisenhower, Dwight D. *Mandate for Change 1953–1956.* New York: Doubleday & Co., 1963.

———. *Public Papers of the Presidents of the United States: Dwight D. Eisenhower 1953.* Washington, D.C.: Government Printing Office, 1960.

———. *Public Papers of the Presidents of the United States: Dwight D. Eisenhower 1954.* Washington, D.C.: Government Printing Office, 1960.

Ewald, William Bragg, Jr. *Eisenhower the President.* Englewood Cliffs, N.J.: Prentice-Hall, 1981.

Fall, Bernard B. *Hell in a Very Small Place.* New York: Vintage Books, 1968.

———. *Street Without Joy,* 4th ed. Harrisburg: The Stackpole Company, 1967.

Ferrell, Robert H., ed. *The Eisenhower Diaries.* New York: W.W. Norton & Co., 1981.

Gelb, Leslie H., with Richard K. Betts. *The Irony of Vietnam: The System Worked.* Washington, D.C.: The Brookings Institution, 1979.

Gerson, Louis L. *The American Secretaries of State and Their Diplomacy,* Vol. XVII, *John Foster Dulles.* New York: Cooper Square Publishers, 1967.

Hackworth, David H., and Julie Sherman. *About Face: The Odyssey of an American Warrior.* New York: Simon and Schuster, 1989.

Hastings, Max. *The Korean War.* New York: Simon and Schuster, 1987.

Hooper, Edwin Bickford: Dean C. Allard; and Oscar P. Fitzgerald. *The United States Navy and the Vietnam Conflict,* Vol. I, *The Setting of the Stage to 1959.* Washington, D.C.: Naval History Division, Department of the Navy, 1976.

Isaacson, Walter, and Evan Thomas. *The Wise Men: Six Friends and the World They Made.* New York: Simon and Schuster, 1986.

Jurika, Stephen, Jr., ed. *From Pearl Harbor to Vietnam: The Memoirs of Admiral Arthur W. Radford.* Stanford, Calif.: Hoover Institution Press, 1980.

Kearns, Doris. *Lyndon Johnson and the American Dream.* New York: New American Library, 1976.

Kennan, George F. *Russia and the West Under Lenin and Stalin*. Boston: Little, Brown & Co., 1960.

Kennedy, John F. *Public Papers of the Presidents of the United States: John F. Kennedy 1961*. Washington, D.C.: Government Printing Office, 1962.

Lansdale, Edward Geary. *In the Midst of Wars: An American's Mission to Southeast Asia*. New York: Harper & Row, 1972.

Layton, Edwin T. *"And I Was There."* New York: William Morrow & Co., 1985.

Leahy, William D. *I Was There: The Personal Story of the Chief of Staff to Presidents Roosevelt and Truman Based on His Notes and Diaries Made at the Time*. New York: McGraw-Hill, 1950.

Maurer, Harry. *Strange Ground: Americans in Vietnam 1945–75, an Oral History*. New York: Henry Holt & Co., 1989.

Nixon, Richard M. *RN: The Memoirs of Richard Nixon*. New York: Grosset & Dunlap, 1978.

Patti, Archimedes L.A. *Why Vietnam?* Los Angeles: University of California Press, 1980.

The Pentagon Papers as Published by The New York Times. New York: Quadrangle Books, 1971.

Perry, Mark. *Four Stars*. Boston: Houghton Mifflin Co., 1989.

Prados, John. *Presidents' Secret Wars*. New York: William Morrow and Co., 1986.

———. *The Sky Would Fall: Operation Vulture: The U.S. Bombing Mission in Indochina, 1954*. New York: The Dial Press, 1983.

Pruessen, Ronald W. *John Foster Dulles: The Road to Power*. New York: The Free Press, 1982.

Ridgway, Matthew B. *Soldier: The Memoirs of Matthew B. Ridgway*. New York: Harper & Bros., 1956.

Roy, Jules. *The Battle of Dienbienphu*. New York: Harper & Row, 1965.

Rust, William J. *Kennedy in Vietnam*. New York: Charles Scribner's Sons, 1985.

Schlesinger, Arthur M., Jr. *A Thousand Days: John F. Kennedy in the White House*. Boston: Houghton Mifflin Co., 1965.

Smith, R. Harris. *OSS: The Secret History of America's First Central Intelligence Agency*. Los Angeles: University of California Press, 1972.

Spector, Ronald H. *Advice and Support: The Early Years of the U.S. Army in Vietnam 1941–1960* New York: The Free Press, 1985.

Stettinius, Edward R., Jr. *Roosevelt and the Russians: The Yalta Conference*. Garden City, N.Y.: Doubleday & Co., 1949.

Taylor, John M. *General Maxwell Taylor: The Sword and the Pen*. New York: Doubleday & Co., 1989.

Taylor, Maxwell. *The Uncertain Trumpet*. New York: Harper & Bros., 1959.

Truman, Harry S. *Memoirs by Harry Truman*, Vol. I, *Year of Decisions*. New York: Doubleday & Co., 1955.

———. *Memoirs by Harry Truman*, Vol. II, *Years of Trial and Hope: 1946–1952*. New York: Doubleday & Co., 1956.

———. *Public Papers of the Presidents of the United States: Harry S. Truman 1947*. Washington, D.C.: Government Printing Office, 1963.

———. *Public Papers of the Presidents of the United States: Harry S. Truman 1950*. Washington, D.C.: Government Printing Office, 1965.

U.S. Department of Defense. *United States-Vietnam Relations 1945–1967: A Study Prepared by the Department of Defense*. 12 vols. Washington, D.C.: Government Printing Office, 1971.

U.S. Department of State. *Foreign Relations of the United States, Diplomatic Papers 1941.* Vol. I. Washington, D.C.: Government Printing Office, 1958.

————. *Foreign Relations of the United States, 1946.* Vol VIII, *The Far East.* Washington, D.C.: Government Printing Office, 1971.

————. *Foreign Relations of the United States, 1954.* Vol. XIII, *Indochina.* Washington, D.C.: Government Printing Office, 1982.

————. *Foreign Relations of the United States, 1955–1957.* Vol. I, *Vietnam.* Washington, D.C.: Government Printing Office, 1985.

————. *Foreign Relations of the United States, 1958–60.* Vol. I. *Vietnam.* Washington, D.C.: Government Printing Office, 1986.

Wedemeyer, Albert. *Wedemeyer Reports!* New York: Henry Holt & Co., 1958.

ARTICLES

Clifford, Clark M. "A Viet Nam Reappraisal." *Foreign Affairs,* Vol. 47, No. 4, July 1969.

Defourneaux, Rene J. "A Secret Encounter with Ho Chi Minh." *Look,* Vol. 30, No. 16, 9 August 1966.

Duncan, David Douglas. "The Year of the Snake." *Life,* Vol. 35, No. 5, 3 August 1953.

Greene, Graham. "Indo-China." *The New Republic,* Vol. 130, No. 14, 5 April 1954.

————. "To Hope Till Hope Creates." *The New Republic,* Vol. 130, No. 15, 12 April 1954.

————. "Last Act in Indo-China," part 1. *The New Republic,* Vol. 132, No. 19, 9 May 1955.

————. "Last Act in Indo-China," part 2. *The New Republic,* Vol. 132, No. 20, 16 May 1955.

Karnow, Stanley. "Giap Remembers." *The New York Times Magazine,* 24 June 1990.

Redmond, Daniel M. "Getting Them Out." *Proceedings, U.S. Naval Institute,* Vol. 116/8/1,050, August 1990.

Ziemke, Caroline F. "Senator Richard B. Russell and the 'Lost Cause' in Vietnam, 1954–1968." *The Georgia Historical Quarterly,* Vol. LXXII, Spring 1988.

INDEX

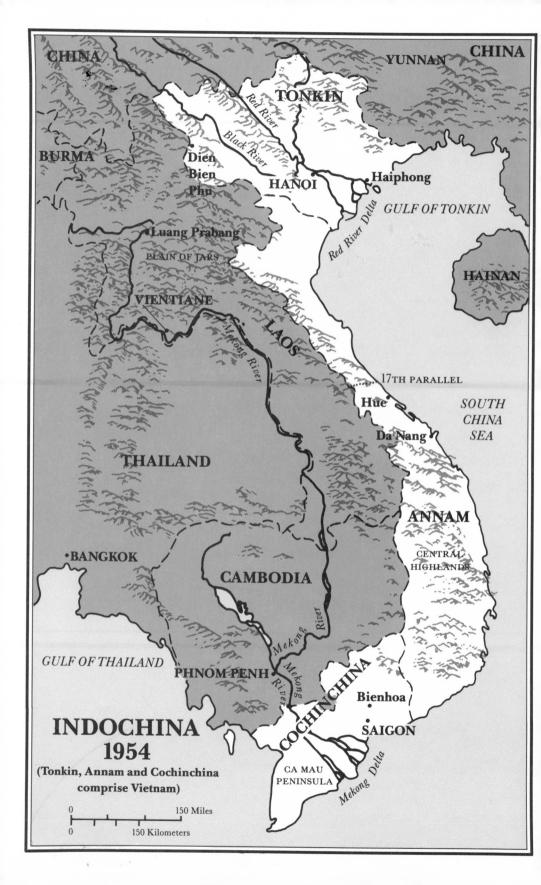